He Dreams What Is Going On Inside His Head

by

Jonathan Cott

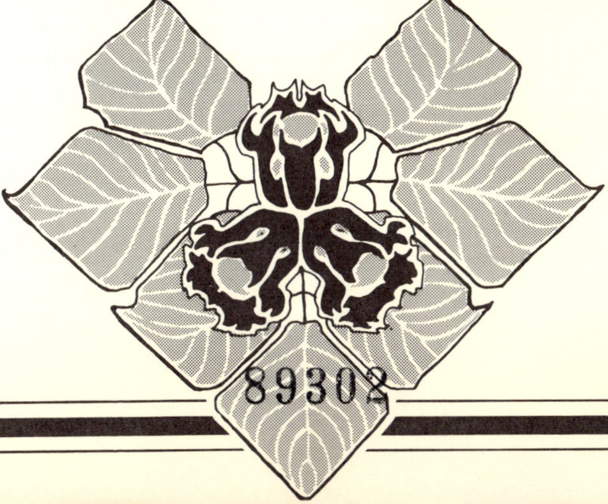

Library of Congress Catalog Car
Number: 73-79839
ISBN: 0/87932/065/6

First printing

Straight Arrow Books
625 Third Street
San Francisco, CA 94107

Distributed by Quick Fox Inc.
33 West 60 Street
New York, NY 10023

Order number: 102065

Production by Planned Production
Printed in the United States of America

For my mother and
In memory of my father

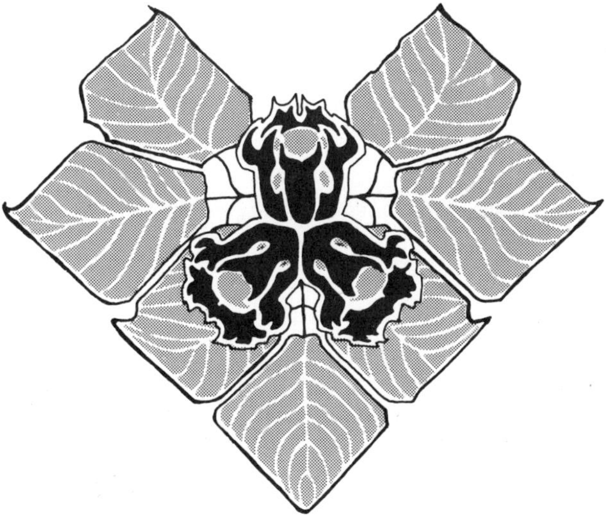

"You can learn something from everything," the rabbi of Sadagora once said to his Hasidim. "Everything can teach us something, and not only everything God has created. What man has made has also something to teach us."

"What can we learn from a train?" one Hasid asked dubiously.

"That because of one second one can miss everything."

"And from the telephone?"

"That what we say here is heard there."

"And the telegraph?"

"That every word is counted and charged."

—Abraham Yaakov of Sadagora

Contents

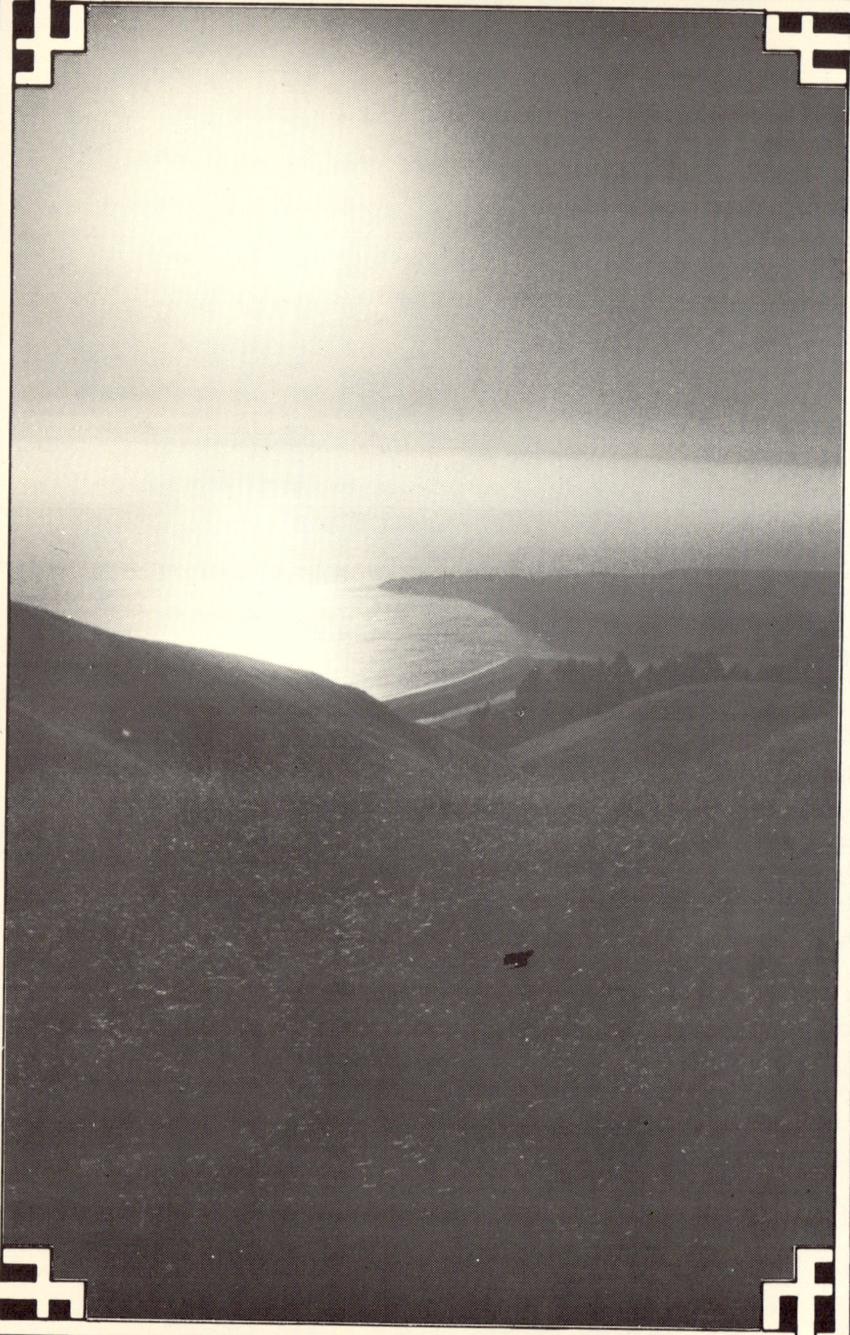

Foreword

This book consists of interviews, essays, reviews, and several poems written between 1963 and 1973 during the time I was living in Berkeley, London, and New York City. Most of these pieces concern themselves with writers, film makers, and musicians who seemed to me not only to have produced extraordinary works in their field but who also, in varying ways, reflected and responded to the sense of the transvaluation of the cultural "norms" of the Fifties and early Sixties.

The Berkeley Free Speech Movement, the Columbia rebellion, Haight-Ashbury, the Yippies, the Black Panthers, and the May, '68 Paris revolt were all reactions to the technocratic barbarism of the *idiot savants* running America and its allies. And though it might sound flippant to notice the connection between the rise to popularity of the Beatles immediately following the assassination of John Kennedy, it certainly seems that around 1964, the relationships between art and politics underwent an important and, to some, unnerving set of redefinitions.

The renewed interest in Eastern mysticism, consciousness expansion, communalism, anarchism, and Maoist theory often led to conflicting and sometimes contradictory ideological stances, but they all insisted on a questioning of the previously accepted notions of what an artist is and what art is for. I still believe that art "evolves," but to say this does not necessarily imply that it "progresses." (Is Tchaikovsky greater than Josquin? Is Ten Years After greater than Robert Johnson?)

Now, whether or not the burning down of banks or the 1968 Chicago convention riots should be seen as kinds of "art"—the ultimate blurring of the boundaries between art and politics—it is certainly true that out of this seemingly rambunctious period came a new kind of poetry, theater, music, and film—much of which helped to undermine the validity of a number of high-toned, arteriosclerotic examples of "fine" art.

And while a poet like Allen Ginsberg and a group like the Living Theater found that their evolving artistic development meshed perfectly with the emerging radicalized social forces, other artists, too, began to respond to these forces in unique ways. A "private" writer like Jean Genet traveled with and wrote essays supporting the Black Panthers. A "romantic" film maker like Jean-Luc Godard started making Leninist-Marxist films and conceived of himself as a worker in the class struggle. John Lennon demystified his "pop" star image and, with his artist-wife Yoko Ono, began to make experimental films and extremely personal and political recordings.

These redefinitions of personality—exemplified at large in groups like the Jesus Freaks or the Hare Krishna people—seem on hindsight to have had their origins in previously unnoticed but perceptible conflicts operating underneath the supposed "fixed" artistic persona. But while the search for new kinds of creative and political freedom was taking place, it was becoming apparent that within this antinomian period lay the seeds of its own destruction. Charles Manson, Altamont, heroin, political fragmentation, and hip commercialism revealed signs of the defeat of some of the more extravagant millennial hopes of the Sixties—and this failure brought forth our latest but not last Emperor of the Last Days, President Nixon, whose top advisers, as the *New York Times* recently reported, admire short hair, *Patton,* and John Wayne and, when not covering up, "relax by worrying and get away from it all by staying where they are."

The articles and interviews in this book are obviously a product of the years during which they were written. (The sower controls the work and the work controls the sower.) At different moments and in varying contexts, these writings certainly reveal a tension between the opposing ideas of closing and opening up: while one review explores the closed world and "internal astronomy" of Jean Genet's *Our Lady of the Flowers* and while the interview with Jean-Luc Godard reflects my nostalgic resistance to that director's break with his artistic and emotional past, the essay on Lionel Trilling's *Beyond Culture* expresses what I felt to be a too-easy acceptance of the idea of repression and social fatalism.

Martin Buber once made a distinction between the idea of Apocalypse—in which everything is predetermined and where the future, since it is already present, does not come to pass and can only be disclosed—and the idea of Prophecy—which confronted man with the alternatives of decision and saw the human being as a center of surprise in creation.

I think that, taken together, the writings in this book have been influenced by both of these ideas, though I have always been most interested in focusing on the achievements of the surprising present and on the possibilities of a vital artistic development—whether in rock music or the music of Elliott Carter, in the films of Kenneth Anger or those of Yasujiro Ozu. These interviews and articles seem to me to reflect a dream about a few persons and several artistic permutations that occurred at certain moments and in certain places during the past ten years.

Most of the writing in this book first appeared in *Rolling Stone* magazine, and I want to thank the editor of this book, Alan Rinzler, and the editor of *Rolling Stone,* Jann Wenner, to whom many of the following words were charged. Thanks, too, to Ralph Gleason, who encouraged my writing.

The following articles were first published elsewhere: the essay-record reviews of the Music of the World's People and of early American music in the *New York Times;* the introduction to contemporary American poetry in Horizon Press's *New American Arts,* edited by Richard Kostelanetz; the review of *A Hard Day's Night* in *Ramparts* magazine; the 1967 film journal in *Sunday Ramparts;* the essays on Jean Genet and J. F. Powers in the *Columbia Literary Supplement;* and the essay on Lionel Trilling's *Beyond Culture* in *The Supplement* to the *Daily Californian.* The poems "He Dreams What Is Going On Inside His Head" and "He Takes a Trip to Southern California" first appeared in *Silo* magazine and later in *Young American Poets* (Follett Publishing Co.) "Air and Angels" was first printed in *Angel Hair* magazine. And "On the Road of Death" has appeared in *Another World* (Bobbs-Merrill).

Jonathan Cott
New York City,
April, 1973

He Dreams What Is Going On Inside His Head

Angel Hair sleeps with a boy in my head.
She says: School is a drawing of your body,
and she paints lectures on paradox when she screws.
The boy has blue eyes but looks like me.
He says my beauty comes from lectures—
especially when they are boring.
In fact, this love of theirs is boring,
and sometimes I cover them with mist to feel
"this true fair world of things, a sea reflecting love."
Below, there is an island where thousands of white balloons
float above a class of high school girls learning grammar.
Earl-Jean sings after supper to the envying nightingales.
And when Angel Hair wakes up even she looks lovely,
and she spends time with me.
The boy is nice, too, and I like him to adore me.
Sometimes I let him in to walk with me by the fountains
and skyscrapers and listen to "Sexy Ways."
He pays court to me, but I am distant every time.
Then when I tell him about our Lord Tennyson,
wrapped round with a cloak while dying in the moonlight,
he has Angel Hair to turn to for his mad yearnings.
But I am jealous when they kiss and I hear their breathings.
They surround me in their sad bliss,
and I watch how the ideas of my legs make them move.
My arms are homework and my blood runs for thoughts.
Still, when I sleep, they watch me, and once
they slept next to me.
They even got used to the smoke in my lungs,
and my heart does not wear them out.
When I read books, they take part in all of it,
and when I want to be alone, they go out for a walk.
They can never leave me, and I hope I will never go away.

1
Interviews

Most questions derive from an interest or even from an obsession. In the latter case, they presuppose a protective, often rigid intellectual armor: one asks a question in order to affirm one's own thoughts instead of as a means of looking around and discovering what is there. Thus, the structure of catechism and, in a sense, many of the questions in some of the following interviews. Much of the time, however, the "art" of interviewing (and the interviews in Kevin Brownlow's *The Parade's Gone By* or in Oscar Lewis's interview novels are wonderful examples of the possibilities of such an "art") hopefully attains to that of the art of translation—an attempt to identify simply with another person (in John Dryden's sense of translation as an act of sympathy).

Ray Davies

The Kinks—with their lead singer, poet, and composer Ray Davies—were in the forefront of the English rock renaissance, singing songs like "You Really Got Me" and "All Day and All of the Night" (later "lifted" by The Doors in "Hello, I Love You"). The Kinks had a number one record with "Waterloo Sunset," after which, except in the eyes of an ecstatic group of devotees, they seemed to fade into the background.

"The world keeps going 'round," Ray Davies once sang, and every once in a while you hear the Kinks and wonder where they've been. Ray Davies used to write gutsy songs about not sleeping at night and getting tired waiting. His directness led him down a quiet and lonesome path that most people turned off as the world turned on. With the release of the Kinks' eighth album, *Arthur,* you might feel like catching up.

Many of Ray Davies' songs have set me thinking of the Taoist saint who fished with a pin and a single silk filament. The man caught multitudes of fish because he was perfectly attuned to—contemplating and participating in—the endless flowing. The means of Ray Davies' songs are small—like the persons he sings about—but the effect is that of a small and quiet radiance that would seem to belie the songs' subjects but which in fact lights them up from the inside. "Sunny Afternoon," "Waterloo Sunset," or "Sitting by the Riverside" suggest the world of T'ang Chinese poets conversing and drinking wine by moonlight or, closer to home, the streams and meadows of Izaak Walton's angler.

This clarity and directness of feeling imbues even Ray Davies' perceptions of the inhabitants of Dead End Street and suburban England—the anonymous losers of anybody's political program. Thus Arthur, the anti-hero of the new Kinks opera, lies on the opposite side of that musical coin where The Who's Tommy is heads. But together, these two characters not only define English life now but also present a composite awareness of successful and failed attempt at self-realization.

Afternoon tea with Ray Davies took place in the garden restaurant (a converted carriage house) of Kenwood House on Hampstead Heath in November, 1969. The setting might have been a Kinks song: gray-lit cool autumn afternoon; children playing, old persons sitting. Signs on the grass positively read: Please Step On The Paths. And in the toilet, a little boy sang cheerily "I LIKE you, daddy," as his embarrassed father outside muttered: "Get a move on." As Chekhov once said, almost defining Ray Davies' method, "I imagine people so they can tell me things about themselves."

After tea, we continued the interview on a bench on the heath, and just as Ray Davies was mentioning how he thought people hated the Kinks, the cassette machine broke down. On playback, you heard a sped-up Donald Duck, voice augmented by the sounds of a squadron of fighter planes reaching an explosion: then silence, as if the loosing of the apocalyptic beast had terminated the interview, even though Ray Davies and I continued to talk, tapes turning, microphones registering.

We concluded our conversation a couple of days later amidst the pigeons in Trafalgar Square.

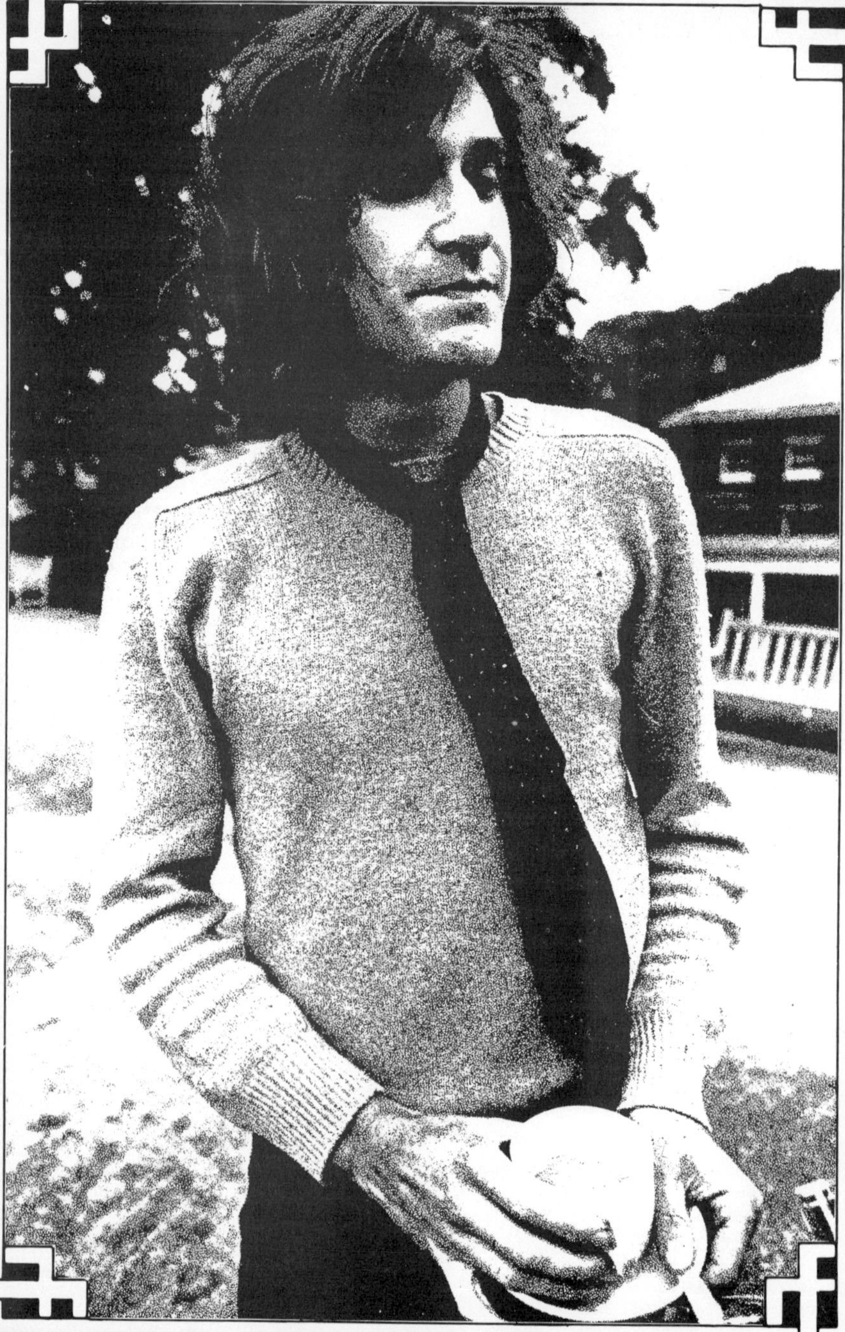

Before your first hit, "You Really Got Me," you recorded "Long Tall Sally" and "You Do Something to Me," the second of which sold something like 127 copies.

Really? Fantastic. How did you know that?

I checked it out.

Then it must be true . . . I was an art student, like thousands of others. Then I got together with my brother and a friend and we decided to go and play dates. The more we played, the more we wanted to do it. And it got to a stage when we wanted to do it all the time. Our repertoire consisted of rhythm and and blues, Sonny Terry things.

For a while when you started, the Kinks were listened to as much as the Beatles and Stones.

No, we weren't, never. 'Cause I think we were more unpopular than they were. In the States, our old image is still lasting, since the last time we went there that's what they remember us doing—the heavy things, the chunk chunk things, you couldn't really miss it. Those three chords were part of my life—G, F, Bb—yeh, it is, it is, and I can't help noticing it. But there have been other things nearly as close to it which people haven't noticed, other songs we've done.

"See My Friends (Playing Cross the River)" moves from those chords to something closer to an Indian drone.

I got the idea from being in India. I always like the chanting. Someone once said to me, "England is gray and India is like a chant." I don't think England is that gray, but India *is* like a long drone. When I wrote the song, I had the sea near Bombay in mind. We stayed at a hotel by the sea, and the fishermen came up at five in the morning and they were all chanting. And we went on the beach and we got chased by a mad dog—big as a donkey.

It sounded as if you were singing about an English river.

I think it was the Indian Ocean.

A number of your earlier songs sound not like places, but like other songs: "I'll Remember," for example, like a Beatles' song.

"I'll Remember"? No, no, bullshit. It's a song written on the sixth, Buddy Holly! I wrote it on a harmonica in Seattle, which is in Washington. I'll remember.

I liked "Love Me Do." When it came out, I thought it was an American surfing song. Totally unsurfer. But I did think it was an American group . . . I like surfers. Their imagery, it's great. And that floating feeling . . . I wrote "Holiday in Waikiki" at the Waikiki Hotel in Hawaii, and admittedly it's like Chuck Berry. We used to do a lot of his songs.

One of your songs reminded me of the Ikettes.

Ikettes? Right. Who were the Lennon Sisters? Do you remember? Were they about the same time as the Inkspots? . . .

I think that song writing changed when groups started spending more time in the studio. See, when groups were on the road, they used to go right in the studio and create the same kind of feeling they had on the road, and the stuff they used to cut was influenced by what they did at gigs. But then groups spent more time in the studio and started to change, the atmosphere changed.

When you're making a record, and if you spend more time over it, you have to record it a tone lower or cut the tones lower because you can't reach some of the notes, I find this. But when you go on stage, you have to put the key up and it really changes the whole thing.

A lot of our stuff recently has been routine for the studio, when it should have been routine for the stage, and that's why it sounds so different. I think the writing's the same, maybe, but it's the fact that we spend more time in the studio and less on the road that's changed the sound of it.

You create an easy driving feeling in "Sunny Afternoon." The guy's had to sell his yacht, his money's gone, and he wants to live life pleasantly. How much are you the person you're singing?

Not at all, really. I'm easy driving. But I'm not a person who loves to live pleasantly above everything else. I'm not that way at all. I might think that I'm that, but I'm not really that. I think the person in "Waterloo Sunset" is closer to me.

"Sunny Afternoon" was made very quickly, in the morning, it was one of our most atmospheric sessions. I still like to keep tapes of the few minutes before the final takes, things that happen before the session. Maybe it's superstitious, but I believe that if I had done things differently—if I had walked around the studio or gone out—it wouldn't have turned out the same way.

The bass player went off and started playing funny little

classical things on the bass, more like a lead guitar; and Nicky Hopkins, who was playing piano on that session, was playing "Liza"—we always used to play that song. Little things like that helped us get into the feeling of the song.

At the time I wrote "Sunny Afternoon" I couldn't listen to anything. I was only playing the *Greatest Hits of Frank Sinatra* and Dylan's "Maggie's Farm"—I just liked its whole presence. I was playing the *Bringing It All Back Home* LP along with my Frank Sinatra and Glenn Miller and Bach—it was a strange time. I thought they all helped one another, they went into the chromatic part that's in the back of the song.

I once made a drawing of my voice on "Sunny Afternoon." It was a leaf with a very thick black outline—a big blob in the background—the leaf just cutting through it.

You sing a lot about sunsets and autumn.

I like autumn things. I did a record called "Autumn Almanac"—I drew pictures of it and everything. After I wrote it, for a whole month I was thinking about it. I wasted a lot of time, really, because I was sweeping up dead leaves and putting them in the sack. I'm susceptible to that sort of thing—to walls and flowers. Walls. You can get probably something more from a wall than from a person sometimes. It's just put somewhere. It's in line, in order, it's in line with the horizon. Ah, ridiculous.

What I try to do probably doesn't come out. What I've worked out, what I do—I might not be right—is to do something very personal, and then suddenly I look at it, up in the air, I look at it. I blow it up and look at it and then I come down again. A better man.

All my records—at one time they've been the most important thing I've ever done. Even the ones that aren't hits. Even the ones that sell one hundred copies. At one time they've been the most important thing to me. So I can't hear our records on the radio, I can't stand it, because they sound to me so *out* of what everyone is doing. You know what I mean? I get embarrassed doing television shows that have lots of people on, compressed, like *Top of the Pops,* one group after another, and we're right in the middle. I feel wrong, not inferior, just wrong. I think we need a bit of time for people to get used to us.

You've also sung about blue skies and suns. "Lazy Old Sun" has what sounds like a hippo groan, almost joking up what you're saying.

Unfortunately, the song just didn't come off, really. When you look at it in writing, it's a lot better. I don't like a lot of the lines. It's nicer when I think about it than when somebody tells me what it's like. I know what I was getting to, but didn't quite get there. It is a joke, it ended up as a joke, a very sad joke . . . too bad. At one stroke it can sound jokey and the next minute I can believe it.

Both at once. As if you're saying something real, don't want to take it seriously, so undermine it with the groan. I could be wrong.

But you're really right.

Are you worried about sentimentality in your songs?

I worry about it because I think other people think I worry. That's the only reason. I like looking at things, remembering things, I like that.

"Dead End Street" sets the theme for a number of your songs. "We are strictly second class." Cracks in the ceiling, sink leaking. At the end of the song, you sing: "Dead End Street / Head to my feet / I can feel it," so that the personal and the social awareness come together.

What you're saying, too, is that it's not only what other people are doing, it's what I'm doing, what I'm feeling. It's a little bit selfish as well. The Beatles are aware that Mr. So-and-so in Northampton is about to buy the record and listen to it while he's having his tea. I think they've always tried to keep that in mind. I'm a little more selfish. I like to do things that involve me a little bit. Sorry, I'm not answering your question directly. We do tend to think about what we're doing . . . too much. And that's what happened to "Dead End Street."

I'll tell you about "Dead End Street." It was about miners, to begin with, because we had a thing in England called Aberfan where a coal tip fell on a school in Wales—they dig for coal and they put all the slack and make a hill. It all fell down on a school and killed two hundred little kids. That's where it all started. I wrote the song about that time, and all that time there were news flashes about Aberfan, and also it was the first year of the economic cutback. I felt it was like the depression days.

"Big Black Smoke" has that mood, too, about the girl who takes purple hearts and sleeps in bowling alleys.

Yeh, it was written at the same time. But it started off to be something different. The big black smoke was there, and I said, Why can't I just say "Big Black Smoke"? There are some songs that *sound* great. You don't know the words—you don't want to know the words—it's the way they roll off the tongue, they might mean anything. And when you look at the song sheet and the words say "I love you, baby" or something very ordinary, they just sound like something good. "Big Black Smoke" had that sound. But I had to put something around it. I had two lines: "Big black smoke" and "She took all her pretty colored clothes," and the song revolves around those lines, really. Because the build-up to the song occurs when she comes into it, or when he comes into it, or when I come into it: "She took all her pretty colored clothes." The beginning builds up to it, and from that line it fades out. There was the first draft, and then I got involved in the story. You've got to have something build up to that line: "She took all her pretty colored clothes."

How did The Village Green Preservation Society *come about?*

Three years ago I wanted it to be *Under Milk Wood,* something like that, but I never got a chance to do it because we had to make albums. Somebody said to me that I preserve things, and I like village green and preservation society. The title track is the national anthem of the album, and I like Donald Duck, Desperate Dan, draught beer.

Johnny Thunder lives on water, he don't eat food, he feeds on lightning [laughter]. Frankenstein. It's not a cowboy song. It would be nice to hear The Who sing it.

Phenomenal Cat went to Singapore and Hong Kong and decided it was just as well to get fat. I didn't, he did, it was completely his own decision. And he came back and sat and ate himself to eternity.

Hope he's there.

He's always there.

In "Animal Farm" you sing: "I want to be back there among the cats and the dogs and the pigs and the goats, where people are people and not just plain."

I like plain Janes. In "Waterloo Sunset" I wanted to use the names Bernard and Dorothy, but it wouldn't work. Terry [Stamp] and Julie [Christie] would have to dog themselves up a bit. They'd have to be less glamorous for a Waterloo Sunset movie. Plain Jane. . . . I'd like to hear Burt Lancaster singing "Big Sky."

"Sitting by the Riverside" is similar to "Afternoon Tea" or "Waterloo Sunset." They have that loosened up, spaces between feeling.

That's the studio. Maybe people should have a winding down session before listening to our songs. Maybe they should be briefed. Or debriefed. I think they should be debriefed.

Listening to lots of your songs, you get a sense that there's a house on Dead End Street with big black smoke around, a guy upstairs with his Harry Rag, the cat always eating. . . .

Do they all live together in a house?

Yes. Plastic Man and Dandy come around to visit. Do you intend to create this kind of world?

I'm not aware of trying to, but it might seem that way. I think on the *Village Green Preservation Society* they were all brothers and sisters. Nobody made love because it was all in the family. I don't think there's a love song on it. Our new record is literally about a family.

You make a perfect family where everyone's friends.

Yeh. The people I'd like to be with are over there—across the river. I'm not left out. I've got a choice, but the easiest one is the one I don't really want. There's a line that says: "Wish that I'd gone with her / She is gone / Now there's no one left but my friends." Yeh, she went over there and I stayed here. [Silence].

Would you say something about your new opera, Arthur?

The opera is about the rise and fall of the British Empire, which people tend to associate me with [laughter]. You could sum up the British Empire in one song. I haven't written it, but it can be done, a little fifteen-minute thing [laughter]. But about the opera: I decided to make it about one person, someone who didn't really count, that's all, and mixed it with a few people whom I knew, put them into one. I told Julian Mitchell, who wrote the script, a story about somebody I know. We liked it and worked on it and it came from there. He was easy to work with.

"Some Mother's Son" contains those beautiful lines: "But still the world keeps turning / Though all the children have gone away." The idea of childhood and the sun join each other in the song.

That's "Lazy Old Sun," see, that's the way it works. It didn't work in that song: "When I'm dead and gone your light will shine eternally." The idea was right to me, and there was a vehicle in "Some Mother's Son" for it to work.

I wrote the song in a kitchen. Wrote it at night, it's not a day song. I had a song which I liked, but which nobody else liked very much called "Wonder Boy," and the lines went: "Wonder Boy, some mother's son / Turn your sorrow into wonder." I had to use "some mother's son" again. It was just one line and it was gone and had to be explained, for me, I was interested in that line. And then I wanted to write about how soldiers must have been frightened fighting and killing each other, but they were just some mother's son. Apart from the line "Head blown up by some soldier's gun," the song could be about executives in an advertising agency.

What do you think of the people you sing about in "Shangri-La"?

I played "Shangri-La" to somebody—an old friend of mine and I knew halfway through it that he was embarrassed by it because it was about him, and he realized it, and I didn't want him to realize it, and I can never sort of talk to him again. I wanted him to hear it, and then I realized: there he is.

I'm not laughing at those people in the song at all. They're brainwashed into that, they brainwash themselves. She says, "That's it, I don't want a new dress," not because she really doesn't want it, but because she can't afford it. Their minds are like that; they're happy, really. It becomes a religion to them. The glory of being boring. It's a glory. He shows you his stamp collection. It's a sense of greatness he's got around him that you can't penetrate because you feel you might upset him, he's got that aura of *stuff.*

The Chorus "Shangri-La" is a bit of a chant—like "See My Friends." It's a religious thing. You accept it as your religion because you can't have anything else, and whatever you've got anyway is what you accept yourself. You let yourself believe it. . . . No, perhaps not. If you lived there [Kenwood] and you accepted this, and this was as far as you could go, you'd be a lot happier. Well, no, perhaps not. See, I've tried living in a big house—and I can't. I'm going back to a little house. I don't think people really want to live in a posh house, as much as a rich person doesn't want to live in a slum. I don't like to say what I've got and be happy with it. I'd wear hobnail boots by my fire rather than slippers. I can't stand slippers 'cause they symbolize giving up to me. But at the same time, I love the people who are like that. But I hate what's handed down when people get into the state where that's all they want. And that can be anybody—toffs, toffs are the worst offenders. Top hats and walking sticks. Cary Grant's a toff. David Niven.

It's like the song "Princess Marina." My brother David said, "I don't know whether you like these people or you hate them." You don't really hate anybody, do you? You only hate people for an instant. They can't help it. "Princess Marina" starts pretty sad, maybe, then it goes into the bit about what it's all about—"I haven't got any money or anything," they're having a hard time. And then they sing the way they did in the music hall, because that's the way they used to express it: "Don't Have Any More, Mrs. Moore." There was a song about poverty. People think I'm taking it out on ordinary persons. But it's about all people. In fact, it's more about nobs and toffs, executives—"Yes, sir, No, sir, Three bags full, sir."

If people are second class, and if, when they start making it, they become dedicated followers of fashion, what alternative do they have, given the way things are?

Be like me and be unhappy . . . We went to Australia and they wanted to take pictures of us surfing, and I thought they only surfed in America. We rolled our trousers up and pulled our overcoats up. It was 100 degrees and we were sweating, but we refused to take our overcoats off. Why should we do it? Surfing in Australia! Rebel at any cost. That's what it seems like, but it isn't really. They'll probably play our song "Australia" at cabaret clubs with maracas and things. That'll be nice. Fabulous!

The line "Australia, no drug addiction" might be too strong for them.

Might have to bleep it out.

The singer in "Driving" sounds like the singer of "Sunny Afternoon."

Can't drive. I probably can. I'm probably a hustler. An American told me I was a hustler: I pretend I can't do things and I can, really. Is that what it means? I probably can drive, but I've never been behind a steering wheel. . . . The song was written for 1938 or 9. "Dead End Street" is written about now, but it could be about the Depression. "Driving" is about the Thirties, but people still take the attitude: Let's just go driving and get away. I don't, 'cause I can't drive.

In "Yes Sir, No Sir," you wrote: "You're outside and there ain't no admission to our play." Again, these people aren't part of what's happening.

Superb line the way you said that. . . . Nothing's happening [laughter].

"Now I've got children and I'm going grey / No time for talking I got nothing to say . . ."

Better with an American accent.

Nothin' to say. That's what you tell the cops.

Most certainly. I was in a lift in New York City and wanted to go to the 50th floor. A woman came in and wanted to go to the basement. She pressed basement and I said, I was in here first, I want the fiftieth floor, and she said "Sue me." Great. I accepted it. . . . A lot more casual, the Americans.

Sometimes they shoot you.

In England they just let you live [laughter]. That's the best way to die. The deadest way.

Greyness is beauty in boredom. I could have given Arthur a limp, I suppose, made him buy funny books, have a secret life. Then, that isn't the important thing—he'd have had control over his secret life, and he hasn't control over what's happening to him. But he thinks he does. . . . When we play the opera in America, I hope people will accept the opera as a musical thing. There's jamming—we do a lot of that, but people don't think we do, since we don't do it on record. As far as the next thing I'm doing, I'm leaving what I've done. That's why I didn't want pictures taken of me reminiscing. I'm not like that, really. I'm going to try something else next. . . . Someone will get me if I talk about it.

How do you go about writing?

Everything has been thrown at me, and paper boats float past me, but something more direct might hit me and leave its mark. I think the things I write about are the things I can't fight for. There are a lot of things I say that are really commonplace. I can't get rid of them. I go into something minute, then look at it, then go back into it.

Have you been influenced by any poetry?

I like a poet who has the same name as me, someone named Davies. And a crummy eight line poem that ends up saying "And that lovely woman is my mother." There's a poem I like, too, whose first line goes "Imagine that life was an old man carrying flowers on his head." And it ends up by saying "And death liked flowers." I'm afraid that's as far as my poetic influences go.

How do you feel about the name of your group?

I went to a studio in a grey pullover and horrible tweed trousers, and the next day I went in an orange tie, and a bloke told me, "Now you really look like a Kink." Maybe it was an unfortunate name—the sadistic image or the things in your arm. It's a good name, in a way, because it's something people don't really want. I think people hate us, they think we betrayed them. Perhaps we have.

But when you recorded live at Kelvin Hall people were screaming and adoring you.

Yeah, it was recorded at a cattle show. There was a large metal roof which gave that effect. Someone said that the audience was more in it than the group. The part I enjoyed was when everyone started singing "Sunny Afternoon."

They must love us really.

1970

Jean-Luc Godard

Having seen over fifteen of Jean-Luc Godard's extraordinary feature films, I seem to have remained hanging on to that aesthetic world created by Godard in which love, conscience, tenderness, and art (values implicit in films as late as *Masculine-Feminine* and *Pierrot Le Fou*) formed the silent horizon—the screen—on which one observed the players disjoined from their creator's idealized perfections. As Godard once said: "Beyond the theater is life, and behind life, the theater. My point of departure was the imaginary and I discovered the real; but behind the real there was the imaginary."

The "imaginary" is the world of love striven for, but the film attests to the impossibility of such striving and then marks death for those whose thin and pure elements gratuitously, violently, and naturally suffer to return to their extinction. Thus the Mozart Clarinet Concerto, heard in *Breathless* and *Masculine-Feminine,* presages death for the wounded, innocent heroes "disguised as princes" (*Pierrot Le Fou*). And the circular camera movements around that beautiful pastoral Mozart piano recital in *Weekend* signifies the end of this aesthetic world. The hippie drum solo near the film's conclusion ends the suggestion of "the film we had dreamed, the film we had carried in our hearts, the film we wanted to make—and secretly wanted to live" (*Masculine-Feminine*).

Like a hallucinating child who sees a page or object that is no longer before him, I failed to realize that Godard was always attempting to break through that mirage in which cinema equaled life—a fantasy shared by his actors. "I know nothing of life except through the cinema," Godard told Tom Milne in 1962. "I didn't see things in relation to the world, to life or to history, but in relation to cinema. Now I am growing away from all that. . . . I thought *Breathless* was a realistic film, but now it seems like *Alice in Wonderland,* a completely unreal, surrealistic world." As Susan Sontag has written: "Life—the world; death—being completely inside one's own head."

In Godard's second feature film, *Le Petit Soldat,* the O.A.S. gunman protagonist quotes Lenin's dictum: "Ethics is the aesthetics of the future." Looking back now, we see that this exile and deserter, in search of his self, not knowing "where to give his heart," ironically was pointing to Godard's recent unswerving and uncompromising concern with using film as a way to "change the world."

There is no more joking self-consciously about the image of films—no more references to *Johnny Guitar.* Godard's new films are not about politics in the way that *Le Petit Soldat* or Resnais' *The War Is Over* are. Rather they present a political consciousness in the guise of quasi-documentary footage and thus attempt to make you watch and listen and think. "To look around one's self, that is to be free," Godard once said. This is true for life. But when one questions (rightly) and then does away with the barest paradigms of the "spectacle" film—action, character, etc.—one finds oneself in undiscovered territory, and the chances of losing the way in the capitalist woods with only little red books in the basket are great.

Godard's new questioning of the relationship between art and politics reveals itself in recent personal confrontations, such as when he asked the audience at last year's London Film Festival to watch the uncut version of *One Plus One* outside the theater on a makeshift screen and return their tickets and send the refund to the Eldridge Cleaver Defense Fund. Put to a vote, only twenty persons decided to walk out. Godard said: "You're content to sit here like cretins in a church." During the shouting that followed, he hit producer Ian Quarrier, who later explained why he added to the end of Godard's film a complete recorded version of the Rolling Stones' "Sympathy for the Devil" ("ten million teenyboppers in America alone").

One Plus One intersperses shots of the Stones creating "Sympathy for the Devil" (from a slow ballad to the final rhythmic holocaust) with scenes of Black Power militants in a Battersea automobile junkyard reciting texts by LeRoi Jones and Cleaver and shooting white nightgowned girls; an interview in lush green woods with Eve Democracy (Anne

Wiazemski) who replies *yes* or *no* to questions defining the liberal temperament; a pornographic bookstore where Mr. Quarrier reads out from *Mein Kampf* while customers give the Nazi salute, then slap two bandaged young men who chant "Peace in Vietnam."

Godard's uncompleted new film, *Some English Voices,* emphasizes one-angle shots in an attempt to demystify image-making. The film includes a car factory production line, the camera conveying the sense of the monotony of automation; car workers at home talking about their life; a speech exemplifying fascist undercurrents beneath the liberal veneer; students talking about the Beatles' "Honey Pie," one saying the more beautiful the music, the more counterrevolutionary the effect, the other saying it's only a song; Godard's dying hand reaching—coming home—for the Red Flag, symbolizing revolutionary internationalism exemplified by Spanish Civil War and N.L.F. songs.

While shooting at the University of Essex, Godard encountered a manifesto published by the Situationists which concluded: "If you see a camera, smash it! It might be *Godard.*"

Nietzsche wrote: "War has always been the grand sagacity of every spirit which has grown too inward and too profound; its curative power lies even in the wounds one receives."

The interview was recorded in English driving out to the airport and during an airport dinner in March, 1969.

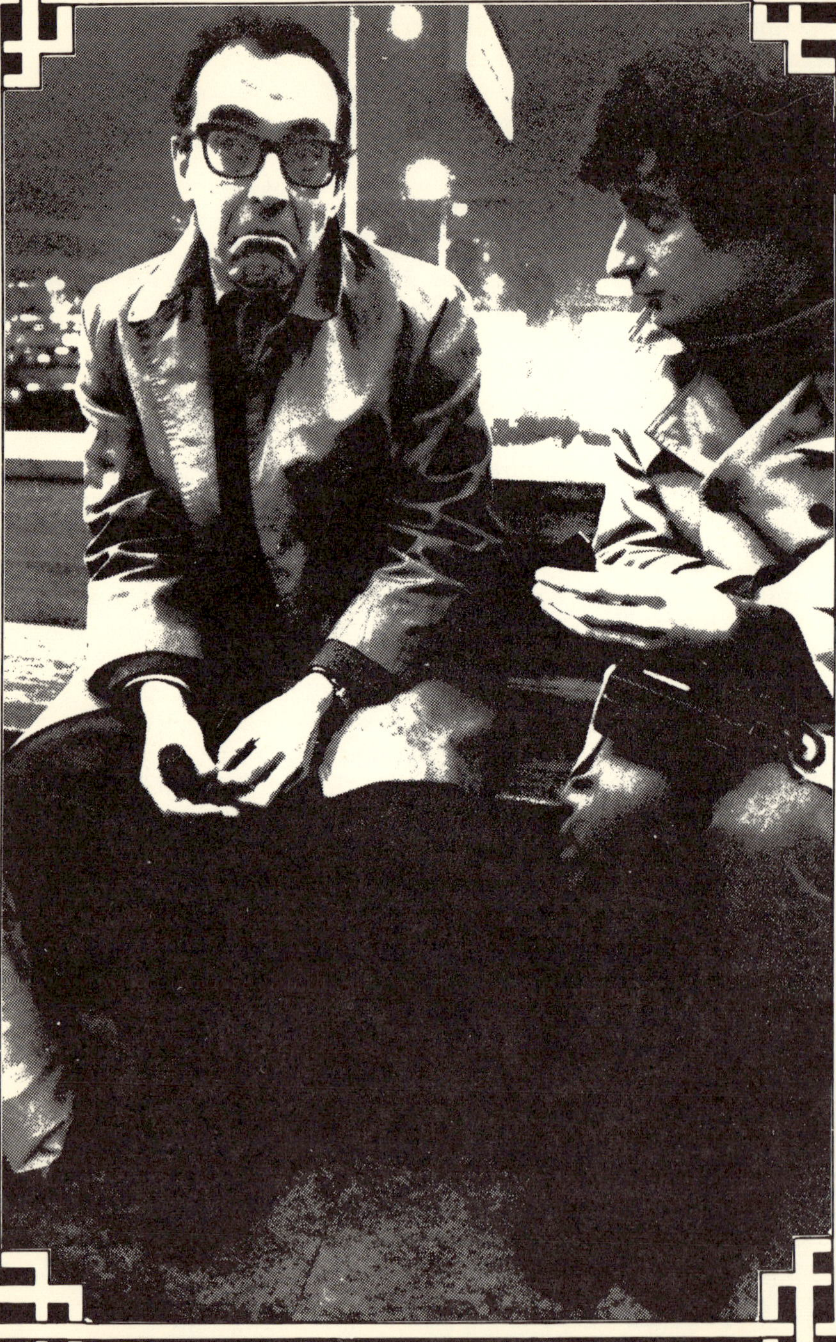

When you were in Berkeley and met some of the students, you made a statement that a film is a practical rifle and a rifle is a practical film.

Well, I gave another definition in an interview I had with a French newspaper: the film is a scientific experiment. I will give you a theoretical example. You need a film just as guerrillas—trekking about in the night, good users of rifles—need a light, a small light, in order to see. But it's not exactly a gun. It's a light which helps you check with your gun. But I still think it's a theoretical gun and I'll keep to this definition.

Why is it that in the last few films, your portrayal of the hippie revolutionaries, in Weekend *let's say, and in* One Plus One, *those two boys in the pornography bookshop. . . .*

They were not hippies. Their long hair isn't necessarily related to hippieness. It could be to clergymen, too. No, they were not hippies. They were just oppressed people.

Well, let's stick to Weekend *then, where you have the band of hippie guerrillas.*

Yes, but that was two years ago and it was the French situation of that time. It was different. It was utopian. And even then, they were more Yippies than hippies because they didn't hesitate to take up guns. Yippies in a French way, maybe. I remember a discussion in Berkeley this year. I had an interview with Eldridge Cleaver and he was reproaching people like Jerry Rubin and Abbie Hoffman. He said, "Those Yippie people like toy guns. We Black Power people like real guns."

One of the problems I felt about the Yippies you portrayed in Weekend *was that I was never sure whether there was any causal relationship between their will and the situation they were involved in, whether they were really a reflection of what was happening, whether they were in fact controlling the situation in some way, or whether they were just victims.*

They were terrorists. Or nihilists. Like the first young Russian nihilists putting bombs under the Tzar. They were nihilists and not really revolutionary, but revolutionaries are sometimes nihilists, too.

Isn't there a similarity between the two characters in Weekend *who wander off on their trip to the mother's home and the two characters in* Pierrot le Fou. *They have that picaresque quality to them. They travel around and things happen to them.*

Maybe, because this movie was done with personal feeling and intuition. After the May-June events I became aware of how late I was. *Weekend* wasn't done with a script. It came from a personal feeling, a personal intuition, as in *Pierrot le Fou.* But the intuition in *Weekend* was closer to the social situation in France than it was in *Pierrot le Fou.* It came from a clear political analysis and was then transformed into a movie.

One Plus One was more of that, and the next one, the American film, will be more yet. The idea is to make the script out of a political analysis and then to convey that, sometimes in poetry, sometimes science, sometimes all it takes is a film. The film itself is less and less spectacular because I think very strongly now that the more spectacular you are, the more you are absorbed by the things you are trying to destroy. You don't destroy anything at all, and it's you who are destroyed because of the spectacle. Some real examples are the films done in Hollywood about Che Guevara and Malcolm X. If Metro-Goldwyn-Mayer is going to do a movie about Che Guevara, the Cubans should be making it, but if Fidel Castro writes the script, Metro-Goldwyn-Mayer won't distribute it. So you can't do it.

After Pierrot le Fou, *your films changed.*

Let's say that early period was my hippie period. I was addicted to movies as the hippies are addicted to marijuana. Now I went through marijuana (I don't smoke marijuana, but I don't need to because movies are the same to me), but now I'm over this movie marijuana magic thing.

All the earlier films were extremely romantic—the sensibilities of all your protagonists were related: all of them seemed to be dominated by the feeling of early death, lack of relationships, and detachment. All those early characters died, except for the character in Le Petit Soldat, *and he was a fascist character.*

Yes, but I'm realizing that only today. Yes, because I was an idealist, and the idea of death relating to love and things like that is not completely fascist, maybe, but if you get too much involved in that, you are going in the wrong direction. It's a bourgeois philosophy, and it's an ideology I was guilty of.

Wasn't it hard for you to give it up?

No, because it was just one step after another.

Don Siegel's films are usually very right-wing. The idea of an action film, which you were obviously influenced by in your early films, usually leads to a kind of right-wing philosophy, whereas now you've gotten rid of the action and . . .

I quite agree with you. The film that made *Potemkin* possible was a fascist American movie called *Intolerance.* But they took out of it just what they needed, from a very technical standpoint, and then they changed it.

You've gotten rid of the action sequences now in One Plus One.

That may be, for the moment. I don't know what action is. I'm trying to demystify the movies at the same time as making them. I'm always amazed that so many of the militants are so fond of westerns, which I hate. They are not bothered by the fact that it's a fascist form. They don't care. They enjoy it. But a lot of people who lack their intelligence or their militancy are poisoned by that. The militants aren't, but the other people, the so-called ordinary people, are. That's why the scientists of the movie or of the theatre or of literature have to work on theory, to try to indicate how to found new bases, a new grammar, a new philosophy, a new mathematics out of it. And you discover how to do that by being linked to the militant people, by being yourself as militant as you can. It's very well explained in a Mao quotation. He said: Where are the right ideas coming from? Are they coming from the sky? No. They are coming from social practice. What is social practice? There are three kinds. There is scientific experiment. There is struggle for production and there is the class struggle. And I discovered, at about the same time as the major events occurred in France, that I was working only in the field of scientific experiment, and I myself have to be related to class struggle and struggle for production, though scientific experiment is still necessary.

This means of course that people who loved your films such as Bande à Part *are going to be disappointed now, aren't they?*

Yes. But movies like *Bande à Part* could still be done, but in a happier society, later, when we've found the right way to do it. Instead of being apart from the society, one will be in it. The fantasy at the end of *Bande à Part* will become real.

Do you think that's really possible?

Yes. We will do it. To make the end of *Bande à Part* possible, we have to have a South American revolution. After they've done that, and if we could help them to do it, the situation in South America will be much better.

It's all or nothing with you now, isn't it?

I prefer all. It's because I take it that all is possible, we don't have to give it away for nothing. Or pretend that since all is impossible, we might as well prefer nothing for the moment, the way hippies and others think.

Towards the end of Weekend, *you use a slogan to the effect that one can only surpass the horror of the bourgeoisie with more horror.*

Yes, I think so. Especially in the scientific experimentation. Not in the struggle for production or power, but in scientific experimentation, yes. You have to burn the opera. Not British Motor Corporation or General Motors, because that's not so clear. You do have to build some cars. But Covent Garden, Lincoln Center, the San Francisco Opera House, yes, we can burn them.

But there are still beautiful operas around.

We've tried other ways, but it's no use. If we don't burn them we'll always be absorbed by going into them.

It's strange that you would be willing to burn Schoenberg's Moses and Aaron *and not General Motors.*

No, not burn them, just forget about them a bit. As Mao said, if we burn books, we would not know how to criticize them.

Is it unfair to say that in Weekend, *the sense of aggression that you feel towards the bourgeoisie might not in fact be an aggression against yourself?*

True. Of course. If it would have been possible to have made the film dirtier pornography, then I would have.

Why did you have to kill those animals?

Well, why not? A lot of people are killed in Africa and Vietnam. Why shouldn't I kill animals? It was not done because animals are animals compared with human beings; it's just that if I had killed a human being I would have been put in jail.

But the killing of an animal is naturally and too easily shocking.

I think an audience will be much more shocked by the death of a pig than by the death of a human being, even if it were told that it was a real human being. One is not used to the idea of shooting animals just for a movie.

In Bresson's film Balthazar, *the donkey is shot at the conclusion. And that death, because it's located in a very Christian, Catholic sense of experience, raises that film to an extraordinary emotional and spiritual height.*

Then it has to be destroyed. Catholic! It's disgusting. I don't think he died. And if it does die, I think it's crueler to kill him later than right away.

You think it's crueler to kill Balthazar than to kill the pig?

You just have to do it because it's a further demonstration. This is the way we are. We are killing innocent people.

Because we're killing innocent people, does it mean you have to show other kinds of destruction?

There's no argument. You do it. Or you don't do it.

You quote Lautréamont in Weekend. *Now* Maldoror *in fact, underneath all the fantasy, is an incredibly strong indictment of the self-destructive processes of the bourgeois family. In other words, the attack on the bourgeoisie has been made often before. What makes your focal attack now different?*

It's no use to talk of attack in *Weekend,* which was just for fun. It was more of a Yippie movie, I think. A toy gun.

But isn't it true that the Yippies in this film are fascistic and nihilistic . . .

Oh, they're just nihilists. They are not fascists, because they attack the fascists.

Well, a criticism that has been levelled against Weekend *is that if you attack the fascists in that way, then you may be slightly fascistic yourself.*

No, I don't think so because you have seen that I'm attacking the fascists.

At the end of Weekend, *the Yippies are shown to be cannibals. How do you justify cannibalism even with the world being as it is?*

I'm not justifying it. You have to criticize it. This is not a Hollywood movie. In a Hollywood movie, after the movie is over, there's nothing more. There is no relationship between the screen and the spectator. There's just a duration. If you don't like it, you go to sleep, the way I do. But in other movies, you can't forget about it. You have to talk about it afterwards.

In Pierrot le Fou *Belmondo says, speaking for you I suppose, that what he's interested in are the colors and the spaces between people. And now apparently you've said that what is alive is not what is on the screen but what is between the spectator and the screen. What do you mean by that?*

I mean that the movie is not on screen. The movie stems from moving. The movie is a mover. The move from the reality to the screen and back to the reality. And the screens are nothing, just shades. It's like a swimmer doing a crawl until he arrives at the end of the swimming pool and then turning and going back again. This is the screen.

Who is the swimmer, film maker or spectator?

They both are. When you arrive, it's the movie maker; and when you start, it's the spectator.

In One Plus One *you show some interviews. There's one with Eve Democracy. And there's Frankie Dymon, the Black Power advocate in the film, being prompted and having statements fed to him . . .*

I wouldn't say fed. They were rehearsing, trying to learn from their comrades in the U. S., who are engaged in a more dangerous fight than their own in England.

But I had a sense of the impotency of the whole revolutionary movement because everyone was quoting something or someone else. There are all these microphones and cameras. Eve Democracy can only say yes or no.

Because she is democracy. What else can democracy say?

But Frankie Dymon too?

Yes, but this is the way it is. And it has to be shown and told frankly so that we can analyze it better and know how to do it. There is no meaning in the movie. The meaning comes before and after. The screen is nothing.

I just had a feeling of futility about everything that happened.

Yes, more or less. But the only ones to escape from that were the Blacks.

John Lennon recently replied to your comments about the

Beatles' not doing anything politically . . .

I'd like to see John Lennon play Trotsky in a film.

What did you mean when you were supposed to have said: "The Jefferson Airplane is me?"

I didn't say that.

How do you feel about the Stones and the Jefferson Airplane? They're two such different groups.

Well, the Rolling Stones are much more accomplished than the Jefferson Airplane, who are more like tribal people. That is, they present something which exists: the music and the hippie. There is some invention, but it should be politicized. The Stones are more political than the Jefferson Airplane, but they should be more and more so every day. The new music could be the beginning of a revolution, but it isn't. It seems more like a palliating to life. The Stones are still working for scientific experiment, but not for class struggle or the struggle for production.

What did you want to do with the Rolling Stones in One Plus One *when they constructed "Sympathy for the Devil"?*

I just wanted to show something in construction. To show that democracy was nowhere, not even constructive. Not destructive, of course, just saying: "We are against war" but doing nothing for peace, not having the strength to follow the Black man who is going to be a revolutionary.

One of the points, too, was that Eve Democracy was walking in a lush green field and the Black people were in a junkyard.

That's true.

And do you think of using colors conceptually in your films? You seem to use color almost symbolically in Contempt. *And in* Made in USA, *the color seems much more aesthetically beautiful than what happens in the film itself.*

They were just plain colors. I don't know that they were beautiful. I think the ideology of beauty should be very well analyzed, first destroyed, and then analyzed. Because we are completely mystified by beauty. So maybe we have to make horrible songs first in order to destroy and then to learn what beauty is. We have been taught what beauty is, but we don't really know.

You're not interested in the idea of the eternity any more?

No, not at all.

You don't feel a sense of loss at all? Are you happier with yourself?

Yes, much.

You're making a lot of film critics and audiences unhappy.

I just forget about that. My idea of film hasn't changed. It's just gone further in its own direction and needs to find the right allies. I would have arrived at the same position I'm at now, but in five years. But because of the May-June events, it came in two months. And I was late and I'm still late compared to other comrades who have simpler ideas about these things.

It was exactly the opposite with Bob Dylan. Maybe he was too early. Maybe he was going in the right direction, but too early for him. And he couldn't stand it, really, even if it was successful. He didn't have the political mind and thought. And now he's kind of broken and he has to protect himself and then go into the woods again.

The door to door theatre in La Chinoise: *is that what you think you're doing in films now?*

Yes. I just think I have fewer ideas, and other less analytical people have better ideas, more militant ideas, in other words.

How do you feel now about your "war" film, Les Carabiniers?

I don't feel. I don't think you should feel about a movie. You should feel about a woman, but not about a movie. You can't kiss a movie. Should you shoot about a movie or a painting? Let's have a look and talk about it, but certainly not feel about it. That's what the Church says, feel about God.

You're attacking culture now the way people used to attack religion.

Yes, it's the same thing.

When Malraux was asked in England about the May events, he quoted Marx and said that revolution occurs first as a tragedy and then as comedy. He said that now we're in the comic phase.

Yes, he is in the comic phase. I quite agree.

He wasn't talking about himself.

How does he know? We just have to take pictures of him. When French television is shooting in Parliament, the cameramen are told not to take any shots of Malraux because the people would laugh.

What do you think now about the disagreement you had with Ian Quarrier at the Film Festival, your punching him and the people heckling you.

I'll protect myself better next time, that's all. I was very disappointed with the Rolling Stones. They didn't even say it was the wrong idea to add the completed version of their song on to the end of the film. I wrote to them and they didn't say anything. It was very unfair for them to accept their being emphasized over all the others in the film. Each group of people is equal to the other, and one shouldn't over emphasize the playing of the Stones by repeating them. If the film is distributed, it will have a new title, the title of their song—"Sympathy for the Devil"—a producer's idea. It's unfair not from a personal point of view, but from a political point of view, unfair to the Black people.

Let's say someone goes to One Plus One *and comes out saying the whole revolutionary movement is useless.*

This is because he doesn't know how to look at pictures, because he thinks he has to say something afterwards. When you open a book of mathematics, if you've never studied mathematics, you can't say anything. And here, just because you have shadows which resemble reality, you think you're the authority about that and that and that. No, obviously, there's nothing to say You can say something tomorrow or two days afterwards. You can talk to other people. But you have to say: I have seen that and that. I've seen a girl in the woods. She was named Democracy. I've seen Black people reading that and that. And then maybe you ask questions about it. Why was it that way? And then you try to see what it means.

The film might not convince you that the revolutionary movement was correct.

The film doesn't have to convince. You shouldn't speak like that. It has to convince that there are better people than others. It's as if in one or two hours of a picture or twenty pages of a book you want the whole truth about the whole society, about everything, and it has to be right. It's absolutely wrong. It's impossible. It took Mao fifty years to write his little red book. Fifty years of fighting. And then it was very natural. It came from everything he had learned.

But the Rolling Stones' song covers a lot of ground, it contains a lot of material.

No, that's wrong. It has very little. That's why I was so angry with that ending. We should know only a little bit of it. We don't know what kind of song it is. It's just words, the beginning of words. It never goes to the end. Because the Rolling Stones are still at the very beginning.

But you hear what they're singing about at the very beginning, about Satan, about the Kennedys, the Tzar, about hippies getting killed before reaching Bombay. There's a lot of content in that one song.

No, there's very little. It's just that you hear it twenty times.

You seem to have such a clear idea of what you're doing, yet there are so many contradictions in the film.

Not in the film, but in the way you look at it. My films are much clearer than they were two or three years ago. They still might be very neophytic, because they're very simple. When you go out of *One Plus One*—ordinary people I mean, people who like James Bond—you might say: This is very complicated, I don't understand anything. But if you go out of the last James Bond film and I ask you, can you tell me what you've seen, you can't. No. There were 20,000 things in James Bond. The movie ran for two hours. I ask, was he in a car. Yes. What color was it? Do you remember the color? He was with a girl. What was he saying to her? And just after he left the girl, what was he doing? He can't remember. Maybe he could remember one or two moments. But he couldn't remember or describe to me the sequence of the story. It's like a mixed salad. You can't describe a mixed salad. There are too many things in it.

And then I ask him, you have just seen *One Plus One.* Do you think it's complicated? Well, let's see if it's complicated. Let's remember what you've seen. People playing music. Yes, you remember that. What else? Well, there were Black people in a junkyard throwing guns and reading things. And there was a girl in the woods. And in four minutes he can remember everything there was in the movie. And there is no more. Yes, but why? he says. I didn't understand why that girl was in the woods just before the sequence of the Black people. And I ask him, what do you think? What's she saying? She was only answering yes and no. Well, what kind of questions was she being asked? Do you remember any? And on and on like that. It's a very simple thing, really very simple. . . . These people have been taught that a James Bond film is a simple movie, while in fact it's really complicated and complicated in a dreadful, in a silly way, because there was no need for complication.

I think you're cheating now because a James Bond film is much simpler emotionally and intellectually than One Plus One.

Yes, maybe, in its reality. The world is more complicated, but not *One Plus One.*

What if a James Bond fan comes out of the movie and says, One Plus One *bored me. You couldn't really disagree with him if that was how he felt.* One Plus One *is a very intellectual film, it makes you think.*

That's because it's the only film like that. If there were a hundred more, made by a hundred different people, it wouldn't be like that. Forget about the film, just think about the Black people, think about the music people.

In the film you say that for an intellectual to be revolutionary, he has to give up his intellectuality; but in order to see the film you have to use your intellect.

You have to give it up at a certain time, but in order to use it again. It's important to give up being an intellectual in the way that the bourgeois conceives of an intellectual. We have to give up being that kind of an intellectual. But you don't have to blow up the world.

Why is it that One Plus One *seems to be telling you what is happening in such a different and more difficult way than Agnes Varda's* Black Panthers?

That is because most of the militants in art are going into the struggle for production and the struggle between the classes. They are forgetting about the scientific experiment, and I'm trying not to do that. Since I came from the scientific experiment, I still have too much of that experiment in me. That's why, when I have the money, I'm trying to make two pictures with other people for every one picture of my own.

Will you be working with more groups like the Jefferson Airplane or Rolling Stones in the future?

No, I don't think so.

What about your idea of using television as much as possible now?

Oh, you can't do that. You get more mystified than ever. Unless you think you can address 20 million people and you have something important to say and think you can go through all this mystification to get to the people, it's very difficult.

So where is there to go now?

You make very small movies to show to fewer people more often. More movies to fewer people, but much more often. So you can survive.

You have a lot of courage.

No, it's very natural. I couldn't do anything else. You have to know how to survive. You have to be optimistic, because the world situation is so bad. Marx said that. The very pessimistic situation makes me feel optimistic. I'm an optimist because things are so bad they must get better because they can't be worse than they are. It's the same today.

Chabrol's Les Biches *is a film that's very far away from any political reality; yet it's a very elegant film. In your terms, what is the correct response to this film? Do you say, this is just bourgeois reactionary indulgence, or that, considering what it is, there are some things going on in it which you're interested in.*

If there are, they're so well absorbed that there's no necessity to say so. I see no difference between that and even a picture like *If,* for example. I really think that a good picture, today, cannot be successful. Maybe a small minority will be good, but even so they won't be shown—*Potemkin* was banned for 30 years all over Europe.

But Weekend *is doing well in the States.*

Yes, but possibly in the wrong way. That's why I'm sorry I didn't make it dirtier.

A lot of what you're saying sounds to me extremely suicidal.

Not at all. Maybe when I was doing *Weekend* I was that way, but not any longer.

I just hate to give up the idea of your old films.

They are what they are, what I was at that time.

What are you going to do after this English film?

We're trying to find a script by Cohn-Bendit to make a film I don't really think is possible—a political Western [*Wind from the East*], that will not be absorbed by the establishment. And we're going to try to make money to make small films.

So really, the film makers like Antonioni and your peers don't interest you any more.

Not at all. I like Antonioni as a person, but I think he's wrong doing a picture for MGM. You can't make a good picture. Or if the picture is good then MGM won't distribute it. Maybe in ten years it will be different, but that's the situation today. Maybe he could do a lot of good things in it as a person, but he has to change his life. One has to. Maybe this is easier for people who have nothing to do than for those who have something to do.

Antonioni is like Peter Brook and those other people. They don't want to change, really. They want to make pictures, they want to make plays. I mean, I'm asking not to be killed but to be able to live with my wife and things like that, but I'm really not especially asking to make pictures. I like other people. I like to work with them and especially so since we are working in a more collective way.

When there's a movie to be done, I can just take the train and say, oh, you're doing a movie, ok, I'm coming, I'll work with you. I can go and discuss it with people, I don't need to be behind the camera. But most of these other people, no, they still want to have that camera. If I'm like that now, it's because I feel more experimental than others. So I take from them the class struggle analysis and then bring in my own scientific experiment. It's not because I'm the director. I really don't care about that.

Do you feel more like a medium now, someone whom ideas go through?

No, more like a worker, a student, or a worker concerned with student power. When you do something bad, you're not ashamed, you're sorry for it. Ok, it's bad, I must do it better, but you sleep very well. It doesn't matter. And if a very good friend of mine says, I hate your picture, I'm no failure at all. I say, tell me why you think it's bad. But five years ago, that response from a friend made me very sad. Which was crazy. I don't understand how I could have felt that.

1969

Dr. Stanley Krippner

A couple of thousand persons at the Portchester Theater were enjoying the Grateful Dead concert on the night of February 19, 1971 when a series of slides appeared on a screen above:

1. YOU ARE ABOUT TO PARTICIPATE IN AN E.S.P. EXPERIMENT.
2. IN A FEW SECONDS YOU WILL SEE A PICTURE.
3. TRY USING YOUR E.S.P. TO "SEND" THIS PICTURE TO MALCOLM BESSENT.
4. HE WILL TRY TO DREAM ABOUT THE PICTURE. TRY TO "SEND" IT TO HIM.

The last slide added helpfully:

5. MALCOLM BESSENT IS AT THE MAIMONIDES DREAM LAB IN BROOKLYN.

Then a color transparency was projected, showing a man in lotus position practicing yoga meditation, with his "seven spinal chakras"—energy centers near the spinal column—portrayed in vivid colors.

At Maimonides, miles away, Malcolm was asleep. A monitoring device indicated he was going through REM—the rapid eye movements which normally accompany a dream. Researchers at the dream lab awakened him, and he recounted his dream: "I was very interested in . . . using natural energy . . . I was talking to this guy who said he'd invented a way of using solar energy and he showed me this box . . . to catch the light from the sun, which was all we needed to generate and store the energy . . . I was discussing with this other guy a number of other areas of communication and we were exchanging ideas on the whole thing . . . He was suspended in mid-air or something . . . I was thinking about rocket ships . . . about an energy box and . . . a spinal column."

The attempt to use an audience as a psychic transmitter was repeated a total of six times during the Dead concerts at Portchester, and a panel of judges, rating Malcolm's descriptions of his dreams on a one hundred-point scale, said he'd made a close correlation four out of six times. (Different pictures were used each time, usually brightly colored slides like "A Synthetic Emblematic Cross" or Magritte's "Philosophy in the Boudoir." The slides were chosen at random by sealing them in envelopes, then choosing two each night from the batch and finally selecting one by a last-minute flip of a coin.)

Another "psychic sensitive," Felicia Parise, tried to pick up the Portchester transmissions while asleep in her apartment, where she was awakened at 90-minute intervals and asked to recount her dreams. She came close only once in six nights, which researchers said tends to confirm that psychic communication works better when the people transmitting know where and to whom they're beaming their thoughts.

The study of psychic phenomena has a long and colorful history—ranging from the Rev. C. L. Tweedale, a Yorkshire vicar who informed the world in 1941 that he had made contact with Chopin and Sir Arthur Conan Doyle, to Astronaut Edgar Mitchell, who during rest periods in the Apollo 14 space capsule, focused his attention on cards showing stars, crosses, waves, circles, and squares, and tried to beam them back to four subjects on earth. (Two of them got 51 correct out of 200, an interesting result since statistically they should have gotten only 40.)

But the man responsible for the Grateful Dead experiment—Dr. Stanley Krippner, director of the Maimonides Dream Laboratory—seems less eccentric than most students of the psychic. A softspoken gentleman who embodies what Santayana called an attitude of skepticism and animal faith, he has been fascinated by psychic phenomena since he devoured ghost stories and science fiction as a child. He did graduate work in psychology at Northwestern, worked with Dr. Gardner Murphy at the University of Hawaii, and taught for three years at Kent State ("I knew something horrible was going to happen, and I wanted to get out of there as soon as possible"). He came to the Dream Lab in 1964. In the following interview, Dr. Krippner talked about his work, beginning with the Grateful Dead test.

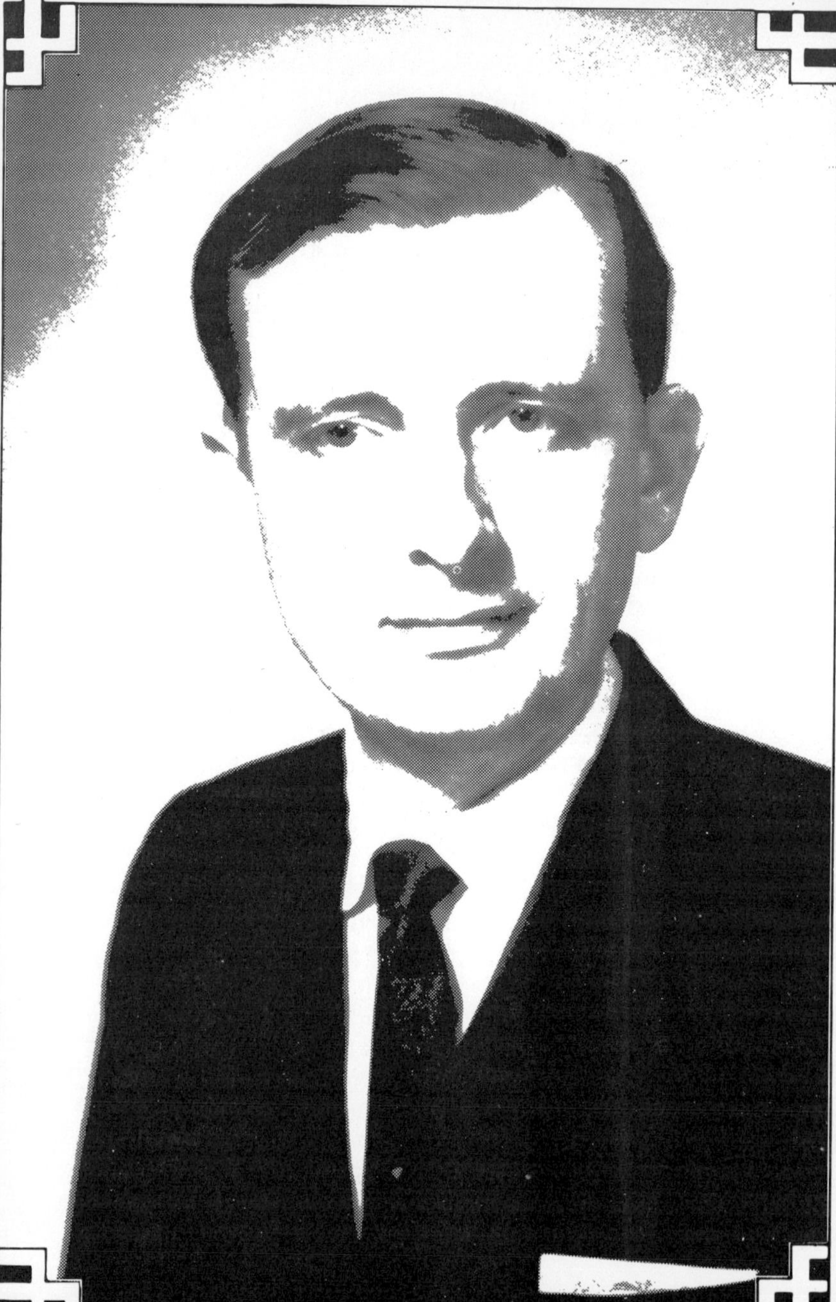

We feel that the music was important for two reasons. First of all, the music appeals to a person's nonverbal nature, to levels of consciousness below the intellect, and we think that this is just the area in which ESP resides. It's basically nonverbal, emotional, and unconscious. And we think the tie-in with music is a very logical one. If we had had a middle-aged concert audience, maybe something else would have worked better. For the opportunity we were given, for the age and condition of the people that we used, we thought that this would really be ideal.

When Jerry Garcia suggested the experiment, I said fine, this is ideal, because having the Dead play the music, having these two thousand people at various states of consciousness in the audience, is going to really test out the hunches we get from nature, from ESP—about where it comes from and how it works. We know that this is just the first step—it doesn't prove anything in and of itself—but it works so well that it gives us some ideas and some impetus for future studies.

You seem at once to sympathize with the idea of supposed paranormal behavior and yet hold to a skeptical attitude concerning the supposed manifestations. You've mentioned that there are psychologists who think that some of these manifestations are the result of a regression to the undifferentiated perceptions of early childhood or, alternatively, a manifestation of super-individual perception, a kind of highly evolved awareness. This suggests some similarity between regression and advanced comprehension.

Now that's a very basic issue. You see, this relates to things that are even more important than ESP. This relates to the phenomenon of transpersonal experience. I think that the infant who is in an undifferentiated state, who doesn't have any sense of ego or self at that point, at some level does feel that he is part of the whole world. He doesn't differentiate himself from his mother, he doesn't differentiate himself from the objects around him. But then he goes through this whole long process in which he develops a sense of self, some sort of ego strength, some sort of competency, and he starts to know who he is, what he wants, and so forth.

Now, if the personality development is mature, if it flows along adequately enough, he will eventually get to the point in his life where he is able to go above the ego and have transpersonal experiences, able to feel himself part of all mankind, part of all living things, part of all creation. And he can do this spontaneously, he can do this through personal relationships, he can do it through meditation, occasionally he can do it through drugs, sometimes he can do it through nature. I think that this is a mark of a highly mature, highly developed person—the capacity for transpersonal experience.

What makes one person a saint and another a babbling baby?

The whole middle part. I think only the person with the strong ego is able to transcend his ego, if the power is given in a wholesome way. Many people who have bad acid trips have such weak egos they shouldn't try to transcend them. They should start building up their own sense of competence first.

If everyone attained a high level of perception, you wouldn't really need to know consciously that an agent was sending you information.

That's possible. Somebody very highly developed spiritually, like a Zen master or a Yogi, would be able to pick up indirectly transmitted messages, and we have a lot of anecdotal instances of that. But we aren't fortunate enough to have this type of person working with us everyday. We have to gear ourselves to the people that we have available, and with most people who are capable of ESP, intentionality does seem to be an important thing. A Yogi or a Zen master would be able to handle a lot of incoming information. He would not become chaotic and would know exactly what was going on and coming in. But those people who were given Yoga for just a short period of time would be inundated, wouldn't be able to separate it out. There would be chaos.

How do you take into account personal unconscious dream material when one of your dreamers is being sent images by an agent?

Well, this is why we have interviews with these people, why we spend time with them helping them to work on all of these things. And from time to time we really feel we shouldn't go further along these lines until they've gotten to know themselves a little better. We feel that sometimes a person overinvests himself in psychic development and that the rest of his development has to catch up with him. So there is some therapy here, sure.

This is why we have post-sleep interviews after the experimental night is over—to get all of the subject's associations developed so that these outside judges can look at the associations. They might think, well, that's basically the archetype that was used in the picture, but he added something to it, or he displaced, repressed, or embellished something. And here again they're not one hundred percent perfect in terms of the tools and judges we have available, but we're quite satisfied that they're understanding most of what goes on in terms of the type of analysis that they have to do.

Do you think it's possible that a group of people can, through black magic, project and commit evil on someone?

Yes, I do. ESP is neither good or bad, but it can be used for good or evil purposes. For the same reasons that I never do any military research, there are certain places where I draw the line constantly. I make moral decisions all the time. The whole folk tradition of possession by evil spirits isn't far off. Rather than these evil spirits being external, I think that they're probably internal and represent a portion of the personality that is out of control and that's taken over an undisciplined individual and wreaked all sorts of harm. But you can still call it possession. The term is very apt. They're all around, both the bad and good witches.

Do you know about the work being done on plants' receptivity to thoughts and pain?

This is why I'm not a vegetarian. I think that plants do suffer when we eat them and I think that what we have to do is the same thing that Peter Rabbit is doing in the Libre commune, for example—using these things for loving and creative purposes. This is the only justification you have for ingesting life, whether it be plant or animal material.

You've written how predatory animals—cats, dogs, men—have more time to go through Rapid Eye Movements—to dream—than hunted animals like antelopes, deer, and rabbits, who can't afford to waste time dreaming.

This is one of nature's compensations. Every aggressive individual has his non-aggressive side and vice versa. And the fact may be that human beings, who are basically aggressive, do have many dreams about gentle creatures in an attempt to reach this level of their personality.

What kind of things are you working on at the Dream Laboratory now?

Oh, every day is interesting in one way or another. We have two psychics from South America coming out to heal some of our people of ailments—backaches, toothaches, things like that. And we're also doing a study in which we teach people to control their brain waves. The brain wave feedback program involves an adaption of the electroencephalograph machine, that allows us to set it for a certain number of cycles per second.

Now, the Alpha wave occurs at eight, nine, ten, eleven, twelve, and thirteen cycles per second. This is the type of brain wave characterized by relaxation, meditation, passivity, calmness, etc. When a person is in that frequency range, the machine produces a pleasant little tone. Then he knows that he's producing Alpha waves, and so he tries to get back to the same state of mind that produced the tone. Many people are able to get that tone to extend longer and longer. Some people are able to get that tone to run for four to five minutes, which means that they are producing nothing but alpha waves for that period of time. This is the type of brain wave that Yoga and Zen produces, and we thought that this would be a natural place to start. Also there are only four basic brain waves, and so the choice really wasn't all that great.

This is the state of the mind with no visual images, no problem-solving type thinking, usually just an awareness of the bodily processes in a very relaxed situation, that differs from person to person. We're trying to find out if there's any relationship between this brain wave and ESP. And the results indicate that there is a relationship, but it's a highly complicated one. So the next study that we're doing at the lab right now also explores the Theta wave frequency, which comprises four, five, six, and seven cycles per second. We're checking a number of these things out together to see how they relate.

You've mentioned that you're doing work with an electrosone machine.

The machine is basically quite simple. It attaches four

electrodes to the head, two above the eyes and two back of the ears on the mastoid bones, and small amounts of current are sent into the four electrodes. This has the effect of slowing down the brain waves somewhat and producing an altered state of consciousness.

It's Alpha plus other rhythms. Now, when I had an experience with the electrosone machine, I had beautiful visual imagery, I felt very relaxed, and after the electrodes were taken off I felt invigorated and alert for the rest of the day. It was very enjoyable, and that after only fifteen minutes under the machine. We're trying to find out if an experience with this machine affects a person's ESP, how different personality types react to this machine, and what their relationship is to the ESP.

So right now we have the brain wave training project going. We have the electro-sleep project going. And then we have a third project going with sensory bombardment, where we have a light machine that flashes lights and stereophonic music. We're trying to find out what effect this has on a person's ESP. We ran a study last year that was highly successful, and it did tend to stimulate ESP, probably by breaking up traditional perceptual patterns and allowing new things to filter in. I think we have produced some very useful information, not only about ESP, but what happens in dreams, in Alpha, in electro-sleep.

Paranormal is anything psychic. One example of that would be pre-cognitive, which means having knowledge of some future event. And you have various types of paranormal phenomena, psychic phenomena. You have ESP, and there are various types of ESP: pre-cognition; retro-cognition, in which you gain knowledge about a past event; clairvoyance; and telepathy. And then you have all of the psychokinesis phenomena, from the spontaneous PK phenomena like poltergeists to the experimental phenomena like influencing the fall of dice, healing phenomena, to thought photography—the influence of so-called mind over so-called matter.

ESP seems to play the same role in your work as the sex instinct did in Freud's.

You see, you have to start someplace with what you think is most interesting. You start one place, and if you keep being broadminded, you will end up in the inner core of reality. ESP is really a metaphor. The Russians use terms that I'm much more impressed by—biological energy, biological communication.

I've told you about three studies that we did, the brain wave training, sensory bombardment, and electro-sleep. Well, we've just finished the fourth study on hypnotic dreams. We hypnotize people and tell them to dream while they're in hypnosis, and they try to dream about the contents of a sealed envelope. They don't have what you would call nighttime dreams, it's a very vivid image which is dreamlike in nature. You might use the term daydream. Hypnotic dream is the technical term for it. Hypnotic fantasy is probably more accurate. We've found out that this is a very efficient way to get results.

And as I say, we just finished a study with that, and we've just finished writing up the Grateful Dead study, which is a dream study. Those five studies give you the five areas of consciousness that we work with. The Alpha state, the hypnotic state, the dream state, the sensory bombardment state, and the electro-sleep state. And there are probably many more that we can go into, but that's where we are right now.

If we lived in a society where ESP was accepted, where children were brought up to develop their powers, then we could run all our experiments in the so-called ordinary way to get good results. But we have the kind of society where creativity is repressed. ESP, originality, and fantasy are repressed, and we feel that all things tie around, go hand in hand and work together. So to study ESP we try to find those moments in a person's existence when typical conditioning is suspended, sleep being one of them.

I think this is a very exciting time to be alive. The old structures are falling apart. They don't work. They're making people miserable. As these old structures fall apart there's going to be a lot of suffering. However, you have both the Yin and the Yang. The advantage is that whenever the old structures fall apart you have an unparalleled opportunity for creativity because people are not depending upon old ways of thinking and behaving. They are able to enter into new things, many of which are going to work, and many of which are going to provide hopefully a more enlightened, more realistic structure for the future. And so if we can just hang with it during these difficult days, I think that something much better is going to emerge.

1971

John Lennon

In 1968, John Lennon decided to become more "public" and to demystify his Beatle persona. He and Yoko Ono (whom he had met in the fall of 1966) were shortly to begin preparations for the series of now-famous Bed-Ins for peace (in Amsterdam and Montreal). And although the Beatles were at the time of the interview just finishing work on their two-record "white" album, it seems in retrospect that John and Yoko's life together necessitated the creation of a new kind of non-Beatle relationship for both of them.

The following interview—one of the first he gave since his meeting up with Yoko—took place at their temporary basement flat in London—a flat where Jimi Hendrix, Ringo Starr, and William Burroughs, among others, had recently stayed. But the flat seemed as much John's and Yoko's as the Indian incense which took over the living room. The walls were covered with photos of John, of Yoko, a giant Sgt. Pepper ensign, Richard Chamberlain's poster collage of news clippings of the Stones bust, the *Time* magazine cover of the Beatles.

We arrived at five on the afternoon of September 17, 1968, said hello to Robert Fraser, who arranged the interview, and to John and Yoko, sitting together, looking "très bien ensemble." We sat around a simple wooden table, covered with magazines, newspapers, sketch paper, boxes, drawings, a beaded necklace shaped in the form of a pentangle.

John said he had to be at a recording session in a half hour, so we talked for a while about John's show at the Fraser Gallery. John wrote some reminders to himself in the wonderfully intense and absorbed way that a kid has painting the sun for the first time: "Were art to redeem man, it could do so only by saving him from the seriousness of life and restoring him to an unexpected boyishness."

When we arrived the next afternoon, September 18, John was walking around the room, humming what sounded like "Hold Me Tight"—just singing the song to the air. Old Fifties forty-fives were scattered about the floor, and John played Rosie and the Originals' version of "Give Me Love." We talked about the lyrics of Gene Vincent's "Woman Love." In spite of having slept only two hours, John asked us to sit down on the floor and begin the interview.

Any suspicions that John would be ornery, mean, cruel, or brutish—feelings attributed to him and imagined by press reports and various paranoic personalities—never arose even for the purpose of being pressed down. As John said simply about the interview: "There's nothing more fun than talking about your own songs and your own records. I mean you can't help it, it's your bit, really. We talk about them together. Remember that."

It's impossible to recapture in print John's inflections and pronunciations of words like "ahppens," for example. Wish you had been there.

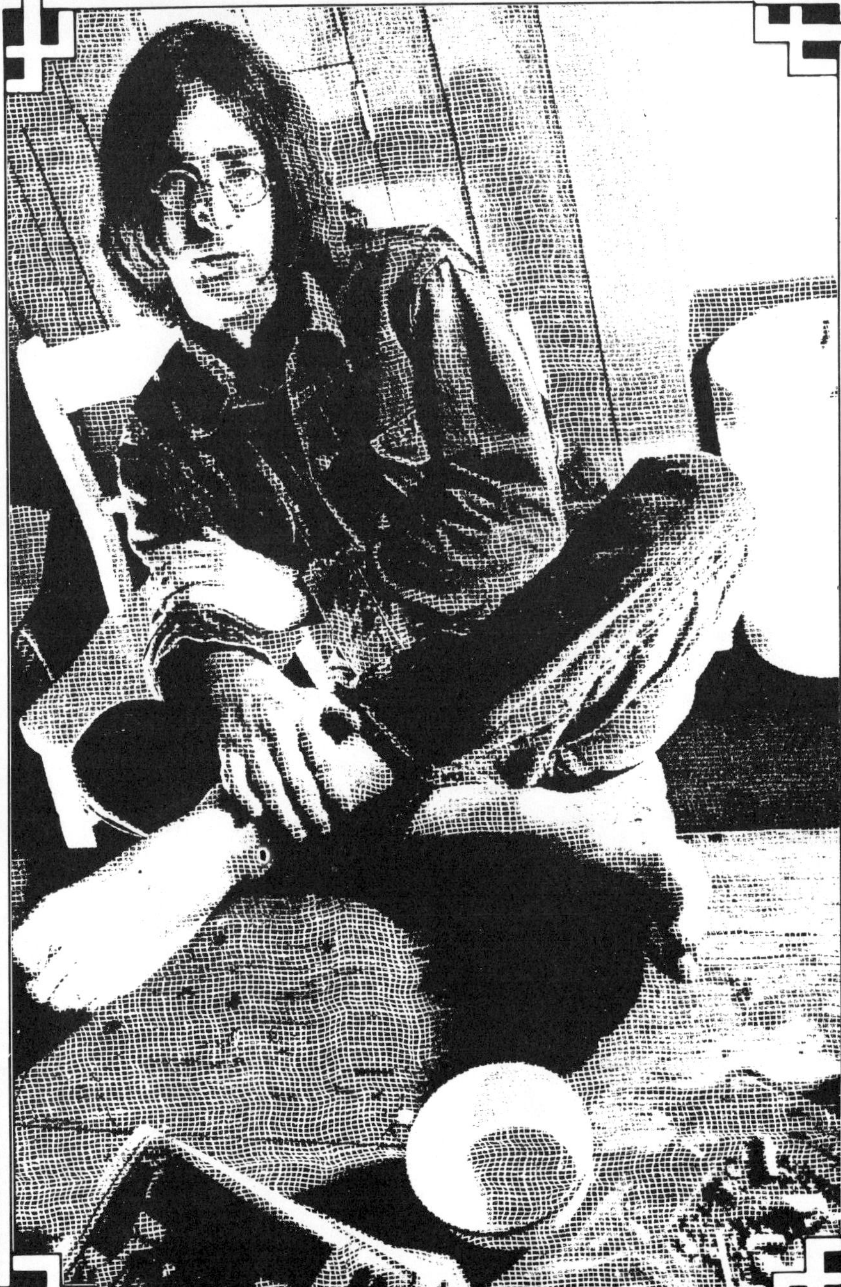

I've listed a group of songs that I associate with you, in terms of what you are or what you were, songs that struck me as embodying you a little bit: "You've Got to Hide Your Love Away," "Strawberry Fields," "It's Only Love," "She Said She Said," "Lucy's in the Sky," "I'm Only Sleeping," "Run for Your Life," "I am the Walrus," "All You Need is Love," "Rain," "Girl."

Ah, yeh! I agree with some of them, you see. Things like "Hide Your Love Away," right, I'd just discovered Dylan really. "It's Only Love"—I was always ashamed of that 'cause of the abominable lyrics you know—they're probably all right. George just came and talked about it last night. He said, remember we always used to cringe when the guitar bit came on, when we did that blamm blam blam-blam-blam, we liked it but there was something wrong.

And "She Said She Said"—yeh, I dug that cause I was going through a bad time writing then and so I couldn't hear it, but then I heard it and so I dug it. "Lucy in the Sky," all right. "Sleeping," it's like that. "Run for Your Life" I always hated, you know. "Walrus," yeah, "Girl," yeah, "All You Need Is Love"—hah, you know that's sort of natural.

The ones that really meant something to me—look, I don't know about "Hide Your Love Away," that's so long ago—probably "Strawberry Fields," "She Said," "Walrus," "Rain," "Girl," there are just one or two others, "Day Tripper," "Paperback Writer," even. "Ticket to Ride" was one more, I remember that. It was a definite sort of change . . . "Norwegian Wood"—that was the sitar bit. Definitely, I consider them moods or moments.

I feel you in these songs more than in a song like "Michelle," for example.

Yeh, right, they're me touch. Well the thing is, I don't know how they'd work out if I recorded them with other people, it would be entirely different. But it's my music with my band when it's me singing it, and it's Paul's music with his band. Sometimes it's halvey-halvey you know. When we write them together, they're together. But I'm not proud of all my songs. "Walrus," "Strawberry Fields," I'll sort of stick my name on them, the others are a bit . . . I think they're more powerful.

I heard that "Strawberry Fields" was written when you were sitting on a beach alone.

Yeh, in Spain, filming *How I Won the War.* I was going through a big scene about song writing again you know—I seem to go through it now and then, and it took me a long time to write it. See, I was writing all bits and bits. I wanted the lyrics to be like conversation. It didn't work, that one verse was sort of ludicrous really, I just wanted it to be like [John sing-talks] "we're talking and I just happen to be singing"—like that. And it was very quiet. But it was written in this big Spanish house, part of it, and then finished on the beach. It was really romantic—singing it, too—I don't know who was there.

Don't you find something special about the song?

Oh yes, definitely yes. It was a big scene, like I'd say "Ticket to Ride" was a big scene, "Rain" was, not so much, but because of the backwards, you know. That was the time I discovered *backwards* accidentally.

It was the first time I discovered it. On the end of "Rain" you hear me singing it backwards. We'd done the main thing at EMI and the habit was then to take the songs home and see what you thought a little extra gimmick or what the guitar piece would be.

So I got home about five in the morning, stoned out of me head, I staggered up to me tape recorder and I put it on, but it came out backwards, and I was in a trance in the earphones, what *is* it—what *is* it? It's too *much,* you know, and I really wanted the whole song backwards almost, and that was it. So we tagged it on the end. I just happened to have the tape the wrong way round, it just came out backwards, it just blew me mind. The voice sounds like old Indian.

There have been a lot of philosophical analyses written about your songs, "Strawberry Fields" in particular . . .

Well, they *can* take them apart. They can take anything apart. I mean I hit it on all levels, you know. We write lyrics, and I write lyrics that you don't realize what they mean till after. Especially some of the better songs or some of the more flowing ones, like "Walrus." The whole first verse was written without any knowledge. And "Tomorrow Never Knows"—I didn't know what I was saying, and you just find out later, that's why these people are good on them. I know that when there are some lyrics

I dig I know that somewhere people will be looking at them, and with the rest of the songs it doesn't matter cause *they* work on all levels. Anything. I don't mind what they do. And I dig that people notice that I have a sort of strange rhythm scene, because I've never been able to keep rhythm on the stage. I always used to get lost. It's me double off-beats.

In "Lucy in the Sky with Diamonds," what about an image like "newspaper taxis"?

That was a Paul line, I think. In a lot of them you'll get so far. You've lumbered yourself with a set of images and it's an effort to keep it up.

Pop analysts are often trying to read something into songs that isn't there.

It is there. It's like abstract art really. It's just the same really. It's just that when you have to think about it to write it, it just means that you labored at it. But when you just *say* it, man, you know you're saying it, it's a continuous flow. The same as when you're recording or just playing, you come out of a thing and you *know* "I've been there" and it was nothing, it was just pure, and that's what we're looking for all the time, really.

What is Strawberry Fields?

It's a name, it's a nice name. When I was writing "In My Life"—I was trying "Penny Lane" at that time—we were trying to write about Liverpool, and I just listed all the nice sounding names just arbitrarily. Strawberry Fields was a place near us that happened to be a Salvation Army home. But Strawberry Fields—I mean I have visions of *Strawberry Fields.* And there was Penny Lane, the Cast Iron Shore which I've just got in some song now, and they were just good names, just groovy names. Just good sounding. Because Strawberry Fields is anywhere you want to go. Actually I've just written a song which goes "I told you about Strawberry Fields / And you heard about the Walrus and me / Told you about the Fool on the Hill . . . ," it's amazing.

How much do you think the songs go towards building up a myth of a state of mind?

I don't know. I mean we got a bit pretentious. Like everybody we had our phase and now it's a little change over to trying to be more natural, less "newspaper taxis," say. I mean we're just changing. I don't know what we're doing at all, I just write them. Really, I just like rock and roll. I mean these [pointing to a pile of Fifties records] are the records I dug then, I dig them now, and I'm still trying to reproduce "Some Other Guy" sometimes or "Be-Bop-A-Lula," whatever it is, it's the same bit for me, it's really just the sound.

What's the flip side of "Angel Baby" called—the song you played before we started the interview?

"Give Me Love" by Rosie and the Originals. An amazing record. It's one of the greatest strange records, it's all just out of beat and everybody misses it—they knocked off the B side in ten minutes. I talk Yoko's leg off telling her this is it, this is what it's all about. There's just one line in this Miracles' record—"I've Been Good to You"—where it goes "You got me Cry-y-y-y-eying"—no breath, a beautiful little piece, I always love to hear it. I think he's [Smokey Robinson] got the most perfect voice, you know. I just think the group's got into such a samey groove that it spoils it really.

In "Penny Lane," you have the lines: "A pretty nurse is selling poppies from a tray / And though she thinks she's in a play / She is anyway." Aside from the little kid's quality of these lines, isn't this what you've been saying recently?

Paul had the main bit of that, but I remember working on those lines. It's always been a bit of "She's in a play, she is anyway, heh heh" because you're saying that again and again, it's a game, man, it's a game, but because you mean it, it's all right, it's OK. There's all that in it. To us it's just Penny Lane cause we lived there.

The Beatles seem to be one of the only groups who ever made a distinction between friends and lovers. For instance, there's the "baby" who can drive your car. But when it comes to "We Can Work it Out," you talk about "my friend." In most other groups' songs, calling someone "baby" is a bit demeaning compared to your distinction.

Yeh, I don't know why. It's Paul's bit, that—"Buy you a diamond ring, my friend"—it's an alternative to baby. You can take it logically the way you took it. See, I don't know really. Yours is as true a way of looking at it as any other way. In "Baby, You're a Rich Man" the point was, stop moaning, you're a rich man and we're all rich men, heh heh, baby!

It's a bit of a mocking song, then?

Well they all get like that a bit, cause there *is* all that in it, that's the point. As we write them or as we sing them that happens you know. And in different takes just the inclination of your voice will change the meaning of the lyrics, and that's why it's after we've done them that we really see what they are. By that time the weight's on it.

I once heard a twelve-year-old girl singing along with "All You Need Is Love," and she substituted the word "hate" for "love" as she sang.

Could be right, you know. Well, it's like the old Peter Sellers gag—"If only I had the Latin"—meaning, if I had the breaks, you know, all you need is love. I just meant it, I felt it, that's what you needed. Of course when I'm down it doesn't work at all, but I believe it in the songs. That's the thing about writing the songs—you say, well, all you need is love, there you go, and it's a bit of a statement, but you've got to do it. You can't live up to it, that's the thing.

I've felt your other mood recently: "Here I stand head in hand" in "Hide Your Love Away" and "When I was a boy, everything was right" in "She Said She Said."

Yeh, right. That was pure. That was what I meant all right. You see when I wrote that I had the "She said she said," but it was just meaning nothing, it was just vaguely to do with someone that had said something like he knew what it was like to be dead and then it was just a sound. And then I wanted a middle-eight. The beginning had been around for days and days and so I wrote the first thing that came into my head and it was "When I was a boy," in a different beat, but it was real because it just happened.

It's funny, because while we're recording we're all aware and listening to our old records and we say, we'll do one like "The Word"—make it like that—it never does turn out like that, but we're always comparing and talking about the old albums—just checking up, what is it? Like swatting up for the exam—just listening to everything.

Yet people think that you're trying to get away from the old records.

But I'd like to make a record like "Some Other Guy." I haven't done one that satisfies me as much as that satisfied me. Or "Be-Bop-A-Lula" or "Heartbreak Hotel" or "Good Golly, Miss Molly" or "Whole Lot of Shakin'." I'm not being modest. I mean we're still trying it. We sit there in the studio and we say, how did it go, how did it go? Come on, let's do *that.* Like what Fats Domino has done with "Lady Madonna"—"See how they ruhhnnn."

Are there any other versions of your songs you like?

Well, Ray Charles' version of "Yesterday"—that's beautiful. And "Eleanor Rigby" is a groove. I just dig the strings on that. Like Thirties strings. Jose Feliciano does great things to "Help" and "Day Tripper."

"Got To Get You Into My Life"—sure, we were doing our Tamla Motown bit. You see we're influenced by whatever's going. Even if we're not influenced, we're all going that way at a certain time. If we played a Stones record now—and a Beatles record—and we've been way apart—you'd find a lot of similarities. We're all heavy. Just heavy. How did we ever do anything light? We did country music early because that was Ringo's bit. His song on the new album just happens to be country and we got this old fiddler in. But we weren't aware of the country kick coming in. But there we go, so it's all right. On the new album we've done a blues.

What we're trying to do is rock and roll, with less of your philosorock; what we're saying to ourselves is get on with rocking because rockers is what we really are. You can give me a guitar, stand me up in front of a few people. Even in the studio if I'm getting into it I'm just doing my old bit, you know, not quite doing Elvis Legs, but doing my equivalent—it's just natural. Everybody says we must do this and that, but our thing is just rocking—you know, the usual gig. That's what this new record is about. Definitely rocking. What we were doing on *Pepper* was rocking—and not rocking.

"A Day in the Life Of"—that was something. I dug it. It was a good piece of work between Paul and me. I had the "I read the news today" bit, and it turned Paul on, because now and then we really turn each other on with a bit of song, and he just said "yeah"—bang, bang, like that. It just sort of happened beautifully, and we arranged it and rehearsed it, which we don't often do, the afternoon before. So we all knew what we were playing, we all got into it. It was a real groove, the whole scene on that one. Paul sang half of it and I sang half. I needed a middle-eight for it, but that would have been forcing it, all the rest had come out smooth, flowing, no trouble, and to write a middle-eight would have been, but instead Paul already had one there. It's a bit of a *2001,* you know.

A critic has written about "A Day in the Life Of" as a kind of miniature "Waste Land."

Miniature what?

Eliot's "The Waste Land."

I don't know that. Not very hip on me culture you know.

So you don't see that song as a peak?

No, I don't. I think whatever we're doing now is past what we were doing then. Even if there is no song comparable to it, say. It's just not the scene now. It was only a song and it turned out well and it was a groove—it did do all that—but there's plenty more.

Songs like "Good Morning, Good Morning" and "Penny Lane" convey a child's feeling of the world.

We write about our past. "Good Morning, Good Morning," I was never proud of it. I just knocked it off to do a song. But it was writing about my past so it does get the kids because it was me at school, my whole bit. The same with "Penny Lane." We really got into the groove of imagining Penny Lane—the bank was there, and that was where the tram sheds were and people waiting and the inspector stood there, the fire engines were down there. It was just re-living childhood.

You really had a place where you grew up.

Oh, yeah. Didn't you?

Well, Manhattan isn't Liverpool.

Well, you could write about your local bus station.

In Manhattan?

Sure, why not? Everywhere is somewhere.

In "Hey, Jude," as in one of your first songs, "She Loves You," you're singing to someone else and yet you might as well be singing to yourself. Do you find that as well?

Oh, yeah. Well when Paul first sang "Hey, Jude" to me—or

played me the little tape he'd made of it—I took it very personally. Ah, it's me! I said. It's *me*. He says, no, it's *me*. I said "Check, we're going through the same bit." So we all are. Whoever is going through that bit with us is going through it, that's the groove.

Was "Hey, Jude" influenced—perhaps unconsciously—by mantras?

No, it's nothing conscious—you mean the repeat at the end? I never thought of that, but it's all valid, you see. I mean we'd just come back from India. But I always related it to some early Drifters song or "You'd Better Move On" or Sam Cooke's "Bring It On Home To Me" or "Send Me Some Loving"—it has that feeling.

Does "Tell Me What You See" have the same singing-to-myself feeling to you?

Not consciously, no. I can't remember, it's way back. As soon as you mention that I just remember running down the stairs at EMI and we went into the middle-eight, because there wasn't one—that's the picture I get. I'd have to hear it to get the rest of it. Otherwise it's just an image of the day I worked on it, what I went through, what I was going through at the time.

Probably paranoia.

It usually is the case—lost paranoias.

In the Magical Mystery Tour *theme song you say "The Magical Mystery Tour is waiting to take you away." In* Sgt. Pepper *you sing "We'd like to take you home with us." How do you relate this embracing, come-sit-on-my-lawn feeling in the songs with your need for everyday privacy?*

I take a narrower concept of it, like whoever was around at the time wanting to talk to them talked to me, but of course it does have that wider aspect to it. The concept is very good and I went through it and said, "Well, ok, let them sit on my lawn." But of course it doesn't work. People climbed in the house and smashed things up, and then you think. "That's no good, that doesn't work." So actually you're saying, "Don't talk to me," really.

We're all trying to say nice things like that, but most of the time we can't make it—ninety percent of the time—and the odd time we do make it, we do it together as people. You can say it in a song: "Well, whatever I did say to you that day about getting out of the garden, part of me said that, but really in my heart of hearts I'd like to have it right and talk to you and communicate." Unfortunately we're human, you know—it doesn't seem to work.

How do you feel now about your first couple of albums?

Depends what track it is. I was listening to the very first albums a few weeks back, and it's embarrassing. It was embarrassing then because we wanted to be like *this.* We knew what we wanted to be, but we didn't know how to do it, in the studio. We didn't have the knowledge or experience. But still some of the album is sweet, it's all right.

Wasn't it about the time of Rubber Soul *that you moved away from the old records to something quite different?*

Yes, yes, we got involved completely in ourselves then. I think it was *Rubber Soul* when we did all our own numbers. Something just happened. We controlled it a bit, whatever it was we were putting over, we just tried to control it a bit.

Do you feel free to put anything in a song?

Yes, In the early days I'd—well, we all did—we'd take things out for being banal, clichés, even chords we wouldn't use because we thought they were clichés. And even just this year there's been a great release for all of us, going right back to the basics, like on "Revolution" I'm playing the guitar and I haven't improved since I was last playing. But I dug it. It sounds the way I wanted it to sound.

It's a pity I can't do better—the fingering, you know—but I couldn't have done that last year, I'd have been too paranoiac. I couldn't play dddddddddddd, George must play or somebody better. My playing has probably improved a little bit on this session because I've been playing a little. I was always the rhythm guy anyway, but I always just fiddled about in the background, I didn't actually want to play rhythm. We all sort of wanted to be lead—as in most groups—but it's a groove now, and so are the clichés. We've gone past those days when we wouldn't have used words because they didn't make sense, or what we thought was sense.

But of course Dylan taught us a lot in this respect.

Another thing is, I used to write a book or stories on one hand

and write songs on the other. And I'd be writing completely free form in the book or just on a bit of paper, but when I'd start to write a song I'd be thinking dee duh dee duh do doo do de do de doo. And it took Dylan and all that was going on then to say, oh, come on now, that's the same bit, I'm just singing the words.

With "I Am the Walrus," I had "I am here as you are here as we are all together." I had just these two lines on the typewriter, and then about two weeks later I ran through and wrote another two lines, and then when I saw something after about four lines I just knocked the rest of it off. Then I had the whole verse or verse and a half and then sang it. I had this idea of doing a song that was a police siren, but it didn't work in the end [sings like a siren]: "I-am-here-as-you-are-here-as . . ." You couldn't really sing the police siren.

Do you write your music with instruments or in your head?

On piano and guitar. Most of this session has been written on guitar cause we were in India writing and only had our guitars there. They have a different feel about them. I missed the piano a bit because you just write differently. My piano playing is even worse than me guitar. I hardly know what the chords are, so it's good to have a slightly limited palette, heh heh.

What did you think of Dylan's "version" of "Norwegian Wood"? ("Fourth time around").

I was very paranoid about that. I remember he played it to me when he was in London. He said, what do you think? I said, I don't like it. I didn't like it. I was very paranoid. I just didn't like what I felt I was feeling—I thought it was an out and out skit, you know, but it wasn't. It was great. I mean he wasn't playing any tricks on me. I was just going through the bit.

How do you feel about his new music?

It's fine, you know. I'm just a bit bored with the backing, that's all. But he's right what he's doing because he usually is. I've only heard the "Landlord" album. I haven't heard the acetate, I keep hearing about it. That's something else, you know.

Is there anybody else you've gotten something from musically?

Oh millions. All those I mentioned before—Little Richard, Presley.

Anyone contemporary?

Are they dead? Well, nobody sustains it. I've been buzzed by the Stones and other groups, but none of them can sustain the buzz for me continually through a whole album or through three singles even.

You and Dylan are often thought of together in some way.

Yeh? Yeh, well we were for a bit, but I couldn't make it. Too paranoiac. I always saw him when he was in London. He first turned us on in New York actually. He thought "I Want To Hold Your Hand"—when it goes "I can't hide"—he thought we were singing "I get high"—so he turns up with Al Aronowitz and turns us on, and we had the biggest laugh all night—forever. Fantastic. We've got a lot to thank him for.

Do you ever see him anymore?

No, cause he's living his cozy little life, doing that bit. If I was in New York, he'd be the person I'd most like to see. I've grown up enough to communicate with him. Both of us were always uptight, you know, and of course I wouldn't know whether he was uptight, because I was so uptight, and then when he wasn't uptight, I was—all that bit. But we just sat it out because we just liked being together.

What about the new desire to return to a more natural environment? Dylan's return to country music?

Dylan broke his neck and we went to India. Everybody did their bit. And now we're all just coming out, coming out of a shell, in a new way, kind of saying: remember what it was like to play.

Do you feel better now?

Yes . . . and worse.

What do you feel about India now?

I've got no regrets at all, cause it was a groove and I had some great experiences, meditating eight hours a day—some amazing things, some amazing trips—it was great. And I still meditate off and on. George is doing it regularly. And I believe implicitly in the whole bit. It's just that it's difficult to continue it. I lost the rosy glasses. And I'm like that, I'm very idealistic. So I can't really manage my exercises when I've lost that. I mean I don't want to be a boxer so much. It's just that a few things happened, or didn't happen, I don't know, but *something* happened. It was sort of like a [click] and we just left and I don't know what went on, it's too near—I don't really know what happened.

You just showed me what might be the front and back album photos for the record you're putting out of the music you and Yoko composed for your film Two Virgins. *The photos have the simplicity of a daguerreotype . . .*

Well, that's because I took it, I'm a ham photographer, you know. It's me Nikon what I was given by a commercially minded Japanese when we were in Japan, along with me Pentax, me Canon, me boom-boom and all the others. So I just set it up and did it.

For the cover, there's a photo of you and Yoko standing naked facing the camera. And on the backside are your backsides. At your "For Yoko" show at the Fraser Gallery you just said, "You are here," showed some things that were there, and then people got the horrors. What do you think they're going to think of the cover?

Well, we've got that to come. The thing is, I started it with a pure . . . it was the truth, and it was only after I'd got into it and done it and looked at it that I'd realized what kind of scene I was going to create. And then suddenly there it was, and then suddenly you show it to people and then you know what the world's going to do to you, or try to do. But you have no knowledge of it when you conceive it or make it.

Originally, I was going to record Yoko, and I thought that the best picture of her for an album would be her naked. I was just going to record her as an artist, we were only on those kind of terms then. So after that, when we got together it just seemed natural for us, if we made an album together, for both of us to be naked.

Of course I've never seen me prick on an album or on a photo before: "Whatnearth, there's a fellow with his prick out." And that was the first time I realized me prick was out, you know. I mean you can see it on the photo itself—we're naked in front of a camera—that comes over in the eyes, just for a minute you go!! I mean you're not used to it, being naked, but it's got to come out.

How do you face the fact that people are going to mutilate you?

Well, I can take that as long as we can get the cover out. And I really don't know what the chances are of that.

You don't worry about the nuts across the street?

No, no. I know it won't be very comfortable walking around with all the lorry drivers whistling and that, but it'll all die. Next year it'll be nothing, like mini-skirts or bare tits, it isn't anything. We're all naked really. When people attack Yoko and me, we know they're paranoiac, we don't worry too much. It's the ones that don't know and you know they don't know—they're just going round in a blue fuzz. The thing is, the album also says: look, lay off will you, it's two people—what have we done?

Lenny Bruce once compared himself to a doctor, saying that if people weren't sick, there wouldn't be any need for him.

That's the bit, isn't it? Since we started being more natural in public—the four of us—we've really had a lot of knocking. I mean we're always natural, I mean you can't help it, we couldn't have been where we are if we hadn't done that. We wouldn't have been us either. And it took four of us to enable us to do it. We couldn't have done it alone and kept that up. I don't know why I get knocked more often, I seem to open me mouth more often, something happens, I forget what I am till it all happens again. I mean we just get knocked—from the underground, the pop world—me personally. They're all doing it. They've got to stop soon.

Tony Palmer, in an article for The Observer, *wrote how he had been predicting the Beatles' failure ever since The Cavern days. All he did was recall the various times he's predicted your failure. And then when he ended this article, he predicted it again. How does he feel?*

I just got a letter from him saying he feels fine. Such a lot of mistakes and lies in the article, saying it was Yoko's show and just some very nasty bits about Yoko, just cruel, you know. I don't know what they think we are. They really do think that we're very hard people. I mean they must be hard to do what they do. You just hold your breath and wait.

Couldn't you go off to your own community and not be bothered with all of this?

Well, it's just the same there, you see. India was a bit of that, it was a taste of it—it's the same. So there's a small community, it's the same gig, it's relative. There's no escape.

Your show at the Fraser Gallery gave critics a chance to take a swipe at you.

Oh right, but putting it on was taking a swipe at them in a way. I mean that's what it was about. What they couldn't understand was that—a lot of them were saying, well, if it hadn't been for John Lennon, nobody would have gone to it, but as it was, it was *me* doing it. And if it had been Sam Bloggs it would have been nice. But the point of it was—it was me. And they're using that as a reason to say why it didn't work. Work as what?

Do you think Yoko's film of you smiling would work if it were just anyone smiling?

Yes, it works with somebody else smiling, but she went through all that. It originally started out that she wanted a million people all over the world to send in snapshot of themselves smiling, and then it got down to lots of people smiling, and then maybe one or two and then me smiling as a symbol of today smiling—that that's what I am, whatever that means. And so it's me smiling, and that's the hang-up of course because it's me again. But I mean they've got to see it someday—it's only me. I don't mind if people go to the film to see me smiling because you see it doesn't matter, it's not harmful. The people that really dig the film . . . The idea of the film won't really be dug for another fifty or a hundred years probably. That's what it's all about. I just happen to be that face.

It's too bad people can't come down here individually to see how you're living.

Well, that's it. I didn't see Ringo and his wife for about a month when I first got together with Yoko, and there were rumors going around about the film and all that. Maureen was saying she really had some strange ideas about where we were at and what we were up to. And there were some strange reactions from all me friends and at Apple about Yoko and me and what we were doing. "Have they gone mad?" But of course it was just us, you know, and if they are puzzled or reacting strangely to us two being together and doing what we're doing, it's not hard to visualize the rest of the world really having some amazing image.

International Times *recently published an inverview with Jean-Luc Godard.*

Oh, yeah, right, he said we should do something. Now that's sour grapes from a man who couldn't get us to be in the film [*One Plus One* in which the Stones appear], and I don't expect it from people like that. Dear Mr. Godard, just because we didn't want to be in the film with you, it doesn't mean to say that we aren't doing any more than you. We should do whatever we're all doing.

But Godard put it in activist political terms. He said that people with influence and money should be trying to blow up the establishment and that you weren't.

What's he think we're doing? He wants to stop looking at his own films and look around.

Time *magazine came out and said, look, the Beatles say "no" to destruction.*

There's no point in dropping out, because it's the same there and it's got to change. But I think it all comes down to changing your head, and sure, I know that's a cliché.

What would you tell a black power guy who's changed his head and then finds a wall there all the time?

Well I can't tell him anything cause he's got to do it himself. If destruction's the only way he can do it, there's nothing I can say that could influence him cause that's where he's at, really. We've all got that in us, too, and that's why I did the "Out and In" bit on a few takes and in the TV version of "Revolution"—"Destruction, well, you know, you can count me out, and in," like Yin and Yang.

I prefer "out." But we've got the other bit in us. I don't know what I'd be doing if I was in his position. I don't think I'd be so meek and mild. I just don't know.

1968

Bernardo Bertolucci

Once or twice a year the New York film critics, as a way of overcoming seasonal occupational identity crises, create occasions to wail and gnash their teeth in a series of intricate and ritualized battle gestures. The "occasion" for this intertribal aggression can be anything from a book like Pauline Kael's *Citizen Kane,* to a "provocative" review by John Simon in the *New York Times*—begging for a counterattack—or even, strange to say, a movie itself. What is most important in all of this is not the specific book, article, or film but rather the opportunity each writer gets to affirm a "critical" position, register an aesthetic preference vis-à-vis the "others," and, last but not least, extract a bit of publicity for everyone concerned.

The most recent shot-at-Sarajevo excuse for another round of the New York critics' skirmish is *Last Tango in Paris*—probably the greatest occasion for critical self-assertion and self-aggrandizement in the past ten, 20, 30 years—perhaps in the history of cinema. Superlatives are of course integral to the history and success of the film. The *New Yorker's* Pauline Kael led the first charge when, after *Last Tango's* premiere at last year's N.Y. Film Festival (for which tickets were harder to come by than for the Ali-Frazier fight or the Bangla Desh concert), she compared the screening to the riotous first-night 1913 performance of Stravinsky's *Rite Of Spring,* calling the film "the most powerfully erotic movie ever made, and it may turn out to be the most liberating . . . Brando and Bertolucci have altered the face of an art form."

Andrew Sarris led the first counterassault against *Tango* in the *Village Voice,* and John Simon started dropping napalm in *The New Leader.* Neutralists like the *New York Time's* Vincent Canby and the slightly more anti-*Tango* Judith Crist of *New York* magazine could hardly get into the action before the *Daily News'* Wanda Hale outflanked them all with a brilliant maneuver: using her "last" review of *Last Tango* to announce her retirement as a critic, she gave the film four stars while reminding everyone that her first foray in the battlefield had consisted of giving four stars to a Shirley Temple movie.

Needless to say, the winners of this particular battle have been the critics and the film's distributor, United Artists. The supposed object of the whole fracas—*Last Tango* itself—has been selling out almost every performance in New York at $5 a head. And on the perimeter of the critical in-fighting—undoubtedly watching the smoke and flares with perplexity and amazement—has been the film's thirty-one-year-old director, Bernardo Bertolucci.

My own interest in Bertolucci began eight years ago when I first saw *Before The Revolution*—the second feature film made by the director when he was 22! This extraordinary movie, partly based on Stendhal's *The Charterhouse of Parma* and partly autobiographical, tells the story of a young man from Parma who, torn between a romantic sensibility—a "nostalgia for the present"—and a theoretical Marxism, falls in love with his neurotic but liberated aunt, only to marry his upper middle-class sweetheart.

Like the foal which, in its first steps, reveals its full-grown characteristics, *Before The Revolution* reflects in microcosm many of the concerns and obsessions with sexuality and politics that Bertolucci would later develop in films like: *A Spider's Stratagem*—a lush, elliptical, almost Brazilian cinema nuovo-textured movie about a young man who returns to his birthplace in order to discover the facts about the death of his father, a martyred anti-fascist resistance fighter; *Partners*—a modernization of Dostoyevsky's *The Double,* starring Pierre Clementi as a young drama teacher who wishes to combine the Theater of Cruelty with political revolution; and *The Conformist*—a film about a sexually repressed Italian fascist (Jean-Louise Trintignant) who is ordered to kill his former professor, now an anti-fascist leader in Paris.

Brought up in Parma, Bertolucci started to make short films as a teenager. At 20 he published a book of poems entitled *In Search of Mystery,* worked as an assistant director on Pasolini's brilliant first film *Accattone,* and made his own first feature *The Grim Reaper*—influenced in part by Pasolini's depiction of the life of Roman pimps and prostitutes. For several years after he made *Before The Revolution,* Bertolucci couldn't obtain financing for his feature films, and during this period he made an industrial film about oil in Persia for Italian television.

Like a number of other Italian film directors, Bertolucci is a member of the Communist party. But, as he told Guy Flatley of the *New York Times,* "I am condemned to be divided. I have a split personality and the real contradiction within me is that I cannot quite synchronize my heart and my brain. One of the two is always ahead of the other one. That is my charm."

Bertolucci is in the midst of Freudian analysis in Rome, and one often imagines, when watching his films, that some of the director's contradictions are a result of a Freudian view of life working against the grain of his Reichian themes and subject matter. At one point when I talked about how I thought the director Max Ophuls seemed to use the camera as if it were an instrument of memory itself, Bertolucci suggested that what was important for him in filming was what was happening "inside" the camera—as if (or so he seemed to imply) the camera itself acted as a kind of unconscious. Certainly, Bertolucci is an instinctive film maker, and you often feel that he uses his "contradictions" to energize his visually virtuosic and very painterly movies.

The director was in New York for several weeks in February in order to answer an interminable number of reporters' questions about his latest film. I arrived at Bertolucci's suite at the Sherry Netherlands Hotel one early Saturday afternoon. Relaxed, gracious, charming, and acting as if he had nothing better to do, Bertolucci offered us coffee and then put on a record he had apparently been listening to over and over again that week—Marvin Gaye's *Trouble Man* film score. "It sounds like Italian rock & roll," he said approvingly. "I love it!" Michele Barbieri—the wife of Gato Barbieri who composed and performs the music for *Last Tango*—helped translate Bertolucci's mixture of seventy percent Italian/twenty percent French/ten percent English, after which the director took a group of us out to lunch at Sardi's—the restaurant which is the gathering place for blooming and fading film and theater stars. Bertolucci seemed to enjoy his anonymity—no one recognized him—and looked excitedly at all the older Hollywood "types" eating their meals.

Over our lunch, he spoke about films. Bertolucci is a real film buff, and he talks about the famous pan shot in Welles' *Touch Of Evil* (the shot begins in Mexico and ends up on the US side of the border) or about moments in Rossellini's *Voyage In Italy,* Resnais' *Muriel,* Sam Fuller's *The Crimson Kimono,* and John Huston's *Judge Roy Bean* with the childlike enthusiasm of someone seeing cinema for the first time. He spoke about his plans concerning the next film he is about to make in Italy entitled *1900*—a movie about the disappearance of the agricultural society and the traditions of the tilling farmers—"the agony of the soil." After he finishes *1900,* Bertolucci mentioned that he expects to direct a version of Dashiell Hammett's *Red Harvest* in this country. (While we were all walking to lunch, I happened to hear Bertolucci casually ask the man who was helping the director get around in New York if he'd consider being in *Red Harvest.* "You'd be perfect for one of the gang members," said Bertolucci. "Really, I hope you do it." A star is born.)

When we began talking at the hotel, I asked Bertolucci about something he had mentioned in an interview with the *Times:* "I fall in love with all the actors in my films," he had said. "They are the prolongations of my penis. Yes, my 'penis.' Like Pinocchio's nose, my penis grows!"

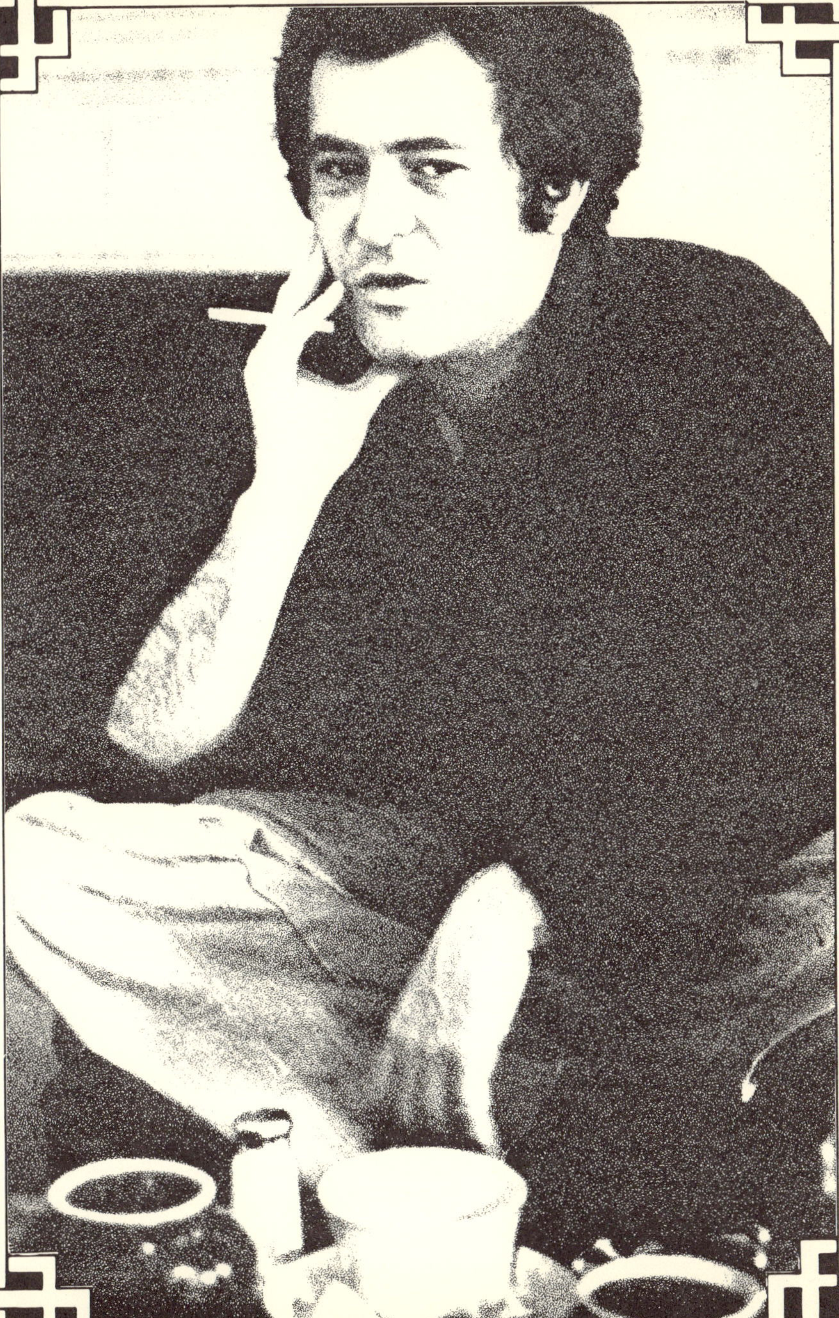

Forgetting the male actors for a moment, how do you relate to your actresses? Is it different from the way you approach a woman you like?

The manner in which we who love the cinema love a woman is very special. It's a very mythological way of loving women—and it's doomed to sado-masochism. There's a beautiful short story I like by Norman Mailer; it appears in *Advertisements For Myself,* and it has to do with what I've been saying. A guy's walking with his girlfriend and he's got a pad on which he writes down everything she does and says, but she really is annoyed by this. So he stops. When she starts to walk ahead of him, however, he starts writing again. She gets really mad, they start fighting, and at the end she leaves him. Very unhappy, he walks through the streets, and in order to console himself, to make himself feel better, he begins writing again on his pad. . . . A very nice story.

Do you feel that way when you direct an actress?

The problem for me isn't when I direct an actress, it's when I love a woman. I love all the actors and actresses in my films—always. I couldn't film them if I didn't love them.

So you have the same problem the character in Mailer's story has.

Luckily there are contracts, agreements, money. . . . I'm the director, they're the actors.

So you have it both ways.

Of course.

The French director Robert Bresson once talked about how he liked to work with "virgin" actresses—actresses who had never acted before—and about how by directing them for the first time he "seduced" them.

It's probably because Bresson has a great sense of sin. I don't. I take the girls who have been seduced by Bresson, dress them in evening clothes, and take them to a dance for the first time. . . . Like Dominique Sanda, who was first in Bresson's *A Gentle Creature.*

The ideas of sexuality and politics come up in all your films—sometimes in a confusing manner. You present a number of characters who seem in many respects to be sexually liberated, yet their liberated actions often seem to emerge from and also reveal a basically unliberated personality. I'm thinking specifically of the neurotic Gina in Before The Revolution; *Dreifa, the mistress and mother surrogate in* A Spider's Stratagem; *the narcissistic Pierre Clementi hero in* Partners; *Dominique Sanda in* The Conformist; *and now Marlon Brando in* Last Tango. *With Marcello (Jean-Louis Trintignant) in* The Conformist *you give us a character in whom fascism is a kind of repressed homosexuality. Wilhelm Reich wrote that fascism is only the politically organized expression of the average human character. Do you agree?*

Yes, I think the average man is fascistic. All my characters are average persons who are conscious of being average, and they're made uncomfortable by being *aware* of this.

If the fascist tendency is universal, why make many of your characters fascists instead of communists?

Well, because the average man *is* fascist. All my characters are predestined. They're doomed, but it's not Destiny that's decided to doom them, it's their unconscious.

Don't you think it's possible to be liberated?

Of course. But I'm more interested in showing the *process* of liberation than in liberation itself.

Don't you think that Brando's character in Last Tango *reflects an unliberated quality?*

I don't think Brando's character is liberated. He's like we all are—someone who feels the weight of his own body. It's interesting to note the relationship between Marlon's body and the space around him. We are usually dominated by space, but Brando strangely *dominates* space. Personally, I need the camera to dominate the "space"; but Brando is the only person I've met who dominates space naturally without the need of a camera or a pen to write or a trapeze or a racing car. And Brando's attitude toward life is different from that of other people because of this fact.

Well, it's a very American idea—dominating space . . . Go West . . . take it over.

But even if Brando is absolutely *still*—say, sitting on a chair—the space around him is dominated by him. Before I even started filming him, Brando had already taken for himself that privileged space that's also occupied by the figures in the paintings of Francis Bacon which you see behind the opening titles of the film. His dialectic with the space is the same as a work of art that's already been achieved. It was very easy to work with Brando.

Isn't this what dancers do, too?

Ballet is the art of the rapport between man and space, but it's stylized, and Brando is "realistic."

Why do you think that middle-aged heterosexual men especially seem to identify with Brando's character in Last Tango?

I think it's because of the continuous danger which is represented by Marlon's virility—the idea of his virility always being in danger, and all heterosexual men can identify with this danger. Homosexuals aren't in danger in this sense.

Well, then perhaps homosexuals are more liberated than phallically anxious heterosexuals.

But I don't think homosexuals are necessarily liberated. They've only regressed—well, not so much *regressed* as *remained* at an anal sadistic stage.

So is the choice only between regression and phallic nervousness?

What you call phallic nervousness has more to do with a *dynamic* quality, and regression has to do with a static situation. Last night I went to a gay club, many guys dancing, and they just seemed totally *frozen*—nothing was happening. I'm not against homosexuality. It's just that I think they've solved the problem even less than heterosexuals. But socially they've achieved a lot today.

Greek and Persian societies, for example, have been homosexual in orientation. Do you consider them regressive?

They were civilizations that needed father images—kings, emperors and tyrants because they hadn't solved their Oedipal problems.

In A Spider's Stratagem *there's one scene in which you show a young boy who's trying to figure out the sex of a rabbit. And complementing this scene is one in which the hero is sitting in the garden and a young girl in a hat brings him something to drink, but at first you're not sure whether it's the same young boy or a girl. It's a very dreamy, lush scene, and you get a feeling of hermaphroditism—similar to moments in* The Conformist *as well. But* Tango *seems to separate the "male" and "female" into two distinct spheres.*

On one side, there's Marlon—absolutely an adult and completely virile. On the other side there's Maria Schneider and Jean-Pierre Leaud. And I personally have both these sides, too—adult/virile and also adolescent. And my adolescent part is bisexual—it's represented by Maria and Jean-Pierre. So I think you can find this element you talked about in *Tango* as well.

To me, Marlon Brando's role in Tango *represents the apotheosis of the American idea of male sexuality.* Tango *is a very American and a very literary film in this sense; it's as if you distilled the "male" ideology of Hemingway, Raymond Chandler, Dashiell Hammett.*

Marlon isn't an intellectual. He doesn't read very much. But, it's incredible, when I looked at him during the shooting I found *in* him a lot of Henry Miller, a lot of Hemingway, a lot of Raymond Chandler—I think he's a living concentrate of American literature. . . . But, you know, I think we should talk about the *language* of the film. I have a kind of nostalgia for an interview where we could go through a unity which is made up of both content and language. All my interviews are always about ideology.

I think this interest in "ideology" comes about because some persons think that you identify with Brando, while others think that Brando is just an actor in a movie, and others that Brando is playing Brando—I mean, if you had another actor in this role you'd have a different movie. But there is an idea about liberation and sexuality in Tango *which gets confused with the Brando "image."*

If someone's looking for a theorem, then it's confused. I didn't want to make a theorem.

That reminds me of the Terence Stamp character in Pasolini's Teorema.

There's the same mystery about the Stamp and the Brando characters. But the first seems to come from paradise and the second from hell.

How do women you've spoken to respond to the relationship between Maria Schneider and Brando?

Women are the only ones who really understand the film.

Because it's a film that's built on the concept of the *inside* of the uterus. Not *just* the room. Marlon in fact makes a voyage back to the uterus—so that at the end he's a fetus. The colors in the film are uterine colors.

In a way it's a bit like King Lear who starts off as an old man, then becomes a woman (suffering from hysteria), then a fool, a child. . . .

Yes, I see what you mean. And I don't know if you noticed, but at the conclusion of *Tango,* Brando has to come back to pick up his chewing gum. You see, he takes a trip from adulthood back to the fetal stage. More than *King Lear, Tango* seems to me closer to one of Jean Cocteau's films, where the hero makes a voyage to the underworld, to hell.

I gather that your original idea for Tango *was a story about a woman and a man—both married to other persons—who get together, not knowing each other's name, and have a totally "free" relationship. But at the end of* Tango, *Brando says: I love you, and then he gets killed. Freud believed that love and affection were ways of controlling socially destructive libidinal energy. And so you're not sure whether Brando has given in to the "conventional" idea of love or whether he's in fact become more "human."*

At this moment you find the whole Hollywood convention. But this Hollywood convention is "life." And I think he finally understands that you can't construct a relationship outside of history. He doesn't want to know her name or anything about her past. And I think *that* is a very romantic concept. After all, we're constructed with a past and a future, and if you don't accept that, you're creating a very romantic, individualistic, and politically horrible situation. Because we're made up of all others. . . . But I don't know if he really becomes more human or more stupid. When you say: "I love you, dummy"—as Brando says—I don't know what you become. I know he's very tender. He can be charming with violence or tenderness—both. But why does she kill him? Is it that she's too bourgeois? Or that she's better than he is and doesn't want to accept his new conventionality? She shoots him with a gun that belongs to her father at the same moment that he puts her father's hat on his head. So in a sense she kills her own father, too.

In the scene in the Metro station, Maria Schneider tells her cinéma verité fiancé Jean-Pierre Leaud that he's using and violating her by following her around all the time with his camera—like the woman in the Norman Mailer story you mentioned before. And yet she's basically really angry at Brando.

Yes. You've a good viewer.

But I'm not sure what this displaced anger on her part was really supposed to suggest.

Do you have a problem having to know what things signify?

Well, it's because films try to make you subconsciously identify with characters—John Wayne, Gary Cooper, whomever.

Tango is a film of total communion between Hollywood and European cinema.

You certainly don't seem to use as many traveling and circling shots as you did in your earlier films.

When I made *Partners* I was sick from the neurosis of style. Now after *The Conformist,* I've accepted myself as a maker of fiction and spectacle. And I've now been able to return to the style and the experimentation of *Partners* but with a new relationship that's more equilibrated and serene.

Jean-Luc Godard has stated that it's important not to make films on politics but rather to make films politically. You really seem to be standing on the opposite side from Godard at this point.

Yes. Godard and I used to be very close friends. He left a screening of *Tango* in Paris ten minutes after it started. And I felt he was in a sense sending me a message by walking out. We continue having a relationship without seeing each other—by symbolic gestures. But I also agree with Godard about the difference between the two kinds of film making. It's just that I'm making films *on* politics. I also made a *political* film, however, last year for the Italian Communist party—about the miserable conditions of hospitals in Rome, and it was shown in the streets, using the walls as the screen.

I know that Visconti, Pasolini and Petri have been or still are Communists. But there is a specifically romantic and operatic quality to many of Visconti's and Pasolini's films.

Well, Marxism can contain opera. In the 1800s, opera was a revolutionary expression and was still extremely popular. I think that Godard in his first film was a right-wing anarchist; now he's a left-wing anarchist. To me, anarchists are dangerous to the fight of the masses. We have to make a distinction between Maoism in Europe—which is a neurosis of the petit bourgeoisie—and Maoism in China, where it's a great fundamental reality.

Many leftists think that's because the Communist parties in Europe have become bourgeois.

That's not true, it's an invention of people like Godard and Gorin—those who are outside of the mass struggle. Considering the world situation today—and the European situation in particular—armed revolution isn't possible. The revolution is being made day by day in the parliament. Every time that the extremists were able to attract a great following and were able to pass from verval delirium to action, the situation itself jumped back 20 years. I think that for the working class, anarchism is dangerous.

How would a working-class Italian audience accept Tango?

When people go to the cinema it's almost as if class didn't exist—it cuts through class.

Coming back to Godard, I know that in The Conformist *you gave to the anti-fascist professor in the film Godard's real address and telephone number.*

I didn't talk about it when I made the film, but now I can. It was a message I was sending to Godard. It was like a game—but a pretty serious game. After all, the film's about a small Italian fascist who plans to kill his teacher and fuck his wife. Godard didn't take it well. But I also wanted to tell Godard at the same time that—*hypothetically*—if I were a fascist and Godard were an anti-fascist, we were both of us still bourgeois. Professor Quadri is a bourgeois anti-fascist, but there is a kind of anti-fascism that isn't based only on the idea of freedom but also on mass struggle and on scientific fact.

Have you seen Godard's and Gorin's Tout Va Bien? *I think it's an important film, and the way the relationship between Yves Montand and Jane Fonda is placed in a social context seems really extraordinary.*

Yes, I was very moved by it. There were some things about it I didn't care for. The characters of Jane Fonda and Yves

Montand were a bit banal to me—they're not in real life, of course. And I could tell when the camera moves when it was going to stop. What I really thought about *Tout Va Bien* was that in this film Godard begins to live again. When Godard theorizes he becomes very simplistic. But when he doesn't do that he's a great poet.

I've heard that because of Godard's accident, Gorin played an important role in the making of this film.

Well, Gorin is more Godard than Godard. . . . You see, I have a political position and vision. We have at the same time to be conscious of the obvious fact that cinema in a commercial context is always used as a tool. And pornography is a tool—it's invented by the distributors. For me, pornography really doesn't exist.

Tango *couldn't be shown in Cuba or China.*

Well, they have other kinds of problems. It would be interesting for a Chinese audience to see *Tango.*

They might see it as being about the death of capitalism.

Tango is my own fantasy about death—and capitalism, too. Both.

Before The Revolution*—which you made when you were twenty-two—seems to me a film that someone in his thirties would make. And* Tango *seems to be made by someone in his fifties.*

Is that good?

It's amazing. It's unusual for a thirty-one-year-old to make a film that understands the dynamics of the sexuality of this kind of character so well.

A tired sexuality [laughing]. Perhaps I'm fifty on the set because I'm like a twelve-year-old in real life [smiling].

Which young directors do you find some kind of affinity with?

I feel close to the structures of Oshima, the lighting of Francis Ford Coppola, to the obsessions about cinema of Bogdanovich, and to the gesticular violence of Glauba Rocha.

As for older directors, I can sense your admiration for Renoir, von Sternberg, and Max Ophuls. Did you ever see Ophuls' La Signora di Tutti?

Just the sequence where Isa Miranda makes a telephone call to her lover. But what influenced me about this sequence had to do with what I could imagine happening *around* that sequence rather than with the sequence itself. It's like a still life by Courbet. You see three or four apples, one pear, the drape; and you can imagine the atmosphere of the house, the table, what's going on in the bedroom downstairs, in the garden. . . . I like to show paintings to Storaro, my cinematographer, before we shoot. In *A Spider's Stratagem* we looked at a lot of naif paintings—like the ones seen over the titles. And we discovered that the way the naif artists painted the *night* was similar to the way Magritte painted it—a night-blue in which you can see everything, discovering each and every detail. So we used to shoot between light and dark. And if you shoot without the filter you get a kind of liquid blue that bathes the people.

The town in A Spider's Stratagem *looked a bit like some early di Chiricos.*

No, I think there was more di Chirico in *The Conformist*—you know, the space, the small persons and the enormous architecture. . . . Incidentally, I saw an incredible film on Italian television a month ago: *The Fountainhead.* Very fascist in its celebration of individualism . . . but Patricia Neal's performance is one of the most beautiful things I've ever seen in the cinema.

I like the way you use bicycles in your early films.

That's because I come from a region in Italy where everyone rides them. Speaking of bicycles, I recently saw Antonioni's footage on China. He just went around filming, and at one point you see a wonderful sequence showing all those people on bicycles. It was so much like the Po Valley where both I and Antonioni were born.

Zabriskie Point *to me was like an Italian movie. Antonioni's depiction of the political situation in this country didn't seem all that effective . . . but the scenes in Death Valley!*

The first time I saw it I didn't like it, but the second time . . . yes, very, very much. And now it's going on in my mind over and over.

Did you notice that written on the hero's plane are the words: "She-He-It": Sheeit!

Shit [laughing].

Right. And I thought that that suggested what the film was about. The heroine (she), the hero (he), and the id (it)—that deepest point in the body of the earth.

That's really interesting. I must ask Antonioni about that. . . . [pause] Do you remember Yeats's lines about the dancer?

It's strange, I was just going to ask you about them: "O body swayed to music, O brightening glance / How can we know the dancer from the dance?" You have all those wonderful dances in all your films.

I was just thinking of those lines. Yes, there are some people through whom culture finds its own continuity, don't you think so? It's a way of allowing things to survive. At this moment we're keeping alive some verses of Yeats. And when we were talking about Japanese films before, we were also keeping alive some moments of Mizoguchi, bringing those moments forward as if they were objects, maybe conserving them as we go about creating. And that, I think, is what we're doing here.

1973

Mick Jagger

The following interview with Mick Jagger was completed by Sue Cox and myself at the *Rolling Stone* business offices in London in June, 1968, shortly before the release of the Stones' *Beggars Banquet* album. Jagger had never previously engaged in long interviews, and I suspect he thought—and probably still thinks—that since they're a waste of time and that, considering he really couldn't or didn't want to talk about anything too portentous, he might just as well submit to them—as to this one—with charm, laconic humor, a sometimes wiseacre wit, and a benign tolerance.

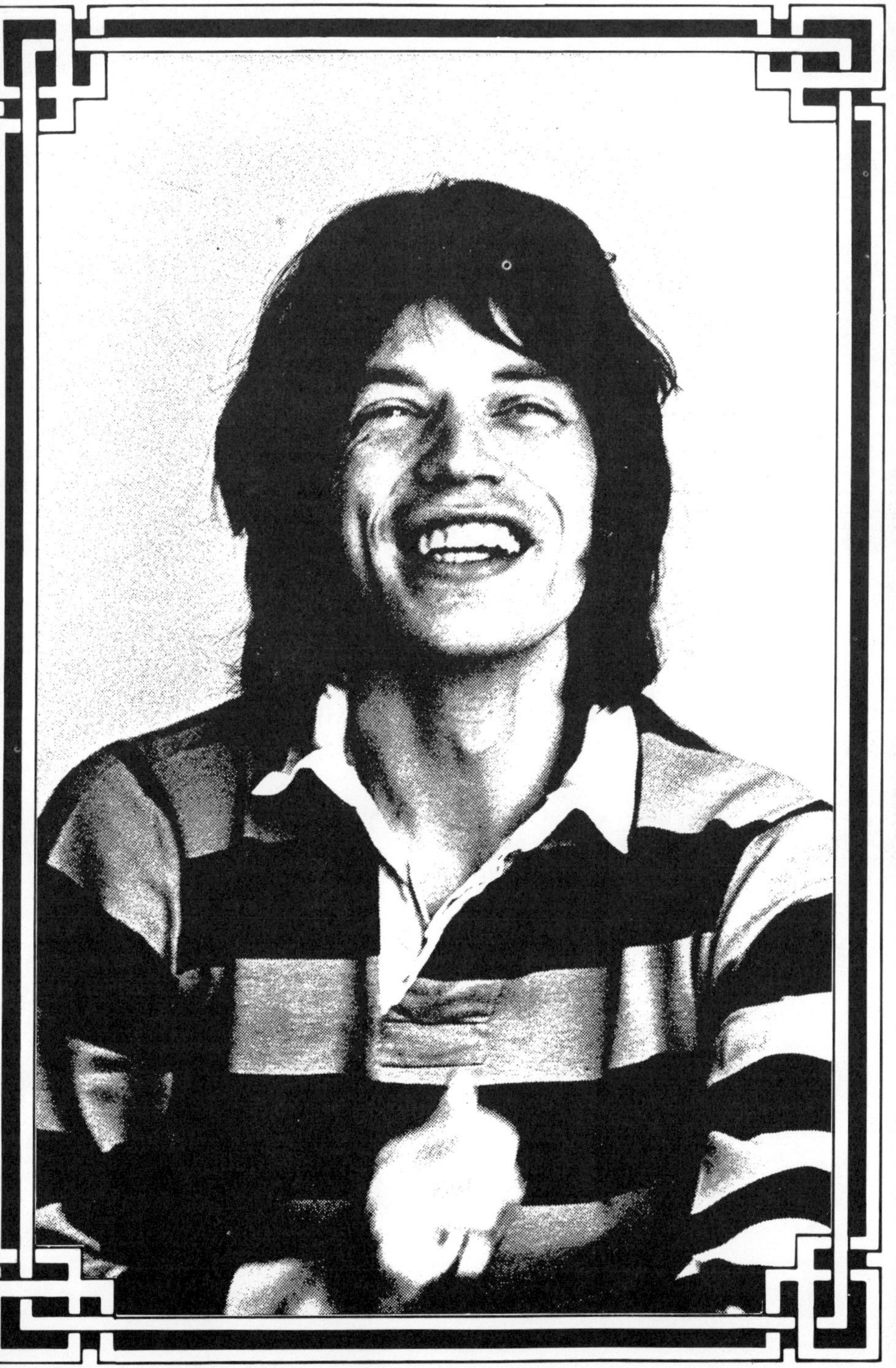

The first thing we would like to talk about are your old songs like "Poison Ivy," "Route 66" and . . .

"Poison Ivy," did we ever record that? Oh, yeah. We did two versions of that. I don't know which one you have 'cause it was never released in this country [England]. Where was it released in America?

It wasn't released in America, it was put out in England. It was a very early recording with three other things, an EP.

Right. "Bye Bye Johnny" and "Better Move On." That was the second version.

Why did you choose that type of material in the beginning?

Well, I mean, we were kids, you know, just kids. We did everything and that was a groove. You see "Poison Ivy" was unknown in this country. It wasn't a hit here by the Coasters, and other songs like "Money" were totally unheard of.

Like "I'm a King Bee"?

Well, that was pretty unheard of in America. What I mean is, there were a lot of these hit records in the states that nobody knew about here, we did them and *after* we thought they weren't good; but at the time it was right.

But the Stones made these songs popular.

No, not really. Everybody did those kind of songs: The Beatles, The Hollies, the Searchers, everyone. I can't explain why.

Isn't it true that with songs like "Come On" and "King Bee" you really re-discovered Slim Harpo and Chuck Berry for a lot of Americans who never listened to that kind of music before?

Yeah. They never knew anything about it and that's why we stopped doing blues. We didn't want to do blues forever, we just wanted to turn people on to other people who were very good and not carry on doing it ourselves. So you could say that we did blues to turn people on, but why they should be turned on by us is unbelievably stupid. I mean what's the point in listening to us doing "I'm A King Bee" when you can listen to Slim Harpo doing it?

At that time did you think you were going to be a writer and get into all your own things as you have?

No, I really didn't think about it much.

Your change in style came about when you thought enough

people had been turned on to blues?

I think our *change* came about the same time a lot of the beat groups *started.* When there were no hit groups and the Beatles were playing The Cavern. We were blues purists who liked ever so commercial things but never did them on stage because we were so horrible and so aware of being blues purists, you know what I mean? You see nobody knew each other in those days. We didn't know the Beatles and the Animals and the this and that and the other group, yet we were all doing the same material. We used to be so surprised to hear other people do the same things we were doing. The thing is that the public didn't know about any of this music because the record companies were issuing hundreds of singles a week so naturally most people missed a huge lot of them.

What were the first things you wrote?

The first thing was "Tell Me." Well, that wasn't the first thing we wrote but it was one of the first things we recorded that we had written. Also, "As Tears Go By," "That Girl Belongs To Yesterday," which was a hit here by Gene Pitney. We were writing ballads, don't ask me why.

How did you come to record "I Wanna Be Your Man," the Beatles thing?

Well, we knew them by then and we were rehearsing and Andrew [Oldham] brought Paul and John down to the rehearsal. They said they had this tune, they were really hustlers then. I mean the way they used to hustle tunes was great: "Hey Mick, we've got this great song" [done with a John Lennon accent]. So they played it and we thought it sounded pretty commercial, which is what we were looking for, so we did it like Elmore James or something. I haven't heard it for ages but it must be pretty freaky 'cause nobody really produced it. The guy who happened to be our manager at the time was a 50-year-old northern mill owner [Eric Easton]. It was completely crackers, but it was a hit and sounded great on stage.

What happened during the time between that and "Satisfaction"?

That's a lot of time, I don't know what happened. You say "I Wanna Be Your Man" and I'd forgotten about it. Next came "As Tears Go By." We never dreamed of doing that ourselves when we wrote it. We just gave it straight to Marianne [Faithfull]. We wrote a lot of songs for other people most of which were very unsuccessful.

Did you write "As Tears Go By" specifically for Marianne?

Yeah, but I could never do it again. I keep trying, night after night. Then we did "Not Fade Away" and went to America and that was really a change.

How did that affect you?

Well we started going back to blues a bit more. I remember we went to Chess Recording Studios and recorded all the old blues numbers we used to do, a lot of which have never been released.

Who was doing your production then, Andrew?

Yeah, but he didn't know anything about blues. The cat who really got it together was Ron Marlow, the engineer for Chess. He had been on all the original sessions. We did "Confessin' The Blues," "Down The Road A Piece," and "It's All Over Now." Murray the K gave us "It's All Over Now" which was great because we used to think he was a cunt but he turned us on to something good. It was a great record by the Valentinos but it wasn't a hit.

That was when you first ran into censorship problems with the words "half-assed games." Many of the disc jockeys in the states just cut that part out.

Did they really? I didn't know that. I really don't know what's considered rude in America cause it's all so different, isn't it! Here you can use Americanisms and people don't know what you're saying. Censorship is weird.

Even though you had several hits before, "Satisfaction" was really the turn on for a vast majority of people. Was there any specific incident that brought those lyrics to you?

It was Keith really. I mean it was his initial idea. It sounded like a folk song when we first started working on it and Keith didn't like it much, he didn't want it to be a single, he didn't think it would do very well. That's the only time we have had a disagreement.

Even when it was finished, he didn't like it?

I think Keith thought it was a bit basic. I don't think he really listened to it properly. He was too close to it and just felt it was a silly kind of riff.

Did you think "Satisfaction" would become the number one pop song of this era as it has?

No, not at all.

Did you think about the problem of writing a song to follow it?

No, I didn't give a fuck. We knew it wouldn't be as good but so what.

Where were you when you wrote it?

Tampa, Florida by a swimming pool.

Did you do a lot of your writing on tour?

Oh yeah, always. It's the best place to write because you're just totally into it. You get back from a show, have something to eat, a few beers and just go to your room and write. I used to write about twelve songs in two weeks on tour. It gives you lots of ideas. At home it's very difficult because you don't want to do anything really but read and things like that.

I'd like to ask you a personal question about "Play With Fire." There are lines about getting your kicks in Knightsbridge and Stepney, and a rich girl, and her father's away and there is a suggestion that the guy in the song is having an affair not only with the daughter but with the mother . . .

Ah, the imagination of teenagers! Well one always wants to have an affair with one's mother. I mean it's a turn on.

Oftentimes when you record, you mumble your lyrics. Is this done purposely as a style?

That's when the bad lines come up. I mean I don't think the lyrics are that important. I remember when I was very young, this is very serious, I read an article by Fats Domino which has really influenced me. He said "you should never sing the lyrics out very clearly."

You can really hear "I got my thrill on Blueberry Hill."

Exactly, but that's the only thing you can hear just like you hear "I can't get no satisfaction." It's true what he said though. I used to have great fun deciphering lyrics. I don't try to make them so obscure that nobody can understand but on the other hand I don't try not to. I just do it as it comes.

For some reason people don't think about the fact that you and Keith are great writers and your lyrics like "Get Off Of My

Cloud," which are really good . . .

Oh they're not, they're crap.

"Union Jacks and Windscreens" . . . It's a nice poem.

It's nothing. Thank you for the compliment but I don't think they are great at all. If a person is that hung up on lyrics he can go and buy the sheet music because it's all there, wrong of course but . . . You should see the one for "Dandelion," they made up another song!

How did you feel when you went on the Ed Sullivan show and had to change the lyrics from "Let's spend the night together" to "Let's spend some time together"?

I never said "time." I really didn't. I said mumble. "Let's spend some mmmmm together, let's spend some mmmmm together." They would have cut it off if I had said "night."

When you first came to San Francisco in 1965, the Diggers put out a proclamation calling the Stones the embodiment of what they represented, the breaking up of old values. This came about after a series of songs like "19th Nervous Breakdown," "Mother's Little Helpers," "Have You Seen Your Mother" . . .

"Have You Seen Your Mother" was like the ultimate freak-out. We came to a full stop after that. I just couldn't make it with that anymore, what more could we say.

But obviously these songs bothered people because for the first time rock songs were saying things that couldn't be said before, not just on a sex level like old blues tunes "I'll squeeze your lemon till the juice runs down your leg." You don't get close to things like that but what you said was strong.

I like that one very much, we used to do it. It's spending all the time in America. All these songs were written in America. It is a great place to write because all the time you are being bombarded with all of it and you can't help but try and put it in some kind of form. I think the Mothers of Invention do it so well. It's all here as well, but not so obvious. As far as I'm concerned those songs just reflect what's going on.

What about people who see your songs a political or sociological statements?

Well it's interesting, but it's just the Rolling Stones sort of rambling on about what they feel.

But no other group seems to do that.

They do, lots of groups.

What other group ever wrote a song like "19th Nervous Breakdown," or "Mother's Little Helper"?

Well, Bob Dylan.

That's not really the same thing.

Dylan once said "I could have written 'Satisfaction' but you couldn't have written 'Tambourine Man.'"

He said that to you?

No, to Keith.

What did he mean? He wasn't putting you down was he?

Oh yeah, of course he was. But that was just funny, it was great. That's what he's like. It's true but I'd like to hear Bob Dylan sing "I Can't Get No Satisfaction."

Did you like Otis Redding's version?

Yeah, I dug it but . . . not . . . well I dug it. I think it's great cause it's sort of . . . no I'm not going to say. Well the sounds were great and he was great when he first started off singing, but then it sort of went into oooh, aaah, gotta gotta gitta which is great because that's his scene, but I like Aretha Franklin's better. I was very turned on that Otis cut it.

Your songs about girls like "Out Of Time," "Please Go Home," "Gotta Get Away," "Yesterday's Papers," "Lady Jane," and many more like "Back Street Girl" seem rather bitter and mean, whereas "She Smiled Sweetly," "Ruby Tuesday," "Like A Rainbow" are all about mystical girls.

Different girls. I don't know what to say except they speak for themselves. They are all very unthought-out songs. I write them and they are never looked at again.

But it sounds as though you mean it at the time.

Well I do, that's the scene. Those songs reflect the day and a few stupid chicks getting on my nerves. "Lady Jane" is a complete sort of very weird song. I don't really know what that's all about myself. All the names are historical but it was really unconscious that they should fit together from the same period.

Satanic Majesties *is probably the most controversial LP you've had, people either hated it or loved it. It seems to be a personal statement rather than a collection of songs. What were your original ideas about putting it together?*

None at all. Absolutely no idea behind it. No, it's wrong to say there is or was no idea at all, there was but it was all completely external. It was done over such a long period of time that eventually it just evolved. The first thing we did was "She's A Rainbow," then "2000 Light Years From Home," then "Citadel," and it just got freakier as we went along. Then we did "Sing This Song All Together" and "On With The Show," "The Lantern," and then Bill's one ("In Another Land"). It took almost a whole year to make, not because it's so fantastically complex that we needed a whole year but because we were so strung out.

That was the year in which several arrests were made.

Yeah that took a lot of time, plus we didn't know if we had a producer or not. Sometimes Andrew would turn up, sometimes he wouldn't. We never knew if we would be in jail or what. Keith and I never sat down and played the songs to each other. We just made that album for what it is.

Were you happy when it was finished?

I was happy, yeah. I breathed a sign of relief because we had finally finished it. It's just there to take it or leave it.

Were any of the songs written after your or Brian's arrest?

I'm very conscious of the fact that it doesn't reflect that in any of the songs. That they aren't all about policemen as they could well have been. But it is an album like *Aftermath* is an album but *December's Children* isn't, it's just a collection of songs.

Is there any one album you consider your best?

Well no. I like our first album very much 'cause it's all the stuff we used to do on stage. Then I like *Aftermath* 'cause I like the songs, although I don't like the way some of them were done.

What about Between The Buttons?

I don't like that much.

Why?

I don't know, it just isn't any good. "Back Street Girl" is about the only one I like.

Going back to Satanic Majesties *for a minute. I've noticed that there seems to be a constant mood of sleeping and dreaming throughout the whole thing.*

I read somewhere else that it was supposed to be about

travelling, which is weird, too, 'cause it is when you come to look at it that way. You heard what? Dreaming and waking up? I don't know, maybe it is. That's great if you get that from it, that's fantastic.

There also seem to be certain words which constantly reappear like ritual objects, for instance "light," "high," and "flower." Am I just reading into it or was that done purposely?

I don't know what to think about it. It's very weird really and doesn't have anything to do with me. It hasn't got any sort of songs in it, all the words are very obscure, no they aren't really. "2000 Light Years" isn't. That is my favorite but it's lousy in stereo.

Do you feel that Satanic *was your first attempt at the "Strawberry Fields" type of music.*

Well, it's a very heady album, very spaced out.

What can we expect to hear in your new album Beggars Banquet?

"Jumpin' Jack Flash" is the most basic thing we have done this time, although that may or may not be in the album. There are a couple of country tunes, 'cause we've always liked country music.

Have you been influenced by The Byrds and Dylan with their country albums?

Yeah, but Keith has always been country. That's what his scene was. We still think of country songs as a bit of a joke I'm afraid. We don't really know anything about country music really, we're just playing games. We aren't really into it enough to know. I think it's going to be a good album.

Are you interested in doing stage performances again?

I'd like to do them, but the thought of going on stage and playing "Satisfaction," "Paint It Black," "Jumpin' Jack Flash," and six others just doesn't appeal to me.

What if you could have a quiet and receptive audience?

I don't think it's going to be like that. I'd like to perform and I think the Stones would, but we're stuck because we feel it's no good having everybody sit down and be quiet. I don't want anybody to have to do anything. They should do whatever they like. Pop concerts are gatherings of people who want to have a good time and I don't think they really have a higher meaning.

People say that audiences are listening now, but to what? Like the Rolling Stones on stage just isn't the Boston Pops Symphony Orchestra. It's a load of noise. On record it can be quite musical but when you get to the stage it's no virtuoso performance. It's a rock and roll act, a very good one, and nothing more.

It is hard to imagine you doing your sexy thing, jumping about, with everyone just sitting there quietly listening.

Right. I certainly don't want to go on stage and just stand there like Scott Walker and be ever so pretentious.

I can't hardly sing, you know what I mean? I'm no Tom Jones and I couldn't give a fuck. The whole thing is a performance of a very basic nature, it's exciting and that's what it should be. The idea of doing it all over again is a drag. I'd like very much to have someone produce a show with us. I'd like that, I'd really like to do that.

Do you ever feel guilty about getting up on stage and pointing to those little girls and singing "Everybody Needs Somebody" when you really don't want them at all?

Of course I want them.

What sort of show would you hope to be able to do with someone producing it?

When I say produced I don't mean slick and corny, I mean crazy and mad. Something to add to the excitement. I loved the show we did at Wembley [The Stones played two numbers as a surprise to an audience who came to see Mick accept an award from the New Music Express as the "best R&B group of the year"] but it was two numbers and that's all I could make. Maybe when we finish the new album and have twelve new songs to do then we can get something together.

You're getting into films now aren't you?

Yeah, well you can do a lot with film.

What is it like to work with Jean-Luc Godard, the director?

I don't now him very well. Godard is a very nice man. I mean I've seen all his pictures and I think they're groovy.

What is One Plus One *about?*

I have no idea really. I know he's shooting with color film used by astronauts when re-entering the earth's atmosphere. I mean he's completely freaky. I think the idea for the movie is great but I don't think it will be the same when it is finished.

What is the idea Godard has told you?

Well it's his [Godard's] wife who plays the lead chick. She comes to London and gets totally destroyed with some spade cat. Gets involved with drugs or something. Anyway, while she is getting destroyed we find the Rolling Stones freaking out at the recording studio making these sounds.

Godard happened to catch us on two very good nights. He might have come every night for two weeks and just seen us looking at each other with blank faces and it would have been the same side of the coin as the chick destroying herself and us sitting there looking bored. One night he got us going over and over this song called "Sympathy For The Devil." It started out as a folky thing like "Jigsaw Puzzle" but that didn't make it, so we kept going over it and changing it until finally it comes out as a samba. So Godard has the whole thing from beginning to end. That's something I've always wanted to do on film. It's probably very boring to most people but when he's finished cutting, it will be great.

When is "The Performance" due to begin?

August something.

Wasn't the script written especially for you?

Yeah, I mean it's very much me. I'm going to make it if I can, different to me. I mean, he is me, the me on that album cover. He is supposed to be a great writer, like Dylan. But he's completely immersed in himself, he's a horrible person really.

How do you feel about acting as opposed to singing on stage?

I don't know. They are both just projections of your ego, which you're not supposed to have, but you can't do without. You certainly can't act without it, that's why the Maharishi had so much trouble. This character in the film has this fantastic ego thing, which is all right 'cause I can make that. If people get the feeling that you are out there with them, and if you come on strong, then you'll make it. It's just a matter of looking confident, being confident, and believing the part, then it's cool.

Do you think this might open a movie career for you?

No, not really. We are doing another film in November which is fantastic. It's called *The Maxigasim.* I can't really say much about it, but it's great.

Who is directing it?

A few freaks.

What did you think of 2001?

It was one of the best movies I've ever seen. It's a very commercial movie. I really got hung up on the audience more than the movie. They kept leaving at the freaky parts 'cause they just couldn't make it. I think the point of the movie is that he [Kubrick] wants to get this whole thing across to the mass audience. He's fantastically interested in doing all these games with the spaceship models and all, that's his hangup, but it's incidental. The point is to freak everybody out, which he is very good at. But if you have already been through all that, then you can turn onto all the other levels.

If you haven't, then you get totally looned out because all the time you are being brought home by all these telephone calls and plastic shoes and you think "ah it's just like home really, it's all right." He lets you identify with it. I mean the toilet thing is the greatest, it's so awful. He spent so much time doing that it's almost heart rending. It's like he's saying, "get it across to those people but give them a bit of relief." Then at the end it all happens. You've forgotten about the stone as soon as you enter the Space Hilton, you can think it was a bad dream, until he brings it back.

People's comments are the greatest: "you need a lot of imagination to understand the movie," "It's a million dollar put-on."

I heard a little girl coming out of the theater saying that the slab was just a big block of hash.

That's fantastic!

Do you find it difficult not having any privacy?

Difficult? No, it's really nice and easy. The only hangup is the fuzz. Now that's a drag. Once you get in trouble with the police, you're always in trouble and that's it. Before, we were never in trouble and they were always very nice to us. They should be looking after people and turning American tourists away from Picadilly Circus. That's the only hang-up but it doesn't have anything to do with being me.

Do you feel that the police made a definite effort to pick on the Stones?

Well, there always has been. Before all the hassle it was just the boring newspapers, but when the fuzz start getting into that, it can be very draggy. They have the wherewithall to do it to you if they want to. The newspapers can only scream from their drunken haunts like The Wig & Feather Club, but they can't do anything, the police can.

1968

R. D. Laing

I first began reading the British psychoanalyst R. D. Laing's *The Divided Self: An Existential Study in Sanity and Madness* on an airplane trip from London to Amsterdam. The plane was delayed taking off, and by the time I was a quarter of the way into the book, the book and I were in the air.

What was becoming clear to me up there was Laing's uncanny ability to decode the "schizophrenic" experience—seeing it from the inside, not as some kind of sickness which demanded a prescribed "cure" but rather as a response to the breakdown of a delicately preserved split between an outer false self and an inner true self. And Laing's diagnosis of this "experience"—the word "diagnosis," as Laing points out, literally means "seeing through"—revealed that a false social sense of reality was not only often socially induced (by means of all sorts of internalizations of other persons' internalizations, as manifested in the family structure), but in fact forced one into fantasies which were unrecognized by that person as such. And when that person attempted to extricate himself from this situation, he was usually branded "bad" or "mad." In one case study after another, Laing brilliantly explored the hidden self images of fractured human beings. "If our experience is destroyed," Laing once wrote, "our behaviour will be destructive."

In a sense, Laing was extending the very beautiful idea which Freud presented in *Delusion and Dream* that if you accept someone's delusion completely, you often do it to free that person from it, and that by treating and investigating the delusion, you can explain its origin. (This is, incidentally, the plot of Alfred Hitchcock's *Vertigo*.) But, as his apocalyptic-sounding *The Politics of Experience* was later to make explicit, Laing was also suggesting that it was in fact our "normal" life—and especially the traditional psychiatric assumptions concerning the symptoms of "mental illness"—that reflected, if not madness, at least a kind of counter-madness, "if by madness we mean any radical estrangement from the totality of what is the case. . . . Our sanity is not 'true' sanity. Their madness is not 'true' madness. . . . What we call 'normal' is a product of repression, denial, splitting, projection, introjection. . . . We do not need theories so much as the experience that is the source of the theory."

And Laing's investigation of the phenomenology of madness metaphorically suggested that madness itself, if not seen as simply some kind of sickness, could reveal certain correspondences with the processes of nothing less than the transcendental experience. As he wrote in *The Politics of Experience:* "True sanity entails in one way or another the dissolution of the normal ego, that false self competently adjusted to our alienated social reality; the emergence of the 'inner' archetypal mediators of divine power, and through this death a rebirth, and the eventual re-establishment of a new kind of ego-functioning, the ego now being the servant of the divine, no longer its betrayer."

Back in that airplane, I began to have trouble breathing. Page after page, case study after case study, the plane began to buckle in turbulence. I remembered John Ruskin's story about how, as a child, he got so frightened seeing the word "crocodile" in a book that his anxiety would only be alleviated when he had turned over the offending page. So I put *The Divided Self* away, and the plane immediately calmed down. Thousands of feet up in the air, a piece of metal between me and nothingness. . . . I picked up the book again—why be superstitious?—and down and up went the plane.

When I arrived in Amsterdam, a ghost of myself, I decided to finish the book—still with a lot of anxiety—and subsequently read some of Laing's other works: *The Politics of Experience, The Politics of the Family, Sanity, Madness, and the Family, Knots,* and *Self and Others* (my favorite—if that's the word—of his books). And it became easy for me to understand why many psychiatrists were calling Laing himself a paranoid schizophrenic, for his books functioned in part as a kind of mirror that reflected the reader's own delicate balance. I mean, if Laing's thoughts were a product of a deluded mind, why get upset or hurl names?

It also became clear to me that Laing's analysis of all our unacknowledged game playing—double-binds, pretenses, as well as the tricky offspring of the "lusion" family: collusions, delusion, illusions, and spiralling elusions—were threads of what in *Knots* he called "the webs of maya." (*Knots* is a book consisting of little dialogue poems that present relationship patterns which Laing calls "knots, tangles, fankles, 'impasses,' disjunctions, whirligogs, binds.") And in *Self and Others,* he wrote: "We are aware of the 'content' of experience, but are unaware that it is illusion. We see the shadows, but take them for the substance. . . . For inner and outer belong to each other. Divided, they become two bewildering aspects of a mystery which we endure but can never solve."

Laing's perceptions concerning the divided experience seem to have drawn him inescapably to a kind of Buddhistic philosophy. And recently, he has pointed out that the "caduceus"—the medical emblem that consists of a staff with two snakes twined about it—is the staff not only of Mercury but also of the great Tibetan yogi Milarepa, while the snakes represent Kundalini (the energy that lies coiled at the base of the spine). Not surprisingly, Laing recently went to Ceylon and India where he continued his study and practice of meditation. And he seems now to be interested in applying some of his recent experiences in new therapeutic contexts, at the same time as he wishes to clarify some of the misconceptions his work seems to have fostered ("freaking out is groovy," "Acid is groovy"—at one time, Laing experimented with the therapeutic use of LSD and mescaline). He has recently completed a coast-to-coast college lecture tour that came a month after the New York openings of Ken Loach's *Wednesday's Child*—a film that is based on and dramatizes Laing's ideas on family madness—and of *Asylum*—a film by Peter Robinson that documents life at Kingsley Hall, the now defunct therapeutic community set up by Laing and a few colleagues in London's East End in which patients, staff, and doctors all lived together without hierarchical distinctions, and which enabled and allowed a person to go through his or her "madness" without the usual tranquilizers/shock treatment/pacification ritual.

I was as nervous visiting Laing in his New York hotel suite at the start of his U.S. tour in December, 1972 as I was in the plane to Amsterdam. To make matters worse, Peter Robinson and crew were going to be filming the interview for a documentary on Laing's trip to the States. On came the lights . . . morning dissociation . . . muddled questions . . . take a couple of deep breaths . . . asked Laing to read William Blake's poem "The Mental Traveller" which reminded me of some of Laing's ideas about the transformation of personality and of the transformations of unacknowledged family "patterns":

I travel'd thro' a Land of Men,
A Land of Men & Women too,
And heard & saw such dreadful things
As cold Earth wanderers never knew. . . .

Laing read the entire 26-verse poem in a quiet but wonderfully modulated, Scottish-accented voice, but didn't say much about the poem except to acknowledge its extraordinary quality.

We talked about several subjects, and later I mentioned I had seen him and Norman Mailer on a WNET television discussion program a couple of nights earlier and thought that a number of Mailer's recent ideas seemed preposterous . . . like the one that went: If you have a really good fuck, the child you conceive will be a boy, but a bad fuck makes a girl.

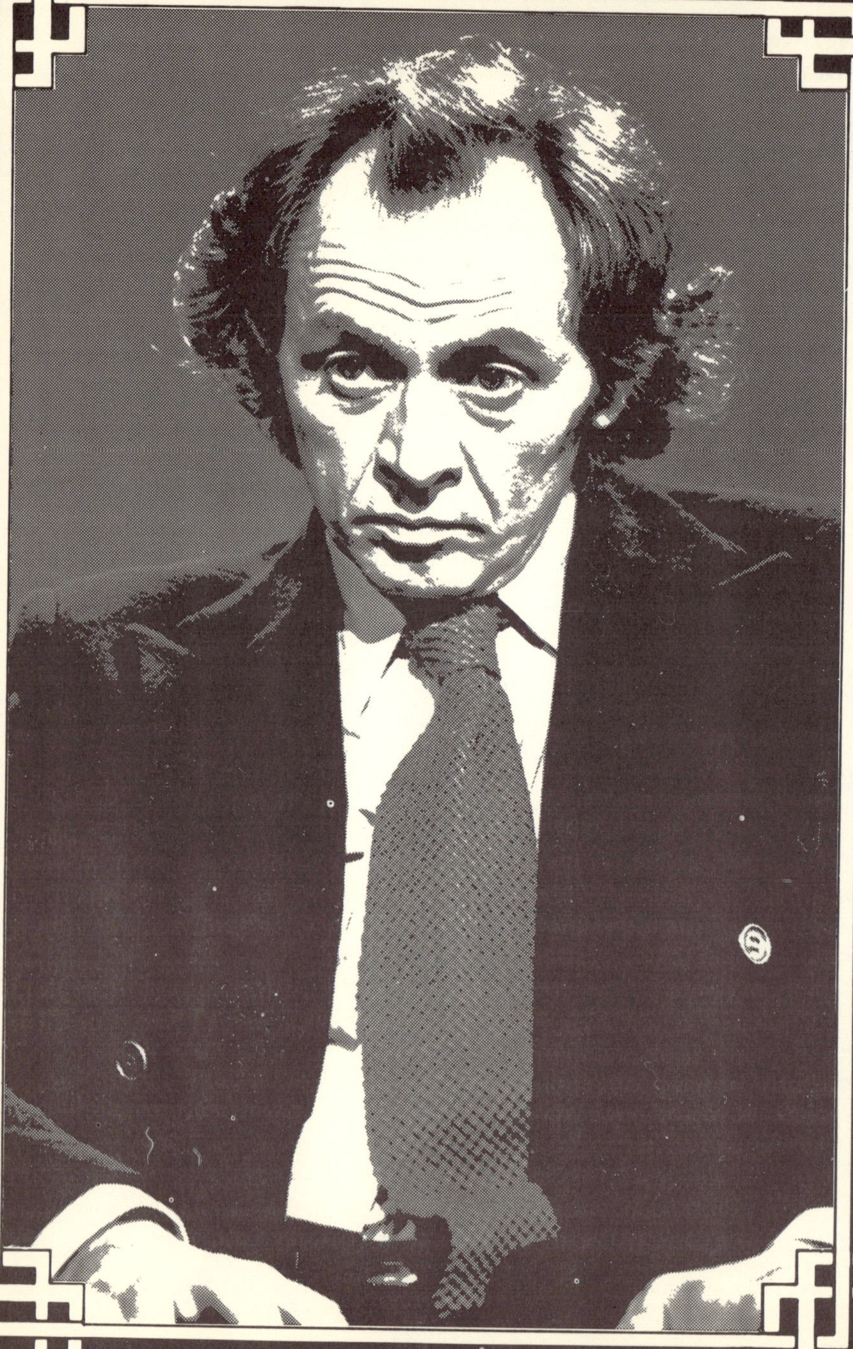

Well, he lets them go. I mean, everyone's got ideas like that: he *says* them. I doubt whether he's really interested in what one calls. . . . well, for instance on the show we were talking about the "cancer" idea, and I sort of mumbled something about this or that paper—and he wasn't interested, and I didn't expect him to be, in actually reading any quasi-scientific evidence on that sort of thing. It's just a thought and an idea, an intuitive presentation, and it also catches people, it makes some people who haven't done so go through a sort of *number*—unlived life, rebellion, revolution of the tissues of Vietnam, the Yellow Peril, the Commies—these are cancer cells in the body politic, as it were, that have gotten out of control and will destroy the Central Intelligence Agency located in the midbrain or the forebrain or wherever you regard the Pentagon as being. The Pentagon has got to keep its control system going, and if you can't drug them, reason, and negotiate with them, then you may have to do a surgical excision—and that would be genocide. . . . Well, I'm not saying I agree with what I've said. Avoid taking a fix on that; a lot of people have identified with that . . .

Well, as a metaphor it makes some kind of sense.

All right, it makes some kind of sense . . . exactly, it makes some kind of sense as a metaphor—so if you don't lose sight of that, and if you're interested in being philosophical, you can work out in philosophical terms, with precision and detail and depth, what kind of sense that makes as a metaphor. But a lot of people, particularly in the left and around the left, may throw out that remark, that *it makes some kind of sense as a metaphor,* and at the same time get very uptight if they come across someone who doesn't appear literally to believe the metaphor! I meet people who've taken what I've written as a *metaphor*—and you *say* that's what it is—and then play it back to me in pretty garbled form, and they've identified with this, they've forgotten that it's a metaphor, they've taken a fix on it, it's become literal truth. And then they get very upset with *me,* because then they wonder if I'm some sort of apostate from my own writing; their mind boggles, it buckles, it becomes confused and bewildered because I don't seem to be identified with my own metaphors. So as long as you remember what you just said yourself, and don't forget it . . .

It's seemed to me that the idea of "madness" in your work plays a slightly similar role as the idea of "guilt" does in a writer like Kafka. That is, in our particular culture, both of these ideas seem to represent some kind of vestigial "human" element . . .

I don't think madness is an exclusive human prerogative, or privilege, or tragedy, or comedy. There are people who are specializing at the moment in finding ways, for instance, of driving monkeys mad as efficiently and as fast as they can. They're spending their lives doing this, and they're producing really freaked-out, crazy monkeys . . . and other sorts of animals.

Don't you suggest that, in a certain sense, madness is the solution to . . .

I never said that madness is *the* solution!

No, a solution . . .

No, I never even said that it's *a* solution . . .

It's a way out . . . ?

Well, it's a way out for the monkey, too! They've taken over double-binds. They put monkeys in environments in which they confuse them and fuck them over, not by physical torture but by giving them the indication that if they pull a lever one moment they'll get something nice, and then the next moment, if they do it again, they'll get an electric shock.

You've talked about how the family does this as well.

Yes, they do, yes, I'm saying that. And so you can also do that to the birds and the bees and the chimpanzees and the baboons and fishes and dolphins: you can set about driving everything in sight crazy, not only ourselves. The people who are doing these experiments are trying to double-bind a monkey, and what can a monkey do except to start to tremble and scream; it finally gives up and becomes catatonic. It's not worth-while raising its hand or feet or doing anything because it's going to be a loser whatever it does, so it doesn't do anything!

I was referring to the way people have used your ideas to aestheticize madness so that it becomes a state interesting in and of itself . . .

Well, why not include monkeys?

I don't know.

All right, people have aestheticized madness in that way. You can drive a beehive crazy, you can completely fuck up an anthill, you can produce gross confusion in any sort of animal or bug or fish that you like: destroy their social system, their ecology, their environment, their network, and scramble their input, and garble the reception of their messages, and then you'd have a comparable situation to what's going on in large sections of the world with human beings.

Timothy Leary once wrote about his first meeting with you in London, and I remember he described an intense and friendly arm-wrestle with you in the kitchen. And in his article Leary also mentioned Aleister Crowley, Alan Watts, the Beatles, John Fowles' The Magus*—his point being that you were part of that special British visionary and mystical tradition which has attempted to "build Jerusalem in England's green and pleasant Land," to quote Blake. And it's struck me that certain English people have seemed able to experience and go through madness and then return "home"—I'm thinking of someone like Aldous Huxley taking peyote and coming back to write about it in that genial, urbane, "civilized" English "style." Perhaps it's just because the repressive, conservative, class-conscious English society serves to sustain and act as a stable background against which someone can dramatically define oneself. Whereas a lot of Americans when they freak out get lost in those "far out" spaces and can't find their way back, just because the American background is so unclearly defined. Also, the "new consciousness" of the Sixties—symbolized by LSD—now seems to have turned into a "downer" consciousness—represented by Quaaludes and heroin.*

I don't suppose it's really possible to gauge the nature of what you call the "new consciousness" without having been at least to some extent in America to witness it. I haven't been in America since 1967. That was before Watts and Kent and all that. I meet quite a number of Americans in England: quite a number of them who have freaked out and gotten on a plane and come over to London. So I've seen a few Americans there—young and old, in and out of the establishment, as well as in different parts of the world—in India, for example. But I haven't seen Americans in America for five years. And it's during these five years that there's been this shift—I don't know how best to characterize it—of the American group consciousness, with its metaphor of acid—as you said—to the metaphor of heroin and downers. So I'm interested to get the feel of it in the actual habitat.

Do you think that drugs were a function of the need for a certain kind of consciousness, and that now the different kinds of drugs themselves have altered consciousness to the extent that people can no longer continue to develop their awarenesses in a kind of spiralling tradition?

I really don't know how profound a sociological or basically personal and intimate effect the drug scene has. My attitude toward drugs and taking drugs was formed before I'd even heard of Tim Leary and the American acid scene. There were people in Europe, where acid was discovered, who were quite well into it in the Fifties in a quiet sort of way and who never thought of reporting it to the media. And of course drugs have been around in India for as long as anyone can remember. Those people made a point of *not* broadcasting certain things because, I suppose, they felt that many people would get more confused than they would otherwise. And also they didn't want books on the subject. There are hundreds of thousands, if not millions, of Americans who sit away and puff away and inhale on reefers and get themselves stoned for the rest of their lives and still not have the faintest idea of what gates can be opened. And then they go out on the street demonstrating and turning that into a political issue. There have been people for thousands of years who have been quietly and unobtrusively using chemicals to some effect.

Wouldn't this be considered a slightly elitist attitude?

Yes, that's the stock, stereotyped response to that. But it's an *open* elite, it's an open secret. Consciousness is not a plaything. And if people seriously want to learn, understand, and plumb something of the depths of their own mind—their own consciousness—then the best way to do it is to find someone who's done it a bit broader and deeper than they have, and to apprentice themselves to that person, whomever it might be. And if their way partly involves the chemical alteration of the brain and the transformation of mental forms that are induced thereby, as well as of the nervous system and the transformation of the tissues—a fundamental, sort of total alchemy—then there are people around who know about that. But because they know about this, they're not making a big song and dance about it; they're not hiding their light under a bushel either, they're just not putting out a neon light. You can set up a crucifix if you like without flashing it on and off in neon. No, I don't think it's "elitist" in the sense that one uses this term as a sort of facile putdown.

Are you in favor of the legalization of marijuana?

I'm not going to say anything about whether I'm in favor of it, because I don't think that's a way to approach the question, bashing the heads straight on. Where I've been involved is with regard to the Royal Commission set up a few years ago in the United Kingdom to advise on the legal question of marijuana, and they came out with the Wooten Report. It's one of those reports that's easy for a certain sort of radical or revolutionary to be impatient with; they despise it because it's a *liberal* report. But it's the most liberal report I know of to have come out until the Canadian one. It was more radical in that respect than the LaGuardia report.

And I gather it's your feeling that drugs should be used not just to get high but rather for the purpose of getting high in order to understand something else?

The drug experience seems to make an enormous point to some people. Because they find, sometimes for the first time in their lives, that the reality that they took to be some sort of fixed, established, solid ground under their feet is alterable by a minute chemical infusion into the body, such that it may undergo a complete transformation. Time may change unrecognizably, space changes into another sort of space, and all the elements of the phenomena of sight, sound, taste, touch, smell, and bodily sensation undergo permutations that might be undreamt of, unimagined, and unremembered ever before. And this proves one very simple point: if one has taken one "fix," a culturally conditioned fix which one shares with everyone else one knows, to be some sort of independently established substantial reality—well, it isn't! It's more like just one take on a kaleidoscope, and you can turn that around and it's just one of an infinite number of transformations, the one that we might happen to identify with from birth to death. One's wearing one suit of clothes, and realizes that it's just one suit of clothes and that there are any number of different ways of dressing oneself up. There are many clothings or veils that can color and clothe and adorn the mind. There's no reason then, ipso facto, to start tearing one's clothes apart because one realizes that one happens to be wearing the fashion of 1972.

What do you mean by "fix"?

Like taking a snapshot. Taking one moment. Or in the Hegelian sense: social-historical change is continual. Nothing ever stays the same, it's all undergoing transformation. Some people think that the laws of these transformations have been fundamentally discovered or set out by Marx, after Hegel. I don't know whether that is the case, but I'm in no doubt—I don't think anyone possibly can be—that there's the question of his socio-economic-cultural transformation. And that's another special domain of transformation; it's not quite the same as the evolutionary law of transformation of forms.

So a "fix" in that sense is that one's mind, which is faced with a set of phenomena which are all the time undergoing change at a certain rate of change, may find itself overwhelmed by the suddenness of a transformation, the sheer quantity of input at any time, the overwhelming degree of pain, a set of circumstances which it tries to alter but can't, such that the mind fixes on one form. That form can be a particular sexual style, a cognitive style, an emotional style, a postural style in walking, talking, and moving, etc. So it fixes on one form and takes that, and then that is a way of coping with such states of mind as consternation, confusion, bewilderment, perplexity, perplexity of mind, bewilderment of mind, confusion. astonishment of heart—those states in which one doesn't know where one is, doesn't know who one is, doesn't know what anything is, doesn't know what to believe, doesn't know what to trust—not only *what,* but down to the primary data of one's sensory input and the phenomena of one's mental environment. Well, that's everything, then—one is at a complete loss, one doesn't know what to take to be the case or what not to be the case, one doesn't know how to construe anything, and one might be in such a state of perplexity or consternation or astonishment that one doesn't even feel in a position to utter anything—even in the form of a gesture or a blink or a noise. I think there's a sort of frenetic, almost, eagerness in the mixture of a peculiar sort of rancid, caseating decay . . .

Caseating?

It's a medical expression for a long-standing tuberculous abscess that might develop inside the middle of a lung, and the inside of this—it isn't supplied with blood any longer—turns into one of the most foul-smelling transformations of flesh that there is. And at the heart of this abscess it goes absolutely rotten, sometimes for years, so that it's like foul cheese—it's turned into really foul cheese, it crumbles, and if it breaks into a blood vessel or into the main artery of the chest, some of it can start coming out of the mouth and it can come out of the breath and you start vomiting with blood. Well, there's something like that about America, on the one hand, and at the same time there's an enormous amount of energy and a freshness and an eagerness . . . so that there's a sort of frenetic, very ambiguous sort of quality about the way Americans freak out.

It may be a romantic idea for an American to see that for a European—maybe there's something in it—there's still a whiff of, or a taste of, or the lingering odor of some sort of social structure which hasn't taken on the thing that seems to be happening over here. As you said, there is no sane background or backdrop to the insanity. One's living in an insane lunatic asylum where the guards are more freaked out than the patients.

I saw a film last night called *Out of Darkness,* which is supposed to reveal a very avant-garde understanding, sort of advanced-consciousness approach to mental illness and the need to treat people as people and persons as persons. It was filmed in a state mental hospital in 1955, and there were shots of the staff, the nurses, the doctors, and the patients. And I don't think that there was any doubt about it: the people in that place who showed the most expression, whose eyes were most alive, whose cheeks and whose mouths were most mobile, were the patients. The staff looked completely zonked out. They had cooled themselves off and were training themselves as hard as possible to sort of cool themselves off completely. But if you looked at a doctor looking at a patient, his face was utterly expressionless . . . except for a slight bend forward—that sort of professional address that says in a completely stereotyped, institutionalized way: I am listening to you, I am here to help you. There were a number of sessions between a psychiatrist and someone who was supposed to be a desperately withdrawn, mute, catatonic schizophrenic, and you could see all sorts of things crossing her face and going on. She was very unhappy and she was very confused. The doctor had completely cancelled himself. The chances for him looked considerably . . . well, certainly no better than the chances for her.

I once read an interview with you in which you said that it might be advisable to let the patients in a mental hospital smoke grass if they wished and have the nurses and doctors be put on tranquilizers. It would be a kind of half-reversal of the typical situation in which the patients are tranquilized.

I didn't say that. No, I wouldn't suggest that anyone be put on anything.

I thought it was a kind of Zen joke to make people aware of the situation as it exists. But what I was trying to get at was the idea of how to transcend a situation honestly instead of, let's say, just reversing a situation you're already in.

Absolutely. I can tell you quite a number of ways in which anyone can start doing that in a mental hospital. It depends where one's transcendence is beginning. If one doesn't see the point of wearing a white coat, then there's no point in wearing a white coat. If one doesn't see the point of sitting behind a desk, then stop sitting behind a desk. If one doesn't see the point of all sorts of things, then stop them. If you start stopping doing most of the things that most people are paid to do and if you carry as many peoples as possible along with you, then quite a lot of things can stop being done to people. It's really a matter of stopping doing things to people. Stop trying to *help* people.

Drugs as a way of life can motivate a lot of a person's life, just giving someone something to do. But I've also noticed that the actual drug experience often becomes self-serving: you take a drug not so much to experience something, but rather have an experience as if to confirm the idea of the drug. So someone listens to a song and says: "This is a speed song," or finally, "It was a trip." And after a while, you'd begin to think that the experience itself was being programmed by the expectations the person had of the nature of the drug, and it becomes a kind of receding-mirror way of dealing with experience itself. Like the parable you tell of the airplanes flying in a formation which is heading in the wrong direction, and one airplane goes out of formation . . .

The Gadarene swine.

Right. And then there's the possibility that that one plane is also flying in the wrong direction. You've often described the situation in which there seem to be no bearings. And likewise the drug experience in this kind of world can actually remind you more of a drug than of something transcending that drug.

Yes, oh yes, that will happen with anything. You get people now who've had some analysis, who've had some encounter-grouping, who've had some . . . well, that sort of bourgeois middle-class sort of thing, or who've dropped into some sort of commune, been out growing organic food, the Jesus freaks, the Sufis, the mantra people, the transcendental meditation people—all these things are, in some circles, bandied around and talked about and compared and tagged—"Oh, that's amphetamine," or "that's hashish," or "that's heroin," or that's whatnot, and so on. Well, the content changes, but the comparatively constant invariant in that is the attitude of mind which will digest and absorb and nullify meditation or psychoanalysis or some political posture or action; and in the same way you can take anything, whether it's a drug or whatnot, an upper or a downer, and tag it, take a fix on it, and finish it off, kill it . . . once you've taken that fix on it, you've killed it—it's dead, it's not moving any more, it's not changing any more, it's finished.

In The Center of the Cyclone, *John Lilly talks about how one "programs" a "trip" and allows for self-metaprogramming.*

Well, I've got a number of reservations about that language, and I have the same kind of reservations about the way Tim Leary used to propound the acid experience and to some extent also about the way Janov tries to rationalize in neurophysiological terms the primal therapy and primal scream experience. Which is that it turns it all . . . it doesn't really matter in Lilly's terms, really, that he puts a *bio* on to the beginning of *com-*

puter or not and whether he makes it sort of intellectually chic by saying *meta* before *programming;* the metaphor is really stopped in the way that . . . who's the Frenchman who wrote *Man a Machine,* which really inaugurated that whole thing?

La Mettrie?

Yes . . . In the cave paintings, as far back as we go, it looks as though the most difficult and perhaps dangerous, fearful, powerful, threatening presence to man were certain animals. They hadn't any instruments, they had no guns or bullets or any technology of killing—let's suppose they had spears or bows and arrows and so on, but one knew that if one went out beyond a certain area, one had to encounter wild animals—I mean wild as far as we were concerned, not domesticated. And you see the earliest pictures that we have of man: he looks as though he's got on the animal pelt, and he's the master of some sort of animal ceremony. He's taken animals *upon* himself, as it were, and has identified himself with the antelope or the deer or the tiger, and with that identification he's turning himself into the forces that he feels controlled by or are controlling him.

Is this a sort of totemic identification you're describing?

Well, after Levi-Strauss I don't want to talk about totemism, any more than I want to talk about schizophrenia—it's very much the same sort of false categorization, I think. Actually, in the beginning of Levi-Strauss's study of totemism, he actually starts off with hysteria as his paradigm for the medical categorization of conduct and experience into disease entities, and, to him, there's an obvious cultural and parochial error that's being made. That seems so obvious to him that he uses *that* point—as if to say: All right, that's established now. And totemism is the same sort of error.

Well, it seems now that it's not the animal that we're contending with—we've killed them all, there are no animals around. I mean, there are nine million rats or more in the Manhattan area that if not kept at bay may take over, but they're certainly kept out of sight of human beings. It's fairly startling after coming back from India where cows are wandering around and where you can see monkeys through the windows. One's still living with other creatures, but we've stripped our space of . . . not even a *fly* in the room . . . which I find really rather disturbing. I like to share the world with other creatures—I won't do anything to them, and if they don't do anything to me, we've sort of reached our modus vivendi. I don't want my sole relationship to animals to be the taste of their flesh in my mouth.

I'm saying about machines . . . the machine in all its aspects, the man-made artifact, the thing that bothered Norbert Weiner before he died . . . Now, we tend to homologize ourselves, or we compare ourselves, or we identify ourselves, or at the very least we analogize ourselves to these human artifacts that we've produced, and we explain ourselves in terms of our own products. I think that's a misleading detour. I mean, I would use it as a transitory metaphor, pick it up and put it down again, but I wouldn't base a whole system of thought upon such a metaphor or analogy because then one's taking what one wants to say from the locus of one's own discourse and placing it in another discourse, and then one's got to take it back again. To talk about the human bio-computer implies that the main function of the human nervous system is analogous to a computer.

One of my former pupils and friends—G. Spencer-Brown—is a very distinguished mathematician, and for some time we did a deal—I became his pupil in mathematics, and he was my pupil in psychology, you might say. Lilly, in fact, quotes quite a bit from his *The Laws of Form.* Spencer-Brown used to design computers, he used to produce the actual designs for them, and he made a point to me which I thought was absolutely dead-on and cogent, that what a computer does is to *compute*—it doesn't do anything else. I mean, we *can* compute, but we're not particularly interested in doing so. That's why we turn over this very low-level activity of computation to computers, so that we can get on with other things. No computer has ever devised or solved or found the proof of any theorem. For instance, in the theorem that the series of cardinal whole numbers is infinite, and even that the series of even numbers is infinite, and that the series of uneven numbers is infinite: no step in the proof that establishes *that,* according to Spencer-Brown, uses any of the operations that a computer is set up to do. There's no computation in the sequence of reasoning used, so that a computer simply computes, but the human mind, although it can compute—we might turn ourselves over to nothing else but computing machines—well, we've got a tendency to identify ourselves with what we wish to control, or what we feel is controlling us, or what we're in danger of being destroyed by. Certainly the human artifacts that we've produced present a major crisis to us, and we're dealing with this by taking it upon ourselves, a sort of machine totemism if you want to call it that.

This reminds me of Kafka's The Metamorphosis. *The Freudian view of the work is that Gregor Samsa introjects and incorporates the parasitism which he experiences and perceives operating in his family situation and becomes a parasitic bug. Paul Goodman, however, once pointed to Samsa's unconscious identification with the animal nature represented by the bug, a kind of unrepressed mode of being. Isn't this idea similar to what you were saying before?*

The word "identification" is very misleading because it implies that there is that which identifies with something else. One can't identify with oneself or with one's true nature, because in being one's true nature there's no process of identification involved. One *is* oneself, one can't identify with oneself. One can identify with one's family, and then the most extraordinary thing to do is to identify with oneself. I mean, that's disappearing in some sort of puff of smoke up one's own fundament, never to come back again. The processes of seeing, hearing, tactile sensibility, breathing, eating, digesting, shitting, sleeping, standing, walking, bending, stretching, moving, stretching out—that is what we do all day long, every day in our life; and we sometimes hear sounds and react to them . . .

Is that yourself doing that? No—if what you're saying is self is *self because you said you'd disappear if you identified with yourself, so it can't be yourself who's doing all these actions. . . . It's a semantic problem, I guess.*

It's a very profound semantic problem as soon as we ever start talking about the *self.* We must be aware that as soon as we do that, the existence of that sound, that word—the "self"—implies that there is an entity, a substance, a being, some *thing* to which that refers, some connotation of that, something—it's very difficult to say that no "thing" is signified by "some" thing—the word is *something,* and what does that signify? Well, the "self," as it were, does not signify a Self. Everyone—Chuang-Tzu, Lao-Tze—knew that "the way that can be named is not the Way." The self that can be referred to as a self-thing is not the Self.

That's not to say that, all right, that Form is formless, or that Form were empty of form. The prime sentence, once one gets to that, is that emptiness, or the Void, is empty of Emptiness.

Well, take the verbal formula "I repeat myself"—when a person says, "I'm repeating myself"—and take it apart: "I repeat my self"—the self is repeating itself, so to speak. So there's something there that is repeating? Where does that repetition come from?

If we're going to take that expression, "I repeat myself," then I don't think there's an "I," and I don't think there's a "self" that is repeated. I don't think the "I" repeats "myself." I would be prepared to say provisionally, at the beginning of a discussion, if we're going to play with words to attempt to convey our meaning or express ourselves, that there is the appearance, at any rate, of a pattern of redundancy, that there appears to be a similarity of form existing over a period of time. Now how to account for the appearance of that persistence? Well, I think there's a very simple-minded explanation of that, which I wouldn't have said . . . that there is something behind that, or prior to that, another redundancy which would have to be another substantial entity, that somehow or other interplays with something else. And then from that, as the origin, there is a pattern thrown up which repeats the *self,* or oneself. There's no self being repeated, I don't think—unless you want to say that we identify (and you've got to then put into inverted commas the "we"), or say that there is a process of identification—without being able to say who or what is identifying with whom or what—where there appears to be a process of identification with part of that pattern. So that one can say that the pattern is itself the appearance of the self, to whatever that appears, that we take that to be our "self." But I don't think for a moment that what is being repeated is the Self.

So in reincarnation, what is repeated there is not the self, but the form that the self takes because of its lack of awareness of itself?

O.K., but again, I'll repeat myself by saying that all these forms of words can't be said to be right in themselves—that depends on the understanding that informs them. Any form of words can be completely misleading, or may mislead, and particularly in this zone. We're talking together, and when you said that it seemed to me that I agreed with you, but if someone else had said that sentence I might not.

When I'm talking to some people, I find that . . . just to take an example: a person who puts out an atheist position or a theist position or an agnostic position or a polytheist position, or who attempts to case his degree of realization of his presence in the world in a particular language, then vis-á-vis one person I might sound like an atheist, or vis-á-vis another I might be a theist or an agnostic.

I wonder whether you think it possible to use methods employed by Indian gurus in order to try to deal with psychological healing on a level higher than what Western medicine is usually aware of. I don't know if this would require some kind of sadhana—*spiritual discipline . . .*

There *are* some people in the world whose minds are relatively, and possibly completely, unconfused. And there's no question of this sort of come-on of what does one think about using gurus. You've got no chance of using gurus: gurus will use *you,* as time and circumstances are most appropriate, and you may or may not have some idea of how you're being used by them, but you don't have to worry about that—you can leave that to them.

Will a guru take on someone who's "mad" rather than one whom one sees as having "God-madness"—isn't there a distinction there for a guru?

God-madness? Meher Baba God-madness?

Well, whatever it is . . .

It's not your problem what gurus do and how they go about it and whether they declare themselves to be such or how they define themselves or with what sort of form they present themselves in the world. They operate as time and circumstance permit with perfect facility and ease . . . If you want to get to that, read *The Platform Sutra* of the sixth Chinese patriarch, Hui-Neng, where that's laid out as clearly as it can be.

All I'm saying in the meantime is just to look at what are the phenomena of one's mind, one's emotions, one's physical frame—*specifically.* For instance, you could get tuned in to really directly experiencing your breathing, so that when you're breathing in, you know that you're breathing in, every breath that you take in, you know that you're doing so, whether you're talking, smoking, or eating—you know when you're breathing in and you know when you're breathing out, and you know if you're taking a short breath in that you're putting a short breath out, etc., without straining or striving to go beyond it or up or down it or beside it, or looking for any effect. If one settles down just to do that, the effect, which is ineffable anyway and can't be put into words and is not a Way that can be named—that's to say, there's no place that you go to from here to another place. The way of experiencing the world changes, and changes all the time—there's an infinite number of different changes that one might undergo—none of these is the answer; none of these is It; none of these is your resting place; none of these has to be hung on to and sort of settled-down in and made your home. The Blake poem we read earlier ("The Mental Traveller") expresses it beautifully well—the sequence, the transformation goes on and continues to go on. And finally, in Eliot's *Four Quartets,* with all the horror, there's also the position one can arrive at where you don't have to worry in that way about transcending it: fish can't transcend the ocean, a bird can't transcend the air, and we can't transcend our Muse, in that sense . . .

But if life, as seen from a spiritual viewpoint, often seems to be a delusional system, and if psychiatry, too, as you've implied, is also possibly a delusional system . . .

Just look at the phenomena before one, without importing any presuppositions or making any superimpositions upon it, including worrying about it or getting yourself to worry about how to get out of this delusional system before it's too late—just settle down to look at it, and it will begin to set itself aright . . . Hmmm?

I'll try. I mean, I won't try.

1972

2
Literature

Of the following essays, the lengthy introduction to comtemporary American poetry (first published in Horizon Press's *New American Arts,* edited by Richard Kostelanetz) requires a few words of special pleading. Written at the beginning of 1964, this essay obviously shows its age. Sylvia Plath's first collection of poems, *The Colossus,* had appeared, but I had at that time only seen a few of the poems, later published in *Ariel,* that would provide the material for what has turned out to be a sometimes necrophiliac obsession and hagiolatry with regard to this obviously remarkable poet. Furthermore, my essay did little, if any, justice to poets like Allen Ginsberg, Gary Snyder, Philip Whalen, Robert Duncan, Charles Olson, Robert Bly, Adrienne Rich, and W.S. Merwin (the poetry of the last three writers has become increasingly more impressive) . . . or, needless to say, to the many younger poets who have now come into their own. My structural classification of three poetic "schools" provided a handy method of what the French call *decoupage*—the cutting-down to size of an enormous amount of detail—and perhaps these classifications now seem a bit schematic. But I hope that, given the reader's indulgence, there still remain some subsisting rewards. The other essays, I hope, speak for themselves.

The New American Poetry

I

What is "new" in the best contemporary American poetry is hardly what we usually think of as new. A "revolution" has occurred, but it is one that returns us to the poetic worlds of four culturally and chronologically disparate writers: Tu Fu, Catullus, Francois Villon, and Charles Baudelaire. They are the seminal poetic models for our time, not only in the most obvious sense that they have influenced poets as diverse as Robert Lowell, Kenneth Rexroth, Louis Zukofsky, and Carolyn Kizer, for example, but more importantly because they assume the stances and gestures which almost all contemporary poets accept as the basis of literary creation. That is to say, their poems are the projections of exacerbated sensibilities; and in their poems we see how the Self—constituting the starting point for the poets' explorations of their own psyches and of others'—enables them to write, although with different techniques, of those feelings with which poets have always been concerned: longing, loss, grief, joy, wonder.

It is fair to say, I believe, that in contemporary poetry, if not in astronomy, the Ptolemaic system—where the poet stands for the earth—is more suitable to creation of important poetry than the Copernican system—where types and myths stand for the sun. One should not take this somewhat heady statement as prescriptive; it is descriptive in the most particular way. Almost all recent American poetry from the most "conservative" to the most exploratory—whether by J. V. Cunningham, James Wright, or John Ashbery—supports this point. It is inconceivable, for example, for a contemporary American poet to write a dream allegory like *The Faerie Queene* or design a gigantic typological structure like *The Divine Comedy.* The two great long American poems of the century—Pound's *Cantos* and William Carlos Williams' *Paterson*—are, for all their disguises, personal in the extreme. Pound does nothing less than incorporate in himself the personae of Master Kung, Odysseus, Malatesta, John Adams, et al.; while Williams discovers man himself to be a city, "beginning, seeking, achieving and concluding his life in ways which the various aspects of a city may embody."

We should realize, however, that we too often value Tu Fu, Catullus, Villon, and Baudelaire for their sensibilities alone without recognizing that these poets' greatness derives in part from their responding passionately to and embodying in unique ways their demoralized ages. Contemporary American poets do so, as well, whether by exploring their "alienated" selves or by fragmenting their syntax and working with confusion in order to reflect truthfully on their positions in disjointed times.

The question finally is not whether widely admired poets like James Dickey, Anthony Hecht, W. S. Merwin—I choose these three at random—are "new," but rather whether they explore their selves, their world, and their language in particularly intense or imaginative ways. I do not think that they do; and we might best concentrate on the most important contemporary American poetry by introducing three types of sensibility and the poets of each "type." These poets have at least one thing in common: they have discarded the exploded mythology and the half-truthful "revelation" and assume the Self as starting point in making issue with themselves and the world.

II

My secrets cry aloud.
I have no need for tongue.
My heart keeps open house.
My doors are widely swung.
An epic of the eyes
My love, with no disguise.

My truths are all foreknown,
This anguish self-revealed.
I'm naked to the bone,
With nakedness my shield.
Myself is what I wear:
I keep the spirit spare.

These two stanzas from Theodore Roethke's early poem "Open House" (1941) suggest the tone and method of our first group of poets—poets who expose themselves and by doing so paradoxically make sense of their predicaments; nakedness becomes their shield. Four poets of recent years have most successfully assumed the stances of the four classic poets talked about above, and together they have produced our most forcible body of poetry: Theodore Roethke, John Berryman, Sylvia Plath, and Robert Lowell.*

The poems of Theodore Roethke, who died at fifty-five in the summer of 1963, explore the world of the "minimal"—a world in which even the dirt breathes "a small breath," a world in which external and internal realities exist on the same psychic terrain and become identical. Roethke searches below the external surface of his self in order to arrive at the inner soul; the "delineation of the ideal" becomes apparent through the poet's scrutiny. With *The Far Field* (1964), a collection of Roethke's last poems, and the earlier collected verse, *Words for the Wind* (1958), we have Roethke's full testament of this search.

The poet consistently presents himself to us, naked and rampaging his Self. "A man's a beast prowling in his own house," he writes in a later poem, "The Pure Fury." And only in an induced dream-state can the poet arrive at what in "Otto" he calls his "lost world." To reach this world, Roethke must make a poetic journey from "exhaustion to exhaustion" (a phrase he takes from Yeats) during which he dives down in his dream state through all layers of his psyche. Re-integration often occurs in the greenhouse, Roethke's lost world, his personal "symbol for the whole of life, a womb, a heaven-on-earth" ("Open Letter," in *Mid-Century American Poets,* edited by John Ciardi). For Roethke, Father is the Great Gardener. After having "returned" to his "heaven-on-earth" in "The Lost Son," the poet cries out: "Ordnung! Ordnung! Papa is coming."

It is almost embarrassing for a critic to interpret Roethke's work in terms of Freud and Jung. Roethke's series of fourteen child-like, dream-like monologues in *Praise to the End* succeeds so beautifully in communicating "the spring and rush of the child—and Gammer Gurton's concision" ("Open Letter") and in revealing secondary elaboration of subconscious roots of thought and feeling that one would rather think that psychologists obtained their perceptions of dreams and childhood fan-

*Owing to necessary space limitations, one can only mention as belonging to our first group fine poets like Stanley Kunitz, Delmore Schwartz (in earlier poems like "The Heavy Bear," "Starlight Like Intuition," and "A Dog Named Ego, the Snowflakes as Kisses"), Karl Shapiro, Randall Jarrell, John Logan, Theodore Weiss, J. V. Cunningham, David Ignatow, Josephine Miles, and Elizabeth Bishop. Here also belong three of our best young poets—W. D. Snodgrass, Robert Creeley, and Thom Gunn (born in England and now residing in California)—and the two most talented "Beat" poets, Gregory Corso and Allen Ginsberg.

tasies from Roethke. Conceptions such as "Dreams as a Form of Ideation" and "Nightmares as Objectifications of Organic Sensations," etc., seem foolish when applied to Roethke's work. To say that the line "I have left the body of the whale, but the mouth of the night is still wide" ("The Longing") has "Freudian overtones" is quite idiotic. The bedrock reality and radically "regressive" images of Roethke's poems are so striking and essential that Freud is superfluous. Roethke's work is the discovery of himself; and his poems need no symbolic correlatives to explain them.

The manifest dream content in Roethke's poems consists of objects existing in the world of the "minimal." "The small! The small! I hear them singing clear / On the long banks, in the soft summer air," Roethke writes in "A Walk in Late Summer." And this is a world of sweet-peas, weeds, stones, meadow mice, little girls. But as we can see from almost any quotation from Roethke's poems, the poetic materials spring up from the greenhouse where the poet spent much of his childhood, from the soil of the garden, from the marsh. "Weeds, too, he favoured as most men don't favour men," Berryman wrote about him. And although in "The Abyss" Roethke writes that "too much reality can be a dazzle," he wants only to tell of his intense love for the objects and events of the natural world. In "Night Journey" he writes how on a cross-country train he "stays up half the night / To see the land I love."

Roethke employs images of the world of the "minimal" in all his love poems (hardly equalled for their passion in our time) or meditations or songs: "Love, love, a lily's my care"; "I remember the neckcurls, limp and damp as tendrils." But this world also includes "A kingdom of stinks and sighs, / Fetor of cockroaches, dead fish, petroleum, / Worse than castoreum of mink or weasels, / Saliva dripping from warm microphones, / Agony of crucifixion on barstools" ("The Longing"). For Roethke's world is his mind; his mind, the world; "A ghost comes out of the unconscious mind / To grope my sill. It moans to be reborn!" And it is reborn. Roethke's poems are the means by which he connects the everyday world with his unconscious ghost. We see, for example, how a creature of the world and the creature of the poet's mind in "Night Crow" become one—

because they are one:

When I saw that clumsy crow
Flap from a wasted tree,
A shape in the mind rose up:
Over the gulfs of dream
Flew a tremendous bird
Further and further away
Into a moonless black,
Deep in the brain, far back.

Ghosts are made real, animals made human; for in Roethke's dream-world there is little distinction between the two. Plants, too, take on human properties. In "Orchids" the flowers have "soft luminescent fingers . . . loose ghostly mouths." In one of Roethke's last great poems, "The Geranium," the poet's relationship with a flower is as human as his love for Jane in his often-anthologized "Elegy for Jane." "The Geranium" resembles this poem in its beautifully cadenced lines and tone of loneliness and grief:

When I put her out, once by the garbage pail
She looked so limp and bedraggled,
So foolish and trusting, like a sick poodle,
Or a wizened aster in later September,
I brought her back in again
For a new routine—
Vitamins, water, and whatever
Sustenance seemed sensible
At the time: she'd lived
So long on gin, bobbie pins, half-smoked cigars, dead beer,
Her shrivelled petals falling
On the faded carpet, the stale
Steak grease stuck to her fuzzy leaves.
(Dried-out, she creaked like a tulip.)

The things she endured!—
The dumb dames shrieking half the night
Or the two of us, alone, both seedy,
Me breathing booze at her,
She leaning out of her pot toward the window.

Near the end, she seemed almost to hear me—
And that was scary—
So when that snuffling cretin of a maid
Threw her, pot and all, into the trash-can,
I said nothing.

But I sacked the presumptuous hag the next week,
I was that lonely.

Roethke writes of such extremes of emotion that one wishes to judge his poems on their power and his imagination alone. Roethke is also, however, one of the great craftsmen of our time. His use of slant and oblique rhymes is wonderfully subtle (lives / leaves; stone / moon; all / temporal); the villanelle form in "The Waking" and his ballad and song forms of "The Saginaw Song," "A Wheeze for Wystan," and "My Papa's Waltz" are extraordinary. In Roethke's poems, finally, the ideal is delineated only by the identity the poet makes between his psyche and the world. As in a dream, we break through to the beauty of "The Moment"—the moment in which events, things, persons, and feelings are transfigured to become All:

We passed the ice of pain,
And came to a dark ravine,
And there we sang with the sea;
The wide, the bleak abyss
Shifted with our slow kiss.

Space struggled with time;
The gong of midnight struck
The naked absolute.
Sound, silence sang as one.

All flowed; without, within;
Body met body, we
Created what's to be.

What else to say?—
We end in joy.

John Berryman's *Dream Songs* (1964) is one of the great achievements of American poetry.

Turning it over, considering, like a madman
Henry put forth a book.
No harm resulted from this.

Neither the menstruating stars (nor man) was moved
at once.
Bare dogs drew closer for a second look

and performed their friendly operations there.
Refreshed, the bark rejoiced.
Seasons went and came.

Leaves fell, but only a few.
Something remarkable about this
unshedding bulky bole-proud blue-green moist

thing made by savage & thoughtful
surviving Henry
began to strike the passers from despair
so that sore on their shoulders old men hoisted
six-foot sons and polished women called
small girls to dream awhile toward the flashing &
                                                  bursting tree!

Curiously, *Dream Songs* perfectly exemplify the suggestions Roethke addressed to himself in his "Open Letter" on how a poet can derive his important powers. The poet, Roethke writes,

> must be able to telescope image and symbol, if necessary, without relying on the obvious connectives: to speak in a kind of psychic shorthand when his protagonist is under great stress. He must be able to shift his rhythms rapidly, the "tension." He works intuitively, and the final form of his poem must be imaginatively right . . . obscurity should break open suddenly for the serious reader who can hear the language: the "meaning" itself should come as dramatic revelation, an excitement.

Berryman, in a note of introduction to his early poems of 1940, wrote of the "strain," the "torsion" of his poetry. In retrospect, we can see how the poet's now-famous twisting, elliptical style emerges in the fourth and fifth sections of Berryman's first volume, *The Dispossessed* (1948); for example, "Rising wind rucks from the sill / The slack brocade beside / the old throne he dreams on," from "The Long Home." *Homage to Mistress Bradstreet,* published in 1956 and unfortunately little read, is a magnificent poem of fifty-seven eight-line stanzas of shifting end rhymes in which the phrasal cadence of the speaking voice conflicts violently with the iambic line. Berryman's latinate diction, wrenched accents, and occasional sprung rhythms combine to produce the haunting study of the torn and deracinated early American poetess. In monologues and interspersed conversations with the poet himself, the poet's heartbreakingly exposed love for and understanding of Anne Bradstreet is revealed:

Outside the New World winters in grand dark
white air lashing high thro' the virgin stands

foxes down foxholes sigh,
surely the English heart quails, stunned.
I doubt if Simon that this blast, that sea,
spares from his rigour for your poetry
more. We are on each other's hands
who care. Both of our worlds unhanded us. Lie stark, . . .
(*Stanza 2*)

Veiled my eyes, attending. How can it be I?
Moist, with parted lips, I listen, wicked.
I shake in the morning & retch.
Brood I do on myself naked.
A fading world I dust, with fingers new.
—I have earned the right to be alone with you.
—What right can that be?
Convulsing, if you love enough, like a sweet lie.
(*Stanza 27*)

It is in the *Dream Songs,* however, that Berryman finds the perfect vehicle for his style and vision. The eight line stanza becomes six-lined. The "roiling & babbling & braining" (a Berryman phrase) is spoken and sung by Henry, the dreamer of the *Dream Songs.* He talks about and converses with himself, but also with Mr. Bones, perhaps of minstrel show derivation, who is somewhat an alter ego: "Easy, easy, Mr. Bones. I is on your side," says Henry. Sometimes Henry becomes an animal like Henry Pussy-cat, or even the tail of a dog. As Roethke wrote:

The revelation of the identity of the speaker may itself be a part of the drama; or, in some instances, in a dream sequence, his identity may merge with someone else's, or be deliberately blurred. The struggle for spiritual identity is, of course, one of the perpetual recurrences. . . . *Disassociation often precedes a new state of clarity.*
("Open Letter"; emphasis added.)

For there is a marvelous clarity to these songs. They abound, of course, in the condensation and displacement of dream-work. But loneliness and despair have rarely been expressed with such quietness and restraint as in the song titled "Snow Line":

It was wet & white & swift and where I am
we don't know. It was dark and then
It isn't.
I wish the barker would come. There seems to be to eat
nothing. I am unusually tired.
I'm alone too.

If only the strange one with so few legs would come,
I'd say my prayers out of my mouth, as usual.
Where are his notes I loved?
There may be horribles; it's hard to tell.
The barker nips me but somehow I feel
he too is on my side.

I'm too alone. I see no end. If we could all
run, even that would be better. I am hungry.
The sun is not hot.
It's not a good position I am in.
If I had to do the whole thing over again
I wouldn't.

Beyond performing in complete darkness "operations of great delicacy/on myself" for the sake only of his Self, Berryman approaches our life today with the moral stature and compassion of Sam Johnson and Givvon. He goes naked to show our "moral nudity." In many respects he has an eighteenth-century mind although his speaking voice is the singing brawl of the declamatory sot (Pope's "sot as hero"). It is through these drunken lurchings of syntax, however, that the extirpation of our respect for ourselves and others is witnessed and proclaimed. I have heard Berryman read his *Dream Songs* in public—intoxicated, slurring, emphasizing words so willfully as to destroy the "line"—yet the majesty of his vision finally broke through like his "flashing & bursting tree." Nothing less than the decline and fall of the contemporary West is revealed in Berryman's "non-tipsyish" drunken songs.

Sometimes Berryman rages against the "teen set":

"Scads of goot eats," dere own t'ree cars, the 'teens
(until of them shall be asked one thing, they romp or doze)
have got it made;
no prob. was ever set them, their poor ol' jerks
of parents loved them, with deep-freeze, & snacks
would keep a Hindu family-group alive.

Well, so they're liars & gluttons & cowards: so what?
. . . It's the Land of Plenty, maybe about to sigh.
Why shouldn't they terrify
with hegemony Dad (stupido Dad) and "teach"? . . .

One waits for the Houyhnhnms to set the "teens" to "hard work."

Berryman realizes that our "squeamish comfy ruin-prone proud national mind" is the small cause from which extend the greater evils. But the cocktail parties go on, parties like the one in which "Henry's pelt was put on sundry walls" (one is reminded of Roethke's "The flying fabric stitched on bone"):

> Golden, whilst your frozen daiquiris
> whir at midnight, gleams on you his fur
> & silky & black.
> Mission accomplished, pal.
> My molten yellow & moonless bag,
> drained, hangs at rest.
>
> Collect in the cold depths barracuda. Ay,
> in Sealdah Station some possessionless
> children survive to die.
> The Chinese communes hum. Two daiquiris
> withdrew into a corner of the gorgeous room
> and one told the other a lie.

And finally we have Berryman's songs of grief for those like Roethke and Robert Frost who are " in friendlier ground"; for their virtues and feelings were so "unusual," patent and open-to-wounding in the face of everyday evils. About Frost, Berryman writes:

> His malice was a pimple down his good
> big face, with its sly eyes. I must be sorry
> Mr. Frost has left:
> I like it so less I don't understood—
> he couldn't hear or see well—all we sift—
> but this is a *bad* story.

Berryman faces ruin and frustration with high comedy and low comedy and sorrow; with "ancient sighs, infamous characters, new rhythms." How can we help but be moved by the courage of:

> The high ones die, die. They die. You look up and who's there?
> —Easy, easy, Mr. Bones. I is on your side.
> I smell your grief.
> —I sent my grief away. I cannot care
> forever. With them all again & again I died
> and cried, and I have to live.

And even when we read lines like these, we know that John Berryman's fortitude and artistic power will endure the clawing degenerations of these years:

these fierce & airy occupations, and love,
raved away so many of Henry's years
it is a wonder that, with in each hand
one of his own mad books & all,
ancient fires for eyes, his head full
& his heart full, he's making ready to move on.

Of the several women who in the past few years have emerged as among the most interesting of American poets, the best of them, Sylvia Plath, who died at thirty-one in 1963, appears already to be one of the most startling women poets of any time.

Her predecessor, the late Dilys Lang, in her *Poems from a Cage* (1961) once wrote of a poetry in which "the idea of a cage, or of captivity, is paramount," as well as a poetry of "release." Her verse, however, only occasionally exemplifies her ideal. The two women who realize these kinds of poetry most successfully, however, are Anne Sexton and Sylvia Plath. The former's collections—*To Bedlam and Part Way Back* (1960) and *All My Pretty Ones* (1962)—display a concern with madness, despair, and the attempted breakthrough out of bedlam. Her poems, like those of Frederick Seidel, too often explore one depressive state without relief or variation and thus dissipate their intended power through a kind of emotional stasis.

Sylvia Plath succeeds in accomplishing what Anne Sexton has attempted and Dilys Lang hoped to accomplish. Like Gaspara Stampa, the great Venetian cinquecentist courtesan poet, Sylvia Plath died terribly young at thirty-one, extending Gaspara Stampa's themes of "fever and love" into the areas of terror and suicide in finished, corrosive poems of almost unimaginable intensity. She published one collection of poems, *The Colossus,* in 1961; but her most startling verse appeared in magazines like *The New Yorker* and *Encounter* shortly after her death.

Sylvia Plath's poems betray her own awareness of an impending early death. "I am terrified by this dark thing/That sleeps in me," she writes in "The Elm Speaks." "All day I feel its soft, feathery turnings, its malignity." In "The Manor Garden," the first poem of *The Colossus,* she shows the influence of the early-to-die Georg Trakl:

The fountains are dry and the roses over.
Incense of death. Your day approaches.
The pears fatten like little buddhas.
A blue mist is dragging the lake.

And her poems do display the deracinated sensibility of many of the German Romantics. One cannot help wondering whether she did not also absorb the child-rhythms and cadences of German traditional rhymes and folk songs which occur as distinctive elements in her work:

The little toy wife—
Erased, sigh, sigh.
Four babies and a cocker!

Nurses, the size of worms, and a minute doctor
Tuck him in.
Old happenings

Peel from his skin.
Down the drain with all of it!
Hugging his pillow

Like the red-headed sister he never dared to touch,
He dreams of a new one—
Barren, the lot are barren!

(from "Amnesiac")

But this aspect of her poems illuminates the grim and dreadful humor with which (more than John Clare and Roethke) she uses the vehicle of childhood to write of her most personal and consuming memories, especially of her German-born father who died when she was ten. In "The Colossus," she attempts to reconstruct him as if she were playing with a jigsaw puzzle:

I shall never get you put together entirely,
Pieced, glued, and properly jointed.
Mule-bray, pig-grunt and bawdy cackles
Proceed from your great lips.
It's worse than a barnyard.

Her most moving poem, entitled "Daddy," significantly begins in nursery-rhyme manner:

You do not do, you do not do
Anymore, black shoe

In which I have lived like a foot
For thirty years, poor and white,
Barely daring to breathe or Achoo!

Daddy, I have had to kill you.
You died before I had time—
Marble-heavy, a bag full of God,
Ghastly statue with one grey toe
Big as a Frisco seal

And a head in the freakish Atlantic
Where it pours bean green over blue
In the waters off beautiful Nauset.
I used to pray to recover you.
Ach, du!

But it concludes with a self-destructive savagery and outraged tenderness that leave one staggered:

You stand at the blackboard, daddy,
In the picture I have of you,
A cleft in your chin instead of your foot
But no less a devil for that, no not
Any less the black man who

Bit my pretty red heart in two.
I was ten when they buried you.
At twenty I tried to die

And get back, back, back to you.
I thought even the bones would do.

But they pulled me out of the sack,
And they stuck me together with glue.
And then I knew what to do.
I made a model of you,
A man in black with a Meinkampf look

And a love of the rack and the screw.
And I said I do, I do.
So daddy, I'm finally through.
The black telephone's off at the root,
The voices just can't worm through.

If I've killed one man, I've killed two—
The vampire who said he was you
And drank my blood for a year—
Seven years, if you want to know.
Daddy, you can lie back now.

There's a stake in your fat black heart
And the villagers never liked you.
They are dancing and stamping on you.
They always *knew* it was you.
Daddy, daddy, you bastard, I'm through.

There is nothing like this in contemporary poetry. Even Stanley Kunitz's and Robert Lowell's magnificent poems about their fathers, as poignant and agonizing as they are, do not come close to the crazy humor and grief and destructiveness of this poem. Sylvia Plath faced ruin herself too many times not to wear it like a glove. From "Lady Lazarus" we read:

I have done it again!
One year in every ten
I manage it—

A sort of walking miracle, my skin
Bright as a Nazi lampshade
My right foot

A paperweight,
My face a featureless, fine
Jew linen. . . .

. . . I am only thirty
And like the cat I have nine times to die.

This is Number Three.
What a trash
to annihilate each decade!

Sylvia Plath is certainly a remarkable poet. Lines like: "My night sweats grease his breakfast plate"; "The air is a mill of hooks"; or "The yew's black fingers wag" are exceptional. Her construction of syllabic verse in "Mussel Hunter at Rock Harbor" and "Man in Black" and the subtle development of images in "Little Fugue" and "Mystic," for example, display a phenomenal technical mastery. Her rich and acute feel for language and disarming use of off-rhyme is excellently illustrated in the following two stanzas from "Watercolor of Grantchester Meadows":

Cloudrack and owl-hollowed willows slanting over
The bland Granta double their white and green
World under the sheer water

And ride the flux at anchor, upside down.
The punter sinks his pole.
In Byron's pool
Cattails part where the tame cygnets steer.

It is a country on a nursery plate.
Spotted cows revolve their jaws and crop
Red clover or gnaw beetroot
Bellied on a nimbus of sun-glazed buttercup.
Hedging meadows of benign
Arcadian green
The blood-berried hawthorn hides its spines with white.

Yet Sylvia Plath continually sees the moon "with the O-gape of complete despair. I live here," she tells us. We must approach her poetry with the knowledge that she suffered a sickness unto death and bore it to the surface through the discipline of her art, unveiling her sickness totally—"I am not cruel, only truthful."

So many fine essays have been written about Robert Lowell's *Lord Weary's Castle* (1946) and *The Mills of the Kavanaughs* (1951), especially Randall Jarrell's "From the Kingdom of Necessity," that it might be best merely to point to what is at once Lowell's most obvious strength and weakness—a somewhat overviolent use of language in his earlier poems as contrasted with the more subtle and powerful diction of Lowell's recent work. From the first stanza of "Colloquy in Black Rock," we read:

Here the jack-hammer *jabs* into the ocean;
My heart, you *race* and *stagger* and *demand*
More blood-gangs for your nigger-brass percussions,
Till I, the *stunned* machine of your devotion
Clanging upon this cymbal of a hand,
Am *rattled* screw and footloose. . . . (Emphasis added)

The slashing aggressiveness of Lowell's verbs and verbals give the key to the tone and intent of most of the poet's earlier verse. "Colloquy in Black Rock," like most of Lowell's religious poems, keeps to the blazing tone to produce a magnificent poem. But in a sense, Lowell tends to limit his experience inversely as he ignites his verbs and images. Lowell's more recent verse—which some persons imagine to be more "simple-minded"—is, on the contrary, an advance over the previous verse, a true "breakthrough back into life." What we find appears at first to be the simpler, quieter, and "looser" structures of *Life Studies* (1959) and *Imitations* (1961):

One dark night,
my Tudor Ford climbed the hill's skull;
I watched for love-cars. Lights turned down,
they lay together, hull to hull,
where the graveyard shelves on the town. . . .
My mind's not right.

A car radio bleats,
"Love, O careless Love. . . ." I hear
my ill-spirit sob in each blood cell,
I myself am hell;
nobody's here—

only skunks, that search
in the moonlight for a bite to eat.
They march on their soles up Main Street:
white stripes, moonstruck eyes' red fire
under the chalk-dry and spar spire
of the Trinitarian Church.

I stand on top
of four back steps and breathe the rich air—
a mother skunk with her column of kittens swills the garbage pail.
She jabs her wedge-head in a cup
of sour cream, drops her ostrich tail,
and will not scare.

(from "Skunk Hour")

But in fact we are discovering, to use out of context Lowell's words from his *Paris Review* interview, a poem like "Skunk Hour" in which "you wouldn't notice the form, yet looking back you'd find that great obstacles had been climbed." Lowell's poems about Ford Madox Ford and Delmore Schwartz; "Memories of West Street and Lepke"; "Man and Wife"; "A Mad Negro Soldier Confined in Munich"—to name just several—manifest the "commanding, deadly effectiveness in the arrangement, and something that breathes and pauses and grunts and is rough and unpredictable to assure me that the journey is honest," to quote Lowell's own essay on Stanley Kunitz.

Lowell has published in magazines like *Partisan Review* and *Encounter* poems (now collected in *For the Union Dead*) about middle age and middle-age marriage in particular. "The Flaw" reveals all the "naked truths"; like Keats, Lowell refuses to "unperplex" bliss from pain:

> Old wives and husbands! Look, their gravestones wait
> in couples with the name and half the date—
> one future and one freedom. In a flash,
> I see us whiten into skeletons,
> our eager, sharpened cries, a pair of stones,
> cutting like shark fins through the boundless wash.
>
> Two walking cobwebs, almost bodiless,
> crossed paths here once, kept house, and lay in beds.
> Your fingertips once touched my fingertips,
> and set us tingling through a thousand threads.
> Poor pulsing *Fête Champêtre!* The summer slips
> between our fingers into nothingness. . . .

But in a group of poems about his Maine cottage, Lowell opens up, as if to the sea air, to write "The Old Flame" or the following poem entitled "Water":

> It was a Maine lobster town—
> each morning boatloads of hands
> pushed off for granite
> quarries on the islands,
>
> and left dozens of bleak
> white frame houses stuck
> like oyster shells
> on a hill of rock,
>
> and below us, the sea lapped
> the raw little match-stick
> mazes of a weir,
> where the fish for bait were trapped.
>
> Remember? We sat on a slab of rock.
> From this distance in time,
> it seems the color
> of iris, rotting and turning purpler,
>
> but it was only
> the usual gray rock
> turning the usual green
> when drenched by the sea.
>
> The sea drenched the rock

at our feet all day,
and kept tearing away
flake after flake.

One night you dreamed
you were a mermaid clinging to a wharf-pile,
and trying to pull
off the barnacles with your hands.

We wished our two souls
might return like gulls
to the rock. In the end,
the water was too cold for us.

It is the poet's clear, open exploration of the presentness of feeling and the true discovery of the beauty and heartbreak of the reality of the "other"—Lowell's Anne Kavanaugh and Bathsheba are mostly Lowell himself—that are providing us now with the poet's fullest and most moving poetry. His unobtrusive slant rhymes (hands/islands; rock/stuck; color/purpler) and gentle but remarkably restless cadences correspond in technique to this new emotional "opening up."

Lowell's exquisite imitations—"reckless with the literal meaning" but "getting the tone"—of Heine:

How confidingly the corrupt twin rocked me in his arms;
his poppy garland, nearing, hushed death's alarms
at sword-point for a moment.
Soon a pinpoint of infinite regression! And now that incident
is closed. There's no way out,
unless the other turn about
and, pale, distinguished, perfect, drop his torch;
("Heine Dying in Paris")

or of Russians like Mandelstam and Pasternak:

Like water pouring from a pitcher, my mouth on your nipples!
Not always. The summer well runs dry.
Not for long the dust of our stamping feet, encore on encore
from the saxes in the casino's midnight gazebo;
(Pasternak's "Sparrow Hills")

all exemplify and extend Lowell's new "tone" and approach. Here is no withdrawal of the power that conceived the poems in *Lord Weary's Castle;* rather it is the unequivocal growth of Robert Lowell's great art. For rarely before have openness, tenderness, and understanding been so naturally wedded in poems that do not reflect self-consciously on themselves but communicate their experiences directly to the reader.

III

"Oh to be seventeen years old
Once again," sang the red-haired man, "and not know that poe-
try
Is ruled with the sceptre of the dumb, the deaf, and the creepy!"
And the shouting persons battered his immortal body with stones
And threw his primitive comedy into the sea
From which it sang forth poems irrevocably blue.

from "Fresh Air" by Kenneth Koch

The so-called "New York poets"—its members consisting of John Ashbery, Edwin Denby, Barbara Guest, Kenneth Koch, and Frank O'Hara—is the most original "school" of poetry today. While the members of this "school" have been influenced by the nineteenth- and twentieth-century European "avant-garde," they have absorbed, but modulated and directed for their own ends, the dazzling and unorthodox syntax, diction, and tones of Mallarmé, Tristan Corbière, Apollinaire, Pierre Reverdy, Vladimir Mayakovsky, and Pasternak.

Frank O'Hara, for example, in his best poems takes off from Mayakovsky's *The Cloud in Trousers,* which begins:

Your thought,
musing on a sodden brain
like a bloated lackey on a greasy couch,
I'll taunt with a bloody morsel of heart;
and satiate my insolent, caustic contempt.

No gray hairs streak my soul,
no grandfatherly fondness there!
I shake the world with the might of my voice,
and walk—handsome
twentytwoyear old . . . ;

and from Mayakovsky's "To His Beloved Self";

With my eyes' rays I'd gnaw the night—
if I were, oh,
as dull

as the sun!
Why should I want
to feed with my radiance
the earth's lean lap!

I shall go by,
dragging my burden of love.
In what delirious
and ailing
night,
was I sired by Goliaths—
I, so large,
so unwanted?

This is a poetry of an explosive, high-pitched adolescent sensibility displaying and celebrating itself alone: "Where shall I find a beloved," Mayakovsky writes, "a beloved like me?/She would be too big for the tiny sky!" Like Mayakovsky, O'Hara never allows the "sluggish fish of the imagination to flounder softly in the slush of the heart." O'Hara begins his poem "Invincibility" with an epigraph from Mayakovsky: "In the church of my heart the choir is on fire." But O'Hara soars even higher and in a more urbane manner than his Russian model. Like the others in his "school," O'Hara "plays" with language with a great deal of *panache:*

Avarice, the noose that lets oil, oh my dear oh
"La Ronde," erase what is assured and ours, it
resurrects nothing, finally, in its eagerness
to sit under the widely spaced stairs, to be a fabulous
toilette, doesn't imitate footsteps of disappearance

The neighbor, having teased peace to retire, soon
averages six flowering fountains, ooh! spare the men
and their nervous companions that melt and ripen
into a sordid harbor of squid-slipping tarpaulin strips,
quits the sordid arbor of community butchers' girth. . . .

O'Hara—and the New York "school" for that matter—has been closely associated with a group of abstract expressionist painters. In fact, O'Hara's poems often communicate the glitter and energy of the paintings of Pollock, De Kooning, and Larry Rivers, the last of whom designed the cover of O'Hara's long poem *Second Avenue* (1960), "dedicated to the memory of

Mayakovsky." O'Hara here handles long lines of fantastic exploding images and skittish humor, dissociative leaps of feeling, with a marvelous control. He is, like Mayakovsky, "just bare lips," open and dizzy in exposing himself to his world:

> My hands are Massimo Plaster, called "White Pin in the Arm of the Sea"
> and I'm blazoned and scorch like a fleet of windbells down the Pulaski Skyway
> tabletops of Vienna carrying their bundles of cellophane to the laundry,
> ear to the tongue, glistening semester of ardency, young-old daring-nesses
> at the foot of the most substantial art product of our times,
> the world, the jongleurs, fields of dizzyness and dysentery
> before reaching Mexico, the palace of stammering sinking success
> before billows of fangs, red faces, orange eyebrows, green, yes! ears,
> O paradise! my airplanes known as "Banana Line Incorpor-ealidad," saviors of connections and spit, dial HYancinth 9-9945, "Isn't that a conundrum?" asked him Sydney Burger, humming "Mein' Yiddisher Mama";
> I emulate the black which is a cry but is not voluptuary like a warning,
> which has lines, cuts, drips, aspirates, trembles with horror,
> O black looks at the base of the spine! kisses on the medulla oblongata
> of an inky clarity! always the earlobes in the swiftest bird's-death
> of night, the snarl of expiation which is the skirt of Hercules,
> and the remorse in the desert shouts "Flea! Bonanza! Cheek! Teat!
> Elbow of roaches! You wear my white rooster like a guerdon in vales
> of Pompeiian desires, before utter languorousness puts down its chisel,"
> and the desert is here. "You've reached the enormous summit of passion
> which is immobility forging an entrail from the pure obstruction of the air."

A poet like O'Hara continues in his writing to get at the "right language," while at the same time illuminating it, and to incorporate everyday "things," like telephone numbers, into poetic diction. One thinks of W. C. Williams' list of typical American ice creams from "Della Primaver Transportata Al Morale." "We poets have to talk in a language which is not English," Williams wrote in *Paterson.* "It is the American idiom. Rhythmically it's organized as a sample of the American idiom. It has as much originality as jazz. If you say '2 partridges, 2 mallard ducks, a Dungeness crab'—if you treat that rhythmically, ignoring the practical sense, it forms a jagged pattern. It is, to my mind, poetry." And O'Hara draws not only on Williams' dicta, but on Mayakovsky's poetic exclamations like: "Yum-yum-yum!" or "Drink Van Houten's Cocoa!" and on the English poet John Betjeman's use of common commercial products' names in his work. Earlier than this, we can also witness a freeing-up of line and tone in the fine, little-read poems collected in *Initial A* (1961) by David Schubert, a true "New York poet," who lived in the city from 1913–1946. But perhaps we might wilfully see this kind of colloquial freedom emerging as far back as Byron's *Don Juan,* especially in those lines T. S. Eliot made famous in his essay on Byron:

> Who queer a flat? Who (spite of Bow-street's ban)
> On the high toby-spice so flash the muzzle?
> Who on a lark, with black-eyed Sal (his blowing)
> So prime, so well, so nutty, and so knowing?

Kenneth Koch's *Ko, or A Season on Earth* (1959) starts off from Don Juan, by way of *Orlando Furioso,* assuming *ottava rima* structure and a fantastic "mythological machinery/And very handsome supernatural scenery," to quote Byron. Koch's mock epic concerns a Japanese baseball star and an assortment of "characters" such as Dog Boss, the Action Poet Joseph Dah, King Amaranth, baseball players, and young lovers. The setting, like the plots, shifts every few stanzas—from Cincinnati to Tahiti to Pompeii to Kalamazoo—all is possible in Koch's world. The following quotation from Canto I should suggest Koch's "method":

> The cabin door shot open, and a man
> (Or was it human?) with a hairy large
> Long sloping face, which was all colored tan
> Except the blackish nose, came in the Arg-
> Entina-purchased cabin with a can
> Of worms he used to fish with from the barge
> And woofed and barked and quite upset the room
> By running 'round. Andrews, alarmed, cried, "Whom . . . ?"
>
> Doris spoke smiling: "Dad's integrity
> Makes him, unlike most poets, actualize

In everyday life the poem's unreality.
That dog you saw on deck with steel-gray eyes
Was but a creation of Dad's terrible musical potency.
Then seeing the dog there made him realize
That the dog was himself, since by himself created,
So in this poem it's incorporated!"

"But," Andrews asked, "what poem? where?" and "Ah!"
Breathed Doris, "don't you know that what you're seeing
Is an ACTION POEM?" "You mean he's Joseph Dah,"
Cried Andrews, "the creator of Otherness Being?"
"The very same," sighed Doris. "That's my pa!"
And Joseph, as if by his barks agreeing
Shook his tan head and frisked back out on deck.
He changed, then smiled: "It's a nice day, by heck!"

Koch's shorter poems, collected in *Thank You and Other Poems* (1962) and mostly appearing in small New York magazines, reveal his debt to Ronald Firbank, Williams, but most of all to Apollinaire. Koch appropriates influences, radically refocusing them, however, in order to assume an adolescent persona in many of his poems, such as the one beginning: "Is the basketball coach a homosexual lemon manufacturer? It is suspected by O'Ryan in his submarine"; or "To You," which begins: "I love you as a sheriff searches for a walnut/That will solve a murder case unsolved for years. . . . I love you as a/Kid searches for a goat; I am crazier than shirttails/In the wind, when you're near, a wind that blows from/The big blue sea, so shiny so deep and so unlike us."

Seventeen years old seems to be the blissful age, a Golden Age, for Koch's poetic heroes—the age to which they longingly look back. Koch's characters, like Spenser's bridal couple in *Epithalamion,* "play their sports at will" and polymorphously delight; but unlike Spenser's couple, they do not accept the "laws of wedlock" as the *telos.* Thus Koch attacks the "restraint and mature talent" of the poetry "establishment" which represents those poets in the "kingdom of dullness" who write "on the subject of love between swans."

As with O'Hara, the word "play" is one of the keys to an understanding and appreciation of Koch's poetry. Koch manipulates language wonderfully, as in lines like: "lilac of angry fudge"; "And the fanning park/In lover's track of clacked-up snow"; or in the marvelous opening of "Summery Weather":

One earring's smile
Near the drawer
And at night we gambling
At that night the yacht on Venice
Glorious too, oh my heavens
See how her blouse was starched up.
"The stars reminded me of youse." . . .

But perhaps the most fanciful word-play occurs in the one hundred, twenty-lined stanzas of *When the Sun Tries to Go On,* published in *The Hasty Papers,* a poem which defies explication and even persistent reading:

And, with a shout, collecting coat-hangers
Dour rhebus, conch, hip.
Ham, the autumn day, oh how genuine!
Literary frog, catch-all boxer, O
Real! The magistrate, say "group," bower, undies
Disk, poop, "Timon of Athens." When
The bugle shimmies, how glove towns! . . .

And so on for two thousand lines! You either enjoy this kind of "play" or you don't. Although the poem is certainly "not serious," it is also finally boring, for the desire to "play" has been played out in the extreme. In "The Artist," moreover, much of the comedy derives from the confusion Koch purposely contrives between the use and mention of the word *Play:* "I often think *Play* was my best work"; "Was this how I originally imagined *Play,* but lacked courage?"

The extraordinary "A Poem of the Forty-Eight States"—especially influenced by Apollinaire's "Zone," and to me Koch's best poem—is a crazily-guided tour around the imagined United States of the poet's true-adolescent narrator, perhaps Koch's alter ego, who has too much knowledge (in Eliot's sense in "Gerontion") to be forgiven because of his "youthful" sensibility:

The electric chair steamed lightly, then touched
Me, I drove, upward,
Into the hills of Montana. My pony!
Here you are coming alone with your master!
Yet I am your master! You're wearing my sweater.
On pony, my pony!

As in a dream I was waiting to be seventh
To smile at my brothers in the happy state of Idaho
Each and every one of them condemned to the electric chair!
What have we done? Is it a crime
To shoe horses? Besides a lemon-yellow stream
There seemed to be compact bassoons,
And I was happy and a crackerjack. . . .

Koch's narrator not only travels through but also becomes the states ("My stovepipe hat! Perhaps you think I am Uncle Sam?/No, I am the State of Pennsylvania . . ."). Koch has of course made this kind of imaginative spatial leap before in "Desire for Spring" (". . . I wish to leap to Pittsburgh/From Tuskegee, Indiana, if necessary, spreading like a flower/In the spring light, and growing like a silver stair. . . .") and this is much like the painting technique of the "felt image of the body" used by Picasso and Chagall, for instance, that extends the torso visually when the torso "feels" longer. Whitman, Mayakovsky, and O'Hara do this kind of thing frequently in their poetry. But as "Poem of the Forty-Eight States" nears its conclusion, Koch's narrator communicates an anguish of outraged adolescence, so frightening and powerful, that we are reminded not only of Whitman, but also of Villon:

5

O Mississippi joys!
I reckon I am about as big and dead as a whale!
I am slowly sinking down into the green ooze
Of the Everglades, that I feared so much when I was a child!
I have become about as flat as the dust on a baseball diamond
And as empty and clear as the sky when it is just-blue
And you are three, and you stand on the rim of the zone of one of the
 United States
And think about the forty-seven others; then in the evening
Air you hear the sound of baseball players, and the splash of canoes!
You yourself would like to play baseball and travel, but you
 are too young;
However you look up into the clear flat blue of the evening sky
And vow that you will one day be a traveler like myself,
And wander to all the ends of the earth until you are completely
 exhausted,
And then return to Texas or Indiana, whatever state you happen to
 be from.
And have your death celebrated by a lavish funeral

Conducted by starlight, with numerous boys and girls reading my
    poems aloud!

8

I did not understand what you meant by the Hudson Tunnel,
But now I understand, New Jersey, I like it fine,
I like the stifling black smoke and the jagged heave-ho of the trains,
I like the sunlight too at the end of the tunnel, like my rebirth in the
    poems of Kenneth Koch,
I like the way the rosy sunlight streams down upon the silver tracks,
I like the way the travelers awake from their dreams and step upon
    the hard paving stone of the station,
But I reckon what I should like best would be to see Indiana again,
Or Texas or Arkansas, or Alabama, the "Cotton State,"
Or Big Rose Pebble Island off the coast of Maine
Where I used to have so much fun during the summer, cooking and
    kidding and having myself a good time,
I like Pennsylvania too, we could have a lot of fun there,
You and I will go there when Kenneth is dead.

John Ashbery, the foremost poet of this school and today's most radically original American poet, writes of characters who operate in a drama without a story. His method is somewhat like that of certain serial composers—a-thematic and discontinuous—but more obviously like that of "abstract" painters who, when they title a painting "White Rose," are concerned more with connoting white roses than in designating them in a more literal or representational sense. Ashbery is not expressly interested in the sound and texture of words, as is Gertrude Stein in *To Do* and *Tender Buttons.* His language is, word-by-word and image-by-image, always simple and elementary: "The pest asked us to re-examine the screws he held"; "Just then the barman squirted juice over the lumps"; "It decided to vote for ink (the village)." The surprise comes when we realize that these three seemingly unrelated fragments comprise the first three lines of Ashbery's "Landscape."

Anyone who attempts to apply Yvor Winters' dictum—that a poet should attempt to make in his poem a rational statement of a specific experience, thus defining it, and manifest in the poem those feelings that constitute an exact correspondence to the poet's particular understanding of that experience—to Ashbery's poems might as well not even begin to read them. Winters' theories help us to explicate Ben Jonson's "Elegy on the Lady Jane Pawlet" or Fulke Greville's "Down in the depths of mine iniquity," but they cannot deal with Mallarmé and certainly not with Ashbery—the first of whom Winters does and the latter of whom he undoubtedly would condemn, unfairly I think, just because their poetry does not "fit" his aesthetic prescriptions.

Ashbery's quiet, elegant, and often refractory lines suggest those of the early poems of England's F. T. Prince and, most especially, those of Pasternak's, one of Ashbery's important influences. When not employing these long lines, however, Ashbery has invented a "notation" that sounds at times like the englyn form of old Welsh poetry: "Boots and aprons and crows and a blowing/and cats from Rome . . . ."; or like some of Kafka's sentence fragments: "Carried forward on the horse—"; "To sit in the corner of a trolley, your coat wrapped around you." *Europe,* a poem in one hundred eleven parts, represents, like Koch's "The Islands," which it somewhat resembles, Ashbery's difficult but adroit construction of a disconnected journey:

1

To employ her
construction ball
Morning fed on the
light blue wood
of the mouth
cannot understand
feels deeply)

2

A wave of nausea—
numerals

3

a few berries

4

the unseen claw
Babe asked today
The background of poles roped over
into star jolted them

55

mood seems the sort
to brag
end

56
songs like
You came back to me
you were wrong about the gravestone
that nettles hide quietly
The son is not ours

Now while it is true that Ashbery discards logic, he does not discard meaning, even if it proves difficult to get at. "Much that is beautiful," Ashbery writes in "Illustration," "Must be discarded/So that we may resemble a taller/Impression of ourselves." About painters like Grace Hartigan and Larry Rivers, O'Hara once wrote:

> In this pocket-abyss where one doesn't know where one is at, where a large red painting may be a Grace Hartigan or a howitzer, where one has nightmares about not knowing what one is looking at, the only thing you have to hold onto is your own natural savagery, and your ability to recognize your own *natural* savagery has been given to you by this art which in turn is the cause of your anxiety about not being able to recognize anything but yourself. And that is the last thing one wishes to recognize. . . . (From *School of New York:* Some Younger Artists; edited by B. H. Friedman)

Ashbery's poetry does not arouse this much anxiety in us, but it has the quality of a dream which begs to be interpreted, since we dream it, and yet whose most fascinating and wondrous quality is that it resists being interpreted—for why else have we dreamt it? As the first lines of *"Le livre est sur la table"* begin:

All beauty, resonance, integrity,
Exist by deprivation or logic
Of strange position. This being so,

We can only imagine a world in which a woman
Walks and wears her hair and knows
All that she does not know. Yet we know

What her breasts are. And we give fullness
To the dream. . . .

And the dreams are "beautiful"; they are more real than reality:

I have lost the beautiful dreams
That enlisted on waking,
Cold and waiting. . . . .

("The New Realism")

But anyone who reads Ashbery's two published collections, *Some Trees* (1956) and *The Tennis Court Oath* (1962), must be struck by the hidden but, as one gets accustomed to making connections and following poetic "leads," the perpetual divulgence of the theme of lost innocence; this theme operates in subservience to and as example of the poet's central idea that "as change is horror,/Virtue is really stubbornness/And only in the light of lost words/Can we imagine our rewards." Thus in many ways Ashbery is concerned with the same feelings and issues found in O'Hara's and Koch's poetry, but Ashbery distances himself through his "hard" tone and problematic syntax from these feelings, becoming in a fashion an "effigy of indifference"—a quality he ascribes to the novice in "Illustration"—for the purpose of dealing with them with greater power.

In *"Le Livre"* Ashbery writes that "Men appear, but they live in boxes." Girls, in the beautiful "And You Know," "protected by gold wire from the gaze/Of the onrushing students, live in an atmosphere of vacuum/In the old schoolhouse covered with nasturtiums." And Ashbery asks in the poem whose first line designates its title: "How much longer will I be able to inhabit the divine sepulcher/Of life, my great love?" The breaking-out of childhood, represented as a box, the sepulcher that "hid death and hides me"—an action which above all insists on the "horror" of change from innocence to experience, and which occurs in "The Picture of Little J.A. in a Prospect of Flowers," "Grand Abacus," "The Instruction Manual," and "Our Youth," for example—exposes the horror of the "dark elders" to the child. In the extraordinary poem "Our Youth," death in the guise of dead animals and decaying objects reveals itself when the bubble of childhood bursts—actually, when we are born:

> Of bricks . . . Who built it? Like some crazy balloon
> When love leans on us
> Its nights . . . The velvety pavement sticks to our feet.
> The dead puppies turn us back on love.
>
> Where we are. Sometimes
> The brick arches led to a room like a bubble, that broke when you
>   entered it
> And sometimes to a fallen leaf.
> We got crazy with emotion, showing how much we knew.

The Arabs took us. We knew
The dead horses. We were discovering coffee,
How it is to be drunk hot, with bare feet
In Canada. And the immortal music of Chopin

Which we had been discovering for several months
Since we were fourteen years old. And coffee grounds,
And the wonder of hands, and the wonder of the day
When the child discovers her first dead hand. . . .

Ashbery employs children's exclamations and a distancing tone to emphasize his sense that death and corruption emerge as our subconsciousness unsuccessfully attempts to ward off the inexorable fact of change, of growing:

Heh? Eh? Our youth is dead.
From the minute we discover it with eyes closed
Advancing into mountain light. . . .

He is dead. Green and yellow handkerchiefs cover him.
Perhaps he will never rot, I see
That my clothes are dry. I will go.
The naked girl crosses the street.

Blue hampers . . . Explosions,
Ice . . . The ridiculous
Vases of porphyry. All that our youth
Can't use, that it was created for.

It's true we have not avoided our destiny
By weeding out the old people.
Our faces have filled with smoke. We escape
Down the cloud ladder, but the problem has not been solved.

Ashbery, writing of "The Pied Piper" in a poem beginning "Under the day's crust a half-eaten child," tells of children "coupling as the earth crumbled." The Piper's love was "strongest" Ashbery writes, hardening his attitude, because the Piper "never loved them [the children] at all . . . his notes/Most civil, laughing not to return." In the face of the horror of growing up, Ashbery finds it necessary to pose himself as distant from the horror, which merely re-emphasizes the horror. This is why the most beautiful and "romantic" images of Ashbery's poems are continually juxtaposed with ugly and terrifying ones or, as Ashbery writes, with the "spoiled, sordid"; as examples, "carnation world" with a "hair or a sneeze"; a "garden in mist" with "mush raging, the stump again."

In this poetic landscape, Ashbery also suggests the necessity of reaching for the "other," and he does so very often by mentioning in his poems the writing or reading of a letter to or by someone else. "The Tennis Court Oath" seems, for all its discontinuity, to be about the writing and the reading of a love letter. One of Ashbery's most moving love poems, "Thoughts of a Young Girl," a poem for an imaginary daughter, begins with a letter:

> "It is such a beautiful day I had to write you a letter
> From the tower, and to show I'm not mad:
> I only slipped on the cake of soap of the air
> And drowned in the bathtub of the world. . . ."

"The Ticket" begins: "The experience of writing you these love letters . . ."—a statement tantalizingly indefinite about time, place, or object. Then, too, in "Rain" we read: "The missing letter—the crumb of confidence," and are reminded of the renovating virtue of "lost words."

What is particularly jolting to us as we read Ashbery's poems is the possibility that his "you," to whom the letters are addressed, may well be Ashbery himself; there is, in fact, no reason to suggest otherwise. And this kind of awareness makes Ashbery's poems more puzzling and disquieting than we might have at first imagined. Nevertheless, that striving for "touching" and meeting never disappears from Ashbery's poetry; and this striving can best be seen in one of the poet's first works, "Some Trees"—a poem of subtlety and beauty that is at once a wish for and an arrival at communion:

> These are amazing: each
> Joining a neighbor, as though speech
> Were a still performance.
> Arranging by chance
>
> To meet as far this morning
> From the world as agreeing
> With it, you and I
> Are suddenly what the trees try
>
> To tell us we are:
> That their merely being there
> Means something; that soon
> We may touch, love, explain.

And glad not to have invented
Such comeliness, we are surrounded:
A silence already filled with noises,
A canvas on which emerges

A chorus of smiles, a winter morning.
Placed in a puzzling light, and moving,
Our days put on such reticence
These accents seem their own defense.

The "New York School" also includes some other fine poets: Edwin Denby, whose *Mediterranean Cities* (1957) shows us how an ebullient and imaginative poet can transform the formal sonnet forms:

A governing and rouged nun, she lifts the cubed
Jewels, garlanded heavy on hair, shoulders
Breasts, on hands and feet, the dark-blue the cell-roomed
Splendor's fountain lifts sunken to Him who holds her;
But the emperor is running to his pet hens
Cackling like a hermit, and his foolish smile
Alone in the vacancy of noon-glazed fens
Haunts a blossoming water-capital's guile;
Holy placidity of lilylike throats
Ravenna of fleets, silent above the cows
A turnip plain and stagnant houses floats
Exultance of sailor hymns, virginal vows;
In a church's tiered and April-green alcoves
Joy rises laughing at ease to love God's loves: ("Ravenna")

Barbara Guest—*The Location of Things, Archaics, The Open Skies* (1962)—who writes of an "atmosphere of wings," of a world somewhere above the "real" one:

Parachutes, my love, could carry us higher
Than this mid-air in which we tremble,
Having exercised our arms in swimming,
Now the suspension, you say,
Is exquisite . . . ;
(from "Parachutes, My Love, Could Carry us Higher")

Ted Berrigan, editor of *"C"* magazine (a kind of "house journal" for the younger poets of this "school," including Joseph Ceravolo, Dick Gallup), whose own poetry displays an exuberant use of language with what is often an underlying penetrating directness:

Time flies by like a great whale
And I find my hand grows stale at the throttle
Of my many faceted and fake appearance
Who bucks and spouts by detour under the sheets
Hollow portals of solid appearance
Movies are poems, a holy bible, the great mother to us
People go by in the fragrant day
Accelerate softly my blood
But blood is still blood and tall as a mountain blood
Behind me green rubber grows, feet walk
In wet water, and dusty heads grow wide
Padre, Father, or fat old man, as you will,
I am afraid to succeed, afraid to fail
Tell me now, again, who I am:

("Sonnet XXXIV")

and Ron Padgett, who has learned most successfully from Ashbery, but whose own poems communicate a unique commingling of humor and of quiet and moving feelings, as his elliptical poem "I'd Give You My Seat If I Were Here" reveals:

The shadows these flowers are making on each other,
The wild and sleepy eyes they make
Are being thrown against the notion *de voyager*
My fingers that are not silver or blue and they point

This keeps happening for eleven months.
But tonight she's in her grave at the bottom of the sea,
Leaving us at that.

If I could tell you why
The delicious crunch of feathers
Through fifteen heads of yours
Can encourage and surround
Then there would be no need for this needle in my head
Or the electricity that is not really mine.

Though it is only real,
My dream to raise no curtain on the other stage
That isn't there, but there
Under the breeze of a handkerchief
That is brushing against the temple you will find
On either side of your head—

And you know and you know.

IV

By the secret that holds the forest up,
no one will escape. (We have reached this place.)
from "Reporting Back" by William Stafford

Our third and last group of poets presents to us a world that is becoming increasingly difficult to see as reality. In this world the most obvious source of value derives from the poet's identification with and acceptance of his environment. The universe is considered neither good nor bad. The poet neither superinduces metaphorical attributions of human emotions to his existing surroundings nor wanders through Baudelaire's hermetic "forest of symbols." The direct contacting of the actual universal situation, whose values never change, reveals the beauty and the ugliness, the joy and the grief that human beings feel when they function as natural living organisms in a world that exists. Plato's philosophical dualism which rejected the material world in favor of that suprasensory world apprehended by reason, or the teachings of the Arabic philosopher Al-Ghazali which stated that if what is present is sought for, it becomes oblique and lost, are not issues—aesthetic, philosophical, or otherwise—for this group of poets. In a time when Hegel's suggestion that man not only exists but also exists as an object of his existence has come to imply an alienation of the self—man observing the movements of his small toe—the poets of this third group assume a quasi-religious role, for they "sing" of that whole natural world of multiplicity and differentiations which is, on the deepest level, the only thing that exists for us; without it there would be nothing, for we would not be alive.

It is not surprising that the poet perceives the importance of Nature and imbues it with a religious consciousness. Scholars of comparative literature who are concerned with the early stages in a society's cultural history have constantly been hard put to distinguish between the functions of priest and poet, whether in pre-Roman Welsh poetry; the Greek tragedies; or the Indian *Rig-Veda* (Verse-Wisdom). Like these early religious-literary achievements, the poems of the writers of this group whom we shall mention later, though they are writing in a much more literarily refined time, are highly religious in the same way as the above poetic examples because in all of them, the individual souls of men and, in fact, of all things are thought of as identical with what the Hindus call the Highest Soul. The Supreme Being or Principle is seen as the whole universe, animate and inanimate; He or It is the originator, the sustainer, and the destroyer of the individual creature. (In his essay, "The Theme of the Three Caskets," Freud conceives of an inherently similar pattern, although psychologically conceptualized in terms of the mother, the beloved, and finally Mother Earth—the "silent goddess of Death.") Poets like James Wright and William Stafford are our poet-priests because their recognitions and realizations of the particular aspects of Nature transfigure and, ultimately, transcend the objects they describe, so that the more acute their involvement, the more "religious" their utterances.

Paradoxically, this "new" development in American poetry returns us to the prevailing esthetic world—the great international sensibility—of the Chinese *Book of Songs,* Japanese *waka* and *tanka,* the *Greek Anthology,* the *Rig-Veda,* Virgil's *Georgics,* the Balkan ballads, and American Indian songs. A poem like the American James Wright's "In the Cold House," for example:

> I slept a few minutes ago,
> Even though the stove has been out for hours.
> I am growing old.
> A bird cries in bare elder trees . . . ;

is of the same "world" as the twelfth-century Japanese Prime Minister Kintsune's:

> The flowers whirl away
> In the wind like snow.
> The thing that falls away
> Is myself . . . ;
>
> (translated by Kenneth Rexroth)

as Sappho's:

> The moon slides west,
> it is midnight,
> the time is gone—
> I lie alone!
>
> (imitated by Robert Lowell)

or as the Papago "Dream Song of a Woman":

Where the mountain crosses,
On top of the mountain,
    I do not myself know where.
I wandered where my mind and my heart
    seemed to be lost.
I wandered away.

Three American poets are predominantly responsible for opening this "world" up for us. All of William Carlos Williams' poems reveal this poet's beneficent relationship with the "natural" world, and thus his indictment of our personal and social demoralization emerges as trenchantly as it does—in the Corydon and Phyllis "Idyll" in Book Four of *Paterson,* for example—because he knows exactly where we have strayed from. Williams represents the world in which one joyfully sneaks "sweet and cold" plums from the icebox in mock-imitation of the eating of the fruit of the tree of knowledge, as opposed to that world where, as in Eliot's *Prufrock,* one does not "dare" to eat a peach.

Yvor Winters' poems, seemingly far from this "world" with their emphasis on "mind" and "will," actually manifest at their best a total concentration of senses and mental faculties on one realization of a particular aspect, a pure distillation, of the "natural" world. His one-line poems such as "The Aspen's Song":

The summer holds me here . . . ;

or "Noon":

Did you move, in the sun?

communicate a subtle but veritable numinosity.

The most adventurous of these three poets (and our most inspiring man-of-letters) is Kenneth Rexroth. His extraordinary essays, translations from at least six languages, and a body of poetry begun over forty years ago comprise the finest testament to a constant uncovering, re-evaluation, and protection of the aesthetic and moral values of Tu Fu, Homer, Samuel Johnson, and anyone else, as Rexroth would put it, "worth his salt."

Some of the best American poets writing today are following the example of these three poets and are returning us to that world which many of us assume to be "lost." Carolyn Kizer's poems "In the Japanese Mode" in *The Ungrateful Garden* (1961) and imitations of Tu Fu; Paul Goodman's "Evening (Gavotte and Variations of Rameau)"; Barbara Howes' "In Autumn"; Hayden Carruth's *The Norfolk Poems* (1962); Robert Duncan's *The Opening of a Field* (1960); Gary Snyder's *Myths and Texts* (1960); and Denise Levertov's *The Jacob's Ladder* (1961); and especially the beautiful *O Taste and See*, published in the spring of 1964, all return us to this "natural" world.

Of all these poets, Denise Levertov seems to me the most moving. Her work from *Here and Now* (1957) and *With Eyes at the Back of Our Heads* (1959) through the two latest volumes named above continues to develop a graceful but intense verse of communion with the "other"—a verse which encounters her subjects in a "green airy space, not locked in." It is in this space that Miss Levertov's poems contact the "natural world" without masks or ambiguities, for as she writes in "The Runes" from her latest book: "In city, in suburb, in forest, no way to stretch out the arms—so if you would grow go straight up or deep down."

Even a poet like Richard Wilbur, who is generally admired for his calculated and "small perfections" of form and content, writes his loveliest poems—"Cicadas," "Winter Spring," "Driftwood," and "The Beautiful Changes"—in this "tradition," even though he too often indulges himself in hollow lines like: "And the soul bathes in warm conceptual lakes" or "A giant absence mopes upon the trees." His simple but unostentatious poem "Exeunt" suggests his kinship with this group:

Piecemeal the summer dies;
At the field's edge a daisy lives alone;
A last shawl of burning lies
On a gray field-stone

All cries are thin and terse;
The field has droned the summer's final mass;
A cricket like a dwindled hearse
Crawls from the dry grass.

The two finest young American poets of this "style" are James Wright and William Stafford. Wright is associated with *The Sixties Press* (edited by the poet Robert Bly) which—with its original publications of the verse of Wright, Bly, and William Duffy, for example, and its volumes of translations of Cesar

Vallejo, Pablo Neruda, Machado, and others—has defined and purveyed these poetic values.

Wright was not originally a poet whose world view or poetic diction would have suggested his affinities with these new-old values of literary creation. His first collection, *The Green Wall* (1957) contained fairly traditional poems written in a torpid, flat style. But in his latest volume entitled *The Branch Will Not Break* (1963)—one thinks of Lorca's "Along the groves of the Tamarit leaden dogs have come to wait for the branches to fall, to wait for them to break by themselves"—Wright breaks through to a verse that sounds at times like Antonio Machado or Francis Jammes, but a verse that expresses a sensibility more kindred to that of the great Chinese poets Tu Fu, Mei Yao Chen, or Su Tung-P'o:

> The white house is silent.
> My friends can't hear me yet.
> The flicker who lives in the bare tree at the field's edge
> Pecks once and is still for a long time.
> I stand still in the late afternoon.
> My face is turned away from the sun.
> A horse grazes in my long shadow.
>
> "Arriving in the Country Again"

This seems to come right out of the Sung period; but Wright has unaffectedly and against all odds made it part of his experience as an American mid-Westerner. His themes of friendship, growing old, lonesomeness, and inebriation are those of the Chinese poets; and although not the "Ancient Chinese Governor"—or any governor—he writes about, he is also as subtly "politically conscious" as the Chinese, in poems such as "Eisenhower's Visit to Franco, 1959" and "The Undermining of the Defense Economy." Wright's worst poems tend to be overly prosaic descriptions. But his best ones are those in which he perceives a correspondence between loss and a phenomenon of nature, as in the beautiful poem "Rain":

> It is the sinking of things.
>
> Flashlights drift over dark trees,
> Girls kneel,
> An owl's eyelids fall.

> The sad bones of my hands descend into a valley
> Of strange rocks . . . ;

or in which he, like Winters, concentrates his senses and mental faculties on one intense realization, so that in the quiet but exultant poem entitled "The Jewel," Wright transfigures and purifies the object into a sacramental hypostasis:

> There is this cave
> In the air behind my body
> That nobody is going to touch:
> A cloister, a silence
> Closing around a blossom of fire.
> When I stand upright in the wind,
> My bones turn to dark emeralds.

William Stafford won the 1963 National Book Award for his *Traveling Through the Dark* (1962), a volume of poems that sees, as one of the poems is titled, the "Universe Is One Place." Stafford is not simple-mindedly "agin' city folks," but rather against the pretensions and lack of genuineness of most of our lives. Stafford is a self-styled "conservative" and against those who live their "city ways" because they "cannot hold thought ways to hold/the old way steady; nowadays/you cannot hear the songs we sang/or know what glaciers told. . . ." Stafford is "for" a contacting of the "real" world—a world of "things we did that meant something," to borrow one of his poem's titles. And Stafford, employing a wonderfully unsentimental, rugged, often elliptical language, reveals in these poems an understanding of death, love, lust, guilt, and making the "responsible act" that gives the lie to the suggestion that this poetry is "naïve." The poet lives in a world in which one has "to stand in absolute rain/and face whatever comes from God,/or stoop to smooth the earth over little things/that went into dirt, out of the world."

Stafford sees the violence of a world where he must push a dead but still-warm pregnant doe over the edge of a cliff, a world where the cheetah kills the deer in that moment of the "one launched look"—the "moment of choice" that occasions a "glance" of love and personal commitment or a life of loneliness and death. Stafford sees life as a "night desert" in which only human connections, which have been betrayed, create any and all of those meanings that enable us to exist in the body of love:

The Apache word for love twists
then numbs the tongue:

Uttered once clear, said—
never that word again.

"Cousin," you call, or "Sister" and one
more word that spins
In the dust: a talk-flake
chipped like obsidian.

The girl who hears this flake and
follows you into the dark
Turns at a touch: the night desert
forever behind her back.

"We shall live again," sing the Plains Indians in their Ghost Dance ritual. In "Reporting Back," Stafford is writing not only of his sense of life but also, we might suggest, of the complexities, strivings, and fulfillments of contemporary American poetry:

By the secret that holds the forest up,
no one will escape. (We have reached this place.)

The sky will come home some day.
(We pay all mistakes our bodies make when they move.)

Is there a way to walk that living has obscured?
(Our feet are trying to remember some path we are walking toward.)

1964

Criticism with the Death Instinct at the High Altar

BEYOND CULTURE: ESSAYS ON LITERATURE, AND LEARNING, BY LIONEL TRILLING

Of Lionel Trilling's recent collection of eight essays, the publisher writes:

> *Beyond Culture* is that rare thing, an integrated work of criticism whose argument can be followed from start to finish with *pleasure* and a clear sense of engagement. The challenging critical stance it takes up is bound to be influential not only in the intellectual community . . . but in the *culture* at large. (emphasis added)

The publisher has a strange and ironic sense of humor. For one of the central purposes of Trilling's essays is to reevaluate our assumptions concerning the ideas of "pleasure" and "culture"; and his reevaluations lead him, in the name of "education," of "trying to see the object as it really is," to an elucidation of a world view that accepts and promotes a psychic state of sempiternal pain, repression, and self-destruction.

If the reader thinks I am being merely captious or even paranoid in my aggravated response to Trilling's book, let him read an essay like "The Fate of Pleasure" which elaborates the idea that the "extruded high segment of our general culture has for some time been engaged in an experiment in the negative transcendence of the human, a condition which is to be achieved by freeing the self from its thralldom to pleasure." Trilling delineates the "extruded high segment's" progress to this "transcendence" partly in linguistic and historical, but mainly in literary-historical terms. He writes of Wordsworth's "grand elementary principle of pleasure" which for the poet constitutes "the naked and native dignity of man" and by which principle man "knows, and feels, and lives, and moves."

Trilling emphasizes that Keats and Dostoevsky most formidably questioned the very nature of pleasure itself. Keats, Trilling writes, arrived at the perception that "there is something perverse and self-negating in the erotic life." And in *Notes from Underground,* Trilling finds that the "painful and scornful conclusions" of Dostoevsky's story (*i.e.,* "that, in the degree that the promises of the spiritual life are made in terms of pleasure—of comfort, rest, and beauty—they have no power over the modern imagination") have established themselves "not only as parts of our moral culture but as its essence, at least so far as that culture makes itself explicit in literature."

Let me respond to several of the statements, proclamations, and interpretations which Trilling makes in this essay:

1. In his discussion of Keats, Trilling observes that the poet attempts to create a pain (unpleasure)-pleasure (specifically sexual pleasure) dialectic. An alternative reading of Keats' poetry, however, enables one to realize that the poet is more specifically concerned with the formulation of a dream-reality dialectic.

Freud expressed the idea in "The Poet and Day-Dreaming" that the poet, like the child at play—one thinks of Keats' "Boyish imagination"—creates a "world of fantasy which he takes very seriously; that is, he invests it with a great deal of affect, while separating it sharply from reality." But we must reinforce the last idea by remembering Lamb's statement that the "poet dreams being awake. He is not possessed by his subject but he has dominion over it." Keats, standing on tip-toe, day-dreams, his "soul lost in pleasant smotherings" ("Standing on Tip-Toe").

Life, one proceeds to understand, is for Keats a dream. But in his poetry—over which Keats has control—the poet realizes how fragile dreams are, for the reality principle does break through finally, just because he has control over his fantasy, and because, in honestly regarding his total response to all dream experience, he realizes, as Endymion says, that "I have clung/To nothing, lov'd a nothing, nothing seen/Or felt but a great dream!" And this understanding is Keats' particular ideology of art. As delight turns to melancholy and as "aching Pleasure" turns "to Poison while the bee-mouth sips," dreams turn to despairs: "Only the dreamer venoms all his days,/Bearing more woe than all his sins deserve . . ." ("The Fall of Hyperion").

It is important to realize that Keats does not question the idea of pleasure *because of its very nature.* Neither is the poet primarily concerned with examining the relationship between the reality- and pleasure-principle, except insofar as he perceives that dreams give him pleasure. Rather, Keats questions the reality of dreams—his "huge cloudy symbols of high romance"—because the poet sees that the dream is often "barren" even as it serves as a means by which the imagination can create its important truths.

2. Trilling asks each of us who feels adverse to the "general culture" to ask himself the question, "Is it true? Is it true for me?" Trilling's analysis of *Notes from Underground* is excellent. But, first, to state that what is true for the Underground Man—that in order for him to be free, he must of necessity feel antagonistic towards the principle of pleasure—is true for me, makes sense neither to my intellect nor to my senses; and, second, to see the Underground Man's position as Dostoevsky's final position without contrasting or even opposing to it Alyosha's position makes little literary sense.

3. Trilling writes that Nietzsche's "humanism," his "naturalistic acceptance of power and pleasure," his love of Mediterranean sunlight, all distance him from our modern spiritual sensibility. "And the converse of what explains Nietzsche's relative marginality explains Dostoevsky's position at the very heart of the modern spiritual life." There are still places and states in which no one is "dying away or fading or paling before the sight of the blue voluptuous sea" (*Beyond Good and Evil*), where libidos are active, and where Nietzsche's four virtues—courage, insight, fellow-feeling, and solitude—are hardly considered outmoded. When Trilling praises the modern spiritual sensibility of unpleasure and calls the aesthetic of beauty so outmoded as to be "worth smiling at," one finds oneself returning the smile.

4. Trilling states several times that there are human impulses "which, in one degree or another, and sometimes in the very highest degree, repudiate pleasure and seek gratification in—to use Freud's word—unpleasure." He states that this gratification in unpleasure is a "leading theme" in *Notes from Underground.* If, however, the principle of negative transcendence of the human upon which the Underground Man bases his actions is a quasi-pleasure principle—in the sense that it provides a delayed gratification—then Trilling's argument entirely contradicts itself, for this condition of negative transcendence is, as Trilling writes, to be achieved "by freeing the self from its thralldom to pleasure." If the ideal of pleasure has, as Trilling says, exhausted itself, the existing psychic energies manifest themselves in self-destructive tendencies as a "means of self-definition and self affirmation." If one does not attempt to extenuate the implications of Trilling's contradiction, one discovers that what Trilling is actually talking about, when he writes statements like those quoted above, is the idea of "primary masochism" which Freud identified with the death instinct.

H. G. Wells wrote a wry, often-quoted criticism of Henry James' novels which reads: "It [any James novel] is like a church lit but without a congregation to distract you, with every light and line focused on the high altar. And on the altar, very reverently placed, intensely there, is a dead kitten, an eggshell, a bit of string . . ." In his essay entitled "Hawthorne in Our Time," Trilling writes of James in somewhat the same manner that he writes about Nietzsche (Who could imagine stranger bedfellows?)—emphasizing the former's, in the person of Strether's, "Live all you can . . ." speech. Trilling writes: "The credence [James] gave to pleasure and the credence he gave to moral sanction together define James' certitude that the world is *there* . . ."

"The "modern reader," however, might well emphasize James' insistently and habitually expressed idea that repression exists coterminously with, if not defines, the quality of maturity, reality, and knowledge. (This idea is central to works like "The Beast in the Jungle," *The American,* and *Portrait of a Lady.*) What seems to me James' finest and most "modern" novel, *The Golden Bowl,* says something quite different: knowledge is cruel—Maggie accepts her breaking into life and marriage with pity and dread, both emotions of which are manifestations of knowledge in action—but the person who attains it is set free.

At the conclusion of "The Two Environments," Trilling praises knowledge and truth, writing that both exist beyond all cultural modes of expression. And he quotes Keats' statement that "an eagle is not so fine a thing as a truth." But what does knowledge draw one's attention to in Trilling's church? High at the altar, very reverently placed and very intensely there, is the death instinct.

Perspectives on Freud's insight

Freud's death instinct theory is a powerful assumption—one of Freud's most audacious and moving formulations of metapsychology. (It is first mentioned—as a formulation—in *Beyond the Pleasure Principle.*) The theory has been ignorantly attacked by a professional like Karen Horney who hardly bothers to understand it. It has also been attacked by persons who *have* bothered to make such an effort.

Wilhelm Reich criticizes Freud for psychologizing biology, for transferring laws which he had discovered in the functioning of the psyche to its biological foundation. Masochism, for Reich, was a secondary drive, a result, not the cause, of neurosis. "Suffering and wanting to suffer," Reich wrote in *The Function of the Organism,* "are the results of having lost the organic capacity for pleasure." In *Gestalt Therapy,* Perls, Hefferline, and Goodman analyze and criticize the death instinct theory in terms of its unsubstantiated biological speculation. They further view it as a manifestation of a psychological symptom in which man resigns the "possibility of present solution," blocks out present needs, and thereby "brings to the fore some other needs of a lower order of structure."

In *Eros and Civilization,* Herbert Marcuse writes:

> The death instinct is destructiveness not for its own sake, but for the relief of tension. The descent toward death is an unconscious flight from pain and want. It is an expression of the eternal struggle against suffering and repression. And the death instinct itself seems to be affected by the historical changes which affect this struggle.

And finally in a brilliant chapter entitled "Death, Time and Eternity" from *Life Against Death,* Norman O. Brown writes:

> Man is the animal which has separated into conflicting opposites the biological unity of life and death, and has then subjected the conflicting opposites to repression. The destruction of the biological unity of life and death transforms the Nirvana-principle into the pleasure-principle, transforms the repetition-compulsion into a fixation to the infantile past, and transforms the death-instinct into an aggressive principle of negativity.

Brown's chapter is the finest criticism of *Beyond Culture* one could imagine, for it suggests the kind of repression Trilling must accept in order for him to endorse the death-instinct formulation without thoroughly examining his reasons for doing so. In Brown's and Freud's terms, Trilling accepts intellectually what is repressed, "though in all essentials the repression persists" (Freud's "On Negation").

In his speech to the New York Psychoanalytical Society in 1955, entitled "Freud: Within and Beyond Culture," Trilling says: "Whether or not Freud's formulations of the death instinct stand up under scientific inquiry, I of course cannot venture to say. But certainly they confirm our sense of Freud's oneness with the tradition of literature." This is a mere preterition, for Trilling believes in the death instinct, and he prides himself in his belief, as we realize at the conclusion of "The Fate of Pleasure."

But when Trilling finally tells us what he understands by this "instinct," he writes: ". . . the assertion of the death instinct is the effort of finely tempered minds to affirm the self in an ultimate confrontation of reality." What does this "effort of finely tempered minds" have to do with homeostasis, the existence of repetition-compulsion, and primary masochism—the three elements which represent the different aspects of the death instinct? Is this affirmation of the self that self-destructive affirmation which Trilling writes about in "On the Teaching of Modern Literature" and "The Fate of Pleasure"? Or is this the affirmation of the ego and super-ego—both of which Trilling sees as biologically-created and based quantities—in their ultimate confrontation of a repressive culture, a confrontation about which Trilling talks in the second part of his Freud anniversary lecture?

What kind of confrontation of reality can one have when one talks about the ego and super-ego and neglects to mention the id and, beyond the id, Eros? What does this confrontation have to do with Brown's statement that "eternity is the mode of unrepressed bodies" or Reich's belief that "only the liberation of the natural capacity for love in human beings can master their sadistic destructiveness"?

In reviewing Margaret Mead's *Male and Female,* Diana

Trilling writes: "The sexuality of *Male and Female* is the sexuality of ego, never of libido. It is directed toward achieving, not toward being." (This essay, as well as the other essays by Mrs. Trilling I will quote from later, is collected in *Claremont Essays*.) Lionel Trilling hardly writes of sexuality and of "the liberation of the natural capacity for love" because, in Otto Rank's terms, the ego—in "spiritual psychic creation"—is opposed to the world and rules it in terms of its will. And Trilling accepts that formulation of Freud's which makes the ego instincts synonymous with the death instincts.

The death instinct theory exists at the center of Trilling's recent thought, but it also possesses his thought. He makes it his subject, but he is subject to its occluding dictates. That is why Trilling suggests that "the fantasy of psychic freedom" can be obtained "through cruelty conceived of as a spiritual exercise" ("Isaac Babel"); and why he writes: "Our modern piety is preoccupied by the ideal of the autonomous self, or at least of the self as it seeks autonomy in its tortured dream of metaphysical freedom" ("Hawthorne in Our Time"). Fantasies of cruelty, tortured dreams—these are hardly the handiworks of psychic freedom. These fantasies seem to have their origin in that "cruelty" which, as the Marquis de Sade writes in *Philosophy in the Bedroom*, is "simply the energy in a man civilization has not yet altogether corrupted." They are, in fact, manifestations of extroverted death, spoken of in the sublimated terms of an apocalyptic spirituality.

When Trilling employs psychoanalytic ideas in his criticism, he can write a brilliant essay such as that on the twentieth-century Russian writer, Isaac Babel—the finest essay in *Beyond Culture* and one of Trilling's best essays anytime—in which he analyzes and connects, as if dream-work elements, displacements and condensations of content and psychological motifs in Babel's stories. Here, Trilling uses elements of the death instinct theory, implying how extroverted aggression (sadism) is derived from "primary masochism," in order to demonstrate how these elements refer to Babel's oedipal situation and to his ambivalent relationship with a sublimating Jewish culture. I am sure that one of the sources of this essay's power derives from Trilling's subconscious identification of his situation as a New York intellectual with Babel's psychically similar situation—the life of aggressive sexuality and violence as it contrasts with, as it reflects and reveals, the values of a life of learning and sublimation.

I feel antagonistic towards the theoretical essays in *Beyond Culture,* not because they offend me on account of their "antisocial" and "destructive" content. In fact, my feelings of antagonism towards them derive from the fact that I could not help but feel relieved after reading these essays the first time. I had the kind of feeling Diana Trilling ascribes to the audience of Albee's *Virginia Woolf*—reassurance that my neurosis and death-wish inclinations were accepted and approved and were even considered to be worthy of admiration because of their "desperate energy" by the highest echelon of intellectual thought.

Yet Trilling, in his essay on the Leavis-Snow controversy, writes that literature makes a declaration about the qualities that "life should have, about the qualities life does not have but should have." And yet Trilling fails to develop precisely this sense of what is possible. He accepts Freud's static dualistic ontology, and as Norman O. Brown writes: "Under conditions of general repression, as long as life is unsatisfactory, death can be affirmed only by those whose life instinct is strong enough to envisage the reconciliation of life and death as a future state of perfection toward which the life instinct strives."

Identifying with Freud

There is little life instinct (Eros) in *Beyond Culture* for two reasons. First, Trilling identifies himself with Freud's "tragic, or stoic, sense of life." "We do well," Trilling writes about the "pains" civilization imposes on us, "to accept (civilization), although we also do well to cast a cold eye on the fate that makes it our better part to accept it." Anyone who has read the Trilling-Marcus abridgement of Ernest Jones' magnificent life of Freud must have felt moved by Freud's powerful intellect, physical courage, and dignity. But Diana Trilling's comments about Freud's followers are much in point here. Mrs. Trilling writes of these followers' "passive or neutral assent in a choice which, as Freud made it, had such harsh resonances." Professor

Trilling's statement about "casting a cold eye on the fate that makes it our better part to accept it" resounds only with the form of Freud's stoical discourse.

Trilling identifies with Freud's *bearing* and self-control and emphasizes the death instinct theory, which is in ways an intellectual correlative to such a *bearing.* He says extraordinarily little about Freud's theory of infantile sexuality. Trilling's stoical advice is just a high-toned way of assenting passively to what Mrs. Trilling in another context calls the "politics of passivity and fatedness"; of saying what practically we already know: produce; do what you've got to do; join the "adversary culture," opt for "fullness, freedom, and potency of life," but remember that here, too, you are conforming to the "presuppositions, received ideas, approved attitudes" of such a "culture." (This argument is presented in "The Two Environments," and in a general sense the argument is quite convincing.) But Trilling is not interested in the idea of manumission. His identification with Freud is, finally, truly a reliance on Freud—a reliance which at once protects him from the vicissitudes of cultural change and yet which hinders him from sensing that the possibilities for "fullness, freedom and potency of life" do not necessarily imply a cultural trap but rather a basis for a life which is freer than one which seeks "autonomy in its tortured dream of metaphysical freedom."

Second, just as Trilling employs an identification with Freud for the purpose of self-protection, so too does he employ the world of books. When he writes of "our present sense of life," he is actually talking about our "literary or spiritual consciousness." Literature, however, has a hard time of making a "criticism of life" if its function now, as Trilling sees it, is to assert the artist's imagination in order to "interpose" a dream between the "reality of the primordial Might" and us, "which, perhaps, in the degree that it terrifies, commands our assent and holds out the promise of freedom." Thus in Trilling's ideology of art, literature is religion whose purpose it is to enable us to attain salvation (freedom). The artist is God—a tyrannical, patriarchal God who terrifies us with a literary "tyrant-dream," holding out to us the promise of freedom. Trilling talks about literature as if it were an imitation of an oedipal situation. There is no longer any distinction to be made between art and life. Art is life, and a life of repression at that.

Here is Trilling writing about Hawthorne—a writer who does not "dominate" us and who therefore "cannot gratify us, moderns that we are. . . . At moments as we read him . . . we have a sensation of having been set at liberty." We look for a "more coercive will, and are insecure in its lack":

> Yet perhaps we feel, too, an impulse of exhilaration charging through our art-saturated minds, a new pleasure in being led carelessly or playfully to one or another dangerous place and being left alone to look at the danger in our own way. The pleasure cannot last long—probably more is needed in the life around us before such independent confrontations of our dependence will seem natural to us, and a kind of joy.

Because we are so dependent on books—because books for us *are* life—we feel a pleasant anxiety when we read a book which does not demand our enslavement to its vision, a book which rather forces us outside of itself into life and ourselves. Without Father or Mother to guide us, we are "left alone to look at the danger in our own way."

But how does Trilling conclude the passage quoted? He writes that the pleasure cannot last long, not because "more is needed in the life around us" in order for us to desire to venture outside of the world of books and back into life, but because more is needed in the life around us before we can feel natural in our *realization* that we are truly dependent on books. Trilling, in other words, makes no attempt to escape from what must be seen as an inextricably neurotic view of the purposes of literature. Brown's words exactly interpret Trilling's "position" in terms of the action of repressing death: "But if death is the aspect of life which confers on life individuality, independence, and separateness, then *a priori* the repression of death should produce symptoms which exhibit on the one hand a flight from independence and separateness and on the other hand the compulsive return of the repressed instinct."

Would it not be more courageous for Lionel Trilling to help begin to discover the ways in which we might be able to attain what we need in the life around us in order to enable us to reach the necessary joy—in life, not merely in books—rather than to tell us repeatedly that a little more "negative transcendence," a finer "tyrant-dream in which we can take refuge" will not only be finer than an eagle, but finer, indeed, than a truth?

1966

Jean-Paul Sartre Meets Darling Daintyfoot

OUR LADY OF THE FLOWERS, by Jean Genet, Translated by Bernard Frechtman.

I engage with the Snark—
every night after dark—
In a dreamy, delirious fight:
The Hunting of the Snark—
Lewis Carroll

There are a number of works of art in which two antinomies—"reality" and "imagination"—confront each other in particular and distinct ways and in which we see the former colored and instructed by the latter. One thinks immediately of *Don Quixote,* Wordsworth's *The Prelude,* and, in this century, of E. M. Forster's *The Longest Journey,* Wallace Stevens' "The Comedian as the Letter C," and Saul Bellow's *Henderson the Rain King.*

There are, moreover, novels in which, to use Shaw's phrase, we can observe the "adjustment of moral and social scales" taking place—novels like *Pride and Prejudice, The Charterhouse of Parma, Parade's End,* and, recently, J. E. Powers' *Morte D' Urban.*

But there is another artistic product, somehow more representative of the way we live, a work of art manifesting that difficult to define sensibility of which the works of Lewis Carroll, Emily Dickinson, and Franz Kafka (in the Fragments, Notebooks, and Diaries) and a novel like Beckett's *Malone Dies* are the most obvious examples. It is a sensibility—cultivated and self-perpetuated—of the closed artistic world of the "singular boy"—a phrase taken from Carroll's *Sylvie and Bruno:* "Then I's very glad I *is* singular boy! It would be horrid to be two or three boys! P'raps they wouldn't play with me!" And Jean Genet's *Our Lady of the Flowers* is one of the most beautiful and perfect examples of this world.

It is imperative to see Genet's greatest novel in this light because one hears so much discussion of Genet as Cartesian philosopher-criminal and evil offspring of the demiurge that, although there are valid aspects to this kind of consideration, one often loses sight of *Our Lady* as a novel—and a particular kind of novel at that.

In all his novels, Genet creates his own "landscapes," internalizing worlds into his psychic system. In *The Thief's Journal* he writes: "Thus my confusion extends as far as that region of myself, which is Guiana"; or, "I intend to report, describe, and comment upon the festivals of an inner prison that I discover within me after going through the region of myself which I have called Spain." Even in this more "public" novel, Genet chooses each "universe wherein I delight."

Sartre accurately writes that *Our Lady* "is the height of aloofness." This novel, more than any other of Genet's works, is the most "closed." And to say that this sequestering of the self occasions the novel's beauty is perhaps deleterious in human terms, but it defines the limits Genet accepts or willingly imposes on himself to enable him to write such a book:

> A gesture that went beyond the room, entered into the night, where it continued on to the stars, among the Bears, and even farther; then, like the snake that bites its tail, it returned to the shadow of the room, and into the child who drowned in it.

This extraordinary statement compresses into a sentence the movement and gestures of the entire novel. Genet's masturbation and homosexual fantasies originate from his mind's prison—in the literal Fresnes Prison—and they terminate there. The novel's pimps and fags are Genet's fantasy projections, but they are astonishing creations even on this level. Strangely, they do let us take hold of their existences. Clement Village, the "real" black convict who serves as model for Seck Gorgui, playing with toy soldiers in Genet's cell, cries in despair when "the foreman brought the soldier that was one to many." Transformed through Genet's imagination, he is, along with Divine-Culafroy, one of the novel's most remarkable creations.

Lewis Carroll's dream characters like the Red Queen and Mad Hatter, and Kafka's Red Indian and Milena—his "real" lover, whose personality, one gradually realizes in the *Letters to Milena,* Kafka creates and constructs willfully as if Milena were a character in his novel and the mirror of his emotions—all exist on the level of projection. Genet differs from these two writers in the way he absorbs characters into himself and transforms them into others, announcing the metamorphosis as part of his aesthetic ground rules.

Thus all the characters exist and operate in an undefinable and intangible area—the *extra muros* extension of Genet's mind—floating uncircumscribed above the ground, but usually unable to fly away. Of Darling, Divine's lover, Genet writes: "A Greek, he entered the house of death walking on air." Of Divine: "Now she is asleep in the lace, and their married bodies are afloat." Or from the magnificent scene describing Divine's funeral procession we read:

> In the rain, this black cortege, bespangled with multicolored faces and blended with the scent of flowers and rouge, followed the hearse. The flat round umbrellas, undulating above the ambulating procession, held it suspended between heaven and earth. The passers-by did not even see it, for it was so light that it was already floating ten yards from the ground; only the maids and butlers might have noticed it, but at ten o'clock the former were bringing the morning chocolate to their mistresses and the latter were opening the door to early visitors.

And, observing two young men in the prison's narrow "Mouse-trap" waiting cell, Genet writes that:

> It seems to me that the two kids were suspended in air, without support, their feet off the floor, and that they were shooting remarks at each other in silence. I am so certain of remembering that they were in the air that in spite of myself my intelligence tries to figure out whether they didn't have some gadget that enabled them to lift themselves up, a hidden mechanism, an invisible spring, under the floor, some kind of plausible device.

Genet's fantasies bathe in elegant and sensuous imaginary waters. White enameled lilies, gilded candelabra, sugared almonds, snow-white petticoats, wax orange blossoms, white tulle, sky-blue denim—all are imagined and continue to extend Genet's daydreams into an infinite and beautiful heaven. "I need merely evoke [a warm, gilded luxury]," Genet writes, "from time to time in its snug details for the vexations of my poor life as prisoner to disappear, for me to console myself, console myself with the idea that such luxury exists." Talking about the luxurious life of Divine—who embodies the most significant "gestures" of Genet's personality—the author writes of Divine's "sinuous, looped existence":

> Then it was Vienna, in a gilded hotel, nestling beneath the wings of a black eagle. Sleeping there in the arms of an English lord, deep in a canopied and curtained bed. Then there were rides in a heavy limousine. Back to Paris. . . . And off again to an elegant Renaissance castle, in the company of Guy de Roburant. She was thus a noble chatelaine.

Everything Genet touches becomes transfigured and purified through his vision. When a character wants to move his bowels, he says: "My two bouquets of violets" or "I've got a cigar at the tip of my lips." And when Darling picks his nose, Genet writes: "From his nostrils he plucks acacia and violet petals." Through his magical use of words, Genet establishes and regulates "a whole internal astronomy."

Needless to say, this kind of analysis of the novel can merely serve to start us off searching for deeper causes as to why *Our Lady* is such a moving work of art. The idea of "internal astronomy" or "closed world of the singular boy" suggests the answer. Genet writes that "to think is to perform an act. In order to act, you have to discard frivolity and set your idea on a solid base." But in *Our Lady,* the "solid base" is in Genet's mind completely:

> The world of the living is never too remote from me. I remove it as far as I can with all the means at my disposal. The world withdraws until it is only a golden point in so somber a sky that the abyss between our world and the other is such that the only real thing that remains is our grave. So I am beginning here a really dead man's existence. More and more I prune that existence, I trim it of all facts, especially the more petty ones, those which might readily remind me that the real world is spread out twenty yards away, right at the foot of the walls.

This allows Genet to write so beautifully that: "At the foot of the prison walls, the wind is kneeling"; but at the same time insists that he realize that "the longest detours finally lead me back to my prison, to my cell" which is himself. "For in every action," Dante wrote, "what is primarily intended by the doer, whether he acts from natural necessity or out of free will, is the disclosure of his own image." Genet is aware of this when he writes:

> We occupy our minds with giving ourselves splendid roles through

luxurious lives; we invent so many that we remain enfeebled for a life of action, and if one of them came, by chance, to be realized, we would be unable to be happy in it, for we have exhausted the dry delights (and many a time recalled the memory of their illusion) of the thousand possibilities of glory and wealth.

Thus action and speech disclose Genet's position. Deprived by his isolation of the capacity to act, he imagines acting and acts only through his imagination, thereby obviating and denying its possibility. Genet desires desperately to act, and as his intolerable longings flood the gates of his imagination, we are drawn into feeling Genet's strivings as powerfully as we do in inverse proportion as he distances himself from us. Genet writes: "If I now try to indulge in a daydream, my throat goes dry, despair burns my eyes, shame makes me bow my head, my reverie breaks up. I know that once again a possible happiness is escaping me and escapes me because I dreamed it." His dreams escape from him because the characters of the novel—embodiments of Genet's desires—attain their own life and destroy themselves just because they are not real:

Darling, Divine, and Our Lady flee from me at top speed, taking with them the consolation of their existence, which has its being only in me, for they are not content with fleeing; they do away with themselves, dilute themselves in the appalling insubstantiality of my dreams, or rather of my sleep, and become my sleep; they melt into the very stuff of my sleep and compose it. I call for help in silence; I make signals with the two arms of my soul, which are softer than algae, not, of course, to some friend firmly planted on the ground, but to a kind of crystallization of the tenderness whose seeming hardness makes me believe in its eternity.

Genet's isolation leads him to cry out: "I feel such a need to complain and to try to win a reader's love!" But we are not the reader who can help Genet; the writer has seen to that. Genet loves the "sweet" prison cell; he loves it "by its being, for my own being."

Yet he suffers. He tells us how he spends whole nights at the following "game": "working up sobs, bringing them to my eyes, and leaving them there without their bursting, so that in the morning my eyelids ache, they feel hard and stony, as painful as a sunburn. The sob at my eyes might have flowed into tears, but it remains there, weighing against my eyelids like a condemned man against the door of a cell. It is especially then that I realize how deeply I suffer." This suffering combines with the most unbelievable longing. "One day at dawn I found myself placing my lips lovingly, though for no reason at all, on the icy banister of the Rue Berthe; another time, kissing my hand."

Eventually Genet tells us he desires to swallow himself "by opening my mouth very wide and turning it over my head so that it would take in my whole body, and then the Universe, until all that would remain of me would be a ball of eaten thing which little by little would be annihilated: that is how I see the end of the world." The need for tenderness without an existing object to receive it becomes so enormous that it destroys itself. Genet's love for the early guilotined Pilorge—whom the author calls "my little one, my friend, my liqueur"—sets Genet off in a reverie of astonishing beauty for one too lovely, too unreal, too distant:

O Pilorge! Your face, like a lone nocturnal garden in Worlds where Suns spin round! And on it that impalpable sadness, like the light trees in the garden. Your face is dark, as if in broad daylight a shadow had passed over your soul. It must have made you feel slightly cool, for your body shuddered with a shudder more subtle than the fall of a veil of the tulle known as "gossamer-fine-tulle," for your face is veiled with thousands of fine, light, microscopic wrinkles, painted, rather than engraved, in criss-cross lines.

Genet resembles his Divine who must retreat "into her shell and regain her inner heaven." His longings lead him to want to free himself from himself, but the nature of them leads him back to himself. That is why he is like Kierkegaard renouncing Regina Olson or Emily Dickinson writing: "So we must keep apart,/You there, I here,/With just the door ajar/That oceans are,/And prayer,/And that pale sustenance,/Despair!" Genet tells us that the "importance of any event in our life lies only in the resonance it sets up within us, only in the degree to which it makes us move toward asceticism." With Genet, there is always on one hand the sense of Emily Dickinson's "Say, sea,/Take me"—Genet's cry "Hold me back! Fasten me!"—but also on the other of her knowledge that ". . . thyself may be/Thine enemy;/Captivity is consciousness,/So's liberty"—for Genet's prison cell like Emily Dickinson's Amherst cottage or Kafka's room in

Prague is "sweet"; there one can feel the "joy" and "ecstasy" which all three writers experienced alone.

But Genet's "gestures" are those which lead to his understanding that love is despair. He tells us that a loving glance is never directed to him; rather it passes through him to another standing behind him. In his one of two moments of seemingly authentic love, Genet—alias Divine-Culafroy—tells how he loved a young girl Solange when he was a child. This girl left Culafroy's home town and returned after a year's absence. He realized after a year that Solange no longer was a part of himself—that she had her own identity. Culafroy thinks: "I'm not the only one who can play at not being what they are. So I'm not an exceptional creature." Solange is just like him but *is* not him, as he thinks is his boyhood love Alberto. Solange, Genet writes, "had formerly been the fairy of the morning spiders."

Spider images occur throughout the novel. Genet describes Culafroy as one of those children whose "slightest gesture proves to them that a crystal mirror, which their fist sometimes bespangles with a silvery spider, encages the universe of houses, lamps, cradles, and baptisms, the universe of humans." And talking of Culafroy's relationship with Solange, Genet interjects the unidentified quotation: "You are your own fate, you have woven your own spell." Here Genet has gotten out of himself far enough to reveal—in the imagery of a spider's web—the truth of his psychology and to portray that subtle and difficult scene in which Solange, jealous, discovers that Divine-Culafroy loves Alberto: "She had difficulty finding enough saliva to ask: 'You like him?' and her swallowing was painful, as if she were swallowing a package of pins."

Loving glances are never meant for Genet; they merely pass through him to the person standing behind him. Yet Genet does not allow himself to receive love:

> Eliminating the elements of mischievousness, levity, and prankishness, I have retained only those which are properly tragic: Fear, Despair, unhappy Love . . . and I free myself from them only by declaiming those poems which are convulsed as the faces of sybils. They leave my soul clarified. But if the child in whom I think I see myself laughs or smiles, he breaks up the drama which had been constructed and which is my past life when I think back to it; he destroys it, falsifies it, at least because he manifests an attitude which the character could not have

had; he tears to bits the memory of a harmonious (though painful) life, forces me to see myself becoming another, and on the first drama grafts a second.

Why will Genet not change? Kierkegaard is much in point here when he writes in *Fear and Trembling:*

For what love to God it requires to be willing to let oneself be healed when from the beginning one has been thus bungled without one's fault, from the beginning has been an abortive specimen of humanity!

Most of Genet's figures of speech suggest God and the Church, but usually to emphasize his sense of his negative state of grace. Yet one cannot help thinking that the purity of his vision, while specifically denying God and Christian grace—the ciborium proves to be hollow—offers the possibility of salvation. "The toilet of the slate house" is Genet's heaven-on-earth:

It was my refuge [as a child]. Life, which I saw far off and blurred through its darkness and smell—an odor that filled me with compassion, in which the scent of the elders and the loamy earth was dominant, for the outhouse was at the far end of the garden, near the hedge—life, as it reached me, was singularly sweet, caressing, light, or rather lightened, delivered from heaviness. I am speaking of the life which was things outside the toilet, whatever in the world was not my little retreat with its worm-eaten boards. It seemed to me as if it were somewhat in the manner of floating, painted dreams, whereas I in my hole, like a larva, went on with a restful nocturnal existence, and at times I had the feeling I was sinking slowly, as into sleep or a lake or a maternal breast or even a state of incest, to the spiritual center of the earth.

Immediately after writing this, Genet states that "if I were sick, and were cured by a miracle, I would not survive it. Miracles are unclean; the peace I used to seek in the outhouse, the one I am going to seek in the memory of it, is a reassuring and soothing peace."

Thus Genet makes peace with himself. We might wish to urge him to "change," to take the leap of faith, but perhaps we cannot demand this of him. In a time when the necessity of enabling us to feel ourselves totally human should be the requisite function of literature, we must honestly admit that Genet's "negative" procedure of blocking himself off from the world is precisely how he preserves his sense of himself as "existing." Genet, if we accept the terms of his artistic creation, *does* communicate longing, joy, grief, and wonder, even when these feelings eventually destroy themselves. *Our Lady of the Flowers* in its immanence does not and cannot, of course, break out of itself, as do *The Brothers Karamazov* or Bach's *Prelude and Fugue in E-Flat Minor,* for example. Genet's novel concludes with a description of a pimp drawing the outline of his penis on a letter. Genet must return to this position—he ends and begins alone with his genitals. Genet knows his book will never be as great as Dostoyevsky's because he is the book, and he is always trying to get outside of himself. "Great writing," Longinus said, "does not persuade; it takes the reader outside of himself." Genet can achieve this only in parts, and writes:

> At times I am shaken with a burst of brutal and unaccountable laughter. It resounds within me like a joyous cry in the fog, which it seems to be trying to dissipate, but it leaves no trace other than a wistful longing for sun and gaiety.

Genet knows he needs a "way out"—as do we all—but until we can make human sense of our cluttered and isolating environment, we should accept Genet as the literary master of the closed world in which each one of us in some way lives. Genet lives in it for us as heroically as he does, as fully and desperately as he does, by denying us entrance to it.

1963

Father Urban: Lancelot in Suburbia

MORTE D'URBAN, by J. F. Powers

Morte D'Urban—recipient of this year's National Book Award—is J. F. Powers' first novel. Yet Powers' two previous collections of short stories—*Prince of Darkness* and *The Presence of Grace*—contained fiction written as far back as 1943. He is, of course, no literary parvenu; and, to those who know the author's earlier writing, the beauty of his first novel comes as little surprise. Powers' "Lions, Hearts, Leaping Does"—often anthologized—is one of the most subtle and moving works of fiction ever written in this country. In addition, stories such as "The Presence of Grace" or, on a lesser scale, "The Lord's Day" and "Zeal" hold up ten years later as almost perfect works of their genre.

As in all these stories mentioned, *Morte D'Urban* deals with priests. Powers becomes oddly cloying and sentimental when writing of young boys, baseball, or blacks: there is something musty and precious—like the aroma of Aunt Millie's living room filled with plastic-covered furniture—about these particular stories. "The Valiant Woman"—Powers' story of Father Firman and his housekeeper Mrs. Stoner—is, on the other hand, a telling account of frustrated middle-aged marriage, narrated from the point of view of a cleric who muses: "Sometimes her underwear hung down beneath her dress like a paratrooper's pants, but it and everything she touched was clean. She washed constantly. She was clean." Powers explores the universal situation by searching into the inner condition of priests—for the same reason that Bernard Malamud and Grace Paley make particular the situations of Jews; Ralph Ellison of the blacks, and John Hawkes, James Purdy, and Flannery O'Connor of the terrible and grotesque.

It is hardly ever mentioned that *Morte D'Urban* is, on the simplest level, a marvelously comic yet sharply indicating picture of contemporary American suburban culture. Father Urban of the Order of St. Clement—the picaresque hero of the novel and literary descendent of such rogues as Boccaccio's Father Cipolla and Machiavelli's Father Timoteo—is, before he is anything else, a modern-day business executive: "Men like Father Boniface talked of 'beefing up' the Order, but Father Urban had another idea—to raise the *tone* by packing the Novitiate with exceptional men." "No," says Father Urban at one point; "let's face it. We're getting the ham-and-sausage-supper types now. The horseshoe pitchers. That's all there is to it. They're the ones who're setting the tone, and it's all wrong." And this kind of approach to the way we work transcends not only religions but also fields of occupation. After all, Father Urban is an urban priest, and a successful one, too: "Father Urban . . . had taken good care to conquer the profane world before tackling the other one, and, for that reason, was able to deal with the clergy from a sitting, rather than a kneeling, position. They loved a winner. It was as simple as that."

Father Urban's "territory" was the Midwest—headquarters in Chicago with "lecture" trips to Minnesota and environs—until bad luck and local church politics shifted him to the "primitive" Clementine retreat in the small rural town Duesterhaus in Minnesota. He was, in other words, "sent to the minors." But even here Father Urban travels around, is ordered to a larger diocese, and, eventually, becomes Father Provincial of the Order in Chicago.

The Church is big business—"second only to Standard Oil"—and it is to make the Clementines into an impressive and consequential order that Father Urban devotes his energies. To this task, he moves in suburban circles and meets all-too-believable characters such as: Mrs. Leeson, "sweet-smelling and made up like a birthday cake":

> "Did you catch the Paar show last night?"
>
> "As a matter of fact I didn't," Father Urban said, when he realized that Mrs. Leeson was talking to him.

There is etiolated Mrs. Thwaites—sitting in a wheelchair near the elevator of her apartment which drops to her fallout shelter—watching television on two sets:

> The only light in the room came from the sets, a dead light, so that Mrs. Thwaites's face showed up like a photograph negative: a little old

woman with the face of a baby bird, all eyes and beak, but with a full head of bobbed white hair. One hand was wrapped in black rosary beads the size of cranberries, and the other gripped the remote control. . . .

"We'd better be running along," Phil said.

Mrs. Thwaites beckoned him over to her then, and asked for his blessing. She bowed her head slightly for it (but Father Urban could see that she was watching the sets), and, when it was over, she handed Phil an envelope. "Take care of yourself," she said.

Father Urban, after opening the door for Phil, smiled at Mrs. Thwaites and cried, "Happy New Year!" But he was too late.

Mrs. Thwaites had turned up the sound.

And almost as extraordinary is Mr. Zimmerman, who keeps a large scrapbook of his "Letters to the Editor," his prize possession:

Most of Mr. Zimmerman's letters had appeared in the *Drover,* with the Ostergothenburg *Times* a close second. Father Urban had reached the point where he didn't know what to say . . .

Mr. Zimmerman returned with a sheet of paper. "Here's one I wrote a month or two ago—no, I see it was longer than that. This went to *Time* magazine," he said, handing a carbon copy to Father Urban.

"But wasn't published?"

"No, it wasn't—at least not yet."

"Has *Time* published anything of yours?"

"No, and I don't have to tell you why."

"No?"

"Pink."

Father Urban didn't reply at once.

While at St. Monica's, Father Urban arranges barn or square dances for the "young marrieds," rock-and-roll dances for "teens," all-cartoon programs for the children and mothers of the parish, and, for the Men's Club, showings of films of Notre Dame football games:

The school nuns were not forgotten. He gave them the use of his (Phil's) car, permission to shop at supermarkets, and occasionally he threw the boss a ten-dollar bill—"Buy yourself some cigars, Sister." They all loved him.

But Father Urban is repelled by most of contemporary America. Out of disgust, he autographs the guest book of a particularly obnoxious suburban family: "Pope John XXIII." His forrays into slothful suburban homes leave him with feelings of dismay.

This is a world not only of TV, *Time,* and washing machines, but also of golf. The most important battle of *Morte D'Urban* occurs on the golf course of Duesterhaus—a match between Father Urban and Father Feld that determines who will rise to leadership of the Clementine Order. Father Urban's mottoes are: "Be a winner!" and "Never say die!"

That was why, for the next three holes, Father Urban's tee shots went off like rifle fire, his approaches soared and dropped like swallows—why even the brass putter turned deadly in his hands.

But Father Urban is as he approaches the last hole in the crucial golf match conked on the head by a golf ball, his head permanently damaged. He tries standing on it, but his attacks persist, arriving and departing "like sections of the Twentieth Century Limited":

When somebody was in the office, and he felt the first section coming down the tracks, he swiveled around in his chair, saying, "I'll be with you in a minute, Father," and opened his breviary, and closed his eyes, and waited until both sections had come and gone. Thus he tried to disguise his condition from others, and thus, without wishing to, he gained a reputation for piety he hadn't had before, which, however, was not entirely unwarranted now.

In a sense, the prototype for Father Urban is Powers' own Father Burner (called "Boomer" Burner—a golf player, too) of "Prince of Darkness" and "Death of a Favorite." He is zealous but lacks devotion:

If questioned, he would display a lot of easy confidence not unaccompanied by a touch of humility, a phrase or two like "God willing" or "with the help of Almighty God and your prayers, Your Excellency." He would also not forget to look the part—reliable, casual, cool, an iceberg, only the tip of his true worth showing.

Some aspects of Father Urban's character are also foreshadowed in the personage of Father Early in Powers' story "Zeal":

"Some people think Catholics oppose progress here below. Look on your garbage can and what do you see? Galvanized. Galvin was a Catholic. Look on your light bulb. Watts. Watts was a Catholic. The Church never harmed Galileo."

Father Urban's speeches sound just like this. Yet Father Early is earnest and—to the Bishop in "Zeal" who is lonely, afraid, bothered by the world—filled with grace "What an intricate instrument for good a simple man could be!" the Bishop says of Father Early.

Moreover, Father Urban is not only Father Early but also, in part, the Bishop. Father Early, Titus in "Lions, Hearts, Leaping Does," and the Pastor in "The Presence of Grace" are all suffused with and mirror grace. Grace—for the Bishop, Didymus, and Father Fabre respectively—is arrived at through their perception of the grace each one of them lacks in the persons of their "simple" counterparts.

Father Urban is not, in the beginning of *Morte D'Urban,* in touch with this presence: "It was all too easy to neglect prayer if you lived at the pace he had in the world." Father Urban's first attitude towards the Duesterhaus retreat is revealed in the following selections:

> "A grand place, this," said Wilf, looking out at the grounds.
> "Yes," said Father Urban, looking at the bare trees and bushes, the dead fields, the trees in the distance like black whiskers on the winter horizon.
> "You cold?" said Wilf.
> "Just numb is all."
> Presently he was in bed again, this time between two blankets, with his shoes on. He had his rosary with him, and began the Glorious Mysteries, but somewhere along the line he forgot what he was doing, and just lay there, watching it get dark in his room.

There was no sense here of a "dark night of the soul," nor even of the gentle yet veiled beauty of any night's darkness:

> With all her eyes the goddess Night looks forth approaching many a spot:
> She hath put all her glories on.
> *(Rig-Veda)*

There is nothing of the above in this early part of *Morte D'Urban.* Yet the novel moves gradually from a merely disparaging portrait of American culture towards a revelation of a world of quiet mysticism—a mysticism that lies at the roots of Powers' art and which impels its subtle substance.

What most critics of Powers' writing fail to see in this

author's work is this definite but unobtrusive religious impulse. Reading Stanley Edgar Hyman's review of this novel, for instance, one would think that miracle, mystery, and authority are the only truly necessary or valid qualities of a religious spirit. This might lead one to say that El Greco and Simone Weil are "religious" while Vermeer and Sei Shonagon are not. Behind the intense personal striving, the apocalyptic turmoil, the eschatological vision lies, perhaps the religious quest. Yet what really is the religious significance of the abysm of the heart? St. Theresa of Avila and Simone Weil thought they knew; and perhaps so. But Powers—like Vermeer and Sei Shonagon—is beyond this; he starts off from a "religious" attitude Simone Weil hopes eventually to arrive at. Powers has transcended the "existential anguish"; his characters are very much at home in this world, and their longings, as we shall see, are for and of the real world—contingent or no.

In his best work, Powers' energetic priests ultimately discover the feeling of quiet mysticism—felt and acknowledged as a living presence, palpable to the touch, truly the "ineluctable modality of the visible." "Grace is everywhere," wrote Georges Bernanos. And the important point to be made about *Morte D'Urban* is that—as it progresses—it shows us Father Urban developing and attaining to this realization. It is a novel that reveals a psychological growth, increasing our awareness of this growth, and thus enables us to see its structural development as corresponding to the religious experience of the entire work—an extraordinary accomplishment.

Father Urban's realization comes through his participation in the "working-day world." At one point, for instance, he drives a sports car down the highway:

> At a stoplight . . . when a girl in a white MG paused alongside him, a girl wearing sunglasses and nothing else—so it appeared from where he was sitting—and with a crisp blue dog beside her, Father Urban experienced a heavy moment, a moment of regret and longing. He wished the little Barracuda were black or white instead of bright red, which just wasn't right for him, and he wished he had a crisp blue dog beside him. So he put on his sunglasses. When he hit open country, he threw away his cigar and gave the little thoroughbred its head.

Father Urban is certainly not Galahad—there is no vision of the

Holy Grail in *Morte D'Urban.* Rather one might say that Father Urban is a modern day Lancelot, inescapably of this world:

> Jack regarded Sir Galahad as the real hero of the book, and had given him the full treatment. He had wished to do more for Sir Percival and Sir Tristam, whom he rated next to Sir Galahad in holiness, but this was impossible, for reasons of space. The biggest problem for Jack, though, was Sir Lancelot.
>
> "There are times when I don't know where I am with him," Jack told Father Urban. "He's the Hamlet of the book." Jack could find no evidence that Sir Lancelot and Lady Elaine had been married before a priest. Sir Lancelot had been under a spell when he begat the child of their union, but the same could not be said for Lady Elaine. Why hadn't their union been regularized later?

In *Morte D'Urban's* homologous "Lady of the Lake" episode, Father Urban watches Sally—Mrs. Thwaites' daughter—remove her clothes and dive into the lake which surrounds the island on which Father Urban is visiting. She throws her shoes at him, hitting him on the head, just before she plunges into the water and disappears:

> He heard the trap door open and shut. He stood the shoes together, and, looking at them there, felt sorry for Sally. Life here below, no matter how much you might wish it otherwise, was shoes—not champagne, but shoes and not dirt, but shoes, and this, roughly speaking, was the mind of the Church.

This is, in context, a strange, somehow terrifying, and altogether startling perception of life as we all know it: this is how it is and also all there is. (Bernard Malamud—one of the few other of our novelists who is always feeling fully concerned with the "working-day world"—suggests the wonder, confusion, and uglyness of this world, coincidentally with Powers, by his use of the images of shoes throughout *A New Life.* Malamud has, interestingly enough, also drawn on the themes and subjects of Arthurian legend in *The Natural* and some of his stories.)

Because Powers accepts the implications of the statement: Life is shoes, he rejects an "easy" mysticism. Small, petty angers and inner dissatisfaction make Father Firman, in "The Valiant Woman," "squash" insects. The extreme projection of violence expressed within a confined area of activity reveals to us again the fact that to make a solitude is not necessarily to make a peace.

Father Burner, we remember, is covetous and bloated with the idea of his own self. And these men turn us back on our own plight. Every day we become more hopelessly aware of the fact that the present Cold War is nothing but our actual violent condition not made manifest—unconfronted and held in terrible abeyance. We do not love ourselves nor our world:

With fearful speed the visible world seemed to slip away from me in a maze of pictures; they were not sad, but rather so full of light and dazzling beauty. How is this? Can I have loved it all so much? mornings, evenings, roads. Mysterious changing roads, full of the steps of men. Have I loved roads so much, our roads, the roads of the world? Is there any poor boy, brought up in their dust, who has not scattered there his dreams? And the slow, stately roads shall bear them on, to what unknown seas—? Great rivers of light and shadow bearing the dreams of the poor. I think it was the word Mezargues that broke my heart.

This appears in George Bernanos' *Diary of a Country Priest,* one of the beautiful books of this century. *Morte D'Urban* does, at this level, compare itself favorably with Bernanos' novel. We think of Father Urban, at the end of his life—"waxed full lean" like Lancelot—too much aware of this world and thinking of the Duesterhaus retreat as his home. This is the home of Father John—for whom the world is too much—who is, early in the novel, invited out to lunch by Father Urban:

"Would you like some coffee?"
"Urban, I would, if you don't mind."
"Shouldn't drink so much."
"No."
"You can't handle it."
"No, and I've never cared for it—not that *this* isn't very good wine. One of the hardest things about the priesthood for me—the wine."

It is the spiritual world of Monsignor Renton with whom "One moment it was 'God is not mocked' or 'Christ, and Christ crucified,' and the next moment it was 'Your ass is out'" yet who is infused with the piety which Father Urban, early in the novel, lacks. It is the world of those who know with sorrow and joy that: Life is shoes. But who also know that coexisting with the hardness of reality is that feeling of quiet mysticism which depends on and can only exist alongside the real world and which leads us to our truest feelings and longings.

"I think it was the word Mezargues that broke my heart," Bernanos' priest writes; and Father Urban, too, is heartbreakingly of this world as he thinks of what he might have done with his life if he had not become a priest:

Recreations: sports cars, history, golf, people. A bit of fluff, yes, but don't put that down. Except for occasional headaches, in perfect health. No, born downstate, land of Lincoln, but consider Chicago my home. New York? All right, if you happen to be a waiter or a cab driver. I don't. No Michigan Avenue and no lake and the whole place has a bombed look. Give me Chicago. The most beautiful sound I know is the sound of whistles on Michigan Avenue at dusk, especially in the fall. I like to sit in Grant Park and listen to the cops calling to each other like nightingales. You know the Chicago whistle? *Wheeeeeeeeeeee-uhhhhhhhhhhhhhhhwheeeeeuhhhh.* I'd say it's a musical instrument, related to the clarinet, piccolo, and oboe, and also related to the old-time train whistle. It'd scare the hell out of you—rightly played, that is—if you didn't see the lights and the people and the Wrigley Building. I like to see Michigan Avenue shining wet at night. I like to come out of the Blackstone or the Drake at dusk, especially in the fall, with two or three good ones in me, and hear those whistles, the mush and the whine of rubber, the distant roar—it always seems to be centered over La Salle Street, to the south, but it's like a haze you can see and never touch. For many years I traveled out of Chicago, and I'm proud to call it my home. Expect from life? Only what any sane person would expect. What I've had from it. I've written my book, I've married my wife, I've made my pile. No complaints, no regrets. Who could ask for anything more?

1963

The Collected Poems of Frank O'Hara

EDITED BY DONALD ALLEN

The arrival of *The Collected Poems of Frank O'Hara* is one of the most exuberant poetry events in recent American publishing history. With its shiny dark green cover, it looks at first like a glutton's cookbook, and its one-poem-after-another layout (arranged chronologically) in fact suggests the supernumerary courses of a Roman emperor's holiday banquet.

Persons who know of the four small but exhilarating collections of verse published during O'Hara's lifetime now have the chance to realize that there is no law of diminishing returns with regard to O'Hara's work. He used to write poems in his letters—and not usually make copies—or jot them down on scraps of paper, then just stick them in some drawer. (One thinks of Rossini tossing pages of a score out the window to a waiting impresario as he rushed to complete an opera.) Donald Allen's detective work and wizard-like editing have enabled him to materialize the close to five hundred fifty poems which appear in this expensive three-and-a-half pound book. Like Andrew Marvell's green thoughts of fantasy, these poems consistently exemplify one of poetry's most beautiful aims—to transform, enrich, and thereby change our language and the world.

O'Hara, who was fatally struck by a car in 1966 at the age of forty, was a prominent figure in the New York art scene. A curator at the Museum of Modern Art and critic for *Art News,* he was a friend of Pollock, Kline, de Kooning, and Larry Rivers, and his work, as John Ashbery states in his introduction, suggested the "concept of the poem as the chronicle of the creative act that produces it": ("My hands are Massimo Plaster, called 'White Pin in the Arm of the Sea'/and I'm blazoned and scorch like a fleet of windbells down the Pulaski Skyway"—"Second Avenue").

Van Gogh once wrote about "that peculiar open-air feeling you get when speaking to a painter." O'Hara's voice, too, emphasizes this "large feeling, like a light in a toe, a voice of the sky." And it was obviously impossible for him to allow his poetic materials to "sit among mattresses of the dead," to quote Wallace Stevens. Like that poet's Crispin, O'Hara embraced, absorbed, and transfigured all the everyday presences of New York City life. Who but he would imagine the seduction of Park Avenue by Fifth (with Madison Avenue the jealous husband in between): "Intercourse!/cried Fifth Avenue, all I want to do is kiss you, kiss/your silver grey temples and your charming St. Bartholomew's ears. . . . Why don't we rendezvous in Central Park behind a clump of cutthroats/near the reservoir and there we'll kiss and hold each other/sweatily as in a five o'clock on a mid-August Friday in the dusk/and after languorously bathe, to sweeten city water for all time."

"Art," Montaigne wrote, "destroys nature and removes man from Grace." This isn't O'Hara's attitude. "Grace to be born," he said, "and live as variously as possible." Like a Waring blender, his poems take in the most diverse and discrete elements and persons—feather cushions and Palmolive Soap, Lana Turner and Mayakovsky, frigidaires and raspberry sweaters, Schoenberg and Rachmaninoff—pouring out the most sensuous concoctions since *The Eve of St. Agnes* and *Rape of the Lock:* white chocolate jars full of petals, and curls tumbling languorously towards a yawning rubber band. What some critics take to preciosity is usually just a munificent inventiveness: "March, the fierce! like a wind of garters"; "The rain, its tiny pressure/on your scalp, like ants/passing the door of a tobacconist."

It's not surprising that O'Hara felt a stronger affinity with poets like Corbiere, Apollinaire, Reverdy, and Mayakovsky than with T.S. Eliot and the Agrarians. Like Walt Whitman, he discovered a truly ecstatic American idiom ("It sails me, I dab with bare feet, they are lick'd by the indolent waves"—*Song of Myself*). And just as Whitman revealed his self as the Self—Brahman—whose manifestations are all the multitudinous creations and creatures of the universe, so O'Hara, more modestly, identifies his self with the language of earthly love (which is really a metaphor for poetry). The poem exists between the poet and the person for whom it's addressed; and, as O'Hara says, "the poem is correspondingly gratified."

Concerning the matter of technique, O'Hara once wrote: "If you're going to buy a pair of pants you want them to be tight enough so everyone will want to go to bed with you." Which is one way of saying that form is to content as pants are to the body. (One thinks of Mayakovsky's "cloud in trousers.") Tone, in a sense, determines the form, not, as in Ben Jonson, the other way around.

Sometimes O'Hara's poems billow out in splended long lines, or else wrinkle up in loose sonnets, rondels, odes, and carefree but always elegant jottings. There is also always room, in the poet's pluralistic poetic world, for extraordinarily deep feelings in reveries such as "To the Harbormaster," "River," or "In Memory of My Feelings."

Readers who weigh this book on a critical scale in order to determine whether O'Hara is a minor-major or a major-minor poet might as well go back to Sturge Moore and Robert Bridges. Along with certain special works by John Skelton, George Gascoigne, Robert Herrick, and Marianne Moore, O'Hara's poems renew our language, feelings, and the ways in which we see things. "I know you love Manhattan," says the Sun to the poet in one of O'Hara's finest poems, entitled "A True Account of Talking to the Sun at Fire Island":

And
always embrace things, people earth
sky stars, as I do, freely and with
the appropriate sense of space. That
is your inclination, known in the heavens
and you should follow it to hell, if
necessary, which I doubt.

Maybe we'll
speak again in Africa, of which I too
am specially fond. Go back to sleep now
Frank, and I may leave a tiny poem
in that brain of yours as my farewell."

"Sun, don't go!" I was awake
at last." "No, go I must, they're calling
me."
"Who are they?"
Rising he said "Some
day you'll know. They're calling to you
too." Darkly he rose, and then I slept.

1971

3
John Lennon & Yoko Ono

Along with the 1968 interview with John Lennon (see "Interviews" section), the following three articles present several moments in the "life and times" of John Oko and Yoko Lennon—as they were first beginning to see themselves. The first two articles focus on John's "primitive avant garde" art show in London in 1968 and on John and Yoko's first—and in some ways their most beautiful—collaborative recording *(Two Virgins).* The third and longest article about Yoko and her work was completed during the couple's first visit together to New York City in December, 1970.

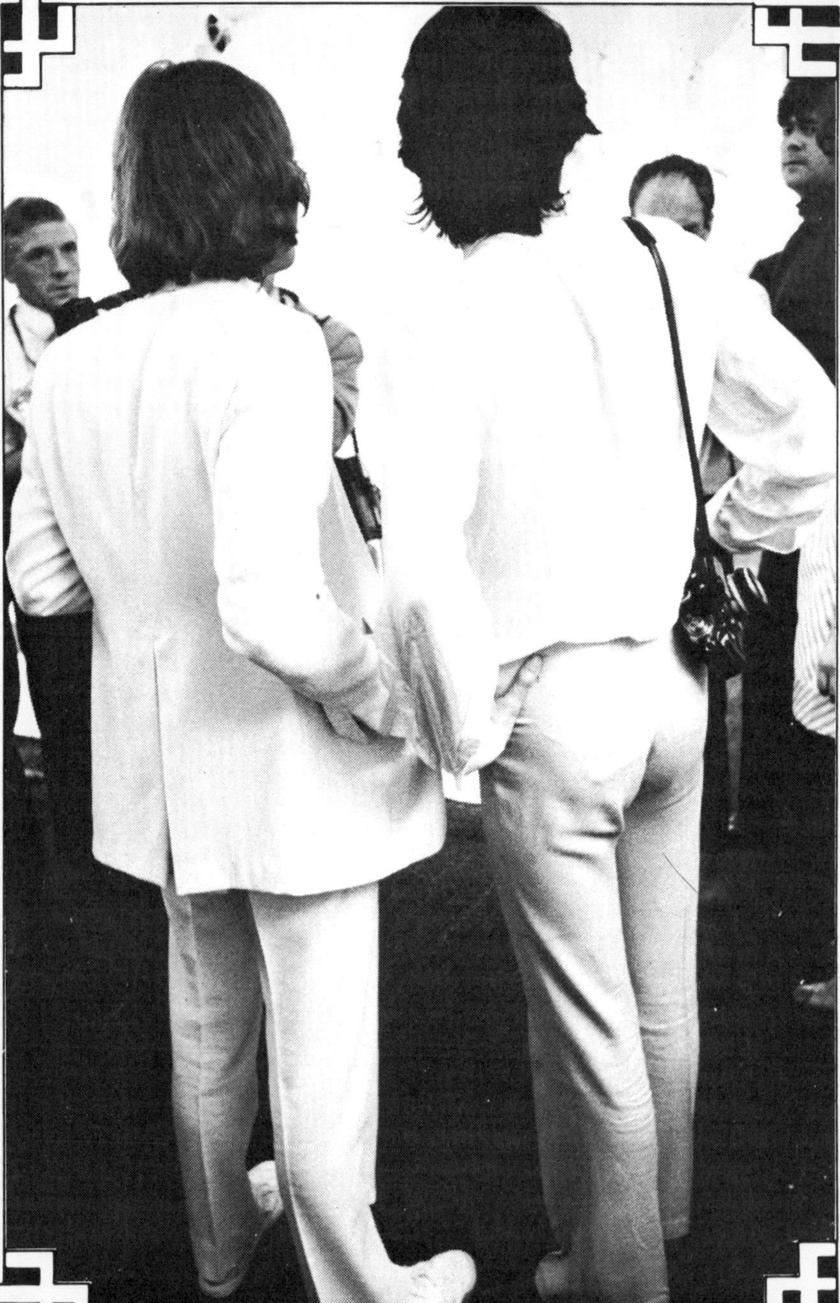

The Eggman Wears White

John Lennon has taken the summer for himself and then given it away. This gift is not a parsimonious "jam yesterday and jam tomorrow, but never jam today." And the fact that the gift is given away with publicity creatures tailing the giver should not obviate the necessity of seeing the gift. Lennon's latest koans are filmed, written about, photographed; and if the point is mutilated, it's the media's fault; and if it's lost, it's yours.

First, Lennon's and Victor Spinetti's dramatic adaptation of Lennon's writings is being presented in a fine National Theatre production, along with works by Henry Fielding and John Maddison Morton. Ronald Pickup, who played Rosalind in the famous all-male *As You Like It,* here plays the protagonist who sets his fantasies against Baudelaire's definition of reality—"that miserable statement of line and surface."

Lennon has taken this reality many times before, fought and questioned it, and now he appears smiling through it. In Yoko Ono's new technicolor film *Number Five,* he smiles for ninety minutes. The directress took two days of shooting to film a two and a half minute Lennon smile, and then with special cameras and effects she lengthened it.

Yoko Ono is quoted as saying: "There wasn't any point in just making love, secretly and everything. We had to make a film which had the same vibrations as making love. . . . A smile for everyone. That's us. Oh, yes, and vibrations." Film Number 6, entitled *Two Virgins,* will present John and Yoko in their "first screen kiss" and music by John.

"John by Yoko—Yoko by John" is the sculpture exhibit now placed in a garden in front of the ruins just outside the walls of the Coventry Cathedral—sheltering works by Moore and Hepworth, among others. The Sculpture consists of two acorns planted by John and Yoko in white plastic pots buried in the center of a circular white wrought-iron seat, around which people sit and watch and feel things growing.

Most people can't take the various senses of growing. It bothers their character armor, as Reich correctly termed it, or rather it reveals all that armor. The whiteness of Lennon's "For

Yoko" show at the Robert Fraser Gallery, which closed at the end of July, exemplifies at least a theoretical simplicity as proportionately bothersome as your insistence on supplying something that is not there.

You enter the gallery to see a movie of the show's "star-studded" opening night, photographed by Bill Waering. (Candid Camera film crews also filmed the guests, but these sequences will be shown as part of a longer film about the opening which will be released sometime in the future.) White balloons are blown up by helium machines on the main floor of the gallery; and attached to the balloons are tags saying, on one side, "you are here" and, on the other, "Write to John Lennon c/o Robert Fraser Gallery." These balloons are released every night in Mayfair and fly away. Lennon tells how as a child he found a tagged balloon from Australia, and it pleased him so much that he decided to imitate the idea. The responses to these found tags have been uniformly imprecatory—like the comments in the guest book, which I'll quote from later.

Down the spiral staircase, you find yourself in the white-walled basement. A white circular eight-foot diameter canvas hangs on a wall, in the center of which Lennon has written "you are here." (You see him in the film upstairs creating the painting on opening night.) "You Are Here" buttons are piled in a jar next to a white trilby hat to which is pinned a notice: "For the artist, Thank you."

Around the room you see cans and boxes for all sorts of charities—Cancer Prevention, League for the Protection of Horses, Tibet Relief Fund—and plastic statuettes—a bandaged plastic dog, white bowed band across his head, holding a red money box saying RSPCA; a plastic blonde girl and teddy bear in her arms with the sign "Please Help Your Local Spastics." Persons are asked to contribute. "For God's Sake, Give Something!" as one of the charity can signs announces.

The show is "For Yoko," but it literally says something about you. If you can't figure it out from what you see or from the "you are heres," ("we are all together" is understood), then you can work it out by glancing at the guest book, blackbound, and also a part of the show.

Wilhelm Reich wrote: "This armoring of the character is the

basis of loneliness, helplessness, craving for authority, fear of responsibility, mystical longing, sexual misery, of impotent rebelliousness as well as resignation of an unnatural and pathological type."

Here are some typical examples of where people are:

"You are as dirty as everybody else—an old capitalist!"; "Long hairred spectical faced turt"; "Best wishes for a speedy recovery"; "Go back to your wife, she loves you"; "Not bad for a 1st try, but get rid of the collecting tins, I like cripples as they are"; "Micky Mouse loves you, so it's alright."

There are also some poems, some pleasant, a few complimentary comments, and some things to think about: "Whispering brutality justifies the sun to falter in reality." But the paranoia that jumps out of the book is worth any number of lectures on "fascist irrationalism."

The conclusion of the animated film *Yellow Submarine* presents the Beatles—"real life shot"—talking to each other, and then John says to the audience: "We've heard there are Blue Meanies in the vicinity of this theater; so go out singing." And the Beatles sing the chorus of "All Together Now," one of the four beautiful new songs heard in the film. I spotted a Blue Meanie middle-aged couple outside the theater saying: "Those goddamned kids lining up to see that bloody Beatles film!"

There you go, John.

As "Hey, Bulldog" goes: "Some happiness is measured out in miles. . . . Some innocence is measured out in years . . . Some solitude is measured out in you . . . Hey, Bulldog, you can talk to me if you're lonely."

If *A Hard Day's Night* was the Beatles' first public-life image, then *Yellow Submarine* is director George Dunning's reinterpretation and also extension of this life into myth. *Yellow Submarine* is the real magical mystery tour, using the emblems of Beatle mythology—a yellow submarine, a nowhere man, a Sgt. Peppers' Band—and verbal ideas which come to life as images, so that the song "All You Need Is Love" is shown letter-by-letter as it destroys the Blue Meanie rocket Glove. ("Now" comes from "nowhere" and "love" from "glove.")

The fascist glove and the stomach full of teeth (both images used in the film) are not new images for character armor. And obviously the director uses the Beatles mythology to reveal a psychic development that proceeds from solitude to community to radiant love. Nothing new here, either. Think of Vergil, Dante, Milton. Or of *The Ramayana,* or *Monkey.* But the point is that *Yellow Submarine* is one of the magnificent archetypal fairy tales.

The art-nouveau-pop-op art style reveals in illustrator-animator Heinz Edemann's conception an unlikely mixing of rigorousness and improvisation. A scene like the "Eleanor Rigby" section which superimposes animated photographs with art images is as powerful as it is because it locates the English malaise as few art works of recent time have done and takes off from them. Similarly, as the critic Kenneth Rexroth has pointed out, D. H. Lawrence in *The Plumed Serpent* writes the first chapter of the novel with a style and diction as flat as a real Mexican dirt town and rises to search for a myth that is shown to be simply a neuresthenic menopausal fantasy.

Where Harry Smith's extraordinary animated *Heavenly and Earthly Magic* (from which certain images like that of the suction machine monster are probably borrowed) stays tuned to a night journey that hardly comes to day—for the nightmare machinery is the world—*Yellow Submarine* attains—as it enters dreams and rises—to the joy of George MacDonald's *The Golden Key,* Mary de Morgan's *Through the Fire,* Herbert Read's *The Green Child,* or even *The Winter's Tale.*

"It's all been written in The Book."

1968

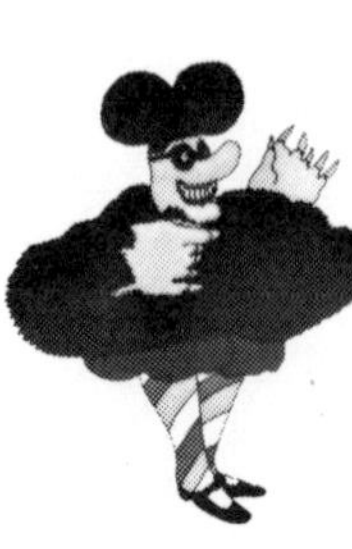

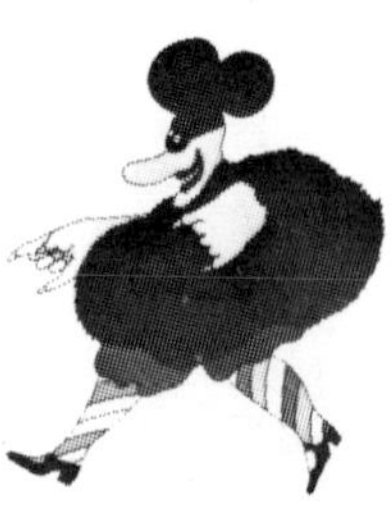

Two Virgins

"What I'm doing is the primitive avant-garde," John Lennon said about his new art and music. *Two Virgins* is really a sophisticated multi-media *menage a trois:* a now famous album cover, a lovely film, and an excellent piece of contemporary music.

Obviously, John's and Yoko's music circulates in that musical air inhaled by composers such as Luciano Berio, Robert Ashley, Gordon Mumma, La Monte Young, Morton Feldman, Cornelius Cardew, and John Cage—composers who generally emphasize sounds over pitches, a mixed-media interacting environment over a performer-listener concert hall ritual, the unfolding of musical events—the way a waterfall falls—over the structuring and permutation of rows and series (as in the music, for example, of Milton Babbit, Harvey Sollberger, or David Del Tredici).

But the music for *Two Virgins* comes without clothes and without clichés—a musical metaphor for two persons seeing each other for the first time and then seeing what's there. The naked album cover is actually an extension of the music, for it exemplifies the idea of confrontation, an interaction between John and Yoko—a real *East Meets West* album.

I suppose that the music for *Two Virgins* moves in close and quiet reach of Feldman's *Durations,* for example. But it is as completely self-realized—in all senses of the phrase—as is John's powerful *Revolution Number 9*—a contemporary music classic that creates its own unfoldings and bearings in an instinctive, natural, and unimpressionable way, as if Cage's *Fontana Mix* had never been conceived.

Yoko told me her ideas about the music:

"This music is a totally new experience for me. John and I did it together. It just happened. It was strict improvisation, no planning. It was a meeting of us, through music, through making music. We were going into an area that none of us really knew. I used voice and John uses everything in the room—old records, piano, percussion.

"He was operating two tape recorders. He was the busy one.

I was just sitting down, doing the voice. The whole concept is called 'Unfinished Music Series Number One.'

"There's a catch, you see. It's an unfinished music. So if you listen to it, maybe you can add to it or change it or edit or add something in your mind. I loathe the idea of giving a set idea to people. So that in my painting, for instance the hammer nailing painting, it's just a process. And this music is just a process. The unfinished part that's not in the record—what's in you, not what's in the record—is what's important. The record is just there to stimulate what's in you, to make it come out.

"I believe in absence. If you have an absence, other people can fill it in. This music is really incomplete.

"Cage was interested in all sorts of sounds. Airport sounds, for instance. I was an extreme case. In the end I was creating Music in the Mind. All my concerts had no sounds in them: they were completely silent. Things were done on stage, just movement, and people had to make their own music in their minds.

"So I came to that point, and that's where I met John. And John brought this old vaudeville rocker-type music to me, and I suddenly realized that my Music of the Mind was getting too Zen, too finished, and I was suffocating, as if I were in an ivory tower and there was nowhere to go. People were silent. I felt the lack of a sense of humor. John was doing this healthy beat music, and I got stimulated with that."

For me, the music on side one of the album—complete or incomplete—is an exquisitely sustained creation. Side two's music is more sectioned; the flow breaks, almost giving the effect of a variation and comment on the earlier music, but disclosing new surprises.

John said that the music was made just as dawn entered through the studio windows. The music appropriately begins with birds singing, and the taped bird loops act almost as a passacaglia and ground base—a continually natural reference point and touchdown for the music. The seeming rhythmic exactitude of the bird sounds and their almost imperceptible variations in fact suggest the music's subtlety, the clear unravelling of multiple threads of beautiful sounds always joining, never tangled.

You'll discover glissandi guitar tones superimposed over

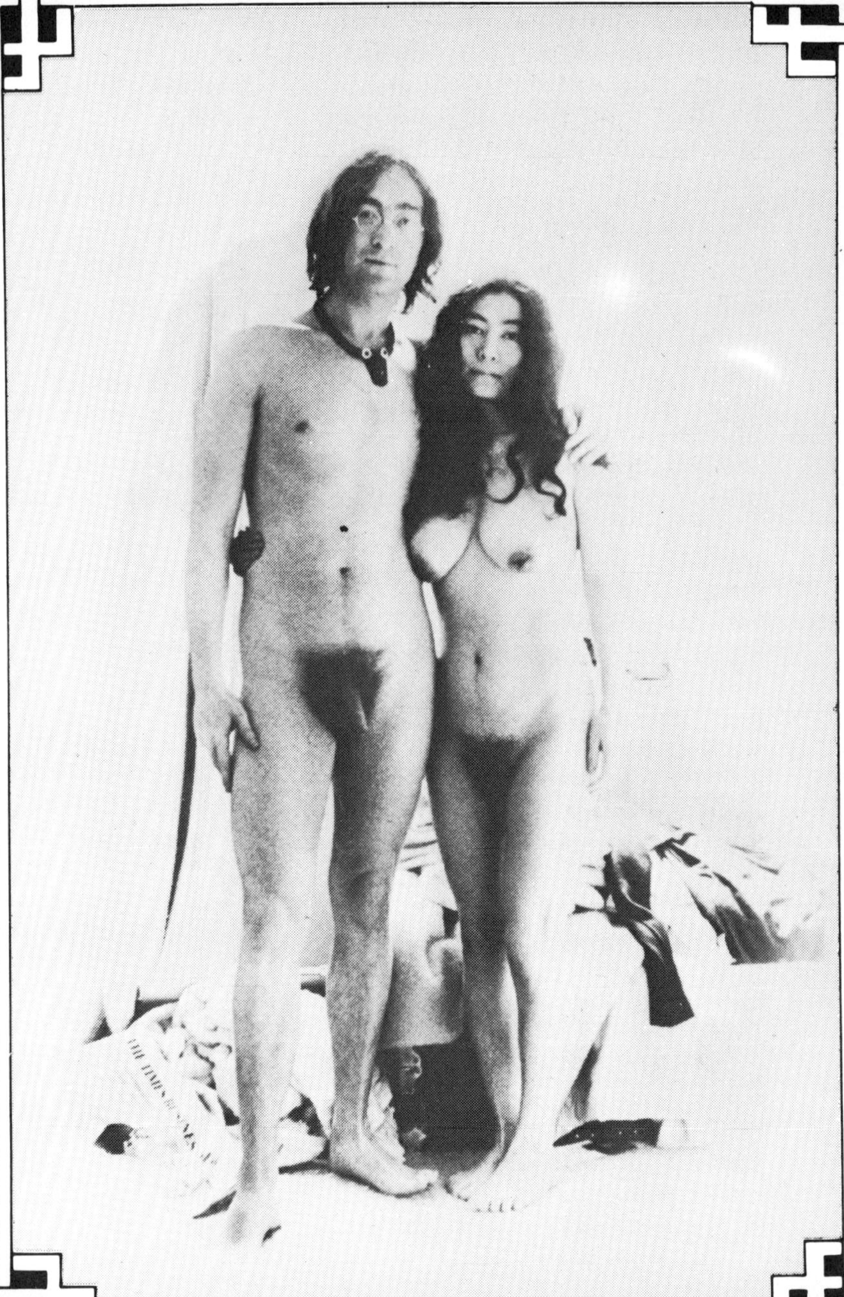

slight old-time music piano chords, Yoko's drawn out crying sound—like one of those ancient shepherd pipes you hear in old, lonesome Swedish herding tunes—a hammer driving a nail into the wall (I'm sure I heard this, but it might be in the mind), and the sempiternal birds. And all these sounds convey feelings close to the night music sections of Bartok's *Out of Doors Suite* or Ravel's *L'Enfant et les Sortilèges.*

While Yoko Ono's voice sounds sometimes like a Japanese *hichiriki* pipe, and while she sings, on the record's second side, a haunting little Japanese song in which the singer says things like "Come on and make me," she has also absorbed the sophisticated vocal techniques of Berio's *Visage* and Cage's *Aria* with *Fontana Mix,* the latter of which she sang with Cage in Japan.

So that while Yoko's vocal East/West symbiosis might seem likely to conflict with John's meletron sounds, his saloon piano and jazz trumpet recordings—cultural gestures forcing each other to grimace—what miraculously happens is that everything simply and unselfconsciously comes together.

Real contrasts seem merely an extension or continuation of a mood. The beginning of the second side, for instance, opens with church organ chords blowing far away—early Sunday morning walking at dawn feelings—and over or under or along with these chords comes Yoko's high-pitched voice, deeply sustained with the longest breath. The effect here as in other moments is that of wonderment; it reminded me of the lament the duck sings inside the wolf's stomach in *Peter and the Wolf.*

Not that Yoko's voice is swallowed up by John's music. Where the tension is played with is in the verbal interplay. "Is that you? Hey there," Yoko wails. "No fucking tin opener," John grunts. And then: "It's me, Hilda, I'm home for tea." And so ghost-haunted lovers in *The Tale of Genji* are transformed into a cozy British family, transfixed in the tea room.

The East/West tension dissolves in the music. And if you hear the lightest of echoes of Satie, Virgil Thomson, Swedish herding tunes, *Visage*—(aside from the obvious quotations and your own music), why not? As in Stockhausen's *Telemusik* and *Hymnen,* all music is heard as one. The confrontation becomes an anastomosis—a running together, as of two streams. The music creates a story, there is a contest, but the music wins—especially those ubiquitous returning rhythms, like those of a person breathing in dreams.

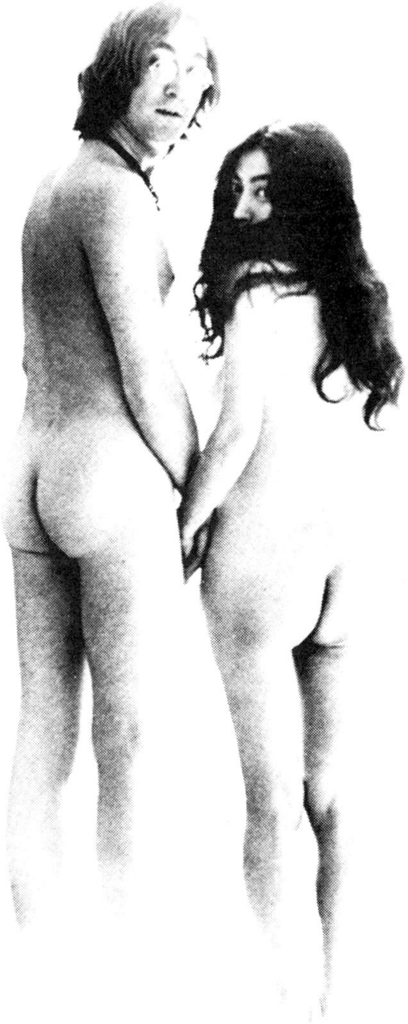

1969

Yoko Ono and Her Sixteen-Track Voice

In December, 1970, John Lennon and Yoko Ono came to New York City—their first time as a couple—where they visited some of Yoko's old friends, went out, as they rarely do in London, to some "entertainment" films like *Diary of a Mad Housewife* and *Lovers and Other Strangers* and to the Muhammad Ali fight, made two new films—*Up Your Legs Forever* and *The Fly*—for inclusion in a three-night John and Yoko minifilm festival at the Elgin Theater, and did some publicity for their two extraordinary new albums.

The following scene takes place in a hotel room one Sunday evening: John is turning on the radio to hear Alex Bennett's WMCA phone-in program on which tonight he's playing tracks from Yoko's album—the first time Yoko's music has been featured on AM radio.

"There are people who are going to love it and people who are going to hate it," Bennett says enthusiastically. "I think that in 1980 music will probably sound like this. Here's a track called "Why," so phone in and tell us what you think of it."

"IT'S TODAY'S TUTTI FRUTTI," John writes on a note pad, so as not to interrupt the music.

"I'm forty-nine years old," a listener phones in, after listening to "Why Not." "Forty-nine and I dig it. I heard trains going through a tunnel, then rain—I'm just using my imagination—then what sounded like a bunch of Indians. I dig it, but I really like songs with a melody."

"It was truly disastrous," a nasal-voiced listener calls up to say.

"It's music, you idiot!" John exclaims to the radio. "Because it's not got da-da-da, there's nothing for him to hook onto."

"You don't mind hearing the program?" Yoko asks.

"I want to," John says. "You see, with Yoko's and my album, we're both looking at the same thing from different sides of the table. Mine is literate, hers is revolutionary."

"Paper Shoes" comes on the air with its train sounds.

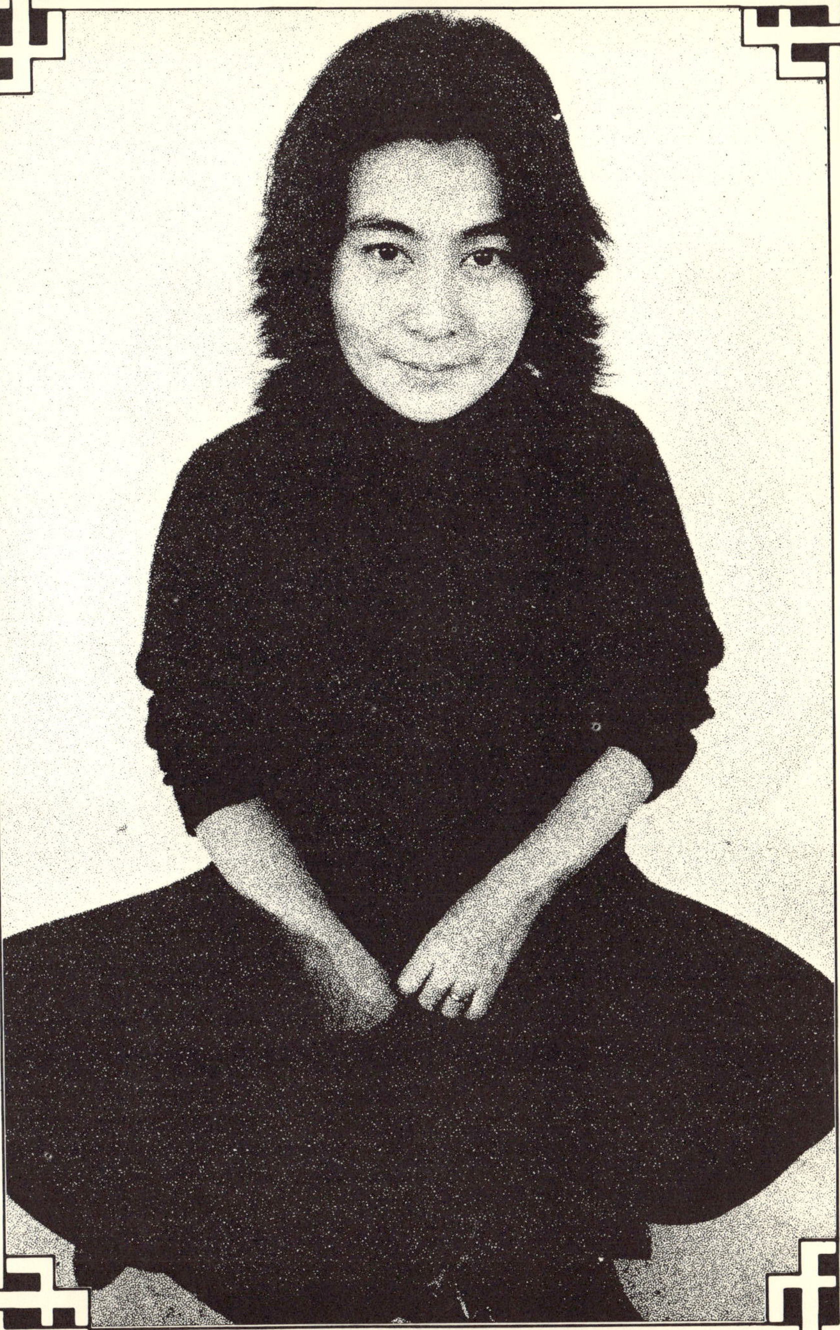

"On one side, at the end of 'Why Not,' you're in the train itself."

"Life is a train, and train is a life," Yoko says.

"She's got a sixteen-track voice," adds John.

The radio program ends, and John and Yoko are relaxing on their bed, John half-watching the soundless television screen and reading an essay called "Concept Art" by violinist and composer Henry Flynt whom John and Yoko have just visited in New York.

"The notion of a concept," John is reading, "is a vestige of the notion of a platonic form (The thing which e.g., all tables have in common: tableness), which notion is replaced by the notion of a name objectively, metaphysically related to its intention (so that all tables now have in common their objective relation to *table*)."

"Before I met John," Yoko is saying, "and when I had become sort of famous because of my bottoms film shots of three hundred and sixty-five backsides for one hour, a film John describes as *Many Happy Endings,* that was the loneliest time in my life. Some people resented me because of my fame and made me feel isolated. Now when my record is played on the radio, I've got someone who's pleased.

"When I met John originally, he said it was OK for me to listen to the Beatles' sessions . . ."

John: "I had to get permission!"

"So I asked John, why don't you use different rhythms, not just going ba-ba- ba-ba. It was a kind of avant-garde snobbery on my part, because my voice was going [vibrating: uhghh . . . ghuhhh], but there was no beat. So I thought to myself (simpering tone) 'Well, simple music!' You see, I was doing music of the mind—no sound at all, and everybody sitting around just imagining sounds. At the Chamber Street Loft concerts I was throwing peas from a bag at the people and I had long hair and I was circling my hair and the movement was a sound. Even then, some people were saying that maybe it was too dramatic. Then there was my Wall Piece which instructed you to hit the wall with your head, and that was called too dramatic as well. But I felt stifled even with that, I was dying to scream, to go back to my voice. And I came to a point where I believed that the idea of avant-garde purity was just as stifling as just doing a rock beat over and over."

"Dear," John interrupts, "one thing that's going to throw you. Henry Flynt is talking about 'Sweets from My Sweet' by the Drifters; he's been rocking for a long time. You know, he played us some fantastic stuff the other night when we saw him. 'Sweets from My Sweet' was a big rock and roll hit, so he's been aware of that for a long time. I don't think he got to that sound pissing about with mathematics. I had to interrupt since I was just reading something he wrote about concept art and it's bloody hard, but he gets to 'Sweets from My Sweet' and I understood him."

"Probably I was the only one who didn't hear it," Yoko says.

"Right," says John, singing, "Dun de dun dun! I'm not putting you down, I'm just very surprised to read this."

"I know you mean well," Yoko replies, "but I get sort of lost."

"You were talking about the 4/4 beat."

"I realized," Yoko continues, "that the classics, when they went from 4/4 to 4/3, lost the heart beat. It's as if they left the ground and lived on the 40th floor. Schoenberg and Webern—Webern's on the top of the Empire State Building. But that's all right. Our conceptual rhythm got complex, but we still have the body and the beat. Conceptual rhythm I carry on with my voice, which has a very complicated rhythm even in 'Why,' but the bass and the drum is the heartbeat. So the body and the conceptual rhythms go together. These days I'm putting a beat under everything I do."

"Yoko and I have clashed artistically," John laughs. "Our egos have smashed once or twice. But if I know what I'm doing as an artist, then I can see if I'm being hypocritical in my reactions. I sometimes am overawed by her talent. I think, fuck, I better watch out, she *is* taking over, I better get meself in here. And I say, are you taking over? And then say all right, all right, and I relax again. I mean, she's going to haul three hundred and sixty-five legs and make a bloody film about a fly crawling over some woman's body, what is it? But it's all right, I know her."

"An artist couple is the most difficult thing," Yoko continues. "On the David Frost program, some guy was saying, 'I like to write music and my fiance likes to write poetry.' The fact is that we both paint, compose, and write poetry, and on that basis, I think we're doing pretty well."

"If you do two LPs there might be a little change!" John laughs. "But until then I don't mind. When she wants the A side, that's when we start fighting. The reason the covers of our albums are similar is that I wanted us to be separate and to be together, too, not to have it appear that old John-and-Yoko is over, because they're dying for us to fall apart, for God knows what reason. It's just that everybody doesn't want anybody else to be happy, because nobody's happy."

"I think it's a miracle that we're doing all right. But we are doing all right, don't you think, John?"

"It's just handy to fuck your best friend. That's what it is. And once I resolved the fact that it was a woman as well, it's all right. We go through the trauma of life and death every day so it's not so much of a worry about what sex we are anymore. I'm living with an artist who's inspiring me to work. And you know, Yoko is the most famous unknown artist. Everybody knows her name, but nobody knows what she does."

Yoko (the Japanese word for "ocean child") Ono ("small field") was born in 1933 and stands five feet two, weighs ninety-five pounds, more or less. "It is nice to keep oneself small," she once wrote, "like a grain of rice, instead of expanding. Make yourself dispensable, like paper. See little, hear little, and think little."

Her life in Japan as the daughter of a patrician family—a banker father, a beautiful hostess mother—which was dispossessed after the war, her education at a school that was the aristocratic equivalent of Eton and which was attended also by Crown Prince Akihito and the late novelist Mishima who had committed hari-kari ("I knew him," Yoko says, "and he was as popular as Mick Jagger in Japan"), her *Gone with the Wind* life during the war when she was selling jewels for food from farmers in the country, and her relationships with her two previous husbands—Tochi Ichiyanagi and Antony Cox—all have been recounted in several magazines, most recently in Esquire, in which she is quoted as saying: "I saw that nothing was permanent. You don't want to possess anything that is dear to you because you might lose it. So I became extremely disinterested in anything material, or in any relationship, in fact. I just kept everything sort of far away."

She seems to like the color *yellow* ("If the butterflies in your stomach die, send yellow death announcements to your friends"), *snow* ("Send snow sounds to a person you like"; "Walk in the snow without making footprints"; "Find a hand in the snow"—"Three More Snow Pieces for Nam June Paik"), and *wind* ("Make a hole. Leave it in the Wind"—"Painting for the Wind"). The biography she once wrote describes one self image:

> born: Bird Year
> early childhood: collected skys
> adolescence: collected sea-weeds
> late adolescence: gave birth to a grape-
> fruit, collected snails, clouds,
> garbage cans etc.
> Have graduated many schools
> specializing in these subjects.

"I dropped out in my third year at Sarah Lawrence," Yoko narrates, "and I started living in New York around 86th and Amsterdam where all the trucks go all the time. I came from a place like Scarsdale, and my new life was very exciting for me, because I was living next to a meat market and I felt as if I had a house with a delicatessen in it. The only thing was that I couldn't figure out how to present my work because I didn't know how to communicate with people. And I didn't know how to explain to people how shy I was. When people visited I wanted to be in a big sort of box with little holes where nobody could see me, but I could see through the holes. So later, that developed into my Bag Piece where you can be inside, and see outside, but they can't see you.

"When I was going to Sarah Lawrence, I was mainly staying in the music library and listening to Schoenberg and Webern; they thrilled me, really. And I was writing some serial works at that time. But I was lazy writing out a whole score. And further I was doing the Match Piece in those days, just lighting the match and watching until it disappeared. And I even thought that maybe there was something in me that was going to go crazy, like a pyromaniac. See, I was writing poetry and music and painting, and none of that satisfied me; I knew that the medium was wrong. Whenever I wrote a poem, they said it was too long, it was like a short story; a novel was like a short story, and a short story was like a poem. I felt that I was like a misfit in every medium.

"I just stayed in Scarsdale at my parents' home, and I was going crazy because I could not communicate with them very well. I was lighting matches, afraid of becoming a pyromaniac. But then I thought that there might be some people who needed something more than painting, poetry, and music, something I called an 'additional act' that you needed in life. And I was doing all that just to prevent myself from going mad, really. And when I had this apartment in New York, what happened was that instead of drying my face with a towel, I used my best cocktail dress. And then I was imagining myself all the time as a kite, holding on to a kite, and when I was sleeping, I'd lose my string, go off floating. That's the time I thought: I'll go crazy. So I just imagined myself holding on to a kite, and the kite was me.

"People asked me what I was doing. I didn't know how to explain that actually I was just holding the string, making sure that I wouldn't let go. This was a trait I had when I was a little girl, too, when my mother asked me what I was doing all by myself, and I would say: 'I'm breathing,' and I was really counting my breathings, and thinking: 'My God, if I don't count them, would I not breathe?' That later became my Breathing Piece. And those events that I was doing in New York were very much connected with necessity."

This sense of disappearing, flying away, flames going out, suggests what David Cooper writes about in his brilliant and disturbing *The Death of the Family,* the effort *not* to see oneself anymore, "to see through oneself as a person limited to relative being . . . Few people can sustain this nonrelative self-regard for more than one minute or two without feeling that they are going mad in the sense of disappearing. That is why people use mirrors in order not to see their selves with the possibility of seeing through, but to see fragmentary manifestations like their hair, eye make-up, and so on. If one did not effect the evasive fragmentation of the mirror image, one would be left with the experience of knowing that seeing oneself means seeing through oneself. There can be nothing more terrifying than that."

"Draw a line with yourself," Yoko writes in her Line Piece. "Go on drawing until you disappear." Many of these "pieces" are printed in *Grapefruit* (Simon and Schuster)—compositions of "Music, Painting, Event, Poetry, and Object"—in which the idea of dismembering and disrobing is seminal. Thus in one of her Events, Yoko asks each participant to cut off a piece of her dress until she is naked. And one remembers John and Yoko naked on the cover of *Two Virgins* and in their two *Self-Portrait* films. Yoko once wrote: "People went on cutting the parts they do not like of me finally there was only the stone remained of me that was in me but they were still not satisfied and wanted to know what it's like in the stone." The point is that the act of taking off one's clothes is merely a metaphor for the uncovering of the self.

And what does it mean to be "naked"? The American sociologist Erving Goffman writes: "The self is not an organic thing that has a specific location, whose fundamental fate is to be born, to mature, to die; it is a dramatic effect arising diffusely from a scene that is presented." And Yoko finally existed in her "scene" by means of a fantastic humor, by transforming her obsessions, memories, and ideas into her special art, and thus realizing herself in her work. "*Grapefruit* was like a cure for myself without knowing it. It was like saying, 'Please accept me, I am mad.' Those instructions are like that—a real need to do something to act out your madness. As long as you are behaving properly, you don't realize your madness and you go crazy." She was accepted also by someone who once sang: "I am he as you are he as you are me as we are all together."

Yoko once wrote: "After unblocking one's mind, by dispensing with visual, auditory, and kinetic perceptions, what will come out of us? Would there be anything? I wonder. And my Events are mostly spent in wonderment."

Before they are anything else, Yoko's poems, events, films, and music exemplify a wonderment which, in some accepted way, suggests childlike awe, a way of seeing things as if you were entering a strange street, invisible until now, for the first time; or as if, for example, you were watching a Western—the sheriff, rustlers, corral fights—through the eyes of one of the horses. More than that, wonderment implies intensity of perception resulting in one's identification with what is seen, not as the "utterly other," but as the utterly same. Thus the inescapable modality of the visible becomes the numinous. And eventually, through hyperesthesia, the perceived object or person disintegrates, for when you see something at this level of clarity, it disappears, and you find yourself asking, what really is there? ("Not the same thing a bit!" said the Hatter. "You might just as well say that 'I see what I eat' is the same as 'I eat what I see'.")

David Cooper writes: "To commence the unuse of the word 'neurosis,' let us regard it as a way of being that is made to seem childish by one's fear of others about one's becoming childlike. . . . The fear is the fear of madness, of being childlike or even being before-one's-origins, so that any act may cohere others against oneself to suppress any spontaneous gesture that has socially disruptive, archaic resonances."

The childlike gestures and awarenesses reveal themselves in Yoko's ways of seeing everything: "An intensity of a wink is: two cars smashed head on./A storm turned into a breeze./A water drop from a loose faucet" ("Wink Talk"). And in her "Touch Poem," Yoko writes: "Give birth to a child/See the world through its eye/Let it touch everything possible/and leave its fingermark there/in place of a signature."

"Sometimes," Yoko says, "I think that some of the things I've done could have been done by John, and vice versa." Together they have collaborated on a number of lovely films (distributed in the US by Film Makers' Cooperative) which, among other things, seem to be about seeing things as if for the first time—the "love that has no past."

Two Virgins shows both of their faces superimposed, separating and merging, revealing love to be the interpenetration of anima and animus; and this scene is followed by a slow motion kiss of the lovers limned against the sky. "When we met," Yoko recalls, "we were so involved with each other that we couldn't see anybody around us. We were just looking at each other and sometimes noticed that people were around us. We didn't have time or space to consider what we looked like to others. We were really in a dream."

Apotheosis is filmed by a camera floating gently upwards in a balloon, rising above a snowy English village, the sounds of dogs barking carried up by the snow fading into the sounds of the wind, as the camera watches the white radiant particles of clouds vibrating on the screen—and then suddenly looks up to the sun.

Up Your Legs Forever, made in New York in one day, shows three hundred thirty-one pairs of legs (those of New York artists, friends of John's and Yoko's, and their friends, all legs donated for one dollar and Peace) shot from the toes up to the thigh. The film forces you to see how different one leg is from its partner and how leg dimples, moles, and scratches suggest idiosyncratic leg personalities, while at the same time the movie exorcises almost anyone's fetishist leg fantasy forever. "When we're counted as legs," Yoko says, "we're very ordinary. We wanted to show we have peaceful legs. And legs are peaceful."

Rape wonders what would happen if a person were followed by a camera to distraction. The camera tracks a German girl through a cemetery, down London streets, into a flat where she runs around screaming "Why me?" At the Elgin Theater, the audience not only waited angrily for the "real" rape, which never came, but also felt raped by the film's progression as they screamed and called for help, hoping the projector would break down.

Number Five has John smiling for one hour. His smile was shot with a high speed camera (20,000 frames per minute) often used to film rockets. A three-minute smile was then slowed down to its present length. "It originally started out," John says, "that Yoko wanted a million people all over the world to to send in a snapshot of themselves smiling, and then it got down to lots of people smiling, and then maybe one or two and then me smiling as a symbol of today smiling. And so it's me smiling, and that's the hang-up, of course, because it's me again. But I mean they've got to see it someday—it's only me. The idea of the film won't be dug for another fifty or a hundred years probably. That's what it's all about. I just happen to be that face."

The Fly, John's and Yoko's most recent film made in New York in two days, shows a naked woman lying motionless on her back as one fly at a time settles on different parts of her body to go about its business—mainly legs tasting and feeling. Some of the flies were stunned with CO^2, having failed to keep calm on sugar water. The woman's catatonia remains a mystery.

It's as if Walt Disney and Jean-Marie Straub had collaborated, for the film's magnified focus on what a fly does if you don't brush it off is shot in long takes with the camera obliquely observing the transformed landscape of a mountainous breast, a hillock nipple, or a desert of fingers on which a fly stands, legs investigating the scene.

At the film's conclusion, you see a long shot of the entire body, seven flies standing here and there, as if on a dead Christ. And this amazing Bunuellian shot implies the idea of the fly as a metaphor for pain. The flies finally fly away, and we're left with a shot through the window of a New York Bowery roof, veiled in a diaphanous blue light like St. Elmo's fire, suggesting the beauty of seeing things anew.

"The idea of the film came to me," Yoko says, "when I thought about that joke where someone says to a man: 'Did you notice that woman's hat?' and he's looking at her bosom instead. I wondered how many people would look at the fly or at the body. I tried when filming to accept all the things that showed up, but at the same time tried not to make the film too dramatic. It would have been very easy for me to have made it become pornographic, and I didn't want that. Each shot had to project more than a pretty image of a body, so it was used more as an abstract line."

Yoko's voice on *The Fly's* soundtrack is a subtle rhythmic embodiment of the Fly's excursions—intersected by John's forward and backward guitar track. And these amazing sounds reveal again those childlike gestures and archaic resonances. For it is most obviously in what John calls her "sixteen-track voice" that Yoko displays her extraordinary art. It is the true distillation of her *sens plus pur,* a kind of psychophysical instrument of amazing disparateness, richness, and range. Yoko's voice is a kind of vocal tachystoscope (the shuttered magic lantern that projects images for a thousandth of a second), immediately and almost subliminally communicating glittering movements of the smallest elements of sound, reminding you of the screams, wails, laughter, groans, caterwauls of both a primordial, pre-birth, premammalian past, as well as of the fogged-over, pained immedicacy of childhood.

Musically, what happens is that nasals, fricatives, registral variants, pitch inflections, and varying timbres all combine, interpolate, and permute to convey the impression of anything from a Japanese *shakuhachi* to bantams in pine woods to swamp animals' madrigals to the feeling of being inside of one's own body cavities. Yoko's voice enters sound to reveal its most basic frequential characteristics and proposes to the listener that if he wants to hear, he might as well stop trying. "She becomes her voice," John says, "and you get touched."

This vocal quality can be heard most powerfully on "Don't Worry Kyoko (Mummy's only looking for her hand in the snow)," the soundtrack for *The Fly,* and her new album on which Yoko is supported by John on guitar, Klaus Voorman on bass, Ringo on drums; and, on "AOS" by Charles Haden, David Izenzon, Ed Blackwell, and Ornette Coleman. Yoko thus brings together and combines the best elements of rock, recent jazz tone roads, and avant-garde musical materials, using them to sustain her adventurous realizations.

With the exceptions of "Paper Shoes" and "Greenfield Morning"—which Yoko constructed from one or two lines and then edited, reassembled, and added some overdubbing—all the songs in the album are performed and recorded live, most in one session without, it's hard to believe, any voice transformation except for the slightest of echoes.

"First of all," Yoko explains, "John and I were going to make individual LPs, and John started his session first. When he was recording, I was in the control room. Sometimes he had to fool around with his instrument just to get inspired or to get into his music, and I'd be thinking, well, he should be doing his song, not fooling about—that's the feeling you get in the control room—but he just kept jamming and then suddenly I realized how beautiful the jamming was. He started something very unusual with the guitar like (high-pitched call). So I couldn't help it, I had to join them. John had said: 'Whenever you feel like joining, join us, and all I have to say is no if I don't want it.' In 'Why,' he inspired me, and I jumped into the room. John sang 'Eyugheyugh!' He was trying to tell me to get in and join them, and I just joined in. I liked the idea of improvisation, going somewhere you don't know, just having something vague planned, like doing something that's slow or quiet and the rest of it decided by the wind or whatever. So I went in and started to scream, and then John's guitar was going along frantic. And I realized that John and I have a very mean streak, it was similar in that sense. There's something about us that's saying: 'Fuck you, I couldn't care less', and I go mad with my voice and John does it with his guitar. Both of us have that side."

"I have that side," John says, "but it's hard to get it on a two-minute single with a technician like George sitting around."

"You see," Yoko continues, "it became a dialogue, we stimulated each other. You don't know who inspired whom, it just goes on. Klaus told me later that he'd realized that I knew about rhythm perfectly, it was right on spot. Of course I knew. In Toronto, Klaus and Ringo were pretty silent about what I was doing, but this time they got really turned on.

"When I say things I stutter a little bit. Most of us kill off our real emotions, and on top of them you have your smooth self. It's like the guy in the film *Diary of a Mad Housewife* with his sing-song voice. There's that unreal tone. But when I want to say 'I'm sorry' in a song—because music to me is something so honest and so real—I don't feel like saying (sing-song) 'I'm sorry, mother,' but rather as an emotion should be (groaning, stuttering) 'I'm so-or-orrrry.' A stutterer is someone who's feeling something genuine. So in 'Paper Shoes' I say: 'Pa-pa-pa-a-aper sh-shooooooes!'

"The older you get the more frustrated you feel. And it gets to a point where you don't have time to utter a lot of intellectual bullshit. If you were drowning you wouldn't say: 'I'd like to be helped because I have just a moment to live.' You'd say, 'Help!' but if you were more desperate you'd say, 'Eioughhhhhh,' or something like that. And the desperation of life is really life itself, the core of life, what's really driving us forth. When you're really desperate it's phony to use descriptive and decorative adjectives to express yourself."

But isn't there another side, such as the seeming gentleness of "Who Has Seen the Wind?"—the quiet little song Yoko presents on the B side of John's "Instant Karma"?

"On that song," Yoko says, "the voice is wavering a little, there are shrills and cracks, it's not professional pop singing, the background is going off a little. There was something of a lost little girl about it. What I was aiming at was the effect you get in Alban Berg's *Wozzeck,* where the drunkard sings, a slightly crazed voice, a bit of a broken toy. In that sense it was a quiet desperation."

Religion is what you do with your aloneness, a philosopher once said. Or with your pain and desperation, one could add. Yoko's music pushes pain into a kind of invigorating and liberated energy, just as a stutterer finally gives birth to a difficult word, since it existed originally at the fine edge between inaudibility and the sound waves of dreams. About her music for *The Fly,* she says, "It's nice to go into that very very fine intricate mixture of sounds and rhythm. It's almost like going into a dream, getting something that doesn't exist in the physical world, unutterable sounds—a kind of metaphysical rhythm."

What Yoko calls "metaphysical sound" seems at first to be the true opposition of her recent unblocked music. Yet it is less an opposition than the idea of the dream of sound from which her new art emerges, a music which Max Picard tells us is "silence, which in dreaming begins to sound."

Yoko's "Music of the Mind"—e.g., "Peel. Peek. Take off." ("Pieces for Orchestra," 1962)—came to fruition in the winter of 1960. She rented a loft on Chambers Street in New York. "All the windows were smoked glass so that you couldn't really see outside, but there was the skylight, and when you were in the loft you almost felt more connected to the sky than to the city outside. It was a cold water flat, $50.50, and it was great. I didn't have chairs or or beds, and so people downstairs gave me orange crates and I put all the crates together to make a large table, crates for the chairs, and at night I just collected them and made a bed out of them. And I started to live there.

"A friend of mine told me that there was a group of artists who were thinking of putting on their works and would I mind if they joined me and did things together. And I said, no, I wouldn't mind, and perhaps they wouldn't mind painting my loft for free. But everyone was lazy and didn't get around to painting it white, but I got used to the grey."

The famous Chambers Street loft concerts featured artists, musicians, poets—a list of whose names reads like a roster of the avant garde hall of fame: Ray Johnson, Walter De Maria, Joseph Byrd, Alansen, LaMonte Young, Jackson MacLow, Iris Levak, George Maciunas, Phillip Corner, George Brecht, Diane Wakoski, Simone Morris, Yvonne Rainer, Terry Jennings, Bob Morris, enry Flynt, David Tudor, and Richard Maxfield.

"But there was no mention that I should have a concert there, and I wasn't going to be the one to mention it," Yoko says. "Somehow my work was still suffering. The idea had been to stop my suffering by getting a place to present my work and at last letting everybody know what I was doing. But it just went on like that. Many people thought that I was a very rich girl who was just 'playing avant-garde.' And some others thought that I was a mistress of some very rich man, which wasn't true either. I think that the reason that some people thought the whole thing was organized by some Chinese man was because La Monte's name is Young. And meanwhile I was just surviving by teaching Japanese folk art."

Within the next couple of years, Yoko had concerts featuring her own work at the Village Gate, the Bridge Theater, and Carnegie Recital Hall, Her first art exhibition took place at the Agnus Gallery, owned by Fluxus originator George Maciunas. And among the instruction paintings there were: "Painting for the Wind," which featured a bag full of seeds hanging in front of a blank canvas, and when the wind blew, seeds would fall out through the bag's small holes; "Smoke Painting," where you lit a match and watched the smoke against the canvas; and "Painting to Be Stepped On," where you stepped on the canvas and made a mark until many marks made up the painting. It was this element of participation, of adding things, of watching things grow and change that enabled you to see Yoko's instructions as a way of "getting together, as in a chain letter." And following this exhibition, Yoko's lecture-concert at Wesleyan College, events in Japan, exhibitions in London like the one on 1966 at the Indica Gallery where she met John, all created a growing interest in her work and an equal amount of incomprehension.

And it was Yoko's and John's extensions of the idea of participating, the "additional act" that would suggest to others how reciprocally to involve *themselves,* that led to the famous Peace events, filmed and reported on many times—the Bed-Ins, the "War is Over" poster that appeared in hundreds of newspapers around the world, and the sending of acorns to world leaders, who were invited by John and Yoko to plant them and watch them grow.

Yoko's first important concert took place at the end of 1961 at Carnegie Recital Hall. "It was a big moment for me," Yoko recalls. "George Brecht, Jonas Mekas, LaMonte Young, Jackson MacLow, just about everyone performed in it. And Richard Maxfield helped me on the electronic side. I set up everything and then made the stage very dim, so you had to strain your eyes—because life is like that. You always have to strain to read other people's minds. And then it went into complete darkness. The week before I had given instructions to everyone as to what they should do, so that there would be a feeling of togetherness but a togetherness based on alienation, since no one knew the other person's instructions.

"So everybody was moving without making any sounds on stage. There was a point where two men were tied up together with lots of empty cans and bottles around them, and they had to move from one end of the stage to the other very quietly and slowly without making any sounds. What I was trying to attain was a sound that almost doesn't come out. I told you about stuttering. Actually I don't really stutter, but before I speak I stutter in my mind, and then my cultured self tries to correct that stutter into a clean sentence. And then it comes out like 'Oh, and how are you today?' instead of 'O-O-Oh-h-how are you?' But before it comes out like that you have this stuttering in you. And I wanted to deal with those sounds of people's fears and stutterings.

"So I thought that if everything was set up in a lighted room and suddenly the light was turned off, you might start to see things beyond the shapes. Or the kind of sounds that you hear in silence. You would start to feel the environment and tension and people's vibrations. Those were the sounds that I wanted to deal with, the sound of fear and of darkness, like a child's fear that someone is behind him, but he can't speak and communicate this. And so I asked one guy to stand behind the audience for the duration of the concert.

"I wanted the sound of people perspiring to be in it, too, so I had all the dancers wear contact microphones, and the instructions were to bring out very heavy boxes and take them back across stage, and while they were doing that they were perspiring a little. There was one guy who was asthmatic and it was fantastic. And in the toilet there was somebody standing throughout the evening. Whenever I go to a toilet in a film theater, I always feel very scared. If nobody's there I'm scared, but if somebody is there it's even more scary. So I wanted people to have this experience of fear. There are unknown areas of sound and experience that people can't really mention in words. Like the stuttering in your mind. I was interested not in the noise you make but the noise that happens when you try not to make it, just that tension going back and forth.

"I think I would never want to go back again to where I was, doing things like that, even though few people have touched this area. Where I'd be so lonely and miserable that nobody understood. And the kind of thing I'm doing now is more understandable. I'm not saying it's better or worse. But now I just want to feel sort of playful sometimes. And when I feel playful, to do something. That's when people seem to understand more or at least accept more.

"I'm starting to think that maybe I can live. Before it seemed impossible. I was just about at the vanishing point, and all my things were too conceptual. But John came in and said, 'All right, I understand you.' And just by saying that all those things which were supposed to vanish stayed.

"Around the time that I met John, I went to a palmist—John would probably laugh at this—and he said: 'You're like a very very fast wind that goes speeding around the world.' And I had a line that signified astral projection. The only thing I didn't have was a root. But, the palmist said, you've met a person who's fixed like a mountain, and if you get connected with that mountain you might get materialized. And John is like a frail wind, too, so he understands all of these aspects."

Instead of Yoko's self disappearing, she now disappears more into her self. "Everybody wants to be invisible," John says. "Yoko just expresses it."

"When the mouth speaks it is as if not the mouth itself but the silence behind it were pressing it into speech," writes Max Picard. "The silence is so full that it would drive the face upwards if it could not relax and release itself in language. It is as though silence itself were whispering words to the mouth. . . . In silence the lines of the mouth are like the closed wings of a butterfly. When the word starts moving, the wings open, and the butterfly flies away."

1971

4
Film

The opening series of short reviews appeared in *Sunday Ramparts*—the bi-weekly San Francisco newspaper that was conceived in 1966 as a kind of combined *Manchester Guardian-Village Voice* offspring of *Ramparts* magazine. *Sunday Ramparts* had a short life (about 15 issues), and the film reviews I wrote for the newspaper appeared between January and May in 1967. Concluding this film journal is a quasi-"wrap up" of the year's films; this article appeared in the then four-month-old *Rolling Stone* magazine, as did the seven reviews which follow. The penultimate essay—a review of *Let It Be*—was co-authored with David Dalton and is an outgrowth of a text David and I had written for a book about the making of *Let It Be* which was included in the British *Let It Be* album. The final essay on *A Hard Day's Night* was first published in *Ramparts* magazine in 1965.

Film Journal: 1967

Blow Up

Blow-Up is not about: mod London, modern Society, pot, rock, high fashion, voyeurism, murder, orgies. Its plot, which every reviewer has related and refashioned, merely attends to actualizing an exquisite parable about the uses of art and the possibilities of the existence of reality.

The hero photographer (David Hemmings) asks a group of fashion models to close their eyes, as we hear "Did You Ever Have to Make Up Your Mind" on the sound track. At a London pot party, the fashion model Verushka tells the photographer, who thinks that she has gone to Paris, that she *is* in Paris. (This scene is only acceptable thematically, since it's a silly depiction of a pot party). The girl in the antique store says she wants to go to Nepal, maybe Morocco. The first two propositions are: *Pick up on one and leave the other behind* and *Right you are if you think you are.*

David Hemmings photographs an old man and a young woman (Vanessa Redgrave) in the park. The man disappears, the woman demands the film. The photographs' shadows and lights suggest a corpse under a tree and a possible murderer veiled in the bushes. The photographer returns to the park, locates the corpse and, in a brilliant cinematic moment, looks directly up at the tree's leaves; but, as the camera diagonally descends to the photographer's face, we realize that it was actually through the corpse's open eyes that we were looking at the trembling leaves. Later on in the film, the photographer witnesses an artist friend and the latter's mistress (Sarah Miles) making love, and one sees merely her eyes staring, like those of the dead man's, emptily into space.

The photographs and negatives are stolen, the corpse disappears. Only the one suggestive photograph remains—an abstract art photo, corresponding to the artist-friend's latest abstract painting. The photograph (the movie) and the painting are composed of dots. And the blow-up is not the murder but the enlargement of formerly compressed chromosomatic specks.

Proposition 3: *What is dead does not exist.* The dead man

does not exist in any form or reality whatsoever.

Proposition 4: *Making love imitates the state of death.* One's eyes (material perceptions) are totally open and totally insensate. The photographer symbolically makes love to Verushka while shooting her picture (a profound ideogram) and then falls, as if sexually exhausted, back on a couch.

Proposition 5: *Art is a form of making love which imitates the state of death,* because in all of Antonioni's films, intercourse leads one not only to a realization of one's deathly isolation but also to the mere material world, not to Antonioni's quasi-Platonic world of Ideal Color, Singleness, and Grace. As Montaigne wrote: "Art destroys nature and removes man from grace." Axiom: *Art imitates the state of death.*

In Antonioni's previous color film, *Red Desert,* colors are emblems of a forgotten world of Color, in which, paradoxically, colors in relation to each other do not exist. That is why the colors in the fairy tale beach scene seem low-keyed—"natural"—as opposed to the colors of Monica Vitti's world of "reality" which are accentuated and over-perceived, just in order to reveal to us exactly how far removed men are from the state of natural grace. (Ironically, the little girl in *Red Desert* sees sand dunes suggesting the forms of human bodies. The state of grace is disrupted once the "other" impinges on one's world—that is to say, as soon as "reality" is perceived.") In *Red Desert,* Antonioni uses color to negate color. The logic is that of the *Diamond Sutra;* the image that of Christ: in a state of immanence, color is its own perception.

Once colors are differentiated, *Life imitates the state of death.* The first sequence of *Blow-Up* juxtaposes masked revelers and derelicts. The former make reality out of what doesn't exist and the latter are the hopeless victims of the reality which insists both they and it exist. When the photographer receives an anonymous phone call, he negates the identity of the caller (my wife, my mistress, my girl friend, nobody, it feels as if I had kids) just after Vanessa Redgrave refuses the photographer's invitation to speak to his "wife" with a "Why should I speak to her?" Her feeling being that of, of course there is someone there to speak to. But none of the characters in *Blow-Up* have any names. So it is appropriate that the photographer, at the conclusion of the film—just after he has thrown the "imaginary" tennis ball back to the revelers—disintegrates and disappears.

Proposition 7: *Life does not exist.* Illogically something comes from nothing. *Blow-Up* is Antonioni's seventh, not last, film.

MADEMOISELLE

Except for his own beautiful *Chant d'Amour,* Jean Genet has been treated badly in films. I gather he had nothing to do with the American film versions of *The Balcony* and *Deathwatch,* but he did write the screenplay for *Mademoiselle,* the film directed by Tony Richardson and starring Jeanne Moreau.

Mademoiselle is a failure in almost all ways. Jeanne Moreau plays a Lamia Woman (a spinster schoolteacher) who floods, burns, and poisons the husbandry of a provincial French town in order to frame, out of frustrated passion, a handsome Italian woodcutter. The woodcutter (acted poorly by Ettore Skinner) had arrived in town with his son, only to find himself desired by the local wives and hated by the men.

He straps a snake instead of a belt around his pants; and against this idea of virility, Genet presents the frustrated impotence of the townsmen. These men beat the woodcutter to death after he and Mademoiselle apparently make it in one of the most sedulously sagging *Weltschmerz* love scenes I've ever seen. One compares it to the extraordinarily filmed love encounters in Resnais' *The War Is Over* or *Chant d'Amour,* or even those in the fourth-rate *Dear John,* and finds it difficult to accept the fact that this great writer on love could have participated in such an unaffecting film.

In novels like *Our Lady of the Flowers* and *Miracle of the Rose,* Genet reveals an understanding of how it feels to be female in such radical and moving ways that one forgets that the "object" women in Genet's works (except in the most recent play, *The Screens*) are usually madams, whores, or nuns. Fontevrault prison, where the "nocturnal mysteries" of *Miracle of the Rose* occur, was at one time an abbey: "At Fontevrault," Genet writes, "the amorous nuns and sisters of God came to life again in the form of pimps and crashers." And in *The Thief's Journal,* it is a decrepit, fish-faced lady thief whom Genet likes to think of as his mother.

The idea of Woman as a kind of Evil Demiurge is not worth Genet's, your, or my time. Lautréamont thought that he was going to get sucked into the vulva of the earth, but seductive fantasy simply becomes idiot psychology when it is presented to us as an actualized dramatic portrayal of Woman, let alone of any particular mademoiselle. One has only to think of the complexity of feeling and the extraordinarily sympathetic understanding involved in the creation of the female roles in such films as Carl Dreyer's *Gertrud* to regret Genet's self-indulgence.

Jeanne Moreau's Mademoiselle is a bad performance. Her unvarying sexuality-gone-sour pout, her methodical changing of shoes and hair styles, her taping adhesive cross-wise across her nipples—all these actions are manifestations, of course, of an unconvincing role; but one fears that she is now in fact taking the La Moreau institution seriously—repeating the cliché gestures of her past great roles in *Les Liaisons Dangereuses, La Notte, The Lovers, Diary of a Chambermaid, Jules and Jim.*

Her "secret wound" and the qualities of her purveyed mystique—self-will, bitchiness, pain—are no longer so easy to identify with. Antonioni, Vadim, and Truffaut, for example, located her mode of expression in brilliantly unified and exploratory psychological frameworks. Tony Richardson merely has her playing herself feeling very evil.

About *Mademoiselle*, Richardson has said, "I am trying to make of it a simple, formal, tragic film." He should have been the last director to make Genet's film. He is temperamentally and technically very distant from Genet's sempiternal world of "internal astronomy."

Kenneth Anger on Lucifer Rising

The following are remarks Kenneth Anger made to Tom Luddy and myself in an interview two weeks ago. I have rearranged the transcription into an essay format. —*Jonathan Cott*

The film *Lucifer Rising* is my answer to *Scorpio Rising*—which was a death mirror held up to American Culture. And for my own sake I had to make an answer to it even though I still see plenty of thanatic elements at work in America. It's a film about the Love generation, but seen in depth—like in the fourth dimension. And I call it a love vision, and it's about love—the violence as well as the tenderness . . .

I began shooting with the spring equinox. I'm type casting in my film, and one thing I've found is that since my film is about demons—but love demons—I have to work fairly fast because they tend to come and go, like gypsies . . .

A demon is just a convenient way of labeling a force, and the demons I'm working with in *Lucifer* are what I and magicians call "elementals"—in other words, these are individuals, they have three dimensions, but their main driving force is demonic. They answer another call . . .

I did an invocation of Alleister Crowley's—"The Invocation of the Bornless One"—I did it in Golden Gate Park at dawn, and this was the time of the autumn equinox of last year and as I finished it, the demon appeared in a flash of blue light. Now the flash of blue light was a ray of sunlight hitting a locket made of a butterfly wing around the neck of an escapee from Napa, and I had this demon named Joe under my control for three days before he split, leaving his boots behind. And during the three days while Joe was my guest, he told me a great deal that will appear in *Lucifer.* But since he had on the back of his jacket a picture of a demon—he had drawn it himself, a torso with two heads, one male and one female—I asked him what this was and he said, "Well, I'm a man in a woman's orbit." He had developed this theory about "orbitism"—his own ideas about Karma, reincarnation, and this is from someone who is completely unlettered—he was a merchant seaman who flipped out—half-Irish, half-Syrian, 23 years old. But he disappeared. He said he'd been sent by Lucifer. And while he was with me, I signed a contract in blood with Lucifer, and Joe disappeared with it. In other words, he behaved exactly the way demons do in medieval books and I've met others since. The problem is to zap them and film them before they get away . . .

We magicians feel that LSD is like a booster rocket. What's going on right now is like storming the astral plane. There's an invisible war going on. It's of Miltonic proportions and it's a war between the forces of life and death, love and hate. The film *Lucifer Rising* is a prophecy. And I see the embodiment of love among the children as winning. Lucifer, the hero of the film, is actually a sunshine child—Little Sunshine . . .

A child's universe is totally magical until this is murdered by society. And such things as the public school system in California are murderers of the imagination and the magic essence of children. A child can quite freely express himself in painting and different forms until a great inhibition falls over him when he's put in the social group. I don't regret at all the passing of Walt Disney because we magicians always considered him the Hitler of children and a destroyer of the true child's imagination.

There is a child in California who is in an institution for the care of so-called retarded children who has a genius I.Q. and has never seen another child. He's cared for by nurses and doctors in a special room because the child is a perfect Cyclops—it has perfect features, it is absolutely beautiful, and it has one eye in the center of its forehead. It has the third eye. And the child is a prisoner for no reason other than it's a mutant, it's different from other boys and girls. But we expect to see more of this sort of thing. In a sense, not completely literally, first we see the hair growing out, then we see the horns starting to sprout, and finally the wings . . .

I see something psychically happening to the youth all over the world. To us, the Red Guards overturning the birthplace of Confucius is just another reflection on a global plane of the riots on Sunset Strip and the mill-ins in the Haight-Ashbury, because the kids are just wearing slightly different costumes. But the thing that is pushing them is an irrational force in both cases. That's why Mao has literally got a tiger by the tail. It's just the beginning of something here in America . . .

Lucifer Rising is the first breaking of the dawn of the new pagan era. *Lucifer Rising* lives in sunlight. He's a lion man-woman/boy-girl child/angel-demon/he-she/god-goddess.

Cinema '67

One might be surprised to realize that both *Blow Up* and *Bonnie and Clyde* share the same audiences. Yet Antonioni's film is a perfectly sustained disquisition into the possibility of the existence of reality, while Penn's return to the gangster genre is actually an attempt to recover a reality which is felt palpably to exist and one which audiences need to have torn apart for them.

But, of course, Penn sees the mother-daughter reunion scene in Bonnie and Clyde as a hallucination of reality—his filtering over-dramatically suggests what the film supposes: that social realities are always dreams. Dreamt by whom? Lewis Carroll and Antonioni look for the Maker, or rather dissolve what people think has been made. Thus in *Blow Up,* the Yardbirds destroy their instruments, breaking down what the photographer tries to re-create, leaving behind only that useless guitar finger board The Who and Jimi Hendrix explode their instruments in their "real" appearances, but this has to do with the idea, that, as Blake modestly phrased it, "Exuberance is Beauty." To Antonioni, raving-up is creation dissolving to chaos. Thus rock and roll is a metaphor for reality as well as for art.

In *Don't Look Back,* Bob Dylan talks to belligerent questioners as if to ask "Who are you?" When he walks onto the stage of Royal Albert Hall, he sees a pretty girl sitting alone and says something like, "At last, a bit of reality." And in the train ride through English industrial towns, charred houses slipping past the window, Dylan just buries his head in his hands—too tired, too many persons buzzing around, too much *thereness.*

Dylan's sense of what is and isn't there is so fine and painful because he knows that one starts from one's own skin. A friend told me a (probably apocryphal) story of Dylan sitting in a New York City cafe seven or eight years ago crying about the destruction of the world—"You were my world"—and it's still the world—Memphis, Mobile, Mexico, and those other names which one calls places, places one is never at when one thinks of them somewhere else. As the Vishvasara Tantra says: "What is here, is elsewhere. What is not here, is nowhere." Social reality can exist, in the sense of an anthropologist's definition: "That movement of all, the living aspect, the fleeting instant in which society becomes or in which men become, sentimentally conscious of themselves or of their situation vis-à-vis others." A draft-resisting activist in London talks of the United States as one giant mind which has to be blown: the state as Consciousness. This sweet American idea reveals itself in films. Jean Renoir's pre-war *The Rules of the Game* is of course about social reality—as defined above. But it's specifically about the persons in it—the Jewish aristocrat, the naive Austrian wife, the game warden, *et al*—persons conscious of their social roles. Recent American films insist on coming across as mythic events.

Thus *The Wild Angels* and *Harper* use the L.A. ambience as an allegorical landscape to depict nothing less than The Decline of the West. Paul Newman's Harper drives a beat-up Porsche as he tries to hold on to the basic American Ideals in the face of religious fanatics, gangsters, junkies, frustrated wives, and girls named Miranda. *The Wild Angels* tells of an anti-Christ angel who rises from the dead with a joint in his mouth. *Cool Hand Luke* becomes a Sisyphus-Job figure in spite of himself.

In this kind of situation, when places are taken for the world or a state of mind, people start turning to *Bonnie and Clyde, In the Heat of the Night* (the wonderful Ray Charles song is heard over a lovely aerial shot of a cotton plantation looking as it probably did in 1810), and "Ode to Billie Joe." One would think that nuclear families and southern agrarianism were going enterprises. (Just think about the similarities between "Billie Joe" and "I Am a Walrus.") But then people see *Festival* or Dylan's film to experience how reality can be used or lifted up to create something more beautiful—like Degas' dancers sweating behind the curtain and then appearing gracefully poised before you. Obviously rock should offer the film maker a way of seeing things physically alive, as in the dance scene in *The Easy Life,* or, best of all, should work formally to intensify and enlarge the meanings of a film, as in *Scorpio Rising* or Warren Sonbert's *Where Did Our Love Go?* The young film maker Alan Clark's excellent "psychedelic" realization of the Butterfield Band's *East-West* also shows what can be done with rock as a subject and object. The feature-length films that use rock still think of it as theme-song material, for these films' sense of "drama" cannot permit that sense of opening-up which documentary approaches to cinema, along with rock, allow.

How I Won the War capitalizes on John Lennon's presence

to draw in an audience not easily amused by an otherwise ponderous exercise in pseudo-Brechtian technique and British class system jokes: a bad unconscious imitation of Godard's wonderful *Les Carabiniers. The Family Way* is another anthropological survey of lower-middle-class English life—impotence trauma and heredity confusion—and Paul McCartney's musical score sentimentally tags the subject along. *You're a Big Boy Now* uses some real Lovin' Spoonful music and requires unbearable instrumental fill ins. This slick film features New York as a summer festival, pill popping in library stacks, adolescent crisis, and a sweet sexy performance by Elizabeth Hartman. *What's Up, Tiger Lily,* the previous Spoonful film, wastes a happy Sebastian score that would have been beautifully placed in a Cousteau underwater film. Listen to the album in this light.

The present "smash" of the London film scene is not Donovan's music for *Poor Cow*—another sociological drama—but Peter Whitehead's *Tonite Let's Make Love in London* (titled after a line by Allen Ginsberg)—featuring interviews with Michael Caine, Julie Christie, Lee Marvin, and Mick Jagger; dolly girls, Alan Aldridge painting up a naked model, and the Animals singing *When I Was Young* to film clips of World War I airplane maneuvers. Except for a slow motion sequence showing the Stones singing *Lady Jane* in concert as screaming girls float up on stage like a chrysalis opening up or a fish trying to shed its gills, a delightful interview with painter David Hockney, and a recording session with a misfortunately untalented "pop star" trying to record a "hit" as his producer looks on at him gangster-style as if to inform him of his certain elimination, *Tonite Let's* exploits certain styles of life to create its own unaffecting scene—corny psychedelic animation dance sequences, murky yellow filters for most of the interviews.

Until we find a happy successor to *Hard Day's Night, What's Happening* (the Maysles brothers' unreleased film of the Beatles' first tour to the U.S.), and *Don't Look Back,* we can only hope that groups supervise or make their own home movies and that a genius film maker like San Francisco's Jordan Belson will allow a film like *Re-Entry* to be shown often in order to expand the possibilities of real cinematic light shows.

1967

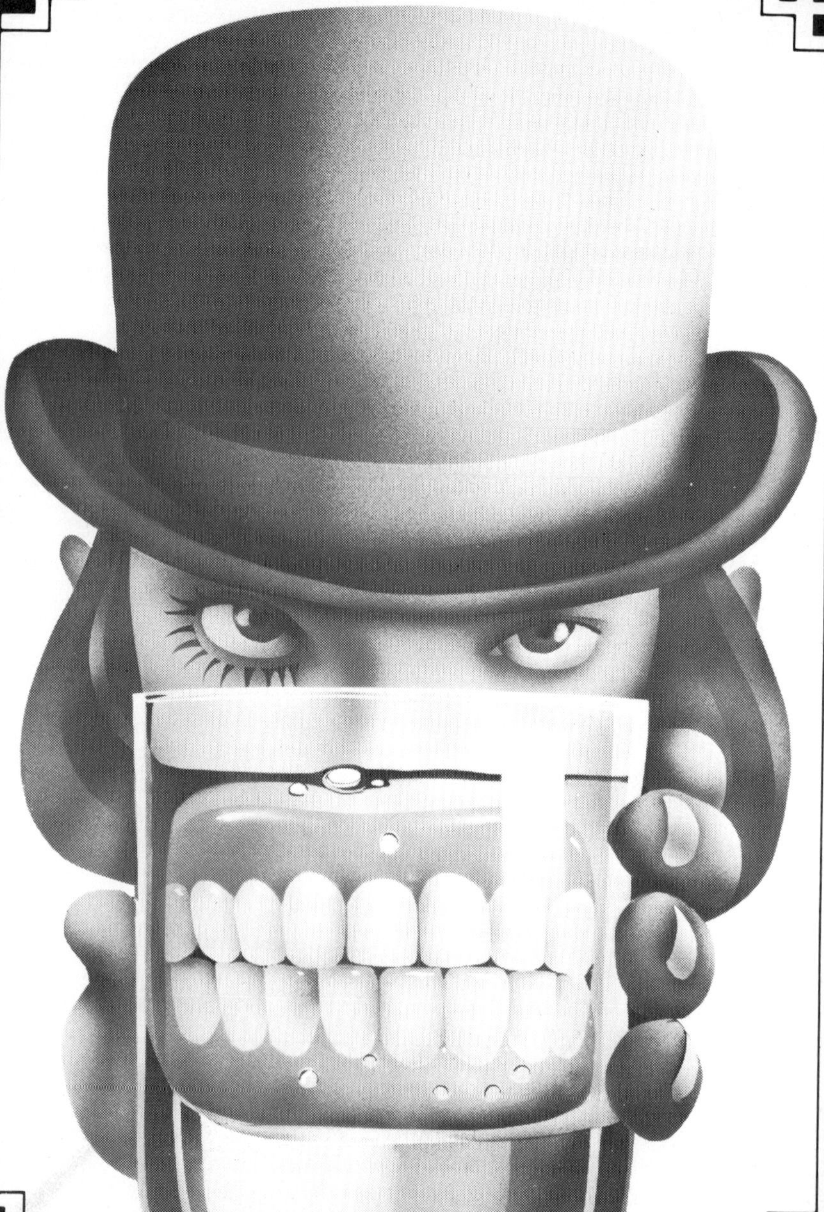

A Clockwork Orange

DIRECTED BY STANLEY KUBRICK

The Best Picture of the Year—if you judge by the noon-to-midnight queues around New York's Cinema I or the critical acclamations of the N.Y. Film Critics poll and almost every newspaper and magazine reviewer—is *A Clockwork Orange,* a mean-spirited film which suggests that in an alienating society self-willed acts of sexual violence and violent sexuality can manifest some kind of affirmation of human integrity.

This bogus idea is coated with futuristic scenery, Anthony Burgess' Nadsat dialect, and Moogsynthesized Ludwig Van. As with a medicinal cachet, Stanley Kubrick forces his "message" down by means of the sucker's plot. The formula is simple: show a situation through one character's eyes, allotting him some vague semblance of human passion, without ironically undermining that character's credibility (as Chabrol and Rohmer brilliantly do in *The Third Lover* and *La Collectionneuse,* respectively). In this manner you provoke the viewers to identify and sympathize with the hero or anti-hero (whether he be Peter Lorre in *M* or King Kong) by the mere fact of their having invested emotional energy in and enduring the hero's tribulations.

Alex (Malcolm McDowell) is a gang leader who goes about with his droogs bashing, stomping, raping, and killing. Betrayed by his pals after he crushes in a woman's head with a giant pop art phallus, our hero is sent to jail, submits to behaviorist "conditioning" by the State à la Skinner (The Ludovico Technique), and when released, gets immediately sick at any sign of his earlier pastimes. He's tormented by one of his former victims—an invalid writer whose wife Alex has raped and killed—who plays him the now abhorred Beethoven Ninth. After attempting suicide Alex is finally allowed to be "unconditioned," and he goes back to do his thing.

Imagine a movie presented from the point of view of an obsessed lepidopterist, desperately searching for butterflies on Park Avenue, who endures a similar series of experiences. The structural idea would be the same (totalitarian control vs.

vibrant human free will), but the results would be ludicrous, banal, and sentimental. Violence, of course, changes the picture into *A Clockwork Orange.* But what Kubrick does is simply to confuse the need for violence with the desire to attain a true sense of self in order to feel one's deepest being. Bashing an old wino has obviously nothing to do with self-liberation. But Kubrick tries to have it both ways: Alex's and his droogs' activities are also seen as "conditioned" by society's dehumani-ation against which smashing someone's balls and violent carnival rape are reactions.

But this explanatory game can be played forever. If the situation and its resulting consequences are despicable, why attempt, as Kubrick does, to attract sympathy for the hero? In interviews the director has compared Alex to Shakespeare's Richard III: "Alex, like Richard," Kubrick says, "is a character whom you should dislike and fear, and yet you find yourself drawn very quickly into his world and find yourself seeing things through his eyes. It's not easy to say how this is achieved, but it certainly has something to do with his candor and wit and intelligence, and the fact that all the other characters are lesser people, and in some way worse people."

This is nothing but a description of bad faith. Relating Alex to Richard III is like comparing the hoodlum mouse in Krazy Kat to the murderers and betrayers in Genet's extraordinary novels. There's hardly any depth in Alex's characterization, while the other persons, acting only as foils for the hero, are nothing but cartoon-strip caricatures.

The American director Sam Fuller has always been criticized for his depictions of "brutality" and for his reactionary politics. Fuller might have some stereotyped ideas about life, but by creating "typical" characters, then respecting their reality, and pushing them into extreme situations he transfigures them by revealing them in such a way that they achieve an intense personal integrity. (See *The Crimson Kimono* or *Shock Corridor,* for example.) By not even half-coloring in Alex's victims, Kubrick minimizes the hero's brutality and thereby defrauds the idea of personality.

Where Anthony Burgess aestheticized and sublimated this personality by means of his dazzling textural use of Nadsat dialogue—so that the language itself becomes the hero—Kubrick uses the dialect as just another decorative element—like the chintzy sexist milk bar—or as just one more super-annuated technical device—wide-angle shots. In *2001* Kubrick's beautifully visualized temporal dimensions provide the medium through which the rebirth and reemergence of consciousness occur after necessary ego destruction. In *A Clockwork Orange,* however, the director affects a "style" as gratuitous as his hero's sadistic acts: he "choreographs" the violence and thus romanticizes it—slow motion bashing, high speed orgy.

In terms of visual energy, however, Kubrick's attempts at "style" are unimaginative: compare them to the powerful murderous moments in say, Kurosawa's *Seven Samurai* or, especially, *Yojimbo,* in which Kurosawa's jolting comic style is wedded to the realization that what people fantasize to themselves—the frightful violent destruction whose brutal pleasure they shirk away from—occurs as actuality when the samurai Sanjuro draws the violence out of them by creating situations that ultimately explode in terror.

Asked about the relationship of *A Clockwork Orange* to contemporary violence, Kubrick is quoted as saying: "I don't think there's anything to be concerned about here. There is a very wide gulf between reality and fiction, and when one is looking at a film the experience is much closer to a dream than anything else. In this daydream, if you like, one can explore ideas and situations which one is not able to do in reality."

Which may be true, except that the distance between dream and reality is constantly shortening. Andre Breton said that the purest surrealistic act would be that of running down the street shooting people. This is already happening. Burgess' novel, written in 1962, extrapolates a future that of course reflects New York street gangs and London rockers. Alex's passion for Ludwig Van instead of some futuristic version of "Rip It Up," "He's a Rebel," or "Midnight Rambler" seems only like a miscalculated piece of outraged snobbery, a poor attempt to obtain spiritual force for the portrayal of one-dimensional evil.

Of course there are other approaches to violence, approaches defined by those who know the limited value of violent acts of frustration. Oppressed and colonialized peoples don't usually have the time or money to cultivate a mystique of violence. And it's not surprising that the most powerful depictions of extreme violence occur in narrative films like the Cuban *First Charge of the Machetes* and the Brazilian *Black God and the White Devil;* or that the most subtle analysis of social violence occurs in narrative-documentaries like the Argentinian *Hour of the Furnaces* and Makavejev's *WR—The Function of the Organism.* This last film, with all its confusions regarding Wilhelm Reich's teachings, attempts to confront in an inventive way those very issues—fascism, sexuality, sexism, and liberation—which Kubrick ultimately avoids, if not distorts.

"The destruction of evil," Kafka once said, "is a lunatic dream by which evil . . . is strengthened and its effect accelerated, because one overlooks its real nature and distorts reality into an illusion founded on one's own misleading wishes. . . . Life is as infinitely great and profound as the immensity of the stars above us. One can only look at it through the narrow keyhole of one's own personal existence. But through it one perceives more than one can see. So above all one must keep the keyhole clean."

1972

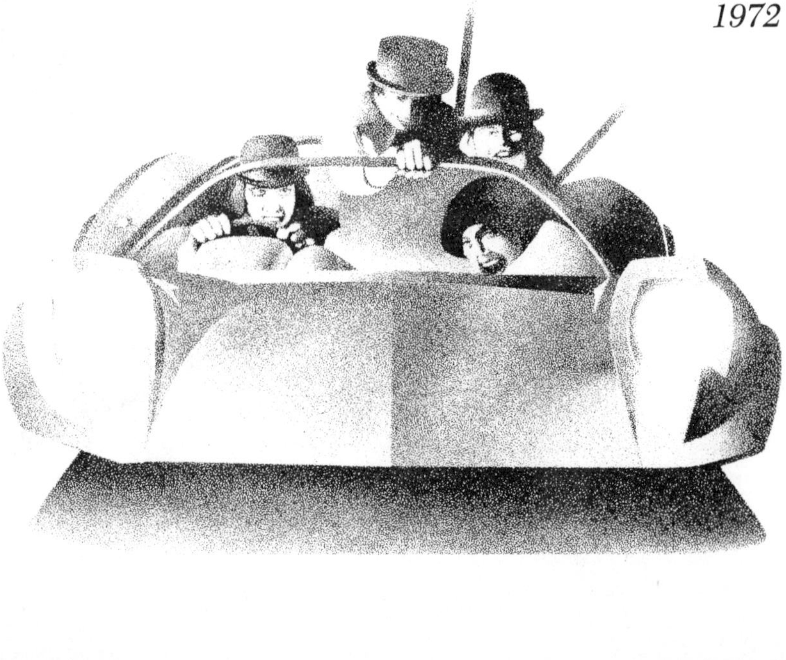

The Heartbreak Kid

DIRECTED BY ELAINE MAY

The Heartbreak Kid is the story of a *yenta,* a *shiksa,* and a *shmuck.* And out of these formidable ingredients Bruce Jay Friedman (who "conceived" it), Neil Simon (who "wrote" it), and Elaine May (who "directed" it) have produced an execrable piece of wiseacre farce that by means of interactional "gag" vignettes forces you to align and realign your sympathies with a bunch of sophomoric characters, while at the same time the film calculatingly amuses itself with what is by now the familiar cynical and self-exploiting attitudes of the Jewish love-hate syndrome. *The Heartbreak Kid* simply uses and manipulates the ethnic stereotypes and generalizations it seems to be mocking, thereby aesthetically feeding upon exactly what it detests.

In a series of quick-cut scenes, we first observe our sports equipment salesman hero Lenny (Charles Grodin) meeting Lila (Jeannie Berlin) in a New York singles bar: they go to bed, but she'd like to "wait" until after the wedding. Cut to Jewish wedding, close-ups of teary relatives, then a honeymoon drive to Miami Beach.

After Lenny and Lila make love at a motel, she demands that he rhapsodize about his undoubtedly blissful postcoital feelings ("Was it as wonderful as you expected? Was it worth waiting for?" she half-asks/affirms). If you haven't yet gotten the message that Lila is a pain, wait until you see her smear an egg salad sandwich all over her face at a diner as Lenny looks on with middle-class incredulity. Wait until she eagerly draws her husband's attention to sclerotic senior citizen "couples" at Miami Beach, intoning things like, "That's the way *we're* going to be in fifty years, Lenny!"

Poor Lenny. Poor Lenny? When Lila gets severely sunburned, our eager beaver hero gets infatuated with fatuous, Waspish, pretty Daddy's girl Kelly (Cybill Shepherd) from Minneapolis (though she could "pass" in La Jolla). "You're lying on my *spot,*" Kelly seductively and imperiously announces to Lenny on the beach as he fights the glare of the sun to see the glorious aura of her face.

Lenny courts her, lying to his bedridden wife at every turn, sets up a meeting with Kelly's agreeably characterless, smiling-zombie mother and stone-age, stoney-faced, patriarchal father (Eddy Albert), during which Lenny explains that although he's just gotten married, he knows he's made a terrible mistake, and he'll be right out to Minnesota just as soon as he's got everything settled, ready to ingratiate himself and make Kelly his wife.

Over dinner, as they wait for a greatly anticipated pecan pie, Lenny slowly breaks the news to a slow-to-catch-on but finally nauseated Lila. Poor Lila. Many persons think that at this moment she attains some kind of dignity in rejection, but as she disappears forever from the film, she remains an unalterably pathetic and ridiculous figure. (*The Heartbreak Kid* is so loaded against Lila that the compassionate National Society of Film Critics in an action of displaced generosity awarded Miss Berlin the Best Supporting Actress of the Year award.) And before you know it, there's Lenny out there in mid-winter Minneapolis, an outsider, alone, courageous, ready—as in a series of fairy tale ordeals—to overcome all obstacles blocking his path to a church wedding and the final embrace of the American Dream (as if he hadn't done that already).

The Heartbreak Kid is often pretty funny, as in the scene where Lenny impersonates a nark in order to scare off a bunch of Kelly's "jock" boyfriends; or in the scene where Kelly's father tries to buy Lenny off and get him to leave town. It's interesting that at this point in the film, the question of Lenny's New York Jewishness loses all motivating significance—except inasmuch as it suggests Lenny's socially amorphous and rootless personality. The humor derives from the fact that Kelly's father detests Lenny because he's finally confronted with someone whose *chutzpah* is as overpowering as his own.

But finally the film's comedy, which is meant to reveal the power of determination (Lenny) in its fight for exclusive and forbidden property (Kelly), serves as a weapon to put down Lila and everything she is supposed, as a caricature, to represent (New York-Miami middle-class Jewish vulgarity), while hardly insisting on a denigration of upper-class Kelly and Dad (seen respectively as merely pretty and self-absorbed, authoritarian and possessive). There is certainly no criticism of the social forces represented by Kelly's banker father whose sole function is to provide the major obstacle in Lenny's way.

At the film's conclusion, we see a wedding reception for our new couple at which Lenny, now in the world he thought he wanted, finds himself nostalgically singing the Burt Bacharach tune he once sang with Lila on their drive to Miami. Such is life, says the film, as Lenny takes on the self-reflective pose of Stendhal's Julien Sorel. It's a half-ironic, ultimately phoney ending—full of self-congratulatory remorse of conscience. But no other conclusion to this film would have been effective—either a happy marriage or a comic duplication of the Lila-Lenny experience.

For the more *The Heartbreak Kid* attempts to explore the theme of "honesty," the more dishonest it becomes. The structure of the film forces the characters' relationships to become merely functions of a story line, enabling the viewer to see Lila's miserable character as a justification for Lenny's rejection, and thereby allowing you to feel free to enjoy the hero's determined triumph over the forces of Wasp exclusivity.

In fact, Lenny's dishonesty—and the audience's sympathy for him—are both meant to increase as Lenny approaches his prize. When he talks at Kelly's father's dinner table about his love of ecology and "clean air," his cliches are supposed to seem not only humorously dishonest but also honestly humorous. And the relationship at this point between "humor" and "honesty" becomes so confused that you begin to realize it's only actor Charles Grodin who's doing a routine: it might just as well be Dustin Hoffman.

Ben Jonson let you laugh at Volpone's greed and hypocrisy without having to ennoble his character. Rather, the playwright ennobled his *audience's* character by means of a formal clarity and a profound sense of indignation. *The Heartbreak Kid,* however, panders to its viewers in all directions. And its basically derisive attitude—and the accompanying snickering laughter that that induces—allows for only the most superfluous and negligible kind of moral and social perception.

1972

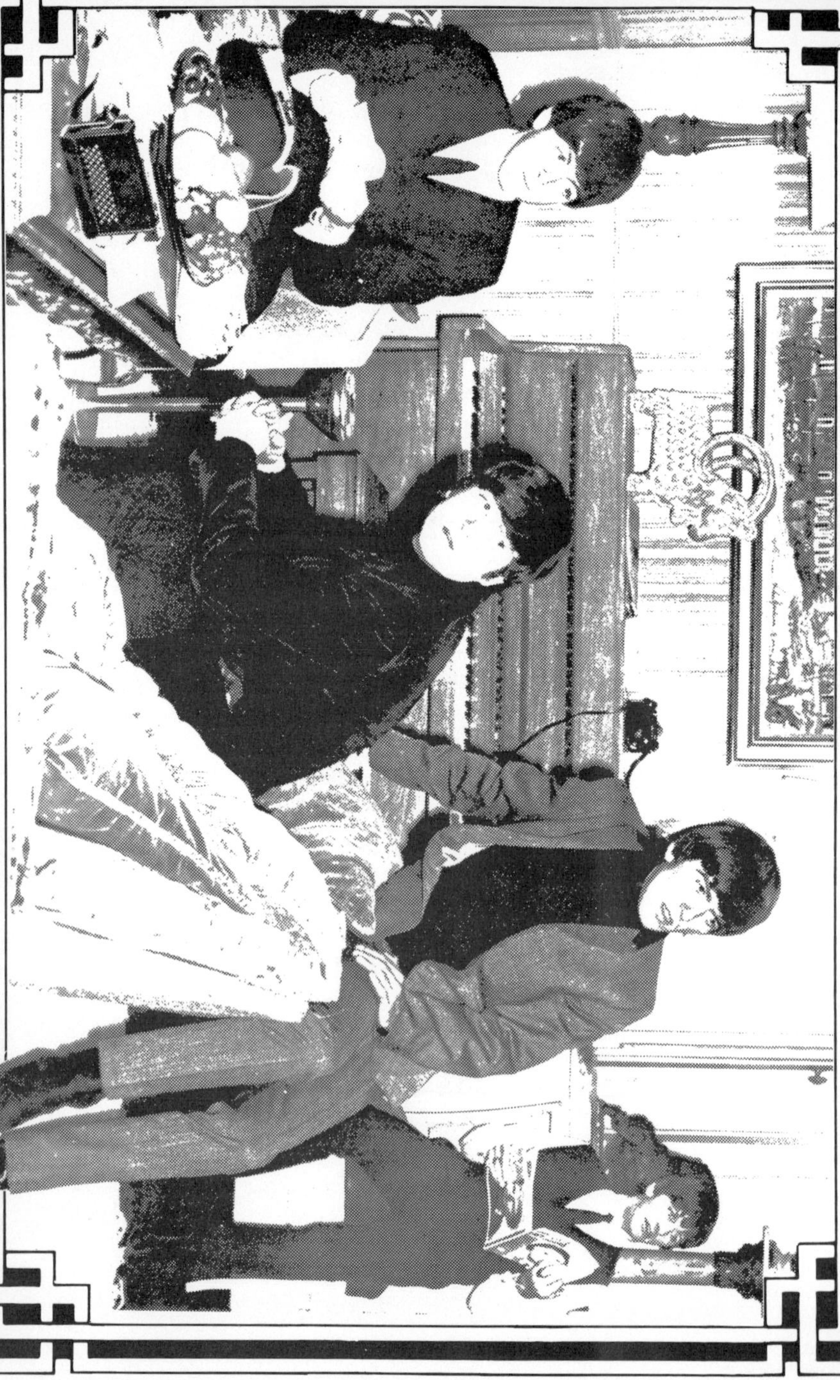

She Takes a Trip Around the World: A Hard Day's Night

"I've been told when a boy kiss a girl,
she takes a trip around the world."
—"Boys," The Shirelles

Introduction

"Come Balthazar, we'll hear that song again."
—Don Pedro in Much Ado About Nothing

The surprise of the Beatles' film is that you need to see it again and again. A friend of mine met a WAC who had seen it fifty-two times: she was standing in the lobby of a movie theater, waiting out the second bill until the Beatles would come for her fifty-third. I have seen *A Hard Day's Night* five times and I will see it again. What does my, and perhaps your, repetition-compulsion mean? Great films like *Ivan the Terrible (Part II), Day of Wrath, Pickpocket, Rules of the Game*—these are movies you see many times. The Bogart, Mae West, and Tarzan fans remain entranced with their idols after innumerable viewings. And films of negligible quality such as *One Eyed Jacks* have their devotees: one friend has seen the Western twelve times. But the *Hard Day's Night* syndrome is hardly cultish or eccentric. The second-run showings are usually packed with persons seeing the film for the third or fourth time. It is not unusual for you to return to one of the great films when you consider their technical quality and emotional power and your newer awarenesses of this power. But there is a law of diminishing returns here; after the fourth viewing of Becker's *Nightwatch* or Olmi's *The Fiances,* you rest for a while before you return. I suppose you need them just so much, even as you realize their magnificence. The question is: why do we need *A Hard Day's Night* so much that we keep showing it as often as we do?

Nakedness

Undrape! you are not guilty to me, nor stale nor discarded,
I see through the broadcloth and gingham whether or no,
And am around, tenacious, acquisitive, tireless,
and cannot be shaken away.
—*Whitman,* "Song of Myself"

On hearing the girls' screaming, you would imagine that the gods of fire, dawn, night, and thunder were manifesting themselves: "Let us adore this Wind with our oblation." But the girls scream so that they do not tear the Beatles' clothes off, for by screaming they alert the police who in turn set cordons up to block them from their desire. The Beatles have come running from the Garden: "I heard Thy voice in the garden, and I was afraid, because I was naked; and I hid myself." The girls think Adam's words. They are naked under their sweaters and skirts and desire to become one flesh with the undressed Beatles. So they are ashamed of this desire and scream loudly enough to be enjoined from their wish.

A Hard Day's Night tempts us with the excruciating hope that, when we see the film again, this time, surely, we shall see the four boys naked.

Childhood and Dependency

When the world is reduced to a single dark wood
for our four eyes' astonishment,
—a beach for two faithful children,
—a musical house for our pure sympathy,
—I shall find you.
—*Rimbaud,* "Illuminations"

Childhood is our goal. Concomitant with being a child exists the pleasure one gets from playing and the intolerable displeasure one gets from realizing one's dependency on others. Thus the Beatles play on the rugby field in that most pleasurable scene which you want to see again and again. Four boys mock space and time—the sequence lasts under three minutes—as they play to "Can't Buy Me Love." Every moment seems spontaneous and joyful. Actions and movements are speeded up and slowed down. What we see is how we truly wish we felt or remember how we once felt or how we once wanted to feel. "Genital

organization is a tyranny in man because his peculiar infancy has left him with a lifelong allegiance (i.e., fixation) to the pattern of infantile sexuality" (Norman O. Brown). If this is correct, why does the playing terminate? After that beautiful scene of exhaustion when the Beatles—lying on the grass, hands under their heads—count or talk silently to themselves? The answer is that 1) Mr. Genital Reality orders them off his field; and that 2) the Beatles have a TV rehearsal waiting for them. They have escaped from their duties: no job, no "Money"—which song comments obversely on that working-day world situation which "Can't Buy Me Love" attempts to fantasize away. The balding TV director ("It's a young man's business") depends on the manager who depends on the Beatles who depend on both, even when they do not wish to admit it. When Ringo gets led astray by the clean old id man, he assumes independence, and, in the tramp sequence, appears comic to us—the Bergsonian object-butt—but we have lost our goal, we laugh at the child in us now. The jokes are on Ringo, but he does not enjoy them. For the Beatles are boys, not bums, and they try their best not to "grow up."

Reaching Our Goal or Goodbye to Beaudelaire's Owls

Such was that happy Garden-state
While man there walked without a mate.
—*Marvell,* "The Garden"

Thus *A Hard Day's Night* does not, in Keats' words, unperplex bliss from pain; still, it strives honorifically towards our longed-for goal of childhood by focusing on the four boys in action. The great Sung neo-Confucianist philosopher Chu Hsi wrote: "Nature is the state before activity begins, the feelings are the state when activity has started. . . ." The verb "to act," in fact—which, in a general sense, means "to begin," "to lead," and eventually "to rule" (from the Greek *archein*) and also "to put in motion" (from the Latin *agere*)—suggests the Beatles' style of life. Their actions and their songs are impelled not from what they know but from what they are—from feelings rather than from states of mind. Boys and girls are naturally active, and it takes a bit of acculturation before they become bored, de-

pressed, and hung-up. Talking at press conferences, taking a bath, dancing, singing, playing cards, running in and out of jail (even the car thief and the cops become game-playing boys again—society's standards are demolished)—all these actions are invested with pleasurable feeling. The Beatles need only themselves for their own resources. Most important is the fact that each Beatle makes an ideal of himself; and that is why we suddenly realize in amazement that the Beatles sing love songs like "If I Fell" and "I Only Want to Dance with You" only to themselves. "You" means "me" in these songs. There is no "other," but they can say "we" to themselves and to each other. The Beatles' state of nature—to refuse Chu Hsi for a moment—is just this state of self-idealized and self-absorbed activity. The Beatles pinch chorus girls backstage, they get married, but that is, as Gatsby said, "merely personal." It doesn't matter. The Beatles' songs are full of feeling because the Beatles like to sing; but it is the singing that is important, for the "feeling" is the state when the singing has started. The girls are screaming, but, as one of the pupils of Heraclitus said perhaps, is this screaming not part of the song?

LOVE

> *". . . . dearest M / please come.*
> *There is no one here at all."*
> *—Robert Creeley*

The Beatles love what they do, so they love themselves. The screaming girls love the Beatles, and the Beatles are the receptacle or container of their love. They also resemble the Greek god of love, in the sense that Kierkegaard speaks of him:

> It is a genuine Greek thought that the god of love is not himself in love, while all others owe their love to him. If I imagined a god or goddess of longing, it would be a genuinely Greek conception, that while all who knew the sweet unrest of pain or of longing, referred it to this being, this being could know nothing of longing.

But the Beatles not only embody love, they are the Incarnation of Love. As Kierkegaard writes:

> In the Incarnation, the special individual has the entire fullness of life within himself,and this fullness exists for other individuals only in so far as they behold it in the incarnated individual. (From *Immediate Stages of the Erotic*)

The Beatles are as extraordinary as they are because they not only represent Love but also contain the "entire fullness" of Love within themselves. They are thus an embodiment and container of Love, and they are also the Love which they contain. There is no one there at all but themselves.

PHYSICALITY

Should time be gone,
and all that is impermanent a mere lie?
—*Nietzsche,* Thus Spake Zarathustra

It has been observed that *A Hard Day's Night* is not strong on plot. This is of course true. But it is not jokes—"campy," anti-Nazi, anti-cops—as good as they are that hold your interest. Rather it is the director's total dependence on showing the physical immediacy of the events and persons observed that generates the film's excitement and pleasure. I can think of no major feature film other than Dreyer's *Passion of St. Joan* that emphasizes the physical fact in such an unmitigated fashion. In Dreyer's film, the fly on Joan's eye, the warts on the interrogator's face, the cripples hanging around, the child sucking the mother's breast just when Joan, about to die, says: "Where will I be tonight?"—all these observed events heighten Dreyer's outraged sense of the flesh, all the more heightened as they contrast with Joan's saintliness. And yet her face, revealing all the confusion and suffering, is the most excruciating of physical facts.

The Beatles' faces and the parts of their faces, however, are the exultantly observed images—if not the heroes—of *A Hard Day's Night:* eyes, noses, hair, teeth. The image of a hand caressing a guitar, first seen on the studio's TV screen, is as close to suggesting a sense of sexual love as the film allows and so eerily reverberates with more force than had it been employed in a different context—say in an Italian comedy, where everyone is touching. The surprise and exhilaration you feel is similar to how you feel at that beautiful moment in Kurosawa's *High and Low* when you first see the kidnapper in his white clothes—as if he were a princess—reflected in the stream of the Tokyo slum.

Then, too, there are the faces of the girls and women. Their faces reveal as much about them as the humors reveal the characters in Jonson's plays. Just a second's sight of them unimaginably expresses the essence of girlhood. As the Beatles sing on TV, you see the girls in the audience, eyes dilating, each one unique from any other in her ecstasy and the force of her early but veritable sexuality. And if the girls seem womanly, the women seem girlish: the wonderfully shy creature talking to Ringo at the press conference, the women dancing at the party, the sexy secretary putting on her shoes who leads George into the shirt designer's office. The Beatles enable the women to become girls; the girls, women—even if only for a moment or the length of a song.

Rock and Roll Music, or at Ch'u Hill When the River Stood Still

And we sail on, away, afar,
Without course, without a star,
But, by the instinct of sweet music driven;
Till through Elysian garden islets
By thee, most beautiful of pilots,
Where never mortal pinnace glided,
The boat of my desire is guided:
Realms where the air we breathe is love,
Which in the winds and on the waves doth move,
Harmonizing this earth with what we feel above.
—Shelley, "Asia's Song" from Prometheus Unbound

Let us take a roundabout path by examining a beautiful ancient Chinese folk song:

> I heard my love was going to Yang-chow and went with him as far as Ch'u Hill. For a moment, when you held me fast in your outstretched arms I thought the river stood still and did not flow.

The sense of stillness and gentleness of the poem's statement brings out the superficial stillness of the emotion the girl says she feels. For there is no sense of passivity here. Rather, the mind and its experiences have been undifferentiated and everything is bursting out from a single source. The past and future combine, with time superseded, so that the present moment becomes eternal. Everything which is flowing remains rooted in this eternal present so that the stillness she feels, while everything is flowing within that stillness, is a bliss and joy that cannot be expressed, only suggested, which this song does so magnificently. Rock and roll songs almost always last under three minutes. The Beatles' songs, like most rock and roll songs, do not develop their musical materials in the way that the sonata-allegro form develops them or in the way that contemporary serial works develop them through permutation. The simple employment of the diatonic scale, usually two themes, and the relatively uncomplicated chord progressions limit development. (The Beatles' songs hint slyly at modal melodic patterns, but they too are diatonic.) Now the reality of Eternity can be felt only in that paradoxical moment of time when time has been superseded so that the present moment becomes eternal. The limited and limiting musical materials out of which rock and roll is created are perfectly suited to the demands of one's perception of Eternity. Everything in the song—in spite of the strophic tension which is undercut or neutralized by means of the continual 4/4 beat—enables you to remain rooted in the eternal present, so that the "river" does in fact stand still.

In this ambience of three-minute timelessness, we are taken outside of ourselves, if we allow ourselves to be so taken. We are taken back to the Garden where the "tragicomedy of love is performed by starlight" and the fireworks light up the sky. It is the blissful peace of the Diamond Samadhi where you feel, like a gentle rain, the soft petals of multi-colored lotus blossoms and those inexplicable, crazy feelings spreading throughout your gums.

Rock and roll is the new mysticism for those too experienced and cynical to believe much in anything anymore—a mysticism which you can accept for three minutes, a veritable even if non-interpersonal giving of oneself, because there is no fear of losing out. (There is here, too, also a return to the undifferentiated world of early childhood experiences.)

The hard day's night, the race to the train, the playing and singing—this is the passion of the world. But in the end, the Beatles in their helicopter fly up to Heaven. Is this not the Easter revelation we all have need of re-experiencing? *A Hard Day's Night* combines radical innocence and religious revelation, inviting ecstasy and salvation to that soul Yeats wrote about: "self-delighting, self-appeasing, self-affrighting"; whose "own sweet will is Heaven's will." Seeing the film again and again, we are the Vulture King seeing Rama in *The Holy Lake of the Acts of Rama:*

As he went on, he saw the Vulture King lying on the ground, meditating on Rama's feet and the marks they bore. Raghubir, the ocean of grace, stroked his head with his lotus hands, and when he looked on the wondrous beauty of Rama's face, he felt no more pain.

Of the Comfort of the Resurrection

"Bring this boy into the world,
and we'll soon make another."
—Grandgousier in Rabelais' Gargantua and Pantagruel

The Beatles have made another film!

1965

On Ozu

Yasujiro Ozu, who died in 1963, was one of the great directors of film, yet few persons have ever seen anything by him. Many of his fifty-four works were lost or destroyed during the war, and it is in the thirteen or so films made between 1949 and 1962—comprising his "late" period—that we can observe Ozu's mastery. Aside from a retrospective organized by Donald Richie in the early Sixties for the Museum of Modern Art, however, showings of the films in this country have been almost nonexistent. *Tokyo Story,* made in 1953, has just opened at the New Yorker theater (which last year premiered *Floating Weeds* and *The End of Summer*), and New Yorker Films is starting to distribute other Ozu masterpieces.

There are obvious aesthetic reasons for this director's neglect. The titles of his films—*Early Spring, Equinox Flower, Tokyo Twilight*—suggest Ozu's kinship with the ink blots of Japanese painting more than with what many persons think of as authentic Japanese movie fare: the samurai swashbucklers, portentous epics like *Chushingura,* or atmospheric romances like *Gates of Hell.* And even devotees of Kurosawa, Ichikawa, and Mizoguchi—the greatest of the three—have been known to be put off by Ozu's style (minimal) and subject matter (the family).

Ozu shares specific cinematic values with certain Western directors: his works touch on the theme of the breakdown of tradition and authority as developed by John Ford. His abiding interest in the interactions of the family group, taken as the World, resembles the concerns of Marcel Pagnol. His extraordinary ability to observe everyday objects and environments in such a way as to reveal their irreducible mystery reminds you of moments in the work of Antonioni (the conclusion of *Eclipse,* for example), Rossellini, and underground film makers like Bruce Baillie. And his technical procedures—the paring down of cinematic techniques—suggests the means of directors as thematically diverse as Bresson, Dreyer, and Andy Warhol. Ozu's last use of the dissolve occurred in his 1930 silent film *Life of an Office Worker.* "The only successful use of dissolve,"

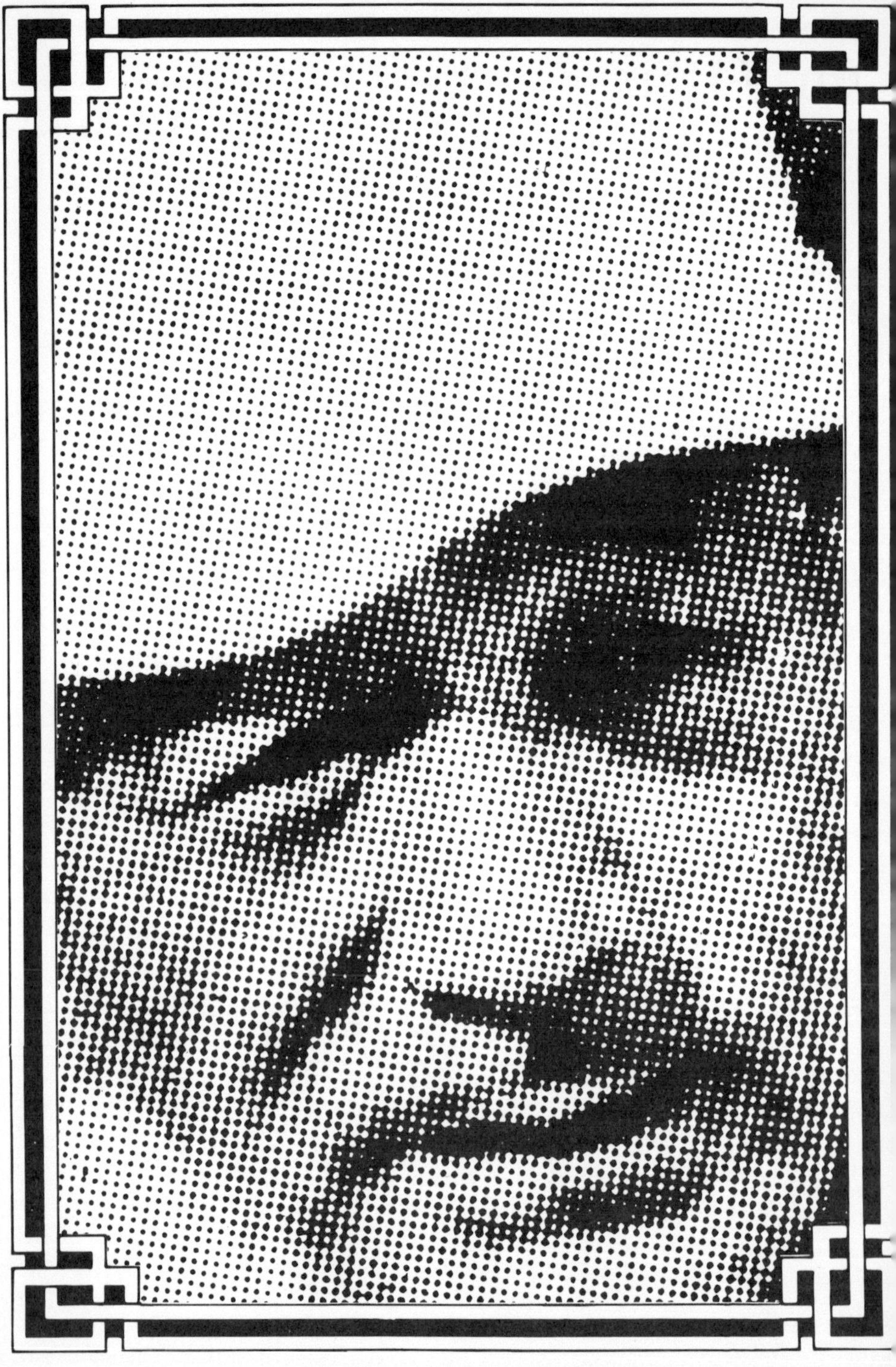

he once said, "is in Chaplin's *A Woman of Paris.* You won't see such a perfect use of technique more than once in twenty years. The others are all cheating." And concerning the use of color in his last films, Ozu stated: "I don't want to bring out every color; I prefer leaving the colors unaccentuated. I would rather 'de-coloraize.'"

These "negative" virtues applied to "plots" that are really nothing but interconnecting webs of family anecdotes, constellations of small intimations that reveal character, suggest such a quintessentially "Japanese" quality, however, that even Ozu's Tokyo distributor felt that no one in the West would understand it. Donald Richie has pointed out that the position of Ozu's camera—always three feet from the ground—is that from which one sees Noh drama or participates in the tea ceremonies. And certainly the time sense in these films is that of the meditative experience rather than that of plot.

I don't know what I was expecting, but I remember walking into a sneak preview of Ozu's *Ohayo* (Good Morning) in 1961, copies of *Lord of the Flies* and *The Sickness Unto Death* under my arm, and watching domestic Japanese family scenes, little boys breaking wind, and a "plot" hinging on the father's stubbornly conceded acquiescence in buying a television set for his children. All this was moreover shot in Ozu's characteristic manner: the camera slightly off the floor as if you were sitting on a tatami mat, no pans, dollies, tracking shots, or dissolves . . . just nothing happening. "Reaching the essence through extreme simplification," Donald Richie had written. Whatever it was, I left halfway through the film and went back to reading and considering Original Sin.

Several years later the veils were lifted when I saw *Early Spring* and *Tokyo Story.* The plot of the latter film is as simple as ever: an elderly couple who live in a small port town near Hiroshima decide to travel to Tokyo in order to see their married children and grandchildren. Their hairdresser daughter and neighborhood doctor son, inconvenienced by the visit, behave in a petty, niggling, impatient manner. "Don't buy such expensive cakes for them," the daughter tells her husband; "they don't need it." The son and daughter send the couple off to a "singles"-type health spa in Atami where all-night partying keeps them awake. They return to Tokyo and are made to feel unwelcome except by the widow of their son who's been killed in the war—a compassionate, selfless young woman—who treats them warmly and lovingly. Returning to their town, the mother becomes seriously ill (she's had a couple of dizzy spells during their visit). The children travel to her death bed, only to rush back to their jobs after the funeral. The daughter-in-law alone remains with the widowed old man, and in a beautiful moment, after he advises her to remarry, she tells of the difficulty she has living alone, of how she seems to be waiting for something. The last scene shows a neighbor, who we've seen making small talk with the couple before their journey at the beginning of the film, now passing by, saying: "You'll be lonely." "Yes," the old man says, as he sits in the empty house. And the film closes with shots of the port and the bay and the boats passing through.

As in almost all of Ozu's late films, *Tokyo Story* uses the nuclear family—the interactions between parents and children, fathers and daughters—much as Howard Hawks used the lives of airplane pilots as a kind of microcosm of the world, a moral center against and in which certain ideas of personality and traditional social roles can be examined and affirmed. Occasionally, Ozu will replace the "family" with an acting troupe *(Floating Weeds)* or a group of office workers *(Early Spring)*, but his world at least on the surface level is not too dissimilar from Jane Austen's.

Whereas Hawks' brilliantly economical and functional camera style perfectly embodies his presentation of what has been aptly called "male professionalism and group responsibility," Ozu's formalist approach is meant—not to "distance" his material in order to demystify it politically (as in the works of Godard, Straub, and Diegues, for example)—but rather to exemplify a secular mysticism which, as Kenneth Rexroth once wrote, "sees experience as its own transcendence."

In Ozu's films, parents and children play out their generational conflicts, but these conflicts suggest not only what Ozu saw as the weakening of traditional Japanese social values but also his sense of the mutability of life. The moral tensions that manifest themselves in the simplest minute-to-minute family transactions finally dissolve (as the shots never do): as you watch the family in its process of "decreation"—by the fact of death or marriage—you become aware of an attitude toward life which the Japanese call *mono no aware*—"sympathetic sadness."

The old woman in *Tokyo Story,* talking to her youngest grandchild, who is picking flowers in a field, says: "I wonder where I'll be when you grow up," but he is self-absorbed and doesn't hear a word. Ozu frames this moment as if observing it from a point of silence: in a long shot you see a wooden hut in the middle of the screen and in the distance, on a level above it, a little baseball-capped head and a stooping figure in the midst of grasses.

The surprising surface tension of many of Ozu's static shots results from both an intense concentration on physical details and the feeling one gets of the impersonality of the viewing consciousness. Every newly introduced room, office, town, or city is announced by simple shots that define the environment: in *Tokyo Story* you see pavillions, train tracks, steam, industrial equipment, empty wet streets, white wash on the line. In Ozu films, bamboo shadows on a mat, dust floating down from the ceiling, objects just lying or placed carefully in a room are all observed with such intensity that the mystery of non-Being and "undertermined consciousness" is paradoxically communicated by just this simple presentation and enrichment of the objects of everyday reality.

And while Ozu avoids any real depiction of "romantic love" ("It doesn't interest me"), he is a master at suggesting a powerful physical radiancy—the rare tracking shot in *Early Spring* of two infatuated office workers walking with a group down a picnic road, the breeze blowing through their clothes; or the breathtakingly luminous appearance in *An Autumn Afternoon* of a daughter trying on her wedding dress to show to her widowed father who, on seeing her, comprehends his loneliness.

This moment resembles the ending of *Late Spring.* A widowed father who forces his dauther to get married, is sitting peeling a pear. As his movements become slower and as he looks around the room, the director intimates to you the fact that there's no one any longer there. As with the grandfather in *Tokyo Story,* this man's social identity ceases as the "family" disappears to re-form as another family somewhere else. Like the irreducible objects shown in Ozu's films—like the black crows tokening death at the conclusion of *End of Summer*—the whole orbit of his life has become concentrated in a moment that unifies existence and activity.

Ozu's "family romance" can be ultimately seen to suggest the interconnecting and interrelated layers of onion skins, under which lies the secret of the Buddha nature. And by this revelation, the meaning of Ozu's technique becomes clear: by eliminating what is developable and exploitable, the director brings you to that point beyond knowing communicated in the Japanese poem translated by Kenneth Rexroth: "The flowers whirl away/in the wind like snow./The thing that falls away is myself."

1972

Chloe in the Afternoon

DIRECTED BY ERIC ROHMER

Chloe in the Afternoon (L'Amour, L'Apres-Midi) is the last of the French director Eric Rohmer's "Six Moral Tales," each of which Rohmer defines as "a story dealing less with what people do than with what is going on in their minds while they are doing it." Beautifully filmed by director of photography Nestor Almendros in Rohmer's characteristically classical manner (simply composed shots, unobtrusive camera work, rhythmically perfect editing), *Chloe*'s formal concentration fails to disguise what seems to me a partial celebration of a kind of moral smugness. Or rather a kind of moral superiority which, in his other features released here *(La Collectionneuse, My Night at Maud's,* and *Claire's Knee),* Rohmer had been happy to examine as the *subject,* rather than exhibit as the *attitude,* of his films.

Thematically similar to these other films, *Chloe in the Afternoon* presents the most straight-forward variation on Rohmer's favorite moral tension: attached man meets attractive, alert, scintillating "other" woman, imagines a possible liaison, then withdraws to home base. In this case, Rohmer gives us Frederic (Bernard Verley), the prototypical but sweet young bourgeois, a businessman who commutes between his suburban Paris home, where his postgraduate wife is expecting her second child, and his office decorated with two "efficient" and pretty secretaries ("It sets a good tone for our business"), into which one day enters a former friend's lover, a free spirit named Chloe (wonderfully played by a French rock and underground film star named Zouzou), furiously puffing on cigarettes and talking about her recent stay in America and about how she wanted to renew an old acquaintance.

Rebuffed at first, Chloe insists on dropping into the office to talk to Frederic about her makeshift jobs (barmaid, waitress), about her current lover with whom she's getting bored. And Frederic, who fantasizes about the possibility of having many lovers—but thinking it impossible to pick anyone up ("What would I have to say to her?")—at the same time as he asserts his love for his wife (who, he assures Chloe, is attracted to no one but himself), finds himself happily awaiting Chloe's afternoon visits. He helps her look for an apartment, talks openly and freely with her (as he doesn't with his wife), takes strolls with her, has lunches, all the while nonchalantly and proudly keeping himself removed from any romantic involvement.

But it is exactly this very detachment that is threatened when he finds himself surprisingly depressed when Chloe breaks an appointment. Puzzled by the discovery of his sexual attraction to Chloe, Frederic visits her in her new apartment above the boutique where, thanks to him, she is now working. Having finally decided to be seduced one afternoon in her room, he touches her thigh, helps her get undressed; and as she gets into bed, our hero goes to take a look at himself in the mirror, then, without a word, rushes out the door and stampedes down the stairs. Rohmer brilliantly shoots this valiant escape with the camera looking straight down the stairwell into the ground floor abyss; whereas when we saw Frederic earlier walking up the stairs to his office, the camera observed him from an elegant horizontal position. Back in his office, visibly upset, Frederic calls up his wife, says he wants to see her—but it's still afternoon!—and we see him immediately back home, crying with her on the couch, sharing with her an understanding that, as Rohmer implies, the bourgeois structure of love can still allow marital happiness to exist.

What Rohmer has lost in *Chloe* is that extraordinary capacity to deal with "moral" problems—those of will, deception, and choice: or, as Shakespeare wrote, of "space, validity, and pleasure"—as he did in his previously subtle and enriching manner. In *La Collectionneuse,* for example—Rohmer's most inventive yet most casual and formally "imperfect" film—the director presents to us a hero whose first-person analysis of his attempt to test his sexual feelings towards the easy-living heroine soon reveals itself as the viewpoint of a supercilious and self-deceiving fool.

In *Chloe,* Frederic's first-person observations are hardly redolent of self-mockery; Rohmer gives us no alternative "reading" of the situation beyond his hero's own understanding of it. But not only that: while in *My Night at Maud's* Francoise Fabian's Maud, as well as Jean-Louis Trintignant's fiancé, are both treated as self-realized and remarkable human beings, in *Chloe,* the "seductress" is shown as being self-aggrandizing and overly impetuous (Chloe says she's simply decided that Frederic is going to give her her baby, no questions asked). And this disparagement of the "third party"—along with the director's complaisant approval of Frederic's wife's half-enforced, half-accepted "feminine" role—loads the dice against any real sympathy for Chloe, and excuses Frederic's "escape" (I mean, he might have said good-bye to his friend!). The film is reduced to the level of an exquisitely textured but simplistic suburban comedy of manners.

At the end of the first part of *Chloe,* there's a lovely fantasy scene in which Frederic imagines he's wearing a magic love amulet which gives him sexual power over any woman he meets. The six "women" of Rohmer's previous moral tales suddenly appear on the street and give in immediately to Frederic's power. All but Beatrice Romand of *Claire's Knee:* "Why should I go off with you, huh?" she demands fiercely and walks off. End of fantasy. End of "moral," as far as I'm concerned. Unless Rohmer intends that you consciously view the whole of *Chloe in the Afternoon* as an ironic commentary on itself, you might be left asking the same question.

1972

The Salamander

DIRECTED BY ALAIN TANNER

A friend once remarked that while nearly all of Europe experienced the bad vibrations of World War II, only Switzerland got no vibes whatsoever. An extraordinary country, whose popular emblems are watches, banks, and chocolate bars and whose postcard landscape is disfigured only by occasional visitors like Tristan Tzara and Tim Leary.

Now along comes *The Salamander (La Salamandre),* which its forty-two-year-old Swiss ciritc-turned-director Alain Tanner calls a "Third World film from Switzerland." The label is amusing but not instructive. For *The Salamander* is simply a lyrical, quietly rapturous evocation not only of the life of the "free spirit" but also of the daydreams set off by the remembrance of the poetic spaces of Truffaut's *Shoot the Piano Player* and *Jules and Jim* and, especially, Godard's *Band of Outsiders.*

"Hello, Paris"—the first words of *The Salamander,* spoken by one of the leading characters on a telephone call to France—suggest Tanner's obeisance to the above films and to the attitude expressed by one of the actors in Godard's *Masculine-Feminine* concerning "the film we had dreamed, the film we had carried in our hearts, the film we wanted to make—and secretly wanted to live." In this sense, Tanner's film is to those of Truffaut and Godard as *The Last Picture Show* is to the works of Ford and Hawks. (It's important to mention, however, that Tanner's pared-down technique and method of directing actors owes more to Eric Rohmer, whose "conservative" sensibility he disdains, just as Bogdanovich adopts Sam Fuller's camera angles, but not that director's obsessions, for his own purposes.)

Like *Jules and Jim* and *Band of Outsiders, The Salamander* relates the story of two young men—in this case a fiction writer/house plasterer named Paul who, when sad, breaks out in song, and a slightly humorless journalist named Pierre—and a young woman named Rosemonde. Their lives intersect at the point when, on assignment from Swiss television, Pierre begins to investigate the reported story of Rosemonde's guilt concerning her involvement in an "accident" in which Rosemonde's uncle was wounded with his own army rifle. The uncle, who represents the Swiss bourgeois mentality, had accused Rosemonde of the shooting, but she has been cleared (and the film suggests that the uncle shot himself as he was cleaning the gun). Paul, living with his wife and daughter in their country cottage, decides to create an "imaginary" Rosemonde in fiction, deducing aspects of her personality, to which end he hopes never to meet her. Both men, of course, finally get romantically involved with her, and the film ends—as their "story" never does.

Rosemonde, who like the mythical salamander can go through fire and emerge unsinged, comes from a large country family. Sent to her uncle's in the city—"one less mouth to feed"—she becomes his "char" and leaves his home after the shooting, gets pregnant, gives the baby to her mother, becomes a salesgirl, quits, and, as the film opens, is working in a sausage factory sticking prophylactic-type looking dough paddies over a tube out of which spurts a continual barrage of grim-looking processed meat. The boss doesn't like her messy hair, so Rosemonde quits her job once again, takes Pierre and Paul to her family's country home (in a car drive reminiscent of the return to the cottage in *Shoot the Piano Player*), returns to the city and gets fired from her new job as a shoe salesgirl because she provocatively caresses all the customers' legs. Her pleasures consist of swimming in an indoor pool, making love, and ritually rotating her head to what is supposed to sound like "psychedelic" rock records. And the last scene of the film picks up on this somewhat corny gesture of "freedom" when we see Rosemonde's weaving slow-motion head smiling as she walks down a busy city street.

It sounds like a pretty ordinary story, but Bulle Ogier's impersonation of Rosemonde (she plays the lead in Jacque Rivette's severe masterpiece *L'Amour Fou*)—sitting on Pierre's bed as he types up an article, she fidgeting with her necklace and cross, turning on the TV, taking off her leather skirt—is an extraordinary revelation of a sometimes plain, sometimes beautiful, lazy, morose, aimless, gentle human being.

Jean-Luc Bideau as Pierre and especially Jacques Denis as Paul (Paris' *Le Monde* critic called him "the most modest actor who has appeared since John Garfield") give wonderful performances. And Tanner's unostentatious gray and white winter colors, purposely imperfect editing, and effectively chosen vignettes—Paul and his daughter, hand in hand, laughing and feeling the wind that blows from passing trains—create a sense of life that reminds us of the possibilities hinted at by the May, '68 Paris uprisings when graffiti spoke of the hopes for a different world: "Be realistic. Dream the impossible."

In this sense, *The Salamander* might be seen as a political film, for as it criticizes middle-class rigidity, it suggests the humane, loving values spoken about by Paul's wife when she quotes lines by Heine concerning the poet's belief in the appearance of a new generation "conceived in freely chosen embraces and no longer in the bed of duty."

Throughout the film, Pierre is seen trying to finish an article on Brazil, and he tells Rosemonde and Paul of his memory of that country's "pimentos, dust, mangos, putrefaction, and the smell of the sea." You might be reminded of Godard's gangster and girl at the end of *Band of Outsiders* heading off to Brazil where "the horizon was a stage, the sky an endless eternity."

All of this has more to do with a few too many viewings of *That Man from Rio* and *Black Orpheus* rather than with Brazil's own important, often infuriating Third World Cinema—styled after the French New Wave. The apotheosis of this Cinema—which includes better-known works like *Antonio das Mortes, Vidas Secas,* and *Macunaima*—is Ruy Guerra's astonishing *The Gods and the Dead,* a film which is just now getting its American release. With its unequaled but fantastically beautiful depiction of violence—the baroque power of which Artaud and even Jodorowsky can hardly have imagined—its staggering embodiment of the bloody dues and demonic retribution owed as the wages of the desires of Empire, it has as much similarity with Tanner's film as a thousand scorpions have with a gentle garden salamander. These two "Third World" works of art perfectly reveal the antithetical possibilities of film. *The Gods and the Dead* is a sustained scream in the midday tropical sun, while *The Salamander,* in a French poet's words, is a "night light in the bedroom of memories."

1972

Two English Girls

DIRECTED BY FRANCOIS TRUFFAUT

Of all the New Wave directors, Francois Truffaut specifically appropriated for himself the subject of childhood. "I realized that I preferred to work with children rather than with adults," the director once wrote about his first two films *The Mischief Makers* and *The Four Hundred Blows.* But it wasn't the ingenue-type of child of *Sundays and Cybele,* the superior and self-possessed brat of Hollywood comedies, or even the poetic, erotic, and cruel archetypal adolescents of Cocteau's films that interested Truffaut. Much as he borrowed from Jean Vigo's schoolchildren in *Zero for Conduct,* his freeze-framed image at the end of *The Four Hundred Blows* of Antoine Doinel (Jean-Pierre Leaud) standing alone at the sea suggested, through that pained gaze, a literal "screen memory" of the eternal child which Wordsworth once perceived as being the father of the man.

It is not surprising that as "Antoine Doinel"—the synthesis of Leaud and Truffaut—grew up in films like *Love at Twenty, Stolen Kisses,* and *Bed and Board,* his childlikeness began to come into conflict with adult "realities" like marriage, and at the same time the films became increasingly self-conscious, reflecting much too often the conventional and sentimental attitudes of domestic comedies. As Doinel got older, the quality of playfulness and percipient humor began to decline, reaching its nadir in the wiseacres of *Bed and Board.*

Throughout the eleven-year period during which the Antoine Doinel series was completed, Truffaut worked on a number of films in which (excepting the clankingly pretentious *Fahrenheit 451*) the aura of childhood awarenesses—manifested in Truffaut's lyrical camera technique—continually remained, if not the subject of his films, at least a kind of moral center from which point the director could observe what might be termed the varieties of human selfishness. In Truffaut's world, selfish love seems to signify and accompany a loss of the childhood feelings of rapturous acceptance and communion. Thus characters like Charlie in *Shoot the Piano Player* and the writer Pierre Lachenay who betrays both his wife and mistress in *Soft Skin* reveal, under their sympathetic veneers, a passive self-centeredness that suggests a kind of moral callousness.*

As Truffaut once wrote: "In *Bed and Board* we are no longer dealing with an adolescent but with an adult, and even though Antoine Doinel and Pierre Lachenay resemble me like two brothers, I am never as gentle with adults as I am with adolescents." Needless to say, Truffaut's own treatment of the child of nature in his film *The Wild Child* (in which the director himself portrays the "educator" doctor) is based on compassion and love. For, as Truffaut knows, the high libidinal price we've paid society and culture has broken our natures, and, as he shows us in *The Wild Child,* the true father of every child is the sun; our mother, the rain and the water of the streams. As the camera pulls back from the wild child as he's escaping "civilization" and disappearing into the forest in order to return to his "real" parents, you understand how, for Truffaut, the idea of childhood inherently stands for that of wholeness.

The director's new beautiful film *Two English Girls (Les Deux Anglaises et le Continent)* recircles and reabsorbs, in order to recapture, the themes and obsessions of earlier films. Based, like *Jules and Jim,* on a novel by Henri-Pierre Roche and set between the 1890s and 1914, the film's depiction of the love of two English sisters for a young Frenchman immediately presents an obvious inversion of the *Jules and Jim* triangle. And just as *Jules and Jim* was primarily about Catherine, so *Two English Girls* is about Claude Roc, played by Antoine Doinel, alias Jean-Pierre Leaud. This young Parisian goes to Wales to

---

*In *Shoot the Piano Player,* for example, the protagonist Charlie (Charles Azvanour) passively witnesses and accepts the suicide of his wife and the death of his girlfriend, avoiding any kind of personal responsibility for matters of the heart. Eight years after the making of this film, Truffaut had Catherine Deneuve relinquish her vanity in the face of the love revealed to her by Jean-Paul Belmondo. Interestingly, Truffaut showed his hero and heroine walking past that same winter cottage in which the gangster brothers of *Shoot the Piano Player* had once holed up and outside of which we once saw Charlie's girl, shot by almost make-believe, childish assassins, sliding dreamily like a sled down a white, ice-coated slope. Truffaut recalls this "world"—much as Proust recalled Venice—to force us to realize how we have unsuspectedly become strangers to the hidden-away landscape of our own childhood, snow, adoration, and grief.

visit the seaside home of a friend of his mother whose two daughters fall in love with him. In spite of her affection for him, the outgoing sister Anne (Kika Markham) instigates marriage plans for Claude and her hypertense, sexually repressed sister Muriel (Stacey Tendeter). We learn that Muriel, guilt-ridden about masturbation, wears dark glasses over her "strained" eyes and, waiting for the fulfillment of her "perfect" love, she in many ways shares the characteristics of an incipient saint.

After his widowed, possessive mother postpones the marriage, Claude, now in Paris and having turned into a diletante art critic and gentleman-about-town, becomes Anne's first lover. Anne, who is a painter, has taken a couple of other lovers but continues to love and see Claude on her frequent trips to France. When one day Muriel decides to visit Claude to try to renew his love for her and discovers that he has been her sister's lover, she breaks down and returns to Wales with Anne. Anne dies suddenly of tuberculosis, Claude later meets Muriel in Calais on her way to Belgium, and, on this night, she gives herself to him, never to see him again.

Truffaut films this story with the voice-over narration he used in *Jules and Jim,* but somehow avoiding what might have become a pretentious self-parodying of both the technique and subject. Making use of slow dissolves and iris dissolves, he emphasizes a Monet-like palette of muted green-grey-sea white hues for the Welsh seaside cottage and daguerreotyped textures, along with soft focus, sometimes radiant Bonnard-like colors for the Paris and Swiss scenes. Again, Truffaut displays his amazing visual powers in seemingly throwaway moments: Anne and Claude, playing a game, getting down on their knees to kiss each other through the bars of a chair, while reflections of lights from the fireplace flicker on Muriel's dark lenses; the wavering cellular water patterns on the hull of the boat in front of which Claude meets Muriel in Calais; the beautiful circling boat shot of Claude's and Anne's lover's hideaway on a small Swiss island; and the bizarre close-up of the gold-red blood stains on Claude and Muriel's hotel bed after her defloration, tokening a sexual repression overcome and the aggressive acknowledgement of earthy love. ("My mouth is full of earth," Anne says on her deathbed. And: "Why do you touch me?" Muriel asks

Claude at the outset of the film. "Because you come from the earth," he replies.)

This emphasis on the images of passionate love of course echoes the feeling of *Jules and Jim.* But while that film was as much about the rise of fascism as about friendship and love,* *Two English Girls* is hardly concerned with its hero as a representative of a particular epoch, ethos, or national "type" (Claude is humorously called *Le Continent* by his English sisters). Rather Claude Roc is Truffaut's most affectionately realized portrayal of the adolescent child who, as he becomes a "man," experiences social existence as a kind of estrangement.

Unlike the passive, uncommitted writer in *Soft Skin* who is shot by his wife or the self-complacent killers of Jeanne Moreau's husband in *The Bride Wore Black* whom the actress, like an angel of death, exterminates in a series of "just" retaliatory murders, Claude Roc's "punishment"—the price he pays for his swerving loyalty—lies simply in the fact of his own survival.

At the conclusion of *Two English Girls,* we are in the gardens of the Rodin Museum in Paris. It is the beginning of World War I, Anne is dead, Muriel is a schoolteacher in Belgium—married and the mother of a daughter—the house in Wales has been sold, and Claude, alone in the world, bespectacled and looking pale and old, watches a group of English schoolgirls running gaily about the statues of embracing lovers. Imagining that Muriel's daughter might be among them, Claude looks for her in every face, then, on leaving, finds himself pushed along with them out through the museum gates.

What we're left remembering are the children running around the dock of Calais as Claude and Muriel meet for their first and last night of love; the flashback to eight-year-old Muriel

*After all that's been said about *Jules and Jim,* it's still interesting to point out that whether or not you think of Jeanne Moreau's enigmatic Catherine as a portrayal of a liberated woman caught between two attractive but finally condescending men, she still seems to embody a kind of proto-fascist spirit. The fact that Jules is German and Jim, French and that the film begins before World War I (during which the two men friends fight on opposing sides) and ends with newsreel shots of a Nazi book burning orgy and with Catherine's and Jim's suicidal car trip (dressed in tie and jacket, Catherine peremptorily orders Jim to her death vehicle) all certainly suggest such an interpretation. And I think that this juxtaposition of social and sexual functions forces us to reexamine *Jules and Jim* as both a love story and social commentary.

discovering sexual pleasure with her erotic little girlfriend; and finally the haunting photograph of ten-year-old Muriel with her "shy, untamed look"—the first image we and Claude have of her in the film (similar in importance to the mysterious statue's face that Catherine embodies in *Jules and Jim*).

It is always the Truffaut child who looks back through the calloused and alienated adult, that child who, the director knows, is the well of being, whose dark pools of water reflect faces we've somehow forgotten. As Jean-Pierre Leaud disappears amidst the schoolgirls at the conclusion of *Two English Girls,* the shock becomes the greater as we remember the fifteen-year-old actor who, in *The Four Hundred Blows,* mingles with his fellow truant "offenders" until he can escape to the sea where, immobilized, he stands staring right at you through the camera as if to ask: Where have I come? Where have you gone? What are you doing?

1972

Daddy Has Gone Away Now: Let It Be

(WRITTEN WITH DAVID DALTON)

HOW TO GROW A TREE AROUND A GOLDEN APPLE.

The idea for a Beatles film came about towards the end of 1968 when Apple was still a kind of nucleus for the group. Some of the Utopian schemes had already been abandoned. The film division was dispensed with as unnecessary, and the electronics division under the supervision of Alexis Mardas, who had promised such miracles as a force field around Paul McCartney's house and a recording technique that would defy bootlegging and baffle illicit broadcasting of Beatles material, had dwindled to a little plastic apple with a transistor radio inside. Earlier in the year, Apple Fashions, the projected spearhead of a Beatles retail empire, had folded and Paul had stopped talking about Apple as "a western form of Communism" and as a "huge commercial/creative complex along the lines of British Petroleum."

Apple's attempts to integrate the Beatle's own personal aspirations with the mechanics of business was proving a fruitless task. As if in evidence of the gulf, you could find Derek Taylor in his third floor office pacifying all manner of creative freaks, journalists, dope-fiends, hustlers, and West Coast expatriates, while on another floor Peter Brown, in his meticulous office, was intoning: "At Apple we are only interested in ideas that will make us a million dollars a day." It was like a labyrinth trying to communicate with itself.

As things got worse, Derek, with his sense of the absurd ("Being born in Scotland carries with it certain responsibilities"), asked Alan Aldridge to redesign the Apple stationery (a peeling apple with the legend "words from Apple") to a peeling pear with the legend "lies from Apple." In this atmosphere, it is amazing that the film got together at all. Neil Aspinall decided the best place to shoot the movie would be at Twickenham studios, where Peter Sellers was shooting *The Magic Christian.*

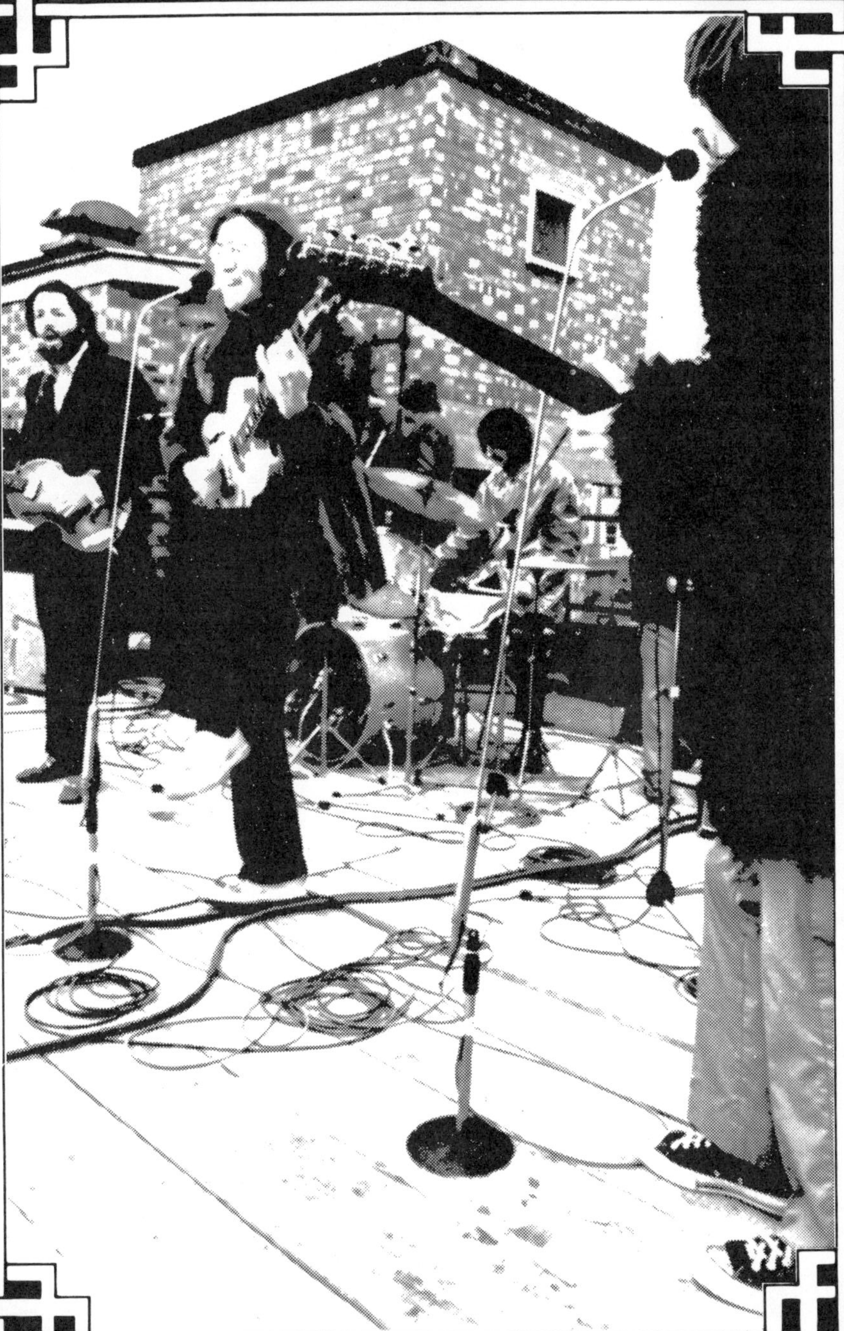

Ringo did not want to go away on location because of his involvement in the Sellers' movie. The atmosphere at the time, influenced by *John Wesley Hardin,* was a return to simplicity (hence the original title: *Get Back*). And after all, it was the easiest thing to do anyway. Director Michael Lindsay-Hogg told them where it was at:

Lindsay-Hogg: Well I think one of those things that's wrong about doing the show here is that it's too easy. Like when we are in the car looking for locations and glorified boutiques, I think that's wrong. But just doing it in the backyard. I mean it's literal. It's almost your backyard. Twickenham. There's no balls to the show at all. I mean there's no balls in any of us, I'm included, and that's why I think we are being soft about it. You are the Beatles; you aren't four jerks. You know what I mean.

THINGS AS THEY ARE, AS A DREAM. AS THEY ARE AS A DREAM.

Paul: It bugs me when they zoom in and out. I'd like it to be like an old movie. If you want to say anything, you walk up to the camera. The only thing that doesn't need to move is the camera. It's like Oriental medicine and Western medicine. We prescribe for the symptoms: they are into preventing it. It's like a switch—get us to do the movement.

Ringo: I'd like it like a country programme where you have one camera, just step in and do your bit, like on the *Grand Ol' Opry,* Flatt and Scruggs; they'd all move in when their solo came around and take the center so they acted out the shots.

Paul: Dreaming in public is the thing. You know those dreams where you go down a Helter Skelter? And the scene changes? But doing that awake. The latest thing from Apple! . . .

So, in January, 1969, The Beatles spent over one hundred hours playing, arguing, rapping, rehearsing in the Twickenham Film Studios, the Apple studio, and on the Apple roof. The film, like the long-awaited album, was first titled *Get Back,* but someone must have realized that after one year of getting back—the film still in the editing room—the best recourse, aside from going forward (which the Beatles did with *Abbey Road*), was just to let it be. The film comes to us in its own good time. If

A Hard Day's Night portrayed the Beatles' "real life" image as fiction, and if *Yellow Submarine* embodied that image mythically, *Let It Be* documents a few moments of the Beatles together "awake" and "for real."

We only get a few moments because with three hundred hours of footage, only the highlights, the more dramatic scenes, and the funnier dialogue are shown. Obviously, most of the original footage is filled up with shots of the Beatles tuning up, running through "Don't Let Me Down" for the fortieth time, off-mike huddles, etc. One misses scenes like the one in which Paul tells how he originally wrote "Get Back" as a political song:

> Don't dig no Pakistanis takin' all the people's jobs
> Wilson said to the immigrants
> You'd better get back to your Commonwealth homes
> Yeh-yeh-yeh you'd better get BACK HOME.*

We also miss the monotonies, the lack-luster workaday yawns, of four people who know each other too well. So if Yoko Ono seems unenthusiastic and listless in *Let It Be,* just imagine sitting through thirty hours of takes and re-takes. Playing and shooting over and over is the context from which *Let It Be* extrapolates its images. Finally, too, one misses the enormous number of Fifties rock and roll classics which the Beatles slipped into—putting them on in the playful and always elegant way that they perform "You've Really Got A Hold On Me" in *Let It Be*, for example.

YESTERDAY, THINGS WE SAID TODAY.

George: In America, ya know, they don't want all new ones . . . they need something to identify with aside from us.

John: I've been doing a lot of "Help" recently.

Paul: "Every Little Thing."

George: "Good Golly Miss Molly."

Paul: "Lucille."

John: When I do it for the fans I'm slinging it like a jerky.

How a group gets into its music can often be seen in the kind of music they play to get into themselves, and in *Let It Be,* this is only hinted at. The Beatles use oldies to get into new songs, not only as warmups ("if it's a slow one we'll omit it . . . if it's a fast one we'll git it . . .") but as a kind of invocation, as they summon up the presences of Carl Perkins, Jerry Lee Lewis, His Majesty Richard Penniman, Antoine Domino, Buddy Holly, Larry Williams, Elvis, and some contemporaries like Mick, Dylan, Pete Townshend, Hendrix, and the Band.

The list of oldies played in these sessions is almost a catechism: "Stand By Me," "Baby I Don't Care," "Thirty Days," "Hippy Hippy Shake," "Short Fat Fanny," "Fools Like Me," "You Win Again," "Turn Around," "Blue Suede Shoes," "True Love," "Wrong Yo Yo," "Sure To Fall," "Tennessee," "Maybelline," "Johnny B. Goode," "Sweet Little Sixteen," "Little Queenie," "Roll Over Beethoven," "Rock and Roll Music," "Singing the Blues," "Midnight Special," "Michael Row The Boat Ashore."

Then there are the frequent and often inane searches for lyrics. Paul working on "Get Back":

> Joe-Joe left his home in Tucson,
> Arizona but he knew it couldn't last

Paul: No, that won't do . . . class, bass, mass, what about looking for another blast.

Ringo: Thought it was going to be a gas.

Paul: Hoping he would find a gal.

Paul: It's just a little production (sings):

Oh Commonwealth?

John (sounding like a Boston matron): Yes?

George's beautiful transcendental song, "All Things Must Pass," influenced heavily by the Band, Tim Leary, Buddhist texts, and St. Augustine, was neither included in the film or on the album.

The Water, Torchlit, Two Thousand Arabs

Michael Lindsay-Hogg, who directed the now defunct *Ready, Steady, Go*—one of British television's better "pop" programs —and the Stones' Circus, directed two to four cameras in shooting *Let It Be.* And since some of the sound track lacked footage, special praise should be given to editor Tony Lenny, who made many of the looser ends meet.

During the shooting of *Let It Be* the Beatles talked about the film they wanted to have made. This Pirandello quality doesn't really come across in *Let It Be.* During one of the early rehearsals, Paul suggested the kind of film he had in mind:

"Get very bright lights so you see everything, instead of moody lighting, that kind of thing. With everything here, it hardly needs scenery. Really, it all should be about him and his drum kit. Look at his drum kit, it really looks great, beautiful, sitting there. Then John and his guitar and his amp, sitting there, actually showing it at that minute. The scenery would just be the other things around, like the scaffolding, the other cameras. It's like in a news event, like on 'Jude' the little screams were more interesting than the postman. If you can think slow, not bang! bang! bang! Instead of getting all the pacing, a chair lift, the flow, the pace is already there. You can glide down from the roof on a one-shot on to Ringo's face, float around, being careful not to miss anything. It's like Warhol's things; he goes to the other extreme, but he reckons there's a pace in *Empire.* Even a Tunisian amphitheater can be boring. I don't dig underestimating what's here. If it's going to be scenery, we should go the whole way and get galloping horses. You should get really close up, like right into one of John's eyes. Can you do that? That direction, rather than John and the moon."

Let It Be is not only a film about the Beatles deciding on the kind of film they wanted to appear in. It also shows them rehearsing for the imagined, debated possibility of their return to public performances after two and a half years. The House of Parliament, a Tunisian amphitheater, a Liverpool cathedral, a hospital, and on an ocean liner, "singing the middle eight as the sun comes up."

George: You know it's going to be the same thing there as here—it's going to be a bit nicer place to be in, but it's going to be even more complicated trying to plug in on all the mikes and tapes and all that crap.

Lindsay-Hogg: First of all visually the thing that interests me . . . naturally . . . Think of the helicopter shot over the amphitheater with the water with the lights and the water, torchlit, two thousand Arabs. Visually it's fantastic.

Paul: But if it was a fan club show. You remember the Wembley, or the Wimbledon one where we were in a cage, and like people were filing past; it was just a different kind of thing from what we ever did. It was terrible. That's not it. But that kind of thing made that show different because it was like playing to a thing, like a fan club.

John: I'm warming up to the idea of an asylum.

After all the possibilities in the world, and after all the transformations and posturings, it is the desire to be seen, to communicate with an audience, to hear the screams that will bring them into the present and pump energy into the myth that drives them onwards playing again in public. It would be an affirmation of the Beatles: "We really have to want to do a show at the end of it. I was saying to Mal this morning, because he had a dream last night of us doing the show, and he just said it was incredible, and I said I'd love to do that, just to play all these numbers one afternoon at the Saville to some people, or all day, or as in ***Hair,*** just setting up, rehearsing as the people walk in, sit down, get sandwiches and drink, and when we want to do a take we'd do sort of a take. Then we could do a couple of other small shows until we hit it and get over our nervousness with an audience" (Paul).

The roof concert is both the conclusion of the film and the solution to the debate about where and if to perform for an audience. The Beatles, wind-swept as if on shipdeck, the crowd of mildly surprised office workers and mid-day shoppers acknowledging the Beatles' first concert in two and a half years:

Lindsay-Hogg: Shall we go on filming until we leave here?

Paul: What we're doing is still rehearsing and we'll get it together.

George: We'll collect our thoughts and you collect yours about where we'll do the concert.

Lindsay-Hogg: What about the roof tomorrow?

Paul: We'll do the numbers. We're the band.

George: I'll do it if you've got us on the roof.

John: I'd like to go on the roof. I'll record the songs when you want to do it.

George: Anytime is paradise.

John: Anytime at all. You suggest where: Pakistan, the Moon, I'll still be there till you don't let me down. You'll be surprised at the story that will come out of this.

YOUR TOAST IN MY MIRROR OR, THE GROGAN AT THE BREAKFAST TABLE.

The unedited *Let It Be,* running to some 800 hours of film (including footage from all four cameras at Twickenham and on the roof), will perhaps someday be donated to the National Trust, where scholars will delve into its meaning. In its totality it is a monster document, revealing, in the same sense as studies of scientists isolated in bathyspheres for months at a time are revealing, or like the slouch of a body cast in plaster that takes several hours to set. It manifests the idiosyncracies, blemishes, acts of vision, and churlishness, the patterns and postures that the Beatles put themselves through while relating to each other and to their public images. The released version can reveal little of this.

Although the premise of the film at its inception was Warholian in the sense that you just turn the cameras on for two months and let it be, the end product is considerably more structured. For one thing, time will not allow what could have been a whole movie in itself, namely, the Beatles creating, working on, refining, and finally distilling *one* song, with peripheral dialogue, old rock, and general studio habits. Instead we have a series of about twenty songs flashing by with occasional "representative" dialogue. This is not to denigrate the quiet, unassuming, even magical moments which *Let It Be* captures, as when the music always ends discussion, each Beatle submitting to it, John and George finally understanding each other in "Dig It" or "For You Blue." But it *is* a sleight of hand (as John says, "Bognor Regis is a tartan that covers Yorkshire") that presents us with this condensation of moments into an illusion of a day in the life. The structure of the film as we see it gives the impression of elation, partly by the very physical progression of scenes from Act I in the murky sublunar atmosphere of Twickenham (rainbows on rainbows) through the intimacy of the Apple sessions and finally, the four evangelists emerging onto the roof to air, light, and the birth of spring. (The roof sequence was shot at the beginning of February.)

What dialogue there is in *Let It Be* suggests we could still be in some snug, day-to-day corner of Pepperland. The order of the day is cheerfulness (Paul: "Hi, lads." John: "Queen says no to pot smoking F.B.I. members.") Just the lads getting together for a bash. But, in the light of subsequent Beatle traumas, the illusion must seem somewhat false. The doubts about their being able to perform again in public, and the threatening clouds that were to break into open hostility with the release of Paul's album, are scarcely touched upon. In *Let It Be* we are given a glimpse of group friction (for the sake of realism), a dialogue between Paul and George which hits on one of the main contentions between them: none of them wants to be session man for the others. Paul: "I always seem to be annoying you. . . ." George: "All right, I'll play whatever you want me to play, or I won't play at all if you don't want me to play."

In another sequence, Paul talks earnestly to John ("now look, son") about how they *can* get it on, if they want to. But, because this is not cinéma vérité but a documentary made by the Beatles themselves, the emphasis is quite naturally not on the tensions. It is one of the paradoxes of reverence that we always wish to know the most intimate details of those we idolize, even when the details are not flattering, and for this reason *Let It Be* is not a completely satisfying film. It presents an "as if" situation that any fairly observant Beatle fan knows does not exist. And, again, it is just this insatiable curiosity, like the probing eye of the camera, staring like a mirror at their every action that has magnified their rifts and sealed their quarrels. Paul: "I get the horrors every morning about 9:00 when I get my toast and tea."

Daddy Has Gone Away Now . . .

One of the strangest phenomena in group situations is who will be "it," who will carry the weight, and here it is Paul, assuming the spectral role of Brian Epstein:

Paul: I mean we've been very negative since Mr. Epstein passed away. That's why. We haven't been positive. That's why all of us in turn have been sick of the group, you know. There's nothing positive in it. It is a bit of a drag. It's like when you're growing up and then your daddy goes away at a certain point in your life and then you stand on your own feet. Daddy has gone away now, you know, and we are on our own little holiday camp. You know, I think we either go home or we do it. It's discipline we need. It's like everything you do, you never had discipline. Mr. Epstein, he said, sort of "Get suits on" and we did. And so we were always fighting that discipline a bit. But now it's silly to fight that discipline if it's our own. It's self-imposed these days, so we do as little as possible. But I think we need a bit more if we are going to get on with it.

If Paul is elected to play "daddy" (and he has grown a beard to play the role), then George gets to play the bad boy, and his answer to Paul is, "Well, if that's what doing it is, I don't want to do anything."

Paul comes across as desperately trying to pull the whole thing together, like the father of a family that has become divided ("it's silly for us at this point to crack up"), while George, with a mixture of apathy and mysticism, appears not to care one way or the other, business versus pleasure:

Paul: We should organize our career now. Like the idea is to get us so we quite enjoy this . . . then what would you like to do next? Would you like to do a live show, lads?

George: It's like hard work really to do it. It's a drag 'cos I don't wanna work really . . . have to get up at 8:00 and get into my guitar . . . "You've got to play your guitar now" and you're not ready for it. But we've got to do that in order to get the goods in . . .

Paul carries the weight, and like an over-serious foster parent occasionally trips over George's punky put-ons:

George: You dig, baby?

Paul: Yeah.

George: You're so full of shit, man.

Paul: What?

George: Before you can pry any secrets from me, first you must find the real me. Which one will you pursue . . . Did you see that?

Paul: What?

George: The Beard.

Paul: No.

George: It's Jean Harlow and Billy the Kid in eternity. It's just the idea of two people on stage and all this audience of different people overhearing what they're saying. Jean Harlow says: "Before you can pry any secrets from me, first you must find the real me. Which one will you pursue?" It ends where she just sits on his knee, and then she sits in the chair and spreads her legs.

FOUR STARS IN SEARCH OF A UNIVERSE.

In the flak between George and Paul, John, enigmatic and profoundly humorous, traces out a cosmic anti-world of puns:

John: It's a feeling . . . it's enough to make a haggis grow legs; but tonight we'll celebrate on Irish Whiskey, said Gene Pitney, the only Sassenach in the group.

Ringo, who is given a token appearance in *Let It Be* singing "Octopus Garden" and a boogie duet with Paul, maintains his deadpan humor and dignity throughout. Derek Taylor once described Ringo as mis-cast in most of the films he has appeared in because "his genius is as a silent actor." And he bears this out beautifully in the sequence where Heather crashes down on his drum kit and his whole body jangles in a flip-flop mime of taken-unawares.

His long suffering face allows him to play a straightman with quizzical intensity to John's ventriloquist:

John: Bognor Regis is a tartan that covers Yorkshire. Rutland is the smallest county. Scarborough is a college scarf . . . And still the boon wasn't over, the Queen of Sheba wore falsies.

Ringo: I didn't know that.

John: Didn't you know that? You weren't there at the time. Cleopatra was a carpet manufacturer.

Ringo: I didn't know that.

John: John Lennon . . .

Ringo: A patriot.

John: I didn't know that.

George rephrases the universe in mystical homilies ("anywhere is paradise") and Paul, who's always "on" (a wink is as good as a nod) can never resist the temptation to play himself. When his head fills the screen, singing the title song on "Let It

Be," his face flashes between tramp and old testament prophet, but it never quite sticks, because he is always a little too sentimental to be believable.

As the unedited tapes run on and on, fragments of their lives fill in a fraction. They watch a lot of "telly": *Late Nite Line-Up* on BBC-2, *Spike Milligan,* science fiction. "I, Me, Mine," in fact, is based on a tune played by an Austrian marching band that George was watching late one night.

IMAGES OF BROKEN LIGHT.

Visually, *Let It Be* is as beautiful as the sum of its accidents: its unbelievable grainy color (generated from 16mm originals) washes about the screen in the Twickenham sequences like video rainbows, giving each his own aura: white for John, purple for Paul, mantra orange for George, and red for Ringo. At times it's like the Beatles in the land of Silver Surfer, especially in one sequence where George, in yellow and brown (and grainy as Dakota), seems to drift in and out of the rust background like a speckled trout.

The camera moves in and out as blindly and perceptively as coincidence itself, picking up with insect eye: fuzz on a microphone while John intones "Across The Universe"; Paul's fingers touching their reflection in the glazed piano board; George's face, pale as wax with downcast eyes, as his guitar gently weeps; Heather rushing into the studio and homing in on a gloppy painting of a flower by Zak, pinned on Ringo's wallboard; and John warbling shrilly as a sparrow on "Two Of Us."

But as often as the lens picks up the beautiful moments of the Beatles together, it misses others that beg to be recorded, and occasionally it blunders into crass word-image links that are just embarrassing. On "Dig It," the camera zooms to Billy Preston as John sings "B. B. King . . ." (they're both black, dig it?) and to Heather on "Doris Day . . ."

Outside, the oblique light reflects from Ringo's orange mac like molten lava and everything looks as if it were shot on a set from *Mary Poppins.* Old men in macs and sweaters gather around like out-of-work miners at the entrance of a colliery. The moments are precious, they know they will soon have to move, and in a gesture of devotion, Peter Asher kneels before John with lyrics on a sheet of paper.

While, in the end, all we have to relate to are the soft, luminous images of *Let It Be,* the Beatles will insist, like the characters in Pirandello's *Six Characters In Search Of An Author* that "the play is in us, sir!" Their voices on magnetic tape, buried in some vault, will always be ready to re-enact their drama, and only they know its true intensity:

Paul (in disembodied voice): The awful tension of being locked in each other's arms snapped last night at TV rehearsal, and Beatles John, George and Harold . . . A few vicious phrases took place.

John: He, the mystical one who lost so much of the Beatles' magic, she the nudie . . .

Paul: It's only the suddenness of their decline from the status of boys next door to the category of weirdies . . .

John (singing drowns out words):

Early in the morning
I'm giving you the warning
Don't you step on my blue suede shoes.

Paul: It would be about the middle of the 1960's
(next few words inaudible)
began to have a few spots of rust. I would deliberately read Ringo out of it, because he never developed any fetish towards the bizarre. Lennon was married happily. McCartney was going steady and George Harrison was about to marry. Everything in the Beatle garden was rosy. But that was a long time ago. Having scaled every known peak of show business the Beatles quite deliberately . . . never came home again. They went their own private way, found their own friends, and became less reliant on each other for guidance and comradeship . . .
(singing drowns out speech)
John (singing):

Early in the evening
I'm giving you the feeling
Everybody's nothing
And nothing to lose.

Paul: Today all of them find acute embarrassment at the stories of one another's adventures and conduct. Harrison's escapades with his favorite mystic from India . . .

John (singing):

Hold my baby as tight as I can
Tonight she's gonna be a big fat man
Oh baby with your rhythm and blues
Everybody's rockin tonight.

(singer and speaker trying to drown each other out)

Paul: Drugs, divorce, and slipping image play desperately on their minds and it appeared to them all that the public was being encouraged to hate them . . . capacity to earn is largely tied up in their performances as a group and until they are either rich enough . . .

(music drowns out voice)

. . . irrevocably doomed . . . all over . . . they will never be exactly the same again.

1970

5
Bob Dylan

Bob Dylan "surfaced" in New York City in 1971 at George Harrison's Bangla Desh benefit concert at Madison Square Garden after what was an almost uninterrupted hibernation of five years. The articles appearing here are really looks-over-the-shoulder at three previously remembered embodiments of the most elusive culture hero of the 1960's. Dylan's film *Eat the Document* was in fact completed in 1967, and the article-review of this film was written the night of its premiere at New York's Academy of Music on February 8, 1971. *Tarantula,* the book Dylan wrote between 1966–67, floated around in several xeroxed bootleg editions until its publication by Macmillan in the spring of 1971. And Dylan's personal appearance at the Bangla Desh Benefit—singing "Blowing in the Wind" and "A Hard Rain's Gonna Fall"—returned us in tone and manner to the image of the freewheelin' Bob Dylan circa 1963.

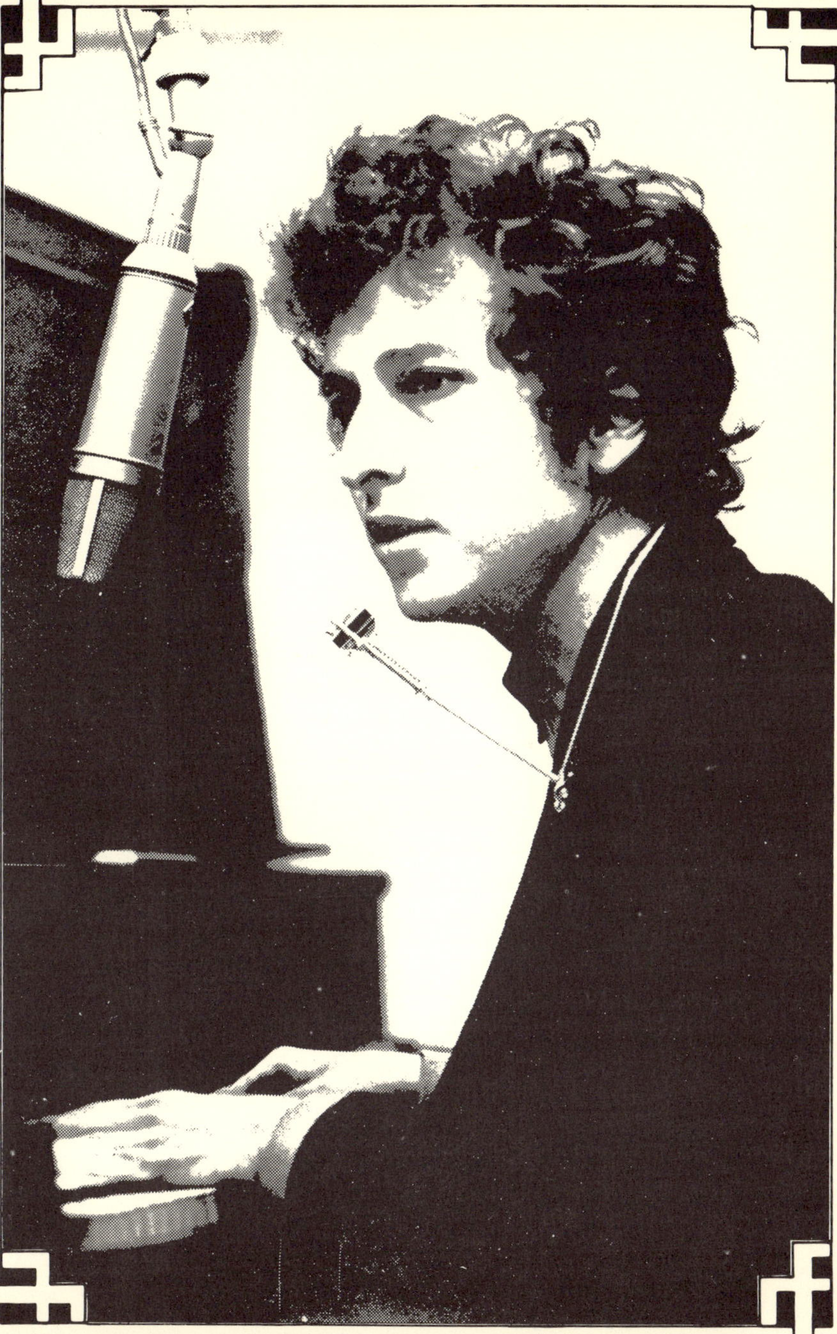

Eat the Document

It was an early evening rain, and merely on the basis of short advance announcements in ROLLING STONE, the Village Voice, and on Howard Smith's FM radio show, a couple of thousand persons showed up at the Academy of Music on February 8, 1971 to catch Dylan's one-hour color film *Eat the Document,* shown twice at 7:00 and 9:00 with proceeds going to a Pike County citizen's group which has been set up to stop strip mining in the South.

Jerry Rubin and Gordon Lightfoot where there. A. J. Weberman ("name me someone that's not a parasite and I'll go out and say a prayer for him"), so-called Minister of Defense of the so-called Dylan Liberation Front, was standing under the marquee wearing his *FREE BOB DYLAN* button and passing out a leaflet which concluded: "The movie you are about to see is about the old Dylan—a beautiful right-on dude who sang the truth and gave a lot of his bread to SNCC, but the new Dylan, the post-accident Dylan, is a stoned Pig."

The Academy of Music, with its cavernous dome and its karmic memories of the Chords and the Valentines, early Fifties rock and roll shows rubbed and ingrained into the seats, was the perfect setting for this revisitation of old Dylan lovers hoping to retrieve their fantasies of their hero who used to "meet on edges." And there everyone was with that "restless hungry feeling," waiting for some miracle, so-called Dylan Liberation Front members in the front rows, confusion boats, kneeling bloodhounds, mutiny from stern to bow—all of Dylan's images coming home to roost.

The Band's manager, John Taplin, who organized the screening, had announced we were going to see a work print. The first images of the film came on the screen, out of focus, no sound, and it was positively 14th Street. "Fix it, you bastards!" some shouted. Other friendly voices screamed: "Get the shit together"; "I see why ABC didn't buy this piece of shit"; "Let's see him shoot up!" Someone behind me was talking about buying the $2 pirate edition of Dylan's "liberated" novel *Tarantula.* A revolution in the Academy of Music.

The projector focused and started again, and on came a very special film conveying the sense of a private diary, both the subject and its filmic embodiment being that of a true night journey through mad, disjointed landscapes, a magic swirling ship of jump-cuts, "ready for to fade." Dylan said: "We cut it fast on the eye."

The quasi-methedrine logic of *Eat the Document* suggests a self-consciously disintegrating structure, an anti-documentary that uses the "star" image in order to de-mystify and decompose it. Thus Dylan's presence is undermined for any easy identification by means of juxtaposing images from Australia with say, a scene in an English train. Needless to say, the film's structure corresponds to what Dylan must have experienced on this mixed-up confusion tour.

Using footage taken mainly by Donn Pennebaker *(Don't Look Back),* during Dylan's 1966 world tour with the Band, both Dylan and editor-friend Howard Alk retired to Woodstock and shortly after Dylan's motorcycle accident, using editing ideas as their map, they constructed a film that suggests the works of Man Ray, Ron Rice, and William Burroughs, with its insistence on perceiving a multitude of concrete details and elliptical progressions. What one remembers are: silhouetted figures, a beautiful, almost androgynous Dylan with cigarette and shades, police dogs brutalizing a man in a bagpipe parade, a man wearing a sandwich board reading: "It is appointed unto men once to die," Dylan reading a paper in bed, a man in a war helmet, a cemetery, dogs on leashes, girls' faces, fans commenting on Dylan's music outside Royal Albert Hall ("It was rubbish"; "He was great, better than Presley"), and above all, the repeating images of travel—a train steaming and whistling across country, scores of cars with their one-too-many windows which one is always looking through. And in a scene which epitomizes the sense the film gives of one's watching postcards of the hanging, the camera pans over people's hands as they drunkenly pass plates across a Last Supper length table, and suddenly at the table's corner is Dylan in shades, shrouded in a private world, looking abstractly and warily to the side.

The soundtrack presents dream-like fragments of speech: "Have you ever heard of me? . . . I heard you booing . . . I can't believe that everyone makes it so difficult . . . I'm sorry for everything I've done." "Are you ever yourself at any time?" someone questions him, and Dylan shrugs. "Why are you here?" another reporter asks, to which Dylan says: "I take orders from someone on the telephone, but I never see him. He calls up and just tells me where to go." And we're back on the Nova Express.

The film's fantastic music is cut off, sometimes returning, in similar elliptical fashion. The audience at the Academy of Music booed when those amazing Liverpool versions featuring Dylan and the Band playing "Like a Rolling Stone," "One Too Many Mornings," and "Just Like Tom Thumb's Blues" were broken off abruptly. Other performances are briefly shown as well: "Tell Me Mama" and "Mr. Jones" with the Band at Albert Hall, three beautiful acoustic numbers by Dylan accompanied by Robbie Robertson, Johnny Cash, and Dylan singing "I Still Miss Someone." But most of the people at the Academy of Music wanted to see a 1966 Dylan concert and not, what is equally powerful, Dylan's particular filmic perceptions.

Most of these numbers, as well as the short fragments showing John Lennon and Dylan zonked out in the back of a car, are small scenes taken from longer rushes that Donn Pennebaker has been working on in "documentary" style, in a wonderful, still unfinished and unreleased film. Both Dylan's and Pennebaker's films go well together.

"I shot most of the film," Pennebaker says, "but it was pretty much Dylan directing what went on. And editing is all Dylan's. Dylan wanted *Eat the Document* to show what TV never does, to snap people's head a bit. It's Dylan's logic. And it's a little like a mystery tour, really an extraordinary event. To worry about whether it's good or bad is ridiculous. I find the film arresting, and I'm knocked out that he did it. Unlike my film, which I'm making in order to see a kind of record preserved, Dylan's film is complete. If someone had bought *Tarantula* and made a film of it that would be one thing. But in *Eat the Document* Dylan is making you see things with his own funky kind of sense."

At the beginning of the showing at the Academy of Music, Taplin announced that the film was "a little too freaky for ABC at that time, and they rejected it."

"That's a lie," said Hubbell Robinson, who was executive

producer for ABC's *Stage 67,* the ninety-minute program to which *Eat the Document* was originally contracted. "We didn't know what we had," Robinson recalled, "because when we saw the film in the fall of '66 it wasn't yet edited. By that time we had to make other programming commitments to producers for the spring of '67 and Dylan didn't know what the film would be and when it would be finished. But we were definitely interested in the film."

There's a possibility that *Eat the Document* will be distributed in the future. When it is released all the Mr. Joneses, whether they're fourteen or sixty-four, will be wondering why Dylan didn't just make a normal TV "music" film which anyone else could have made, when in fact *Eat the Document* is a near-visual equivalent of some of the songs Dylan was singing on *Highway 61 Revisited and Blonde on Blonde.*

1971

Tarantula

Once in a while, you can cross a street, walking down the backward abysm of time, and hear the sounds of early Byrds, *Meet the Beatles, Bringing It All Back Home.* Today, after having seen the succession of Dylan's new faces on *Nashville Skyline, Self Portrait,* and *New Morning,* you might again feel the mystery of time's reversing warp as the beautiful, androgynous, light-dark 1966 Dylan face stares in bookstores out through the cover of his five-year-old *Tarantula.*

Macmillan's editor-in-chief, Bob Markel, who wrote the book's preface, recently added some details to explain *Tarantula's* delayed appearance:

"Dylan had written about 12 pages of typed, single-spaced material in 1965. He later finished the manuscript, and we set it in galleys. This was about July, 1966. When I talked to Bob at that time, he mentioned that the book didn't look right and that he wanted to improve parts of it. We agreed, but then he had his accident and couldn't work; he was having difficulty reading. So I knew the schedule was shot. Now we had the legal right to publish the book then. But I felt it would have been a lousy thing to do. Dylan didn't want it out, and we also knew that he never would have darkened our doors again if we had gone ahead.

"About two years ago, a reporter from the Toronto Globe and Mail called to ask me if I knew about xeroxed bootleg copies of the book going around. And then the underground papers got hold of it, perhaps from one of the places we'd sent galleys—*Time, Life,* Grossman's office—maybe a copy was stolen from my desk, I don't know. We decided that we couldn't take any legal action, so we decided to do nothing. But soon there were other editions coming out, and Bob became annoyed. Last year I suggested he take a look at the book again and make some marginal notes. He tried, and it didn't make any sense to him. But late last year, he finally decided just to put the book out instead of having people think that Macmillian or he had suppressed it. Because these accusations didn't hold well with him or me. So the five years' wait is over."

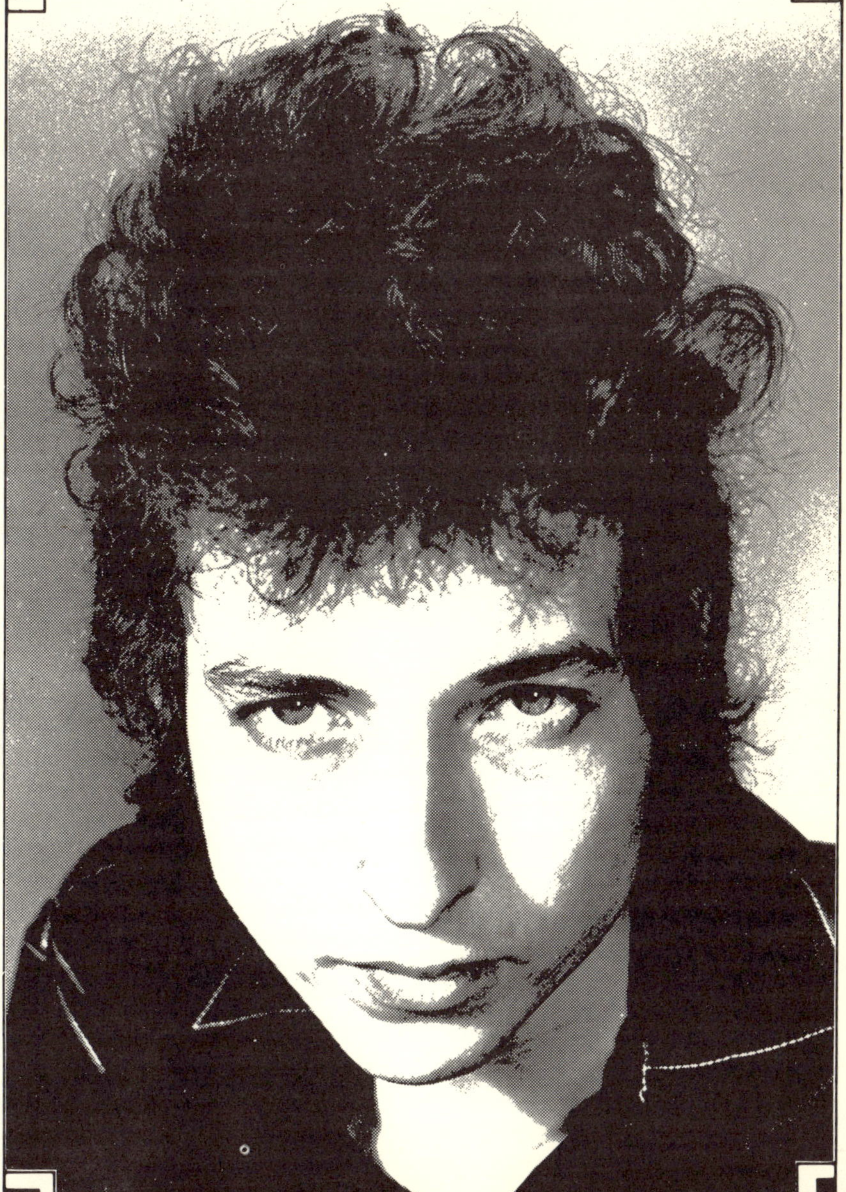

It's difficult to know how *Tarantula* would have read five years ago. The relationship between cultural disintegration and its literary exemplification in *Tarantula* might have been considered very far out at the time. Today, *Tarantula's* close to fifty schismatic and disjointed "fables," "poems," "scenes," "hallucinations," whatever, suggest only an imitative fallacy, for they are literally about too much of nothing. And one can simply imagine Dylan waking up one morning five years ago, turning over to see the galleys of *Tarantula* lying next to him, and thinking: "No way, man. It's only fit for covering your head. Let's not publish."

Suppose, as one anti-formalist critic does, that "art is simply what occurs in a setting and situation appropriate to a certain kind of attention." Then, by that measure, what is there to attend to in *Tarantula?* It mirrors, of course, the Dylan world; it is a notebook in which Dylan jots down some of his best-known characters (Mona, Rain Man) as well as cadences ("why are you always wearing your brother's clothes? think about it kid, but don't ask your father"; "the punch-drunk sailor with a scar below his nose suddenly slaps and kicks little sally . . . you Know he knows something's happening").

The prose-poem fables, which have titles like "Mouthful of Living Choke" and "Somebody's Black Nite Crash," describe or transmit flashing episodes in the life of a pantheon of new Dylan characters like Twinkle Clown, Tao, Simply That, and Mr. Clap—characters who often split themselves like protozoa into others (Mona, for instance, becomes Moan and then Monk).

Inserted among the fables are scores of letters from persons like Zorba the Bomb, Simon Hord, and The Law, and these letters sometimes give clues to the nature of the enterprise: e.g., "unfortunately my friend, you shall not get the information you seek out of me" (letter from ivan the bloodburst), or "it's where it's not at that you gotta know" (letter from Funka). "Real" persons like Bo Diddley, Adlai Stevenson, Jack Paar, Lord Buckley, Freud, and Baby Huey are glimpsed in short takes. And, hovering over the entire desolate crew is Aretha, goddess, siren, the mysterious queen who at one point is used as a trump card by one of the players. In fact, *Tarantula* often seems like the hallucination of a methed-up poker player, rapidly dealing the cards, all of which reveal only parts of himself in a cosmically tricked deck.

The book suffers from hypertrophied images: "a bearded leprechaun . . . wearing a topless mafia cape"; freak and goon show humor: Cunk selling "fake blisters at the world's fair," "a sauerkraut hits him in the face"; punched-out allegorical names: Plague the Kid, Weep the Greed, Tom the Wretched; and wiseacre wit: "ed Sullivan and Fresh kid, a relative of Prince Rainier and visiting this country as a guest of Cong Long, a grandson of Huey Long—seen escaping with catchers' mitts."

There are, of course, stunning episodes, like the story of Simply That, or the section beginning "back betty, black bready" with its "blam de lam!" chorus. And, at the heart of the book, there's the dream of the burning building, in front of which the hero is singing, unable to put out the fire "because both myself & the fire were in the same/Time all right but we were not in the same Space . . . i could not feel any guilt about just standing there singing for as i said i was picked up & moved there not by my own free will but rather by some unbelievable force." A woman named Justine tells him he's correct not to feel guilty, for "only God can be everywhere at the same Time & Space." And this episode is related to the dialogue about the House in Doomstown (p. 116), which in fact turns into a debate between the ideas of social commitment and personal accommodation.

Whereas writers like Lautréamont, Rimbaud, and William Burroughs insist on combining a careful delineation of the minute particulars of their demonic visions with a tone of insouciant, often lyrical cruelty, Dylan's Season in Hell reveals too often merely the fragments of an exploding conscience drifting away from any moral or asthetic center. His assaults against the "wall of dollar" and "the intoxicating ghosts of dogma" are rebuffed as his "hipster's dictionary" suffocates him with too many words.

Dylan, who in his songs has captured and distilled as true at representation of the American idiom as Mark Twain, William Carlos Williams, or Chuck Berry, suffers in *Tarantula* from a case of self-inflicted tarantism—a jittery uncontrolled language dance. In a way, the book's manifest self-indulgence can be seen as a painful consequence of what must have been for Dylan a period of near self-abolition.

There's a passage in *Tarantula* when the author uncovers his confidence-man persona to present his epitaph: "Here lies bob dylan/killed by a discarded Oedipus/who turned/around/to investigate a ghost/& discovered that/the ghost too was more than one person."

"If a dervish remained in a state of ecstasy," a Sufi saying goes, "he would be fragmented in both worlds." It's no surprise that a year after Dylan completed *Tarantula,* he wrote: "Strap yourself/To the trees with roots/You ain't goin' nowhere."

1971

I Dreamed I Saw Bob Dylan

You might see me on your roads
When I'm a-passin through
Remember me how you wished, too,
As I'm a-driftin' from your view.
—"Long Time Gone"

Bob Dylan has been passing through people's minds more often than he's been in view. Abbie Hoffman saw him in Woodstock. A. J. Weberman sees him almost anyplace, anytime. Dylan, in fact, has become an archetype—the *hallucination publicitaire* of millions of Dylan acolytes.

People resent A. J. Weberman not so much because of what some think is his self-serving parasitism, but rather because he thinks he has decoded and "mastered" Dylan, murdering to dissect in an act of self-appropriation. "I'm not Dylan, Al," Bob told A. J., "you're Dylan." And everyone wants to have the option of seeing the Dylan that's himself.

With everyone trying to absorb him, it's not surprising that Dylan, in order to make some space for himself, became a bit of the archetypal Trickster. Someone tells of seeing Dylan in a Boston supermarket, leaning on a shelf of canned goods and jotting down notes. "Hi," the guy said. "Ho," Dylan responded. With too little room in which to exist ("What's worse is this pain in here, I just can't stay in here"), Dylan has often emptied himself out, "evaporated," as he says in one of his songs, only to come back in new suits and trappings, but very much in his wits. Dylanophiles, meanwhile, hang onto reassuring categories—pre- and post-accident, "new" and "old." The underlying fear is: what if Dylan just goes away? So people see him everywhere.

Since his accident in 1966, Dylan has made only four concert appearances: the Woody Guthrie benefit at Carnegie Hall; a concert with the Band in Edwardsville, Illinois; the second Isle of Wight Festival; and now the Bangla Desh benefit. His feature appearance at the Isle of Wight before two hundred thousand

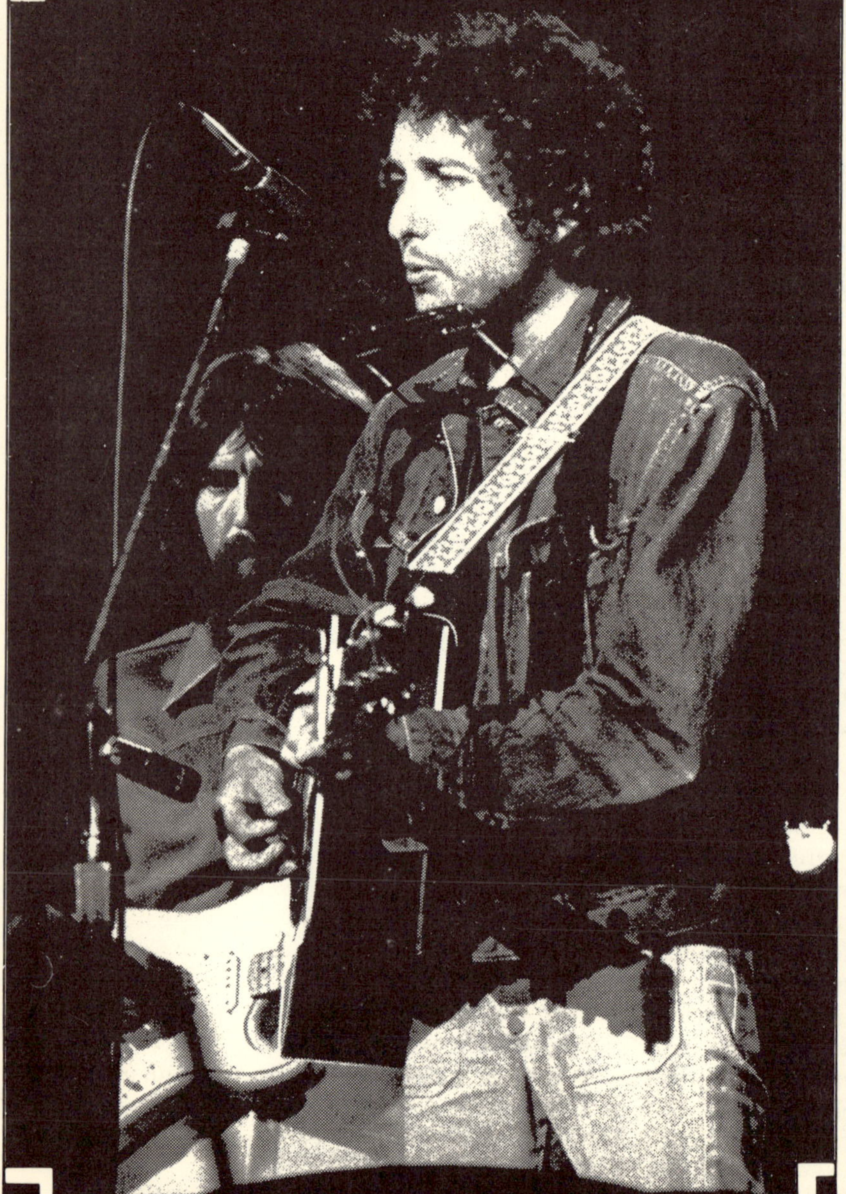

persons seemed like a mirage. Dylan came on stage and backed by the Band, sang for an hour, then disappeared. One reporter wrote that Dylan wore a green shirt; another, a yellow one. One critic heard him sing "Baby Blue"; another, "Positively Fourth Street." (He sang neither.)

Dressed in a white linen suit, a bit nervous and edgy but looking as if he had just put down a glass of mint julep, Dylan sang with his new "tonal breath control"—musically accenting every word of a song so that lines like: "Bow down to her on Sunday/Salute her when her birthday comes" were no longer phrased de *dah* de *dah* de *dah-dah* (iambically) but *de de de de de de-de*—like a person dancing very small steps.

In that concert, Dylan slid on one line from major to minor and back again, and when singing by himself, telegraphed harmonies so that omitted modulations created new melodic lines. Although Dylan ended his solo numbers, as of old, strumming while backing up from the microphone, you felt that he remained outside of the song, viewing it from a nearby distance. Sometimes he lingered on a note, furnishing it with the lightest of melismas, vocalizing and decorating one syllable. Dylan drew out and softened his lines while the Band musically pared down the rhythm, subdividing beats. Robbie Robertson added functional—not decorative—guitar solos, illustrating what Dylan must have meant when he described Robertson as "the only mathematical guitar genius I've ever run into who does not offend my intestinal nervousness with his rear guard sound."

Their version of "Lay Lady Lay" was charged with a more urgent weight than that heard on *Nashville Skyline.* And this particular aura and those magnificent musical confines within which the Band surrounded Dylan strangely seemed to detach him from his material further than he might have felt towards it. Or felt that night. People expected Dylan to embody musically those rattled experiences which his older songs spoke of, whereas Dylan just sang his songs with a clarity that radiates from inside the lines, lighting up the words like eyes: "Once I had mountains in the palm of my hand/Rivers that ran through every day."

Which all goes to say that the Isle of Wight Festival enabled you to eavesdrop on Dylan playing with the Band one summer evening. To people who thought that Dylan was themselves, the event entered consciousness as the mythical Return of the Hero from the Dead. But this Return was merely the symbolic substructure underlying a lovely concert—with a few flat notes—by an extraordinary artist.

Sometimes you find yourself sinking through memories like water, imagining it's yourself you're discovering. At the bottom of the wishing well, you see only what you wanted to find—an Idol mirroring your fantasy of him. But Dylan never accepted himself as someone's mirror. He told how Woody Guthrie was his first and last idol, "shattering even himself as an idol." And he once wrote: "I will never chase a living soul/into the prison grasp/of my own self love."

From the start, Dylan invited you to share his dream: "You can be in my dream, if I can be in your dream—I said that." The dream is that of self-realization. He never meant: "Pilfer me, become me." So at the Isle of Wight he raised his hand suddenly at that moment in "One Too Many Mornings" to emphasize the line: "Everything I'm saying you can say it just as good."

In a sense, Dylan puts on his various selves as easily as most people put other people on. There are three words in the *Book of Job* translated as: "For the fainting—from his friend—loyalty." At Madison Square Garden, Dylan was loyal not so much to the expectations of his admirers as to the meaning and beauty of his songs. There was no forcing of rhythms, no Isle of Wight "invention." He sang as effectively as he ever has, and probably improved on "Love Minus Zero" and "It Takes a Lot to Laugh."

He appeared on-stage in the dark: curly hair, Levi jacket, guitar, and mouth harp. People cheered, but they didn't believe it, responding the way one does after having obtained something deeply hoped for with a kind of passionless disbelief.

"Oh where have you been, my blue-eyed son?" Dylan began. Why was he taking us back? Just when we were getting used to A. J. Weberman's business exec-sometime record maker, out came the freewheelin' 1963 Bob Dylan, singing more beautifully than ever, his voice suggesting Hank Williams' intensity, Roy Acuff's vocal coloration, and the famous Dylan phrasing—all of this blended into a controlled, deep-flowing lyricism, balancing the expressiveness of *Blonde on Blonde* with the elegance of *Nashville Skyline.* What was this new incarnation? Lazarus rising from our dead memories? Coyote impersonating some highway rambler? Was he really singing the lines no one ever expected to hear him sing again: "How many years can some people exist/Before they're allowed to be free?"

Like John Wesley Harding, Dylan can't be tracked or chained down. And he doesn't make foolish moves. Perhaps Weberman's "cop out" imprecations had gotten to him. Perhaps Dylan chose at least two songs that literally express his feelings about Bangla Desh ("Where hunger is ugly, where souls are forgotten"—"Hard Rain" or "How many deaths will it take till he knows/That too many people have died?"—"Blowin' in the Wind"). One wondered whether Dylan had reached a level of consciousness where, in Jung's words, he could "detach the earlier state from himself and objectify it, that is, say anything about it. So long as his consciousness was itself trickster-like, such a confrontation could obviously not take place." Or perhaps Dylan simply decided to reappear in the guise of the person who used to sing at civil rights benefits in the early Sixties.

"He's an inscrutable cat, man," one of Dylan's friends said the day after the concert. Anyone who thinks that Dylan will now start writing more "protest" songs had better wait and see what self-portrait he draws next. Behind all his protean changes and disguises, it's possible that Dylan, as one person commented, was singing his older songs because Leon Russell just happened to like them. As Dylan waved so long to the crowd, you sensed that this might just be his way of saying goodbye to New York City once again, looking a lot the way he did when he was living on Fourth Street almost ten years ago.

1971

6
Poems

He Spends Time in Southern California

I could ride the Disneyland sky ride forever.
It is always tea time or perpetual autumn,
My Duino, fireworks above my head.
The poets' girlfriends ride the bobsled—Maud, Milena . . .
Fenimore sits alone.
I see them all blondes, flighty pink ribbons,
threes in their convertibles zooming home.

Down south, a love note on my door:
"Your intellectuality is so strong it destroys my womanhood"
or "Your mouth renders me mad."
Instead, they open up the surf with their dizzy teeth,
thousands of sprinklers light rainbows on the lawn,
even poison pink oleander trees make me cling.

They come again and stay.
In twenty years they look up, mild with pleasure,
and in fifty, too, back like the sea,
back with their careless limbs.
They are always coming to me like Friedrich's
great beautiful cats of prey.
How they leave me with their wrists,
yet I fly above it.

In my heart of daughters they look lovelier than
   wild peacock feathers,
shoots under moss, arms, stems. . . .
They come to the breathing names, watering the brush:
Borrego Springs, Mesa Grande, Escondido, Solana Beach,
and there is always a happy day,
and now you abandon me.

Air and Angels

1

My head can't fit the moths.
Come at me. I'm dependent on you.
When I call, the water is at my ears.
In fact, when it's raining all over,
I lie, feeling I'm water, sensations before orgasms
prolonging this all afternoon.
I listen to songs like
You told me so many many lies,
but I didn't want to hurt you.
Today the Rolling Stones are breaking up,
tomorrow they're breaking up—perpetual fall.
Moths come off flowers to my sweaters.
You say, They don't hurt you.
But because my blue and green sheets,
which everyone sleeps between,
turn suddenly white, you tell me,
Take care of yourself, anyway, love.

2

There are words that slip out of you
(thinking:
    the action of a "leaf falling"
    helps you lie with her
    in slower fucking)
like "erect" (hearing "direct")
or "green eyes" which is my own rising.

"Earth" . . . your blue veins flow to the side.
Your hips are too small.
"I guess they'll have to cut me open."

Jacob fought "his" angel.
"Today I feel nothing
but am afraid of losing you."
Other times, when you light the oven,
bending down,
I have you close the curtains in a night shift,
as I stand outside and ask you to come in.

The Big Bopper told me:
"Girls are mirages."
"Trips cross country are mirages."
"Eyes through the head are mirages."
Still, I want to walk through West Berlin with you,
near the opera house, listening to *Moses und Aaron*—
losing our words.

On the Road of Death

AFTER HENRI MICHAUX

On the road of Death,
My ma met this huge iceberg;
She wanted to talk,
But it was too late,
A huge iceberg of cotton.
She looked at us, my brother and me,
And then she cried.
We told her—what an absurd lie!—that we
    understood perfectly.
She had such a lovely smile then, a young girl's smile,
Which was just like her real self,
Such a real pretty smile, almost demure;
And then the Opaque swallowed her up.

7
Music

Between 1966–67, a few friends and I took turns presenting open-ended, late-night radio programs for KPFA in Berkeley. One night a week I used to interview various persons—whether the Diggers, Kenneth Anger, or Susan Sontag—and intersperse the conversations with different kinds of music: a Bulgarian love song followed by the Beach Boys' "Barbara Ann," Luciano Berio's *Visage* followed by The Byrds' "It Won't Be Wrong," a late Brahms Intermezzo, James Brown's "Prisoner of Love," and an example of Japanese *gagaku.* But except for the Pacifica and several college radio stations, this eminently reasonable and aesthetically pleasing kind of catholic programming is almost non-existent.

As I wrote in a review of Elliott Carter's *Concerto for Orchestra* which appears in this section: "Each piece of music is its own medium, but whether you listen to Pygmy music, Balinese gamelan music, Machaut, Chopin, or Arnold Schoenberg, your awarenesses and feelings are a function of your perceptions: you have to allow yourself to hear what is there and not expect or demand something that isn't." Many kinds of music are, of course, disappearing. The "single vision" Top-40 approach to music appreciation simply reflects a more universal homogenization of musical styles. Fourth-rate rock bands from Bali and Zagreb imitating The Doors attest to the efficacy of the transitorized onslaught directed against many authentic and vital non-Western classical and folk traditions. Fortunately, recordings of the music of the world's peoples are becoming more popular, and an increasing number of musicians and composers like Harry Partch, Lou Harrison, Phillip Glass, Karlheinz Stockhausen, and Ornette Coleman have been discovering and working with non-Western music.

The articles on "ethnic" music and on early American music first appeared in the *New York Times.* The other articles and essays on a varied number of composers and musicians were originally published in *Rolling Stone* magazine.

Leonard Crow Dog and the Music of the World's Peoples

Those who think of "ethnic" music as anything from the Kingston Trio to Simon and Garfunkel's adaptation of Peruvian Quechua songs, a koto record, or Ravi Shankar at Monterey will be amazed by the range and beauty of many recently recorded examples of music of the world's peoples. For the first time we are attaining a standard of technical fidelity and a perceptive selection of music that will shortly disappear or be transformed into what Westerners usually think of as the "norms" of musical tradition.

Not that there's anything egregiously corrupting about the transmogrification of, say, the American black gospel and blues tradition into R and B and contemporary soul music. Any acculturation that produces Aretha Franklin or B. B. King reveals the expressive power of evolving tradition.

What most people forget about is the original and most basic American tradition—that of the American Indians. And with the recent rediscovery of continuing practice of peyote shamanism (in the writings of Huxley and Carlos Castaneda, for example), it's not surprising to observe a renewed interest in Indian peyote ritual music. Structurally, peyote songs are some of the least complex in the American Indian tradition; their beauty lies mainly in the way, by means of periodic incantatory repetitions, they manifest and heighten the efficacy of a magic verbal talisman of affirmation. As in most Indian songs, just the simple revelation of the details of personal and sacramental reality attains, especially in our sophisticated times, an unmediated profundity: "In the great night my heart will go out. Toward me the darkness comes rattling" (Papago Death Song, translated by Frances Densmore).

A Sioux Indian named Leonard Crow Dog is an unusual but not untypical shaman. Eighty years ago Leonard Crow Dog's

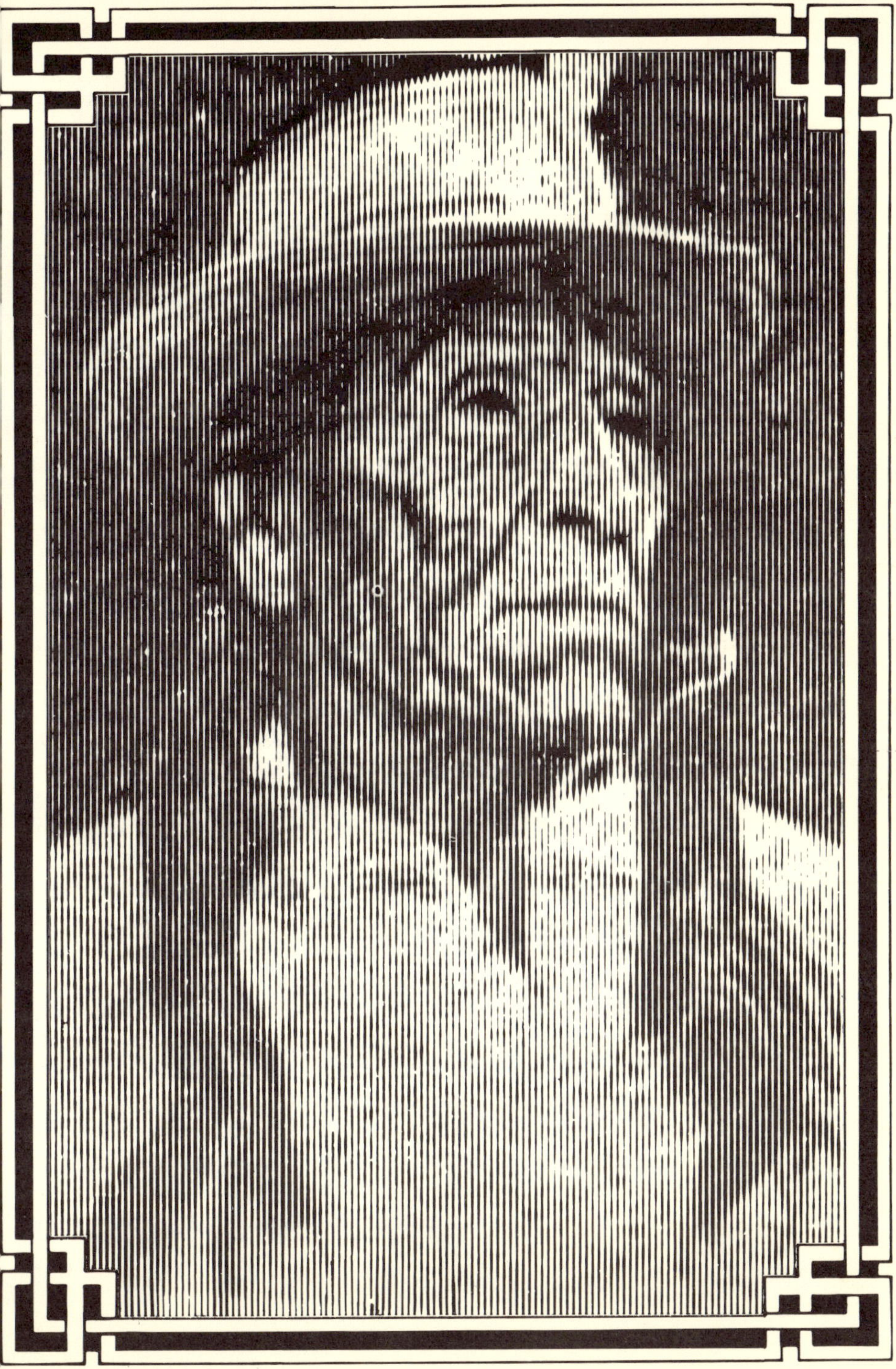

Ghost Dancer grandfather shot Chief Spotted Tail, whom he thought to be a U.S. Government flunky. Sentenced to hang, he began singing his death song until, at the last moment, his lawyer discovered there was no law under which an Indian could be executed for killing another Indian. The Crow Dogs have since continued to practice their religion and rituals, meditating in a vision pit dug into a hilltop, and performing both Yuwipi and peyote ceremonies. This ceremonial music—sung by Leonard and his father Henry Crow Dog—makes up *Crow Dog's Paradise* (Elektra), an album which takes its name from the Crow Dogs' home in Rosebud, South Dakota, a grassy hollow surrounded by pine-studded hills.

Leonard is a medicine man and chairman of the Native American Church, which is incorporated under the state laws of Arizona, Montana, Kansas, and South Dakota, enabling it to use peyote, the hallucinogenic cactus, as a sacrament. Leonard has performed as a dancer at New York's Electric Circus, Philadelphia's Electric Factory, and at the anti-poverty demonstration at Resurrection City in Washington, D. C., but he spends most of his time in the Rosebud reservation, welcoming strangers who wish to partake of his Saturday morning services.

Recently, Leonard visited New York and stayed with his friend and biographer Richard Erdoes. He sat on the edge of Erdoes' living room couch, his strong Mount Rushmore face framed by long black braids, his shirt open, saying:

"I had peyote when I was 7, and I haven't turned into any monster. By partaking of it, you research peyote and it researches you. You will see all your qualifications. It's the chief of all medicines and with it you will see your soul and yourself and find out how far you are from the universe.

"I almost got put away a few years ago for having whites in the ceremony. But now we have documents to make peyote a sacrament. We don't use it as a drug, abusing and misusing it. I'll have a service with people who come to see our family. There are leaders and helpers behind me. And you've got to learn peyote's ways and learn the songs. I want to share the visions I have with the white man. Peyote can speak any language.

"The Indian almost lost his culture. I tried to take off where my people left off. Bring it back and let the people go from there. This is where we stand, and a white man can then come to understand. I sang one of my songs on the record in English, but you will feel what I'm singing in the others if you're spiritually aware of the sacrament."

The songs on *Crow Dog's Paradise* are thought to be "racially inherent" in Indians and shared by all of them. This isn't correct. The music of the Kwakiutls or Hopi, for example, differs from that of these Sioux peyote songs, which feature a fairly relaxed vocal technique, tile-type melodic contours, small durational values, isorhythmic phrasing, and a continuously regular rhythmic pulsation. Like most peyote music, Leonard's songs use the water drum and rattles which are at the service of the incantatory and visionary sacramental experience. Peyote was introduced to the Sioux and Navajos by the Apaches about a hundred years ago, and the music on Leonard's record can be compared to that heard on Folkways' "Music of the Sioux," recorded in the Forties by Willard Rhodes. Henry and Leonard Crow Dog make their own musically unsophisticated songs—finding them in the midst of vision—but they are part of the oldest and truest American musical tradition.

Sioux music, like Cajun or Balinese music, suggests a world where art and life continually interpenetrate, erasing the boundaries that most of us think must exist between work and play, sensual communion and spiritual experience, the musician's ego and his tradition. The Sioux, and almost any other so-called primitive people, value songs of work, love, worship, and death equally. Recent performances at the Brooklyn Academy of Music of Cambodian, Senegalese, and Moroccan dancers and musicians all confirm the aims of the Greek tragedians, as well as of great Eastern theaters like the Kathakali, Balinese Barong, and the Thovil of Ceylon—a social healing, the purification and well-being of the community achieved by means of communion with the divine.

Music played the same sort of role during Bach's time and even for the first couple of years of the San Francisco rock scene. But you can't create such a community with music. And with rock now lost, for the most part, in a state of torpor and entropy—tedium sounding off against nostalgia on almost every side of every record—it's enlightening and more joyful to turn to the many recent examples of unadulterated "ethnic" music recordings.

One of the most dazzling of these recordings features the music of the master Moroccan musicians of Joujouka, recorded and edited by the late Brian Jones, and just released on an album entitled *Joujouka* (Rolling Stones Records—Atlantic). These excerpts from a truly Dionysiac Moroccan Pan Pipe Festival reveal a subtle alternation and overlapping of intensely resonating periodic motifs cascading into a sound mass of what one imagines to be a thousand screaming ecstatic birds. It is astounding music, worthy of the apocalyptic Beast from the Land.

In a gentler mood, Nonesuch Records' *A Bell Ringing in the Empty Sky* presents a Japanese *shakuhachi* (vertical bamboo flute) recital performed by Goro Yamaguchi, quietly manifesting the diaphanous qualities of a tone's inner life. Articulations, timbral modifications, pitch inflection, fluctuations of intensity all combine to produce an extraordinary meditative experience.

This record is part of the Nonesuch Explorer series, a project which outstrips the relatively few commercial attempts that have been made to present accurately the music of the world's peoples.

Columbia's World Library of Folk and Primitive Music of the middle Fifties presented mostly fragmentary, low-fidelity ethnomusicological samplings. Folkways Records set the popular recording standard in the Forties and Fifties with its enormous monaural catalogue including fine musical examples of the Ituri Forest Pygmies, Mexico's Cora Indians, and Nepalese tribal music. And recently there have been some good stereo recordings from the UNESCO collection of Oriental and African disks, the excellent French-produced Ocora African series, and the scholarly Anthology of the World's Music collection, Including Tibetan tantric and traditional Chinese music.

The five-year-old Explorer series, under the aegis of coordinator Teresa Sterne and A&R producer Peter Siegel, has so far released forty-five albums. And except for several of the first ten disks, leased from European labels, they set a new standard for the presentation of this music.

It's impossible to describe or define briefly the forms and

types of music heard on the best of these albums. Nonesuch has just released a two-record Explorer Sampler, *The Nonesuch Explorer—Treasures of the Explorer Series,* containing thirty cuts from its catalogue. It's a good introduction but the selections are, of necessity, often merely excerpts. Until you can afford most of the Explorer Series recordings (at a reasonable $2.98 per record), I would suggest that the finest of the controlled studio recordings, made with musicians who have at one time visited Wesleyan University's World Music Center or the University of Washington's School of Music, include: the *shakuhachi* record already mentioned; the Indian *tanam* and *sarangi* recitals and the four South Indian instrumental and vocal albums; the folk fiddling from Sweden; and the African *mbira* recital.

The Explorer field recordings feature a collection of Tahitian music; two Bulgarian albums in addition to the reissue of the amazing *Music of Bulgaria;* Peter Siegal's and Jody Stecher's *The Real Bahamas;* South American *Black Music* and Peruvian albums; and the magnificent Balinese records—*Music for the Balinese Shadow Play, Javanese Court Gamelan, Music from the Morning of the World,* and *Golden Rain.* These last two albums present the Ramayana Monkey Chant (the extended version is on *Golden Rain* a dance of exorcism know as the *ketjak*—two hundred men squatting in concentric circles chanting *tjak* with an overwhelming controlled rhythm thrust.)

David Lewiston, who recorded the *ketjak* as well as the marvelous South American albums, is an Englishman who lives in New York. "I'm going to the field as much to learn as to make recordings," he says. "I'm making a record, rather than looking for some esoteric significance that would interest only half a dozen scholars, I try to think how I can help the reasonably intelligent layman to enjoy this lovely music. Some people may say this is a popularizing approach, but I don't think that's a bad aim.

"It's only recently that it's been feasible to make really decent recordings in the field. In the Thirties they would have to take record cutting machines out into the fields, and very often the equipment would fail. The important thing is good mikes—studio condenser microphones. This was the key. Every recording situation is different, and you have to know how to listen to what the sound is like in any particular place. It's a once-only situation. I take two pairs of microphones, twenty hours of recording tape, camera, and film. This with a change of clothes amounts to seventy pounds, much better than the previous two hundred pounds people had to carry. It's still a major undertaking going out into the field, but it's possible now to go by oneself."

For listeners tired of manic rock or imitation folk, the Explorer series is proving to be one of the most vital and important recording projects of the past decade. The real is never a hype, and, as the ancients said, it enhances life values.

Our Musical Past Rediscovered—From Fuging Tunes to Sousa

Nineteenth-century American musical life—a mixture of carnival exhibitionism, parlor recitals, and tepid academicism—presented an unlikely environment for the conception and development of any kind of important compositional practice. And it certainly seems as if the idiosyncratic twentieth-century tradition represented by composers like Charles Ives, Carl Ruggles, Henry Cowell, Ruth Crawford Seeger, Harry Partch, John Cage, and Elliott Carter were spontaneously generated.

Yet it was the early American composer William Billings (1746–1800) who, when asked about the Rules of Composition, wrote: "Nature is the best Dictator, for all the hard, dry, studied rules that ever was [sic] prescribed will not enable any person to form an air . . . . I think it best for every composer to be his own Carver"—words which suggest the later attitudes of both Ives and Ruggles.

Of course, Billing's anthems and fuging tunes (which I'll return to later) were products of a Jeffersonian way of thinking by which composers considered music a "craft" like any other (Billings himself was a tanner as well as a musician). In the nineteenth century, however, musical life was often seen simply as a form of entertainment.

The pianist Anton Rubinstein, for example, was advised to blacken his face in time for his "show" in Memphis, Tennessee. A pianist named Hatton would appear on stage with a string of sleigh bells attached to his right leg and would proceed to shake it at some moment during the piece, thus earning him "a storm of applause which had no end" until the act was repeated several times *da capo*. The widely loved orchestral composition entitled *The Fireman's Quadrille* included the clanging of fire bells, the simulation of a stage fire, and the trooping on stage of a

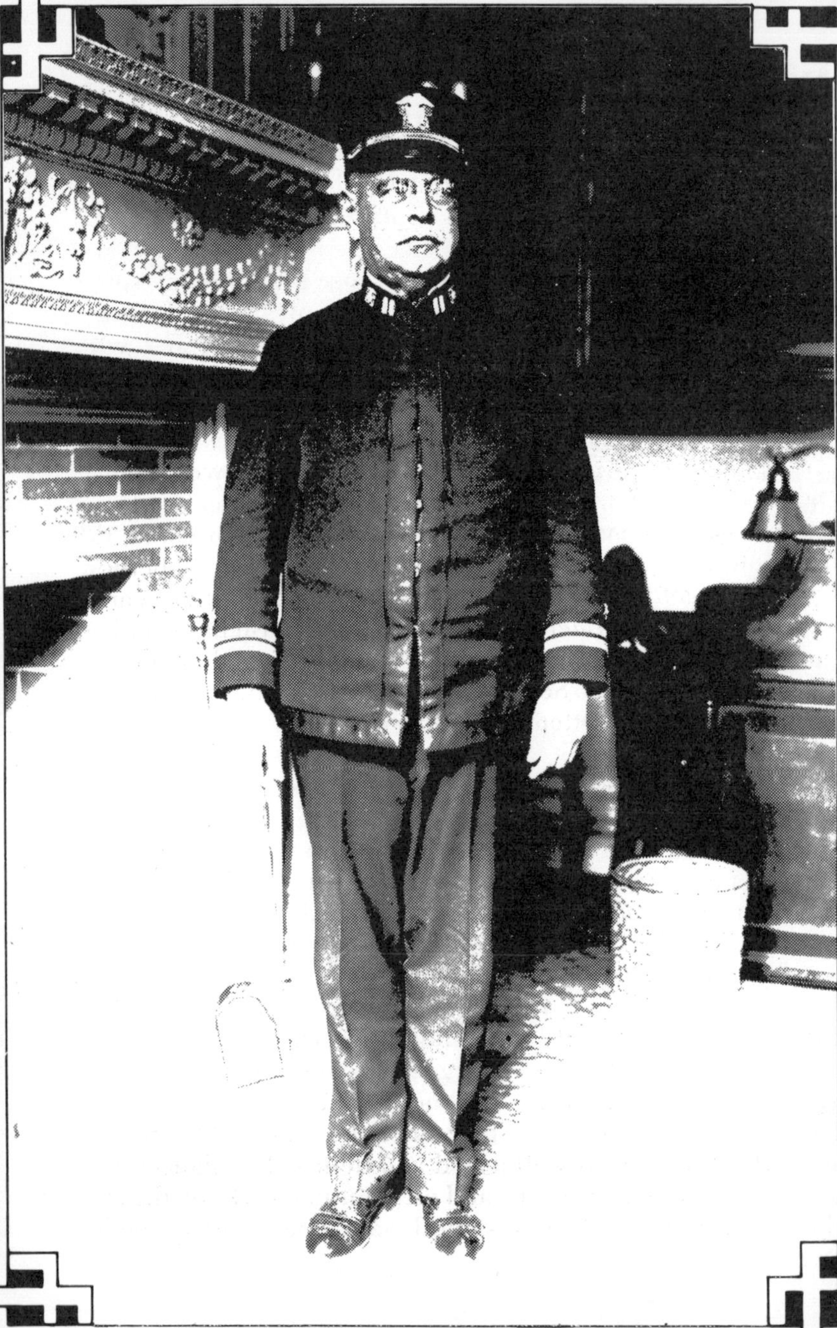

fully attired fire brigade that extinguished the blaze forthwith. Is it any wonder that Jenny Lind was managed in this country by P. T. Barnum?

The aesthetic alternative to these antics—antics which might, in fact, be seen as correlatives to the financial chicaneries of magnates like Oakes Ames and Jay Gould—was usually either a heavy-handed and stultifying acceptance of Teutonic musical models imitated by composers like George Chadwick and Arthur Foote or the cultivation of those sentimental songs performed by traveling "singing family" troupes which featured young "lady" pianists playing on instruments covered with brocade and lace in "rooms stifling with fashionable scent" (Walt Whitman).

John Philip Sousa—whose boyhood ambition was to become a circus performer—represented this era perfectly, writing over a hundred marches many of which were enthusiastically played during America's many popular military actions in Cuba, the Philippines, and even Peking during the Boxer Rebellion. Robert Offergeld has written that Sousa "became the nearest thing to a real *Kapellmeister* that the White House has ever had (he knew eight or nine Presidents personally)." And "Stars and Stripes Forever" and "Semper Fidelis" are probably the best-known works ever written by an American.

Technically brilliant, Sousa's marches are today appreciated as either uplifting patriotic masterpieces, exemplars of authoritarian inebriation, or as "camp" perversities—sometimes as all three, as witness the legendary Vladimir Horowitz transcription of "Stars and Stripes." For something rather more authentic try the extrordinary performances by the Czechoslovak Brass Orchestra, conducted by Rudolf Urbanec (Nonesuch H 71266), a recording which features eleven marches, including Sousa's portentous contribution to the Masonic order entitled "Nobles of the Mystic Shrine." By clarifying the instrumental textures *à la* Boulez and thereby revealing all of Sousa's cranking and syncopating musical gears, Urbanec and the Czech Brass Orchestra have given us what is at once the most *echt*-Teutonic, razor-edged, yet subtly delineated and delicately balanced presentation of these uproarious and elephantine works by the man who once said that a "march should make a man with a wooden leg step out."

As Europeans like Berlioz have shown us, elephantiasis is hardly endemic to America (though it's interesting to see works like Ives's *Fourth* Symphony and John Cage's *HPSCHD* as the extensions and apotheoses of this contagion). And today, in the country that spends four million dollars on a presidential inauguration, it certainly seems appropriate that the "monster Concert" is back in the news—exactly one hundred years after Boston bandmaster Patrick Gilmore organized an orchestra of two thousand and a chorus of twenty thousand for the 1872 Mammoth Festival in Boston.

Last year, members of the Eastman School of Music Piano Faculty, graduate piano students, and soloists Eugene List, Frank Glazer, Barry Snyder, and Maria Luisa Faini (all conducted by Samuel Adler) gave a triumphant ten piano sixteen pianists concert at philharmonic Hall; and now some of the music presented that evening can be heard on a new Columbia recording entitled *Monster Concert* (M 31726). "Stars and Stripes" starts it all off (I still think that the two-handed Horowitz outdoes all twenty-two hands playing here—aside from the density of the sound, who can tell the textural difference between four and fourteen pianos?), with hundreds and hundreds of piano keys contributing to other versions of the "William Tell" Overture, "Thunder and Lightning" Polka, "Maple Leaf" Rag, "Blue Danube" Waltzes, "Semiramide" Overture, "La Gallina," and "Ojos Crillos."

These last two pieces—"The Hen" and "Creole Eyes" in translation—are by the American avatar of monstrous musical imaginings, Louis Moreau Gottschalk—America's first great "rock star"-type pianist and composer. About his Havana Festival Concert of 1860, Gottschalk wrote:"My orchestra consisted of six hundred and fifty performers, eighty-seven choristers, fifteen solo singers, fifty drums and eighty trumpets . . . nearly nine hundred persons bellowing and blowing to see who could scream the loudest."

Born in 1829 in New Orleans to a Jewish-English father of German descent and an aristocratic French Creole mother, Gottschalk went to Paris as a teenager where he studied piano and was praised by Chopin, Berlioz, and Liszt. At twenty-four, he returned to the States and proceeded to give hundreds of piano recitals in cities and mining towns around the country. drawing enormous and excited crowds, hangers-on, and all types of groupies (his affairs were notorious, and he was often forced to skip town). Indulging in what he himself called "the full force of chromatic grapeshot and deadly octaves," Gottschalk was one of the first American musicians to adopt the stance—now highly cultivated by rock musicians—of Phallic Aggressor at the keyboard.

His own music—Latin and French Creole in flavor, veering from the sentimental to the bombastic and full of flashy arabesques and Lisztian embellishments—exhausts as it exploits its treacherous romantic emotions. Gottschalk's best pieces are those like the two Cuban dances featured on *Monster Concert*—both of which are airy, kinetic, and based on an unpretentious cultural tradition that fostered neither an academic lassitude nor a self-consuming egomania.

After the exhibitionism of Sousa's and Gottschalk's vertiginous musical styles, it is a calming experience to turn to a recent recording of the *Songs of Stephen Foster* (Nonesuch H 71268). Aside from the familiar "Jeanie with the Light Brown Hair" and "Beautiful Dreamer," the album presents infrequently heard songs like the lovely "Ah! May the Red Rose Live Always," the ebullient "If You've Only Got a Moustache," as well as two wonderful mini-operatic dialogues: "Wilt Thou Be Gone, Love?" (with a text adapted from *Romeo and Juliet*) and a comic duet between "Mr. and Mrs. Brown."

This album forces us to re-evaluate Foster's heretofore easily-dismissed role in nineteenth-century American music. For the first time, Foster's songs have been presented with an integrity, clarity, and the kind of musicianship usually reserved for works like Brahms's "Liebeslieder" Waltzes. Using the composer's original sheet music and featuring the straightforward and sympathetic instrumental arrangements by composer and ragtime pianist Bill Bolcolm, the songs are recorded with the historical instruments at the Smithsonian Institute (an 1850 Chickering piano, and 1864 melodeon, a one-keyed flute, and a keyed bugle) and are sung with simplicity and grace by baritone Leslie Guinn and the extraordinary mezzo-soprano Jan De Gaetani.

The transparency of the performances reveal the ways in which Foster distilled and transformed the cliches of minstrel show songs, Sunday School hymns, and parlor melodies and unconsciously created a distinctly American folk art tradition.

But beneath the nostalgia of "Gentle Annie" and the existential gaiety of the marvelous "Some Folks"—both heard on this album—lies the story of not only the nineteenth-century American music but also of the by now easily identifiable archetypal "dreamer" trying to fit into the exploitative scene of the rising American middle class. Like most song writers and composers, Foster was almost always underpaid by his publishers, his songs were often pirated. And having become an alcoholic, he died broke and alone in New York. Having provided the necessary musical ethos for a homesick nineteenth-century industrial society, he was among the first whom that society considered expendable.

It is good to know that a century earlier, composers like Billings and Justin Morgan had many admirers and that their works were often published in Tune Books which were used in singing schools and village choirs. Since the nineteenth century, however, these compositions have been continually critized for their supposedly faulty voice leading, an incorrect use of leading tones and diminished sevenths, archaic constructions, and the over-use of parallel fifths.

Compared to the sturdy eighteenth-century American Moravivan musical tradition which was influenced by Handel and Haydn (excellent examples of which can be heard on *Music of the American Moravians*—Odyssey 32 16 0340—and in performances by the Fine Arts Quartet of *String Trios of John Antes*—Columbia MS 6741), the music of Billings and his colleagues does sound slightly "off."

But choral societies which have tried to "improve and correct" the harmony and voice leading of this early music are obviously missing the point—much as literary "experts" once unconvincingly tried to alter the bizarre and personal metrics of poets like Sir Thomas Wyatt and John Donne. For as Wilfrid Mellers has suggested, Billings and other New Englanders—along with composers of eighteenth-century southern folk humns—had in fact developed an "instinctive folk-organum," one which displayed an extraordinary admixture of English Medieval and Renaissance musical characteristics, half-remembered Reformation musical forms, and a rich and independent melodic modal invention that occasioned some amazing harmonic textures.

Three excellent commercially available recordings give us distinct and fascinating perspectives on the music, *The New England Harmony* (Folkways FA 2377) presents works of Billings, Justin Morgan, Jeremiah Ingalls, and others of the period as performed by the Old Sturbridge Singers—an amateur group which consists of mechanics, storekeepers, doctors, and housewives. And their clear, straight-forward, but sometimes rhythmically heavy interpretations are probably quite similar to those heard during eighteenth-century village choir presentations.

The Continental Harmony (Columbia MS 7277) features nineteen anthems and fuging tunes by Billings as sung by the professionally precise and spirited Gregg Smith Singers. Aside from a lovely rendition of the patriotic song "Chester," the chorus gives us versions of rarely performed songs like "The Bird," "Kittery," "Cobham," and, most surprising of all, a short piece entitled "Jargon" which is perhaps the first totally dissonant work ever written by an American and sounding as if it were composed by Charles Ives himself.

The most extraordinary of these three albums is the recent *Early American Vocal Music* (Nonesuch H 71276)—to my mind the most beautiful and important recorded contribution to the performance of early American anthems, plain tunes, set pieces, fuging tunes, and folk hymns. The performers are The Western Wind, a group of young singers who specialize in Medieval and Renaissance music. And here they perform these pieces with an expressive shading and dramatic approach usually reserved for the works of Medieval motet composers and the compositions of Thomas Tallis and Orlando Gibbons—thereby opening the veils which heretofore often seemed to hide a music of astonishing directness, iridescence, and spiritual depth.

Justin Morgan's brief plain-tune "Amanda"—with its ravishing cross-relations—and his epic-sounding "Judgment Anthem"; Billings's "I Am the Rose of Sharon" and "I Am

Come Into My Garden"; and various short and haunting Southern folk hymns like "Power," "Canaan" and "Animation" (the last of which features a terrific hoedown duo between a countrified bass viol and violin) are all given subtle and totally sympathetic performances.

Hearing these Southern hymns, moreover, we are reminded of the almost forgotten inter-relationships between and mutual interpenetrations of the white and black "spiritual" and "revivalist" traditions, which seem to have their roots in the Baptist backwoods of New England as well as in Africa. And the ecstatic white folk-hymn tradition that developed from the music heard on the Nonesuch recording is still preserved and practiced today in parts of the deep South. Known as Fasola or Shape-Note Singing, this four-part communal singing can be heard on a primitively recorded but joyfully performed album presenting the *All-Day Sacred Harp Singing at Stewart's Chapel in Houston, Mississippi* (Asch Mankind Series AH, 4151—distributed by Folkways)—attesting again to the irreducible and ineradicable power of what we now often cynically call the American musical heritage.

1973

The Last Poets and the Apocalypse

Like Noah or Daniel, we're feeling the Last Days eerily approaching us again. Some think of creating their arks (Soleri's utopian cities) or of realizing their prophetic dreams (Manson's apostolic desert tribe). John Lennon sings "Instant Karma" and the Stones, "Gimmie Shelter." Dennis Hopper makes *The Last Movie,* and who's to say the Peruvian earthquake isn't an echo of the fantasy?

The idea of an imminent, total, miraculous apocalypse has been around thousands of years, always to be disproved but never discredited. Top 40 radio blares out the obligatory this-week's version of "Aquarius" and the desperate getting it/doing it/feeling it together songs, most of them nothing less than Good Citizen Milk commercials which merely fill the vacuum left since people lost faith in vacant ballads. The Last Poets, however, are chanting:

> Time is running out on bullshit changes
> Running out like a bushfire in a dry forest
> Like a murderer from the scene of a crime
> Like a little roach from DDT
> Running out like big niggers run on a football field
> Run nigger! Screwin' your woman!
> Run nigger! Whippin' your ass!
> Run nigger! Stealin' your culture!
> Run nigger! Takin' your life!
> Run nigger! Killin' your children!

The Last Poets recording on Douglas Records consists of poets Omar Ben Hassen and Alafia Pudim and the percussionist Nilaja. (The fourth poet, Abiodun Oyewole, who is heard on the Douglas record, has left the group.) With little radio airplay, *The Last Poets* album has already sold 160,000 copies, most of them in New York, Detroit, Chicago, Los Angeles, and, with an upsurge a few weeks ago, in Miami! They're recognized and admired as stars in Harlem where they live. But as Omar Ben

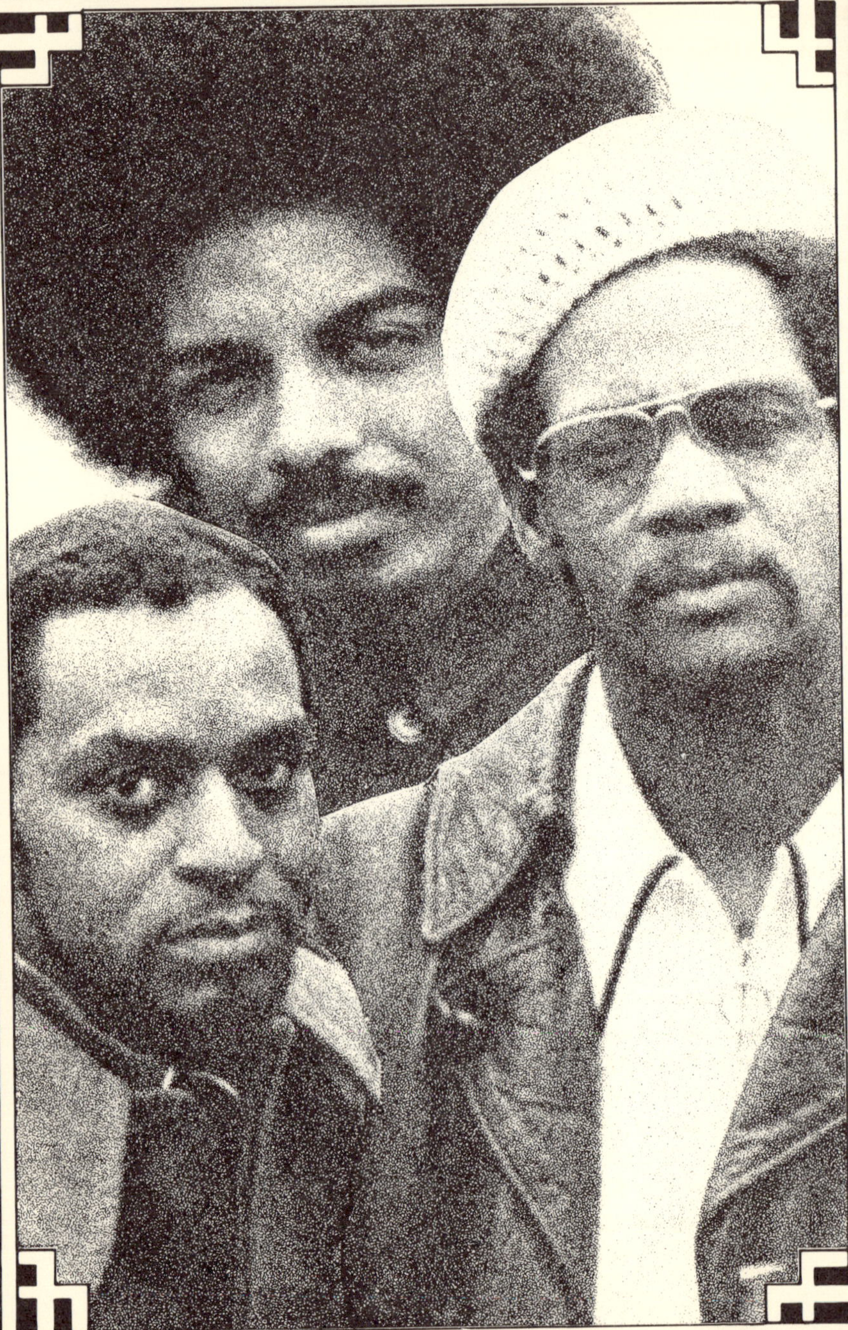

Hassen says: "If people dig us, that's boss, but they'll dig *us:* Omar, Alafia, and Nilaja, not as leaders. The people are the leaders. We'd just like them to react to our poetry in a positive way—no Cadillacs."

"A word hasn't been coined to fit what we're talking about," Alafia says. "For the time being we use the word 'poet' to characterize what we do. But I'm really just trying to get it off." "This is the last age for poets," Omar Ben Hassen adds. "After this age only spears piercing the marrow of the villain's heart."

The world The Poets walk through is one that a lot of people think is some kind of hallucination. In fact, it's the reality of black and white urban life and the hallucinations *that* life produces. It is a world decorated and desecrated with "Gilbert erector set houses," "public mausoleums," "vomiting sinister buildings," "chitlin-brained queens," "gash men" ("dudes who use their revolutionary status to take off our sisters"), "transit cops," "dope in the arm and Clairol on the brain," and "Jones comin' down."

This joining of minute particulars with what Omar calls "the projection of vision" reminds you of a merging of purified and intensified street rap—meant to develop revolutionary consciousness—and a sense of life similar to that of Poe's in stories like "The Pit and the Pendulum:" the death sickness, inquisitorial voices, grotesque white lips of black-robed judges.

In fact, Omar Ben Hassen, who started writing wall poems at eight ("I'm Omar the Lover/If you don't believe me/Ask your mother"), was influenced by Poe. "I dug 'The Raven' and 'Annabel Lee,' the way they told people about themselves in a very eerie and mysterious manner. I just used to read 'The Raven' over and over. And then later, Le Roi Jones took a heavy hold.

"I'm a universal man," Omar adds, "because I receive knowledge from the universe. What's happening in the universe and on earth is the same thing. Man hasn't learned to *be* yet. You have to get under the planetary influence that causes men to love each other. There are war influences, love influences. It all depends on what influences man wants to be influenced by.

"It's the energy I get from my people when I walk down the streets. We say how bad it is, but there's certain energy and knowledge you get from the ghetto. If you're a beautiful person you can see beauty in the ghetto. See, it's got something to do with the fact that love of inner self can evoke the same love out of self. In a recent poem 'This is Madness,' I say: I begin to hate with love and love with hate. It's really all the same thing. It's he who legitimizes the difference, you dig, who makes the mistake. What makes me write is not hate, but the love for my people, my love for righteousness."

At the end of May, 1970, The Poets, billed with Carolyn Franklin and Jerry Butler, performed to a cheering audience at the Apollo Theater, although the Apollo's manager and a few others got squeamish about The Poets' language. The performance is reminiscent of Artaud's conception of the Balinese theater—words, gestures, a pulsing rhythmic ritual with The Poets bending, stretching, collapsing, the congas insistently forcing the energy out as the audience cheers and laughs with shouts of Right On!, everything embodying a shared social outrage burning away the kindling of false selves.

But what The Last Poets do onstage is nothing more than heighten the form of a new black urban street poetry. At a New York high school assembly commemorating Malcolm X's death two months ago, the "predominantly black" students hooted the principal down, and kids got up on stage and read their poems—charged statements like those of The Poets, rhythmically asserting black consciousness while revealing the breakdown and proving unworkable the New York City school system. And why haven't you shown up for class this term?

At the Apollo, while The Poets rose into their words and wailed, Nilaja, wearing a dashiki and his talismanic necklace-like elikis (he's a follower of Yoruba, a Nigerian Voodoo sect), played congas, putting you in an attention trance and letting you move with and listen to The Poets' words.

Have you seen the skinny little boy
That chases the white ghost at night?
Face puffed up tracks in his arm and his mind blown
His momma somewhere drinking
And talking about survival
Pop's in jail or downtown at the Y
The little boy chases the white ghost with his friend

And they get *High* and they get *High*
Like cloud nine
Where everything is fine

The Poets have chased the white ghost—the "junk" that's the metaphor for living death—and exorcised it, breaking the "mental hold," as Alafia Pudim says in a poem. They go inside the self-mutilating, self-denigrating, sometimes fatuous roles which humiliated blacks and all humiliated persons are forced to play, embody these roles, and aesthetically blow them up.

Alafia Pudim says: "By writing the poetry, we become and are what the poetry is about. It's like taking the inside of yourself and bringing it out and looking at it and saying, wow, this is really what's going on, and then making the improvement, molding and shaping it. I started writing in order to have an explosion. To channel off the frustration, the oppression, the implosion. We're just a minor valve in the ghetto.

"It's coming to a head. We had our work, our art, so we could get some of that stuff off, but there are millions of kids who can't. You can't have peace before power. If we don't get no positive reaction coming from the words, then we've got to *make* a reaction. It's not going to be an organized thing, it's going to be improvised.

"I'm above the hatred thing. I hate the actions and deeds of some white people. Malcolm was saying, let's not get caught up in hate because it's a negative energy, it's a self-destructive thing. But I don't love my enemies, don't get me wrong. I ain't taking nothing off anybody, because that's the law of survival which says, give back what you receive."

"A slave," Omar says, "is somebody who thinks like a slave. You start to slump, you become slobbish, you don't really care about yourself no more. And other people begin to treat you like a slave. I know I'm not a slave. I have my poetry to tell everybody that I am free.

"I used to sit down with other people who were trying to discover themselves. We would like to sit down and tell the truth to each other. If someone fucked a faggot, he'd say he fucked a faggot. If so and so liked white women, he'd say; if so and so was taking dope, he'd say he was. We tried to work with each other. We pulled that shit out of each other—it became a truth society, you dig?"

Whites who have tried to see into themselves have perceived the shit, but when was the last time you walked around 128th Street? Few New York City cabs will head up to the Apollo, and the separations are as deep as the real human horror of humiliated people trying to make do in Harlem.

"If I were white," Nilaja says, "I wouldn't come hear us. Just like I wouldn't go hear George Wallace. You've got to have a lot of soul and a lot of heart to dig us." "You've got to get yourself together, Mr. Cott," Omar said to me. "As Jerry Butler says, 'Only the Strong Survive.' But, you know, our poetry is for our brothers. We want to give our people something to look into, to really look into a word in a different sense than the way the word's been legitimized."

The Last Poets' most recent poems, [included on their second Douglas album] include "The White Man's Got a God Complex," "In the Meanwhile," "I Must be Insane," and "This is Madness"—and they carry The Poets' energy, truth connections, and perceptions much further on down the line. Like the thirteen poems already recorded, they force you to make yourself your own truth society. They inform, advise, warn, charge, judge.

And they do so with an extraordinary intensity and a kind of outraged exuberance and comic dignity. As the academics would say: these poems are a symbolic criticism of value. As Emily Dickinson would say: they make you feel physically as if the top of your head were taken off. Like the most amazing apocalyptic art, they are poems for the righteous living and for the righteous dead.

1970

Virgil Fox at the Fillmore

Organist Virgil Fox played an all-J.S. Bach program on his portable electric organ to the accompaniment of Joe's Lights and a cheering, sold-out audience at Fillmore East December 1, 1970.

Fox was encircled by one hundred and forty-four speakers which hummed during whispering chorale preludes or else roared with fortissimo effects during the "Passacaglia and Fugue in C," as if couplers, swells, pistons, and crescendo pedals were overpowering the theater. "Do you begin to see the secret of this man Bach?" Fox asked exultantly when he was near the end of the concert. The crowd gave the organist the kind of standing ovation usually reserved for Eric Clapton, calling out for more, and Fox happily played six encores. Both this concert and the again sold-out repeat December 14th performance have been recorded by Decca, and are being released as a "Heavy Organ" album through its rock division.

According to publicity hand-outs and radio ads, fifty-eight-year-old Fox was supposed to bring Bach's genius to youth culture heads at the "East Village rock mecca" dressed in a billowy white crepe shirt, silver-brocaded vest, crushed-velvet bell bottoms, and rhinestone-studded pumps. In fact, he appeared wearing a modest light brown suit and interspersed his performances with short, excited, hand-punctuated quasi-ministerial remarks about the "genius of this man Sebastian Bach" and the "perfection of the human soul manifested in you and me."

Fox, who plays seventy concerts a year ("Have organ, will travel, that's my motto") in places like Cody, Wyoming or New York's Philharmonic Hall and who claims to have learned to play the organ in a previous incarnation, talks with a raved-up gusto and the expressive American nuances reminiscent both of Little Richard and James Purdy's amazing Midwestern characters.

"I got down on my knees behind Joe's Lights just before I went on stage," Fox says, "and asked the great power to pass *through* me the message of the greatest composer of all time. And when I came down those steps, baby, my physique was completely exhausted. I'd only had a few hours sleep, but it was that *power,* sonny boy, that took over. You've got to come the whole way. And those kids know. To have a composer of Bach's depth walk into the Fillmore and get over to those kids is amazing. They're honest people who are trying to get through when the rest of the world is going blotto. The Aquarian Age is coming on, and everything is finished—concert halls, the *New York Times,* everything. It's the jet stream, it goes twice as fast.

"You've got to illumine the greatness of Bach on this dumb mechanical instrument called the organ. The Scotch call it the kist of whistles. I don't like Bach performances that sound like a typewriter. The professional organists are so green-eyed to think that an organist like me is in the mainstream. Every concert management and all those big festivals say we're so sorry, there's no audience for the organ as a concert instrument. Listen, I face two thousand people every three nights. That proves to me that the way the average concert organist plays is a crock of shit—no nuance, no gradation, no expressiveness.

"The people I address live in the twentieth century. They listen to the accelerated action of the Steinway, for instance. There's no such thing as 'authentic' Bach or Beethoven. What if Bach said, 'I can only do what was done two hundred years ago.' That music was infantile."

"Mr. Fox," I said, "do you think the music of Dufay and Josquin is infantile?"

"Of course, my child, you're a creature of the creator," Fox said sweetly, "and you're entitled to your opinion. But the important thing is that we had something absolutely fantastic the other night at the Fillmore. That gives us common ground, brother. So just tell them what happened, sweet child."

"Mr. Fox," I said, "you were far out the other night, and it's terrific to have an informal setting where you can hear great music, but like maybe one can play Bach not just with highly contrasted and sharply alternating loud-soft volumes of sound, but by clarifying the structure and the textures and not using so many rubatos and retards and twisting the phrases, you know?"

"Listen, Johnny," Fox replied, "we had a few problems

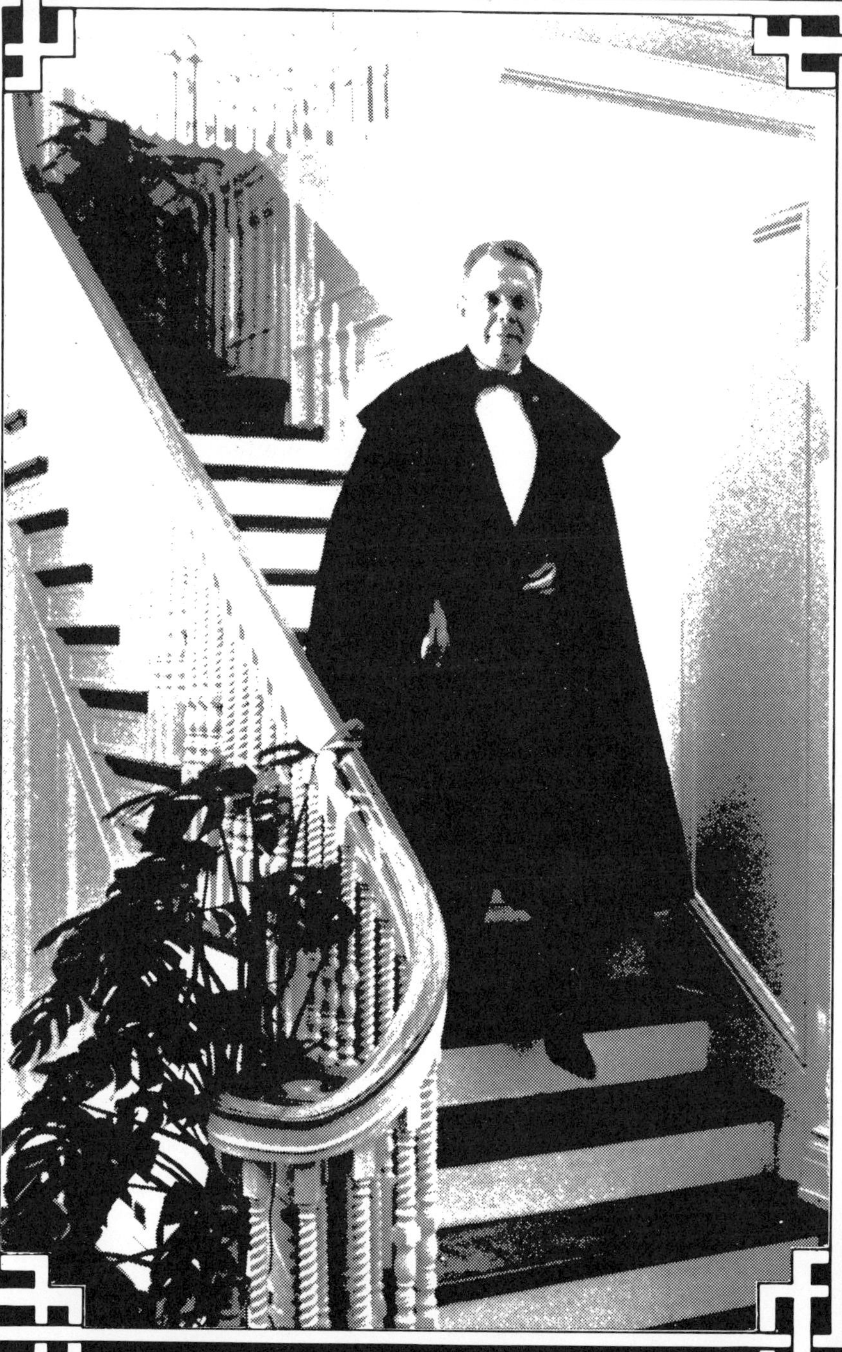

getting all the equipment set up right at the Fillmore. I need three days and only had half the time, so there was an artificial ring of sound around the hall, and the backstage fans and air conditioning added to the hum of the speakers. But I was aware that kids at the Fillmore wanted to be reached at the same volume scale that they're used to.

"As far as what you call the overuse of rubato, I like it. I'm not concerned with a cerebral approach to music. If you have ice cubes laid on a windless plain, you have no reach to humanity. If you don't have living, breathing, honest, musical, emotional, warm, expressive playing, it ain't music. Mountain peaks of power is what I aim for.

"I was the pupil of Wilhelm Middelschulte who, along with Max Reger, was the greatest organ contrapuntalist between Bach and our time. I had a psychic happening with him in church, brother. We touched the mountain tops, and he branded me when I was sixteen with an illumined thing across my brow. My mission was to go beyond the organ's mechanical limitations and create true music and do what few organists ever do.

"I played in Cody, Wyoming, where Buffalo Bill is sitting on the plains and you run all over the sage brush, and I played Bach, just as I did for kids in Nashville and Hollywood High, where I quieted everybody down by playing the lowest C pedal note and pointed to a girl sitting up front and said, 'That girl and me can fit in that pipe.' That got them. And the kids got the music sight unseen."

"Mr. Fox," I said, "your publicity and program notes say you're the 'greatest living interpreter of Bach's organ music.' What about Lionel Rogg and Helmut Walcha? Do you think you might be immodest?"

"I think I'm terribly immodest," Fox said. "I'm the only non-German organist ever to have played at Bach's last church in Leipzig, and a critic there said that, and I quote, 'This youth proved to us that he has an understanding of the innermost secret of the art of Bach.' Nobody plays it like me. Lillian Russell, who was Diamond Jim Brady's girl friend, once said: "It would be absurd for me to pretend I'm not beautiful. I look in the mirror and can see that I am.' That's right. And I think she would have added, as I do about myself, that 'to be beautiful is another story, and I wish to be a beautiful character.' I've been called the greatest performing organist, and any publicity firm that doesn't use that recognized opinion is just plain foolish.

"The composer of *Hair* is going to write a piece for me and orchestra, and I'm going down to the White House to play for a reception for Prime Minister Heath soon. And then there's the repeat Fillmore concert. Just tell them what happened, baby!"

1970

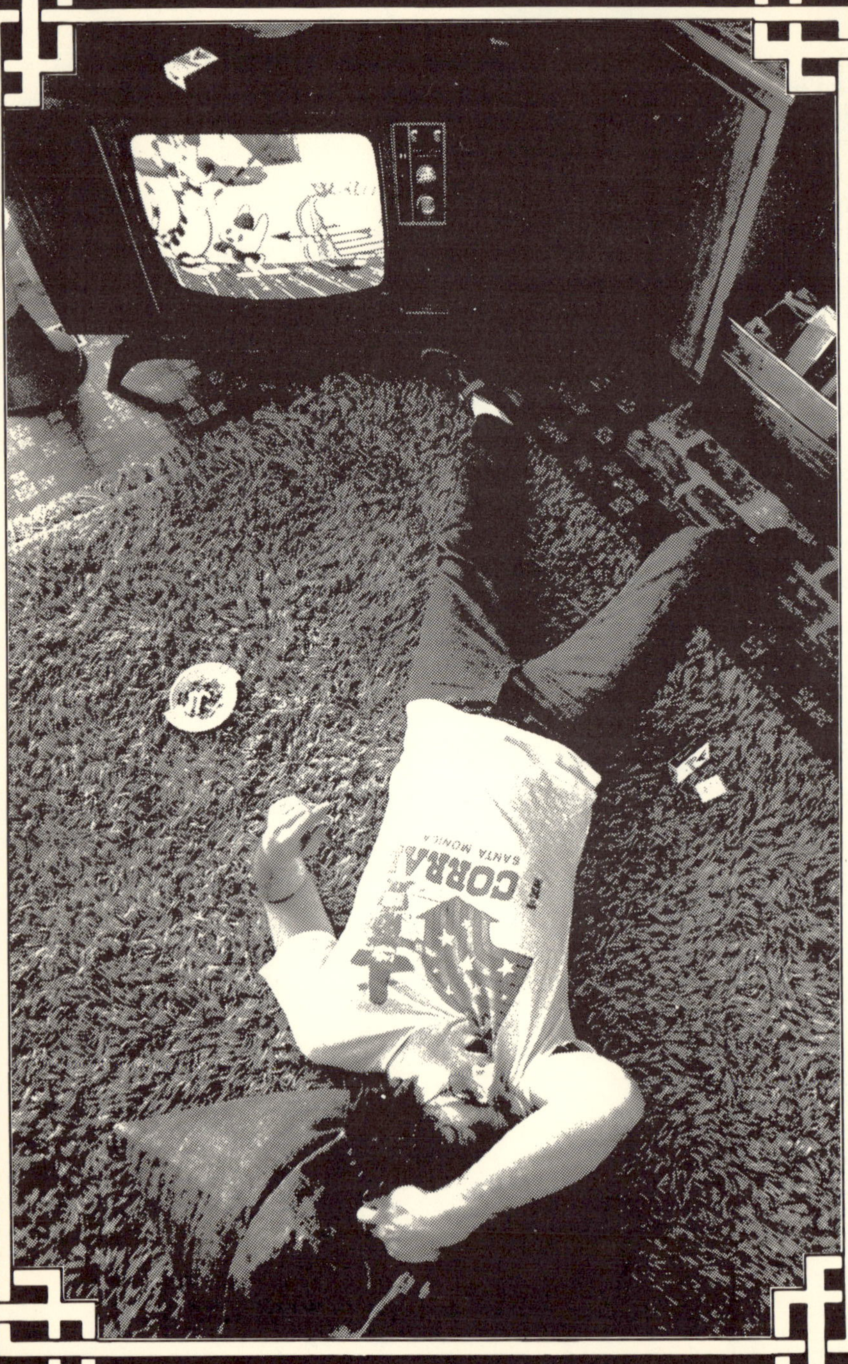
SANTA MONICA

Randy Newman's Dream

White suits, Panama hats, rambling country estate with polished marble floors, northern hemlocks swaying sedately on the grounds. Jeff and Martin in early morning sunlight in the parlor with roaring fireplace and open French windows. They are dancing together to very soft big band music, but only because all the girls have gone to sleep.

A large stuffed owl, knocked over by the dancers, catches fire. THE POLICE, *represented by the local sheriff and his raiding party including federal narcotics agents, watch through the windows, without making a sound, as Jeff and Martin stop dancing and stamp on the owl until the flames are out.*

As they carry the smouldering bird out onto the lawn through the French windows, to douse it with a garden hose, the police retreat into the shrubbery, out of sight. Turning to go back in, Martin, out of the corner of his eye, sees a badge glittering in the bushes. "We'd better wake the girls," he says softly.

—Michael Brownstein

Randy Newman performed with his piano for two weeks at the Bitter End at the end of September, 1970 in one of his infrequent appearances outside his L.A. living room.

"I could have disappeared and no one would have cared," Newman says. But among his attending admirers in New York were Bob Dylan, Alan Jay Lerner, Odetta, and Barbra Streisand. "I was talking to a guy at a table at the Bitter End who said 'I really like your work,' and then realized it was Dylan. I really was pleased by that. But when people compliment my songs, I usually never think about it, I just say, 'Thank you, thank you.'"

A poet once wrote, as if describing the distinctive quality of Newman's songs: "A metaphor is what happens when one looks in a certain way, just as a sneeze is what happens when one looks at the sun." Along with the Beatles and Ray Davies, Newman creates his wonderfully short and small songs, nurturing, compressing, and perfecting them with a passion for the particular: "The milk truck hauls the sun up/The paper hits the door/The subway shakes my floor/And I think about you" ("Living Without You").

Listening to the songs Newman sang and played on the piano at the Bitter End—culled from his two albums (which drew on a melange of blues, country, Thirties, and vaudeville musical styles, and a phrasing and perception sometimes reminiscent of Kurt Weill)—you sensed how Newman's fantasy worlds seemed to result from the intersection of an inner obsession and a fortuitous event, or of a musical style and one strange reflection of reality: high school graduating Lucinda flattened out in the sand by a white beach cleaning truck or a pusillanimous voyeur, singing his blues, waiting in the shadows to catch the eye of his muse, Suzanne, discovered as a name scrawled in a telephone booth.

You often find a purposeful disparity in Newman's songs between the mood and the content. In "Suzanne," for instance, you find nostalgic major/minor blues cadences supporting a description of a voyeur who fantasizes rape while the music and the mood of the song convey the sense of a pale, hollow-cheeked German romantic poet pining in the Black Forest. In fact you're realizing all along that the character is, as Newman says, "spectacularly unromantic." Newman adds: "It's a weird song. The guy singing says 'I don't mean to get too romantic' after he's said all this horrible stuff. There's something funny in his type of desperation, something pathetic, too. He wouldn't get far as a rapist.

"The reason I sing songs like 'Suzanne' is that the character is more interesting to me than the heroic figure you find in most songs—the tough guy or romantic hero. Where I went to school everyone liked the surfers, the guys who were great at pool, football players. I never had a hero. And I don't like them. There's something degrading about it. Actually, there was once a baseball hero I admired—Roy Campanella, if you want to know. But there's not enough left for yourself."

Listeners often imagine that the person impersonating a character in a song is equal to the person singing it. When Lennon sings "I'm So Tired" or Newman sings "Fat Boy," they are taking a part of themselves or someone they imagine and putting that part or person on themselves. In this sense, Newman could theoretically say: "I don't sing, I am sung."

"That person singing in 'Fat Boy,'" Newman says, "is so callous that it's almost kind of funny. My attitude to the guy singing about the fat boy is obvious from what I have that guy saying. I don't think a great deal of him. I don't love him.

"Sometimes you might not be able to tell what my opinion is. That's all right.People could laugh at my songs for the wrong reasons. But I have enough faith in people to realize that most of them aren't diseased. I don't know many people who think exploiting a fat boy is the thing to do.

"I often have a response that I want people to feel. In 'Fat Boy,' I wanted people to recognize what a bastard that guy singing that song is. And I think he's one."

"Underneath the Harlem Moon"—written by Gordon and Revel for blacks to sing in the Cotton Club in the Twenties and a song which Newman performs straight-forwardly and elegantly—also insists on a double-edged response: "Creole babies walk along/Rhythm in their thighs/Rhythm in their hips and in their lips and in the eyes."

"What the song has to say is kind of repulsive," Newman states. "It's a great song—'You may call it madness/But I call it hiedy-ho!'—but you have to know the historical context: I sang the song at the Bitter End. But I'm hesitant to sing it, frankly."

One of Newman's finest gifts is his ability to use and transform styles, like that of the Busby Berkeley Chinese production numbers or Anna Mae Wong movies, for "Yellow Man," and also clichés, twisting and slanting them slightly, something Newman does as well to the situations that he depicts. "You describe something that exists and leave it at that," Newman says, and adds: "Often something that doesn't quite exist, but almost does. My songs take a step to the right—not politically—just a little bit off. It's a bit dangerous when I use clichés because some of them don't get far enough to the right."

Probably Newman's finest example of this kind of song, "Uncle Bob's Midnight Blues," is actually just a series of clichés transmogrified by the context. "I was originally going to call it 'In Defense of Alcohol' because I could understand why alcohol came down through the ages bigger than hemp: 'Goin' down to the corner/Gonna have myself a drink/'Cause this shit that we been usin'/Sure confuse my thinking.'

"I put in that part about buying myself a goat and tying him in my front yard, 'for all my so-called friends to see.' You see, the song's about a wiped-out come-down: I been up so long/That it looks like down to me; Please don't talk about me when I'm gone. All the clichés are there. I added 'When the blue of the night meets the gold of the day' for Bing Crosby. And the 'We Love You' lines that end the song came about because I had this fantasy after hearing the Rolling Stones' 'We Love You.' The fantasy was that the Stones were in their decline and McCartney and the Beatles were singing on the record, which they were, and saying: 'Sure, man, we'll sing with you, so long!'"

The idea of reality in Newman's songs is lightly questioned by the nostalgia you feel in a recreated or invented dream of the lost world—often seen in Thirties colors—and by means of a resonating simplicity ("Let's burn down the cornfields") that suggests as it recreates certain familiar but self-detaching identity perceptions in certain spaces ("Some ships without a sail/Some cats without a tail/Boy it's weird here on this spooky old pier at night/But I'm not frightened because no one is"—"Linda"). This same spatial awareness is revealed in the highly contrasted black and white album cover photo depiciting, on some abstracted L.A. lawn, a TV on stilts being observed by a baby chair next to a rocking chair.

"The whole idea of a song is a real situation," Newman says, adding: "Any type of creative endeavor isn't of its essence real." How does Newman bridge the thought levels here? "Well," he says, "it's true that's a bit metaphysical. Let me just ask you: Is a bee a domestic animal?"

Michael Tilson Thomas

When Michael Tilson Thomas was attending nursery school in Los Angeles, he remembers that a woman came two times a week to play music for the kids on the piano. "We all had an assortment of sticks and noisemakers," Thomas recalls. "One time she was doing some sort of Spanish piece. I was filling in with my drumsticks all kinds of complicated rhythmical riffs *à la* castanet parts. Most everybody else was going *click-click-click.* And I remember thinking: Wow, that's so boring! Here I was, five years old, thinking: What's going on, why don't they fill in what's in between the beats?" It was at this moment that Michael Tilson Thomas recognized the conductor's mentality.

Today, the twenty-seven-year-old Thomas is music director of the Buffalo Philharmonic, associate conductor of the Boston Symphony, and conductor of the New York Philharmonic Young Peoples' Concerts for the next two seasons. He was named Musician of the Year by *Musical America* magazine and was awarded an honorary doctorate by Hamilton College. And last year Deutsche Grammophon released five albums on which Thomas revealed a mastery of an enormous range of musical styles: his performances of Ives' *Three Places in New England* and Tchaikovsky's *Winter Dreams Symphony,* for example, are the most beautiful interpretations available on records, demonstrating Thomas' sense of instrumental balance, intonation, articulation, and voicing, and his disposition to allow each work its own musical space and gestures.

Thomas is also an excellent pianist—as is witnessed by his vibrant performance with pianist-friend Ralph Grierson of the original two-piano version of Stravinsky's *Rite of Spring* (Angel Records).

Between tours, Thomas' home base is a small, three-room Back Bay apartment just a ten minutes' walk from Boston's Symphony Hall. From the tiny terrace of the apartment, there is a view of the city. Inside, eaves slant up to meet cathedral ceilings. Like the nuances Thomas brings out in his best performances, the furnishings and art objects in the living room are a testament to Thomas' sense of balance and contrast. A belt made of little bells is strewn on the floor. Graduated gongs hang from the ceiling. Sacred ornamental chimes and other instruments lie on coffee tables, stereo speakers, and the floor.

The visitor's eyes wander from rock crystals and geodes to an African ceremonial mask and then to a strangely vague and foggy Thirties oil painting showing a section of an audience—twelve or thirteen persons—painted in earth tones. In contrast to this are two mammoth aluminum polymer Japanese paintings, geometric cube constructions that, when leaning against the wall, suggest shifting two-to-three dimensional effects. "Objects to be contended with," Thomas calls them.

Anyone wanting to interview the conductor has to contend with his seemingly twenty-hour-a-day schedule. We decided to meet in front of Symphony Hall. Constructed in 1900, this quiet, almost ascetic building—simple lights, wooden plank floors—is spruced up only with torsos of famous Greeks like Apollo, Sophocles, and Demosthenes in niches around the walls of the second balcony. Symphony Hall features perhaps the best acoustics of any concert hall in this country.

While I was waiting outside the hall, a blue Porsche Cabriolet with racing engine, steering, and suspension zoomed up to the stage entrance. Thomas got out, and the car sped off.

"I thought we'd talk in the car," Michael said. "I just got in from Buffalo and haven't seen my car for awhile. I had an accident and it's getting fixed, but the mechanic who just drove it off is a real artist and he isn't satisfied with it yet. . . . Sometimes I really like just listening to the sound of the engine."

Thomas had to attend some meetings and conductors' auditions in an hour, so we went inside to his office to talk. I had read that Michael, who often goes dancing after conducting a concert, had seen James Brown at Boston's Sugar Shack and had immediately followed James and his band to Washington. Brown's show, according to Thomas, is "the closest thing to a genuine *Gesamtkunstwerk* [a term Wagner used to describe his all-inclusive music dramas] in the twentieth century."

"When I went to see James Brown in Washington," Thomas says, "people asked me if I wanted James to do something with the Boston Symphony. But I just wanted to see and learn; I was so excited about his show. You know, it's music, singing, dancing, but on the other hand, more than anything else, it's a personal rap between him and you. That's what's so incredible about it. You never feel he's on stage doing a number. I've seen him with the rhythm section playing and him talking in rhythmical cadences against this. He has a really antecedent consequent way of talking."

"Pardon me?"

"I mean he'll say: [pitch rising] 'andsothatsthe*wayits-GONNABE'*—it's all in the length of the phrase and how he pitches his voice—it's all worked out with the rhythm.

"There was a young black painter who had done some pictures which James had seen and liked. So he had the paintings brought out on stage and asked the audience to look at them. Then he introduced the guy and said something like: 'each man's got to get himself together in whatever it is he does, and there are people right amongst you doing what they're doing and it's so important to us.'

"Can you imagine any other rock performer showing paintings to the audience? He really focused them in on these paintings. And when he had the artist come up to take a bow, I sat there and wept. What he was doing was at such an exalted level of sophistication, in the sense of *transcending* sophistication—the way he dealt with the idea of community; of the arts being together; his generosity; and transmitting all of this with the means of a rhythm section and an improvised rap against it—it was unbelievable!"

What had Michael learned musically from the James Brown show?

"One of the big things that fascinates me most in music is the idea of what rhythmic unit in a piece propels it. A composition can be in 4/4, but there's a question of what level in the rhythm is driving the piece—is it at the 16th or 8th note level, maybe at the bar level—all these situations produce a very different kind of feeling. And feeling where this is in music gives it its excitement. . . . In James' band you can hear all this in the way the bass line and rhythm section work. It's the way those guys can put down twenty minutes of continuous 16th notes absolutely like a rock."

Thomas's acceptance of all kinds of music was encouraged in part by his Los Angeles school education and in part by his family. He is the grandson of Boris and Bessie Thomashefsky, two of the founders of New York's Yiddish Theater, from whom actors like John Barrymore learned many of their bravado techniques. Michael's uncle was Paul Muni. His father is a writer and film director and producer, and his mother, a teacher, was once head of the research department at Columbia Pictures.

When Michael was three, he remembers listening not so much to children's "classical" music records such as *Tuby the Tuba* or *Sparky's Magic Piano,* but to favorite albums such as Bach's D minor *Piano Concerto,* Mozart's *Fortieth Symphony,* Prokofiev's *Second Violin Concerto,* and Stravinsky's *Rite of Spring.*

"The only thing I liked about *Sparky's Magic Piano,*" Thomas says, "was the voice of the piano going *Sspoorarkie.* That was fantastic! I used to play that over and over again, but the rest of the record I didn't listen to. My reaction to music as a child was very physical. I used to dance a lot to *Le Sacre* and Bach."

He learned to read music at seven, and his serious study began at ten or eleven. "Until I was eighteen," Thomas says, "I studied music without thinking of being a professional. I was going to be a chemist or a crystalographer." His uncompartmentalized high school education introduced him to both virtuoso rock & roll and classical musicians. Michael went to school just in time: Governor Reagan has since cut funds for the unrestrictive public school arts program in California.

At the University of Southern California he studied with composer Ingolf Dahl and pianist John Crown. Thomas played piano for Piatigorsky's master cello classes, met the French composer Pierre Boulez at the Monday Evening concerts, conducted at the Ojai Festival, and assisted Boulez in rehearsals of the famous *Parsifal* production at Bayreuth. He later went to Tanglewood to conduct Stanley Silverman's multi-media opera *Elephant Steps.*

Like Leonard Bernstein, who made his debut by replacing Bruno Walter in 1943 with the New York Philharmonic, Thomas started his amazing rise by stepping in for the ailing William

Steinberg midway through a Boston Symphony concert at Carnegie Hall in 1969. "Michael reminds me of me at that age," Bernstein says, "except that he knows more than I did."

Thomas is one of the first American conductors to place himself in the twentieth century tradition exemplified by conductors like Mahler, Scherchen, Mitropoulos, and Hans Rosbaud—a tradition in which vital contemporary works are performed not out of an attitude of "dues paying" but out of a recognition of and trust in the on-going processes of music.

At a time when most orchestras obligingly perform about forty nineteenth century "standards," Thomas has experimented. What else would you expect of someone whose musical tastes encompass Japanese *gagaku* music, Carl Ruggles, the Stones, Perotin, Hendrix, the Indonesian gamelan orchestra, Dylan ("in his antagonistic moods"), Lou Harrison, a Dorian *Kyrie* from the medieval *Liber Usualis,* and the idling sound of his Porsche Cabriolet? "I'm always snooping," says Thomas about his range of musical interests.

Last season he designed and led four experimental Spectrum concerts with the Boston Symphony. All were attended by sold-out audiences consisting mainly of young persons, many of whom had never before entered Symphony Hall. The first Spectrum program featured Mozart's *Notturno for Four Orchestras;* Liszt's *Hexameron* for six pianos and orchestra; Bartok's *Music for Strings, Percussion and Celesta;* and Steve Reich's *for four rock organs and ensemble of maracas.*

"There's an idea behind each concert," Thomas says, "but they're non-academic ideas. It doesn't interest me so much to do a pedantic historical progression. I like creating a program where you see similar situations being approached in shockingly different ways.

"The Liszt is a narrative kind of work—it's a variation piece in which all the pianists wrote their own variations to show off their own techniques and, in a sense, their personalities. You have a good idea of how each tries to make himself appear by the kind of variation each writes. Liszt wrote his own variation, an introduction, transitions, and a finale for all of them. This is almost a nineteenth century literary idea—they play introduction and theme together, each one comments, and then it turns into a big conclusion.

"Now, Mozart is interested in the idea of echoes. The orchestras are deployed around the hall, sounds die out, and phrases overlap—it's a more abstract idea. But Bartok is interested in an antiphonal process and also in using the orchestra as a whole sound mass. What I find most interesting is not so much the stereophony—it goes back and forth—but the fact that there are cellos all across the stage—not just treble on your left and bass on the right. And in the third movement there are sections where there's just a unified wall of sound, every part's coming from almost every point on the stage, it's a different acoustical situation from the one you usually encounter. And Reich's piece is totally different."

The second Spectrum event in January presented a two-concert Stravinsky retrospective. Among the works heard were the *Symphonies for Wind Instruments, King of the Stars, Symphony of Psalms* (dedicated by the composer "To the glory of God and the Boston Symphony"—in that order), and *Requiem Canticles* (the most exciting performance of this piece I've heard, especially with the *Libera me* section which, when each member of the chorus whispered the text in different pitches, suggested the Tower of Babel or the birth of language). The first concert concluded with *The Rites of Spring.* After a slightly rough-edged opening, Thomas, looking like a mad chef throwing all kinds of strange spices into the orchestra pot, stirred the piece together and raised it to its ecstatic apotheosis. He received a standing ovation equal to those Janis Joplin used to get after "Piece of My Heart."

The presentation of the Spectrum concerts differed from the fusty and stifling "cultural" social outings typical of most symphonic and operatic events. At Symphony Hall people were standing around talking. Slides showing Stravinsky at work and with friends were flashed against a screen set up against the organ pipes above the stage. Musicians, informally dressed, ambled in. Thomas walked to the podium and talked into a microphone, mentioning how Stravinsky conceived of time as kinesthetic motion, of how he tried to find the wrong note at the right place, of the gestural phrase. He and the orchestra played examples of such a phrase from one early and one late work.

Thomas often adds unannounced works to the program. He inserted one of Stravinsky's last small works, the "Owl and the Pussycat" song, as a foil before the portentous *Symphony of Psalms.* And his commentary, like his conducting, combined Boulez's precise, functional approach and Bernstein's looser, more emotionally colored one—without the latter's occasional sentimentality or attitudinizing.

"When the troubadours were around," Thomas says, "you knew you were in the presence of a person who knew a piece of music he could play for you. It wasn't a matter of whether he could play it better than Joe so-and-so. It was just a matter that he knew it and could play it at that moment. And this is the idea of Spectrum: we have these pieces at our disposal and like them and would like to share them."

What does Thomas think of recent mergings of orchestral and rock groups, as with Deep Purple and a London orchestra?

"I can't stand these pieces where a rock group comes in and does its usual number and the orchestra plays A flat in the background—it's like an old Mamas and Papas date except realized live on-stage with orchestra. It's so uninteresting. Both people have to give and a lot has to be learned on both sides.

"I've found, generally, when I've talked to rock performers that I've known a good deal more about rock than they've known about classical music. When I talked to Clyde or Bootsy Collins in James Brown's band about certain things that were going on in Messiaen rhythmically, it blew their minds. But on the other hand, even if most rock musicians have fairly stereotyped ideas about classical music, I think it's the ultimate condescension on the part of the symphony orchestra to criticize rock; because if a rock group is really good, it's totally together in what it is, and the orchestra can only make it less tight.

"The pieces by Del Tredici, Stanley Silverman, and Bob Selig are the ones that interest me the most because they really do have a contact and feel for what rock is, and they've created a situation where there can be a real interchange."

When asked about the tightness of a group like the Stones, Thomas replied: "The kind of thing I like is the way the Stones produce their records, the way they do this slight delay, reverb, or their double tracking. I love how *im*precise it is. So that instead of hearing a voice which is absolutely synched with its echo a certain precise fraction of a second behind, it's almost like a vague general melodic line that's being drawn which has all kinds of little peaks and points on all sides—*this* time Jagger decided to delay a little bit where the L goes, *that* time the K comes a little sooner—so that the relationships within the lines to themselves are changing all the time."

Thomas's sense of constructing a program is subtle. He talks in terms of conveying a certain density, color, brightness. In fact, his programs are often itineraries for a special voyage. In one recent New York Philharmonic concert, he started with Handel's *Water Music*—the glitter of the wave crests; followed it with Ruth Crawford Seeger's *Andante*—where the displacement of rhythmic pulse reminded one of being inside a wave; Ruggles' *Lilacs*—a music of erotically shaped, resplendent underwater coral; Berg's *Seven Early Songs*—sending the listener back up through shadow-flecked, romantic, after-the-storm colors; and the concluding Mozart *34th Symphony*—emerging into the air.

"I don't sit down and think whether I want the program to work in this way, but there's just a feeling I have about it," he said. "I look at it on paper, I see and hear it in my mind, and either it's right or not. And if not, I'll fool around with it over and over again. What I like is when a piece that you know in a certain context suddenly does something totally different because of the new context in which it's placed.

"I've been told that I'm continuously reinterpreting the same data to arrive at completely opposing conclusions. I really am a syncretist—I can devoutly believe in two opposing ideas. Maybe that's what I subconsciously like to do in programming, saying:'This is the way it is, except *bang,* suddenly it's the other way around.' I really don't believe in ultimate or definitive readings.

"In Buffalo I programmed a work by Perotin, Josquin's *Deploration,* Varèse's *Integrales,* and a Schumann melodrama which I resurrected, *Schoen Hedwig*—Beautiful Hedwig. It's about a knight talking to a maiden, a super-campy, romantic piece, but the music is really beautiful. And I staged it with lights and candles, going back into that period, then *bang,* the lights go on, and there you are with a Schumann symphony taking place. There's that enormous jump of time in the first half of the program—the Middle Ages and Renaissance to the present, and with the Schumann you get a totally unexpected form."

Thomas will sometimes also program what he calls an "old-time religion" concert—Borodin, Chopin, Wagner, and Liszt. And recently he's obtained a clavichord—the precursor of the harpsichord—which he'll use for improvising and making some recordings. He'll continue the Spectrum series, expanding the ideas of the series "into even farther out things." He'll be involved with concerts that will present Asian music—*gagaku* and *gamelan,* perhaps. In addition he'll spend more time performing contemporary music, especially works by Boulez, Stockhausen, and Carter, along with pieces by lesser known composers.

"I love to work in new music," he says, "because when you're doing something that few people have done before, you're creating the tradition, you're dealing with it in a fresh, open way, there are a lot more decisions to be made and fewer presuppositions.

"The 'Here are the fifty greatest moments of classical music' approach, listening to it while you're ironing . . . I doubt young people are attracted to that. It's better to say: Look, it exists at all levels, you can never exhaust its possibilities—what's in it as well as its limitations are *you,* they're in your mind. Through these pieces is a path to a heightened understanding not only of art but of life."

1971

Elliott Carter's Concerto for Orchestra

CONCERTO FOR ORCHESTRA

Elliott Carter, Leonard Bernstein, N.Y. Philharmonic

Elliott Carter's *Concerto for Orchestra,* commissioned by the N.Y. Philharmonic for its one hundred twenty-fifth anniversary, is one of the masterpieces of twentieth century music. This will surprise no one who has been aware of Carter's development (he was born in 1908) from early "American"-textured works like *Pocahantas* (1939) to pieces like the *Cello Sonata* (1947), the extraordinary two string quartets (1951 and 1959), and the *Double Concerto,* in the last four of which first explored relationships between "internal dream time" and "external time," discovered new linear and textural shapes and harmonic fields, purveyed a radically new employment of polyrhythms, and, most important, uncovered ways in which psychological contrasts between and among instruments could be revealed.

If all this sounds fairly dense and complicated, you might as well realize that every piece of music is its own medium, but whether you listen to Pygmy music, Balinese gamelan music, Machaut, Chopin, or Arnold Schoenberg, your awarenesses and feelings are a function of your perceptions: you have to allow yourself to hear what is there and not expect or demand something that isn't. "Different strokes for different folks." In this regard, Elliott Carter's music is to Tchaikovsky's as the Band's music is to Grand Funk, for the former insists on an awareness of a formal complexity and beauty against a more one-dimensional, merely mood-suggesting, or augmenting complacency.

Where Carter differs from avant garde composers like Cornelius Cardew, John Cage, or Morton Feldman is in his control of all aspects of his materials and in his insistence on the creation of developmental energy in a structured vision that has more in common with Beethoven's *F Major Quartet* than with Feldman's *Out of Last Pieces,* for example.

Carter also differs from composers like La Monte Young, Terry Riley, or even Ligeti in that he works with pitches and their inter-relationships ("populating time with pitches") instead of presenting and manipulating sound objects or cyclic patterns or frequential reverberations. All these distinctions might suggest that although you may enter Carter's musical world, it doesn't insist on entering you.

Rather than being restricted by his chosen medium, Carter uses a complicated musical language to open up levels of perception equaled by the great Western European composers. The *Concerto for Orchestra,* Carter's most recent work, extends his musical ideas of transformation and interpenetration. "I regard my scores as scenarios, auditory scenarios, for performers to act out with their instruments," Carter says, "dramatizing the players as individuals and as participants in the ensemble."

In the *Concerto,* Carter allows four orchestral ensembles to share materials so that each single voice celebrates the whole. In this sense, the *Concerto* resembles Ives' *Concord Sonata,* in which variations and states of transformation suggest the center from which they emerge. And in Carter, the context is most important. "The matter of succession of material," Carter writes about the *Concerto,* "becomes very important, since how the ideas are formed and how they are related and connected gives expression to the poetry they evoke. Thus, the individual instant, the characterized sound or brief passage, like trees in a storm, gain an added meaning by their contexts." And these individual instants reveal nothing less than the imaginative power by which "airy nothings" are given "local habitation."

The final effect of this magnificent multi-layered and textured work is that of a conceptual and charactological strength and a shimmering ecstasy, like the thousand flowers with which, a poet once wrote, all valleys are ablaze. It is a difficult and beautiful work of art for the happy few.

1971

Igor Stravinsky (1882–1971): An Appreciation

Igor Stravinsky tells of a dream in which he wanders outside a house, trying to enter. In his parable "Before the Law," Kafka writes about a man begging admittance to the Law. At the conclusion, the doorkeeper, seeing that the man is at the end of his strength and that his hearing is failing, bellows in his ear: "No one but you could gain admittance through this door, since this door was intended only for you. I am now going to shut it."

On the spiritual level, it's obvious how boundaries and doors are inexplicable ego projections, the haze of primordial delusion through which people walk blindly, for everyone creates his own doors. If one pushes interconnections and interpenetrations far enough, everything becomes everything. But in art as in nature, differentiations and divisions paradoxically function at the service of a fundamental unity. When it was requested that Stravinsky, ill in a hospital last year, compose even two notes, he said, "But which two?"

Debussy once called Stravinsky a "natural" and "instinctual" composer. Stravinsky concurred. But it is Stravinsky's concern with specificities, what Reich would have termed a condensation of mobile orgone energy—a self-willed instinctive, "natural" choosing and discovering of musical limits—that defines all of Stravinsky's musical procedures.

Kafka saw a freedom which could exist for him only when it became unobtainable. Just the opposite of that is the vision Stravinsky expresses in his music. "You are free and that is why you are lost," one character in Kafka's *Fragments* says to another, and this thought is duplicated many times in *Amerika* and *The Castle.* Stravinsky's music, conversely, conveys the sense of breaking down the obstacles to that freedom which Kafka never attained.

Here is the key to Stravinsky's musical personality: the composer wants to and succeeds in breaking into the house—a

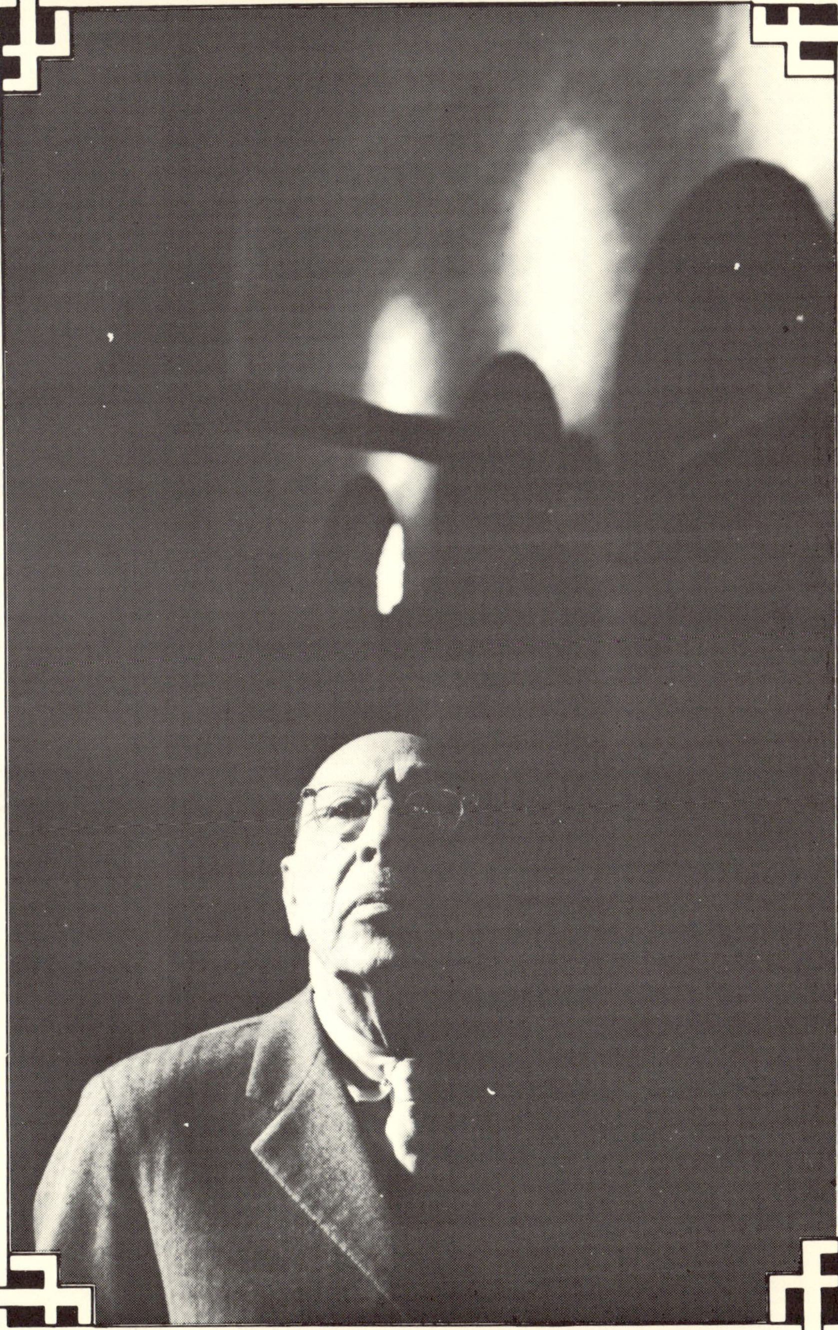

house which can be seen as a metaphor for Stravinsky's self-determined musical choices—right away. His employment of *staccato, marcato,* and sharp *ostinato*—his musical attack, in other words—all suggest the typical Stravinskian sound. The conflict between metrical and rhythmic materials, the unresolved *appoggiaturas,* the superimpositions of conflicting modalities, the juxtaposition of rhythmic cells, all create an enormous musical tension and exhilaration. And it is this unique violent sound that unifies all of his music from *Fireworks* (1908) to the building of the ark section in *The Flood* (1961).

The hullabaloo that is made of Stravinsky's so-called "primitive, neo-classic, and serial periods" by both critics and audiences is mostly oratorical pretension, on the one hand, and negligible academic dickering, musical historiography, on the other. Masterpieces such as *Renard* (1916), the *Piano Concerto* (1924), *Movements for Piano and Orchestra* (1959), and the magnificent *Variations for Orchestra* (1965) reveal the same musical power and kinetic energy, transcending annalistic periodization. "The true purpose of linear historicism," Stravinsky writes, "is simply to open up more Midwestern territories of the mind to Ph.D. candidates." And Stravinsky's striking and recognizable musical inflection is always the same. As he writes in *Dialogues and a Diary:* "I do not understand the composer who says we must analyze and determine the evolutionary tendency of the whole musical situation and proceed from there. I have never consciously analyzed any musical situation, and I can follow only where my musical appetites lead me."

When Stravinsky uses Pergolesi, Tchaikovsky, Weber, Wolf, or Gesualdo, he employs the old in order to renew his already strong musical personality. Milhaud's adaptations of Lully or Richard Strauss's borrowings from Couperin reveal to us more about the originals than about the adapters. But Stravinsky's *Pulcinella, The Fairy's Kiss, Monumentum pro Gesualdo,* or the harmonization and arrangement of "The Star Spangled Banner" (which, when it was first performed in 1944, got the composer into trouble with Boston officials who accused him of "tampering with national property") are pure Stravinsky. Like Nerval, Eliot, Pound, and Duncan in poetry or Mingus and Coltrane in jazz, Stravinsky takes from his musical forebears in order to renovate and enrich his own singular vision. Everything is there: the unique inflection and stylization, the freezing of the leading tones, the stricken gestures, and the violent rhythmic attack.

For Stravinsky wants to get into the house—and he breaks in. Like the Russian spring he writes about, Stravinsky's music is like the "whole world cracking," opening up consciousness and enabling us to contact vital and hidden-away feeling. But the violence in Stravinsky's music is usually playful. It's an open, child-like "aggression," in its literal meaning of "approaching" (the house). It is the aggression of Chicken Little, Gargantua, and The Frog Prince.

Stravinsky has said that his music is best understood by animals and small children. I once played *Agon* for three kids under the age of six, and they called it "noisy." Dogs like what their masters like. When Stravinsky rightfully talks of Schumann as being the composer of first childhood, he implies that he himself is the composer of a true second childhood, of a music for older children that creates a sense of beginnings. And like the games and actions of children, his compositions cannot be predicted and judged according to a predetermined aesthetic code. Stravinsky writes: "My agenbite of inwit is that I do not know while composing, am not aware of, the value question. I love whatever I am now doing, and with each new work I feel that I have at last found the way, have just begun to compose. I love all of my children."

Pleasure, delight, and play infuse his music. Building and acting are at the base of composition. "My knowledge is activity," Stravinsky says. "I discover it as I work, and I know it while I am discovering it, but only in a very different way before and after." The building of the ark scene in *The Flood* is the finest part of this ballet because the act of building, as of composing, is as exuberant as child's play. It is a music of intense activity, an aural manifestation of the muscular system of motion and locomotion.

This physical vitality suggests the sexual excitement of Stravinsky's music, and this is usually what is inside the house. Here we run into much bickering, philosophizing, and nonsense. Adorno called Stravinsky's art reactionary, saying that it embraced the negative forces, trying to "exorcise" them by identifying itself with them. Roman Vlad's study entitled *Stravinsky,* which the composer calls the "best study of my music," is concerned with this problem. Vlad writes that "if at one particular time Stravinsky allowed his art to become identified with a tragically negative situation, he did so in order to give expression to this situation and thus restore the balance on the basis of pure aesthetic reality."

Throughout the book, Vlad repeats his thesis, which is that the "underlying sense of tragedy" of Stravinsky's earlier music, such as *Le Sacre* and *L'Histoire du Soldat,* gave way in the religious works and in the "neo-classic" period to a "vehement repression of the dramatic impulse, and finally by oblivion and escape into Arcadian bliss. In *Petrushka,*" Vlad continues, "and particularly in *Le Sacre,* rhythm was already on the way to becoming the symbol of the power of evil. In the Triumphal March of the Devil from *L'Histoire* this is fully realized."

What can one say of all this? Admittedly, Stravinsky's concern with orthodox religion (*Mass, Threni, Canticum Sacrum*) and his partiality for Greek themes (*Apollon Musagete, Persephone, Oedipus Rex*) reflect an awareness on his part of evil and the need for inner peace. "Must one be a believer to compose in these [religious] forms?" Robert Craft asks the composer. And Stravinsky replies:"Certainly, and not merely a believer in 'symbolic figures,' but in the Person of the Lord, the Person of the Devil, and the Miracles of the Church."

Children and Stravinsky believe in the Devil, but one wonders if they're worried. Stravinsky's true religious music may be that of *Le Sacre, Les Noces,* and *Agon*—a kind of musical Trinity—which all convey a playful but powerful sexual energy. (Certainly Ballanchine's brilliant choreography for *Agon* hints at this.) The rhythm in these works seems more exuberant than religiously evil. What Vlad sees as evil can be taken to be manifestations of an ideal norm of self-regulating organic rhythms, the quanta of musical love. And this love complements and mirrors the macrocosm of an eternal universal spiritual love. The late Beethoven quartets, Stravinsky writes, "are my highest articles of musical belief (which is a longer word for love, whatever else), as indispensable to the ways and meanings of art, as a musician of my era thinks of art and has tried to learn it, as temperature is to life. They are a triumph over temporality."

D. H. Lawrence talks of "religious chastity" as the peace which comes of physical love. From the *Ebony Concerto* to *Dumbarton Oaks,* from the *Symphonies for Winds* to the *Septet,* Stravinsky's music conveys a sexuality and a joy in being that weds it to the religious hypostasis of the *Song of Songs* or the *Gitagovinda.* "I myself having been created," he writes, "I cannot help having the desire to create." Like Grandgousier who said to his wife, pregnant with Gargantua: "Bring this boy into the world, and we'll soon make another," Stravinsky kept (one wants to say 'keeps") on composing one powerful work after another. And this work includes not only the close to one hundred pieces of music available on recording, but his *Poetics of Music* lectures and, most important, the five books co-authored with his friend and assistant Robert Craft, more politically awake but as rich, moving, and beautifully written as the novels of Nabokov:

"How does a man grow old? I don't know; or why *I* am old, if I must be (I don't want to be), or if 'I' am 'he.' All my life I have thought of myself as the 'youngest one,' and now, suddenly, I read and hear about myself as 'the oldest one.' And then I wonder at these distant images of myself. I wonder if memory is true, and I know that it cannot be, but that one lives by memory nevertheless and not by truth. But through the crack of light in my bedroom door, time dissolves, and I again see the images of my lost world. Mama has gone to her room, my brother is asleep in the other bed, and all is still in the house. The lamp from the street reflects in the room, and by it I recognize the simulacrum as myself."

Stravinsky recalls how Augustine, having grown old, appointed the priest Eraclius as his successor. "Eraclius stood forward to preach, while the old Augustine sat behind him: 'The cricket chirps,' Eraclius said, 'the swan is silent.'"

1971

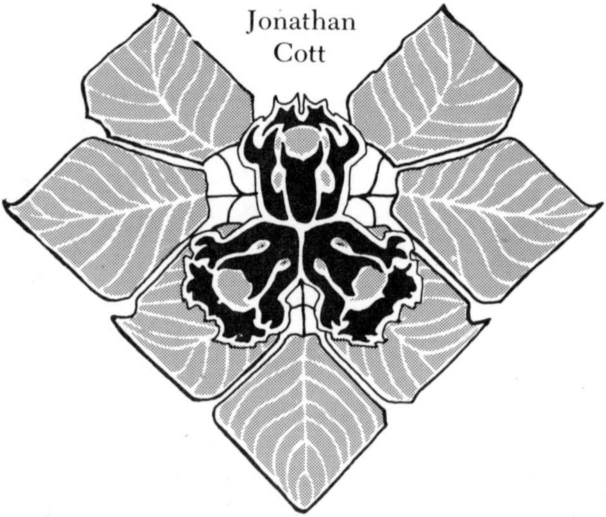
Jonathan
Cott